CHARLES IVES
"MY FATHER'S SONG"

CHARLES IVES
"MY FATHER'S SONG"

A PSYCHOANALYTIC BIOGRAPHY

STUART FEDER

Yale University Press • New Haven & London

Permission to reprint material from the following works is gratefully
acknowledged: *He Is There* © 1956, *The Housatonic at Stockbridge* © 1954,
Slow March © 1953, *Spring Song* © 1954, and *The Things Our Fathers Loved*
© 1955. Peer International Corp.
Majority © 1935 and *Mists* © 1933. Merion Music Inc.

Frontispiece: Charles Ives at fourteen. Yale Music Library, Ives Collection.

Set in Century Expanded type by Keystone Typesetting. Printed in the
United States of America by Vail-Ballou Press, Binghamton, New York.

LIBRARY OF CONGRESS CATALOGING-IN-PUBLICATION DATA
Feder, Stuart, 1930–
Charles Ives, "my father's song" : a psychoanalytic biography /
Stuart Feder.
p. cm.
Includes bibliographical references and index.
ISBN 0-300-05481-5 (alk. paper)
1. Ives, Charles, 1874–1954—Psychology.   2. Composers—
United States—Biography.   I. Title.
ML410.I94F4 1992
780′.92—dc20
[B]   91-42317
CIP
MN

The paper in this book meets the guidelines for permanence and durability of
the Committee on Production Guidelines for Book Longevity of the Council on
Library Resources.

1 3 5 7 9 10 8 6 4 2

*To Carol
and to Susanna, Adam, and Aaron*

CONTENTS

Illustrations are on pages 41, 96, 197, 295, and 350,
and following pages 130 and 272.

PREFACE

I first encountered the music of Charles Ives in the autumn of 1950 through Henry Cowell. Cowell, himself an innovative composer and my teacher at the Peabody Conservatory of Music, performed the good offices of curator and promoter of other people's music. He was editor of the *New Music Quarterly* and with his wife, Sidney Robertson Cowell, was already at work on what would become the first biography of Charles Ives.

Nicholas Nabokov, the composer and writer, held a weekly seminar on modern music at the Peabody where one evening Cowell presented the music of Ives. He first gave us an account of a life that sounded both legendary and anomalous. The legend, which Cowell was already instrumental in creating, was that of Ives the businessman composer, now a New Yorker but with roots in small-town New England, where his father had been a village bandmaster. The anomaly to those present, an assortment of impecunious students and professional musicians trying to earn a living through a variety of academic and other musical occupations, was that Ives was more than comfortable financially. Although Cowell tended to mute the fact, referring to Ives's modest style and charitable disposition, it was clear that he was actually wealthy. Cowell spoke with reverence about the composer, now seventy-five and ailing, who had created a body of unique music earlier in his life, around the same time as such musical innovators as Stravinsky and Schoenberg.

Cowell then played us some private-label 78's. The music of Ives was not performed in Baltimore in those years; through all the obligatory Friday afternoon concerts and Baltimore Symphony evenings, I had not heard a single Ives work. Ives's *The Unanswered Question* was eloquent and like no other music presented in Nabokov's seminar that year, and the experience proved to be memorable.

It was some years before I heard that piece or thought of Ives again. In the meantime, I had been drafted into the army and stationed with the First Army Band, where I had ample opportunity to observe the military version of the American band tradition. I scarcely noticed the death of Ives in 1955 as I was immersed in premedical studies. Involved in another world, I lost touch with Henry Cowell, who had been of help earlier when I was considering a career in music. By the time of his death a decade later, I had completed medical school, internship, and a residency. I was practicing psychiatry and in psychoanalytic training.

It was only at the end of my training that I returned to Ives. By then, I had published a few papers relating psychoanalysis to music. I found myself interested in biography and the nature of auditory representation in mental life and in art. It seemed to me that, in the case of composers, analysis of the representation of idea and affect in the auditory sphere—in effect, music—might yield cogent biographical material. In a sense, this approach was no different from that of many biographies of composers, except that my method would be specifically psychoanalytic. In the context of other biographical materials, the music might serve as a point of entry into the affective and symbolic aspects of the mental life of the composer.

Ives is an appropriate subject for such an undertaking for two reasons in particular. First, the complex generational relationship between father and son raises such varied and diverse issues as early memory, identification, and mourning. Second, the surface of the music as heard often gives the impression of something beyond itself, a fictive or perhaps autobiographical element. This feature goes far deeper than the programmatic elements inherent in titling and the composer's comments. It is nonverbal, a part of the music itself.

The memory of this quality from my initial hearing of Ives's music persisted in my mind through the decades. I came to see that Charles and George Ives were a biographical father-son pair second to none in music (comparable perhaps only to Mozart *pére et fils*), and that Ives's music should be approached biographically, not only through the usual materials, but also through the symbolic products of one of them—the composer.

While it was immediately clear to me that the truest biography of Charles Ives must subsume that of his father, none existed. The life of George had to be reconstructed from materials that were an intrinsic part of his son's story. George would have to be sought there as much as in conventional biographical sources such as family documents and newspapers of the time. The search for George Ives leads to the further recesses of the composer's mental life—to the reconstruction of memory and to the symbolic products of the artist in the music itself. Ultimately, two coordinates of a dual biography suggested themselves— the 110-year span of their combined lives and the psychic life of the composer son, in whose mind all that related to both of them was reflected and concentrated.

That its central focus is the mental life of the artist is what entitles this book to be called a psychoanalytic biography. It is an example of applied analysis in that it applies principles and formulations derived from clinical psychoanalysis to biographical data. Additionally, it stresses the critical role of early childhood experience insofar as it can be determined or reconstructed, and recognizes the importance of adolescence in fixing character and setting the stage for adult love and adult work. But further, the form the biography assumes roughly follows certain features of a clinical analysis (in some respects, even those of a psychoanalytic session). That is, little of a strictly interpretive nature appears at first; there is much history taking and data gathering initially and throughout the book. Indeed, as in the psychoanalytic hour, a good deal is frankly banal, the stuff of everyday life. Only gradually do formulations suggest themselves and interpretations become available as lines of meaning coalesce.

The psychoanalytic thinking proceeds along classical lines, with particular emphasis on ego psychology. I make no attempt to be comprehensive in applying various alternative psychoanalytic points of view. Nor is research in human psychological development adduced gratuitously—only that which has explanatory value for biographical purposes.

The biography is divided into four parts, the first two comprising the nineteenth century, the second the twentieth. Book One covers the life of George Edward Ives until the birth of Charles, and Book Two the life of Charles until the death of his father and graduation from Yale. Book Three deals with the creative lifetime of Ives both before and after his marriage to Harmony Twichell, the second most important person in his life; Book Four, the summing up in two idiosyncratic autobiographies and the final years.

Not all of Ives's music is considered in this biography. More precisely, the works are not taken up in a comprehensive or systematic way although virtually all of the major works, many of the minor pieces, and most of the songs are brought into the discussion at some point. The chief criterion for consideration is the connection of the particular piece to some aspect of Ives's relationship to his father. Accordingly, a few minor, youthful, or obscure works receive extended and repeated treatment while some major works are considered relatively less. Since the function of composition subserved an ongoing intrapsychic relationship between father and son, musical quotations of nineteenth-century tunes known to Ives from childhood and received as it were from his father are given consider-able attention. These tunes are frequently woven into the fabric of works with consequent psychological association. Between the polarities of the received and the created lie the many subtle examples in which aspects of the father achieve auditory representation in musical form. Such are the features that are inherent in the music of Charles Ives and at the core of the human experience of its composer. They are at once a part of art and a part of life.

ACKNOWLEDGMENTS

Firist thanks are to Gladys Topkis, who, over the nearly ten years this book was in the making, became my friend as well as my editor. Her special blend of straightforwardness and tact, uncompromising professional skills, and sensitivity to both music and psychoanalysis were of inestimable help. Richard Miller's keen intelligence and finely tuned ear added much in the final editing.

An exchange of introductory postcards with Sidney Robertson Cowell in the early 1970s reminds me how long this first biographer of Charles Ives has encouraged my own Ives studies. I thank her for many informative and pleasant afternoons in Shady, New York. No study of Ives could be complete without the scholarly contributions of John Kirkpatrick, whose work at once opened the field of Ives studies and put it on firm footing. I am grateful to him for this as well as for his generous sharing of time and materials entrusted to him. Vivian Perlis's fine work on the Charles Ives Papers at Yale University made access to primary materials feasible. I also appreciate her sharing of transcripts from the Ives oral history project. J. Peter Burkholder was helpful with conversation and materials in the early stages of my work. The late Bigelow Ives is appreciatively remembered for a day-long interview.

I am grateful for the cooperation of Harold E. Samuel, librarian of the John Herrick Jackson Music Library at Yale. Kendall Crilly, public service librarian, patiently provided the needed Ives papers at the Beinecke Rare Book and Manuscript Library and the Yale Music Library. William E. Devlin, formerly curatorial assistant at the Danbury Scott-Fanton Museum and Historical Society, was a valued partner in the study of Danbury history and Ives family background. I thank Allan H. Unger for medical consultation on Ives's cardiological problems. Geoffrey Block kindly made portions of his Ives discography available.

Longtime friends Herbert D. Saltzstein and Donald L. Gerard faithfully waded their way through an early draft and were generous with suggestions as well as encouragement. I have benefited from ongoing discussion of mutual psychoanalytic projects with Emanuel Rice. Leonard Shengold helped me see previously unexplored dimensions of Ives's family relationships.

I was fortunate to have dedicated word-processing assistance from Karen Miller in Great Barrington for the final drafts. During earlier, pre-electronic stages, Susan Morance typed the old-fashioned way in the city.

I thank my wife, Carol, for putting up with the Ives family for what turned out to be fully a third of our married life. (Ordinarily, one set of in-laws is sufficient.) Her tolerant attention to domestic detail, which should rightfully be shared, freed me for many weekend hours of work, while her encouragement, loyalty, and loving support enriched those hours and the entire endeavor.

CHARLES IVES
"MY FATHER'S SONG"

PROLOGUE

REMEMBRANCE

The music in my heart I bore
Long after it was heard no more.
Wordsworth

In 1921, Charles Ives at forty-seven was working on a unique autobiography. He was compiling a collection of songs drawn from every phase of his life ranging widely in text and topic and in musical style. His creative life was shortly to come to an end although he would live to be close to eighty.

He had already had some intimations of failing capacity; yet he was in the midst of an extended creative period which, characteristically for him, was ultimately to have an extraordinary yield: a piano sonata (Ives's second), called the *Concord*;[1] a work of prose, *Essays before a Sonata*, defying brief description but incorporating elements of biography and personal philosophy;[2] and the collection of vocal music he called simply *114 Songs*.[3]

The songs, like the essays, challenge definition. Drawn from music and thought over a thirty-year period, the collection is at once a catalog, a commonplace book, a diary, and a journal—in essence, a work of autobiography, although Ives did not intend it as such. A second, deliberate collection of autobiographical prose writings a decade later came to be called the *Memos*.[4] In fact, all three in this final harvest—in effect, Ives's trilogy—contain elements of music, personal philosophy, and biography, although each best and most charac-

1

teristically represents one facet. The songs in particular, but in a way Ives's entire work, constitute a singular American autobiography in music. The collection is full of ideas, musical and other, but above all it is full of memories.

The song *Remembrance*, for example, was originally a short piece for small orchestra, called *The Pond*, when Ives completed it in 1906. Returning to it in 1921, he had little to change in the music when he made the vocal transcription. The principal additions were the new title and a quotation from Wordsworth (see epigraph). *Remembrance* is about Ives's father, George Edward Ives, as was *The Pond*.

On the printed page, *Remembrance* is simplicity itself. Only nine measures in length, it is as distinctly an Ives piece as is any of his apparently more complex compositions. It is also characteristic of a group of Ives's compositions in which the presence of George Ives is made manifest through some reminiscence in music—a tune, the sound of a band, a favorite musical quirk of George's—or some elusive emotion, usually within the spectrum of nostalgic feelings, encoded in music and related to Ives's memories of his father. In *Remembrance*, the words are explicit. In fact, the earlier, orchestral *Pond* was in a sense a song as well. In his sketch for the piece, beneath the melody of the trumpet (the closest relative to George Ives's cornet), Ives wrote a lyric. It remains unclear whether he intended it as an optional vocal line or a musical idea—an imagined instrument, a trumpet, with words whispered subvocally:

> A sound of a distant horn,
> O'er shadowed lake is borne,
> my father's song.

A sense of timelessness is evoked by the supporting arpeggios, sustained and muted. The melodic line, slowed beyond recognition and intoned with a leached-out simplicity, actually was derived from an Irish love song, *Kathleen Mavourneen*, popular during Charlie's boyhood. The original song is unabashedly sentimental in words and music.[5] It tells of the parting of lovers, the singer imploring his beloved to waken, for dawn is coming and they must say farewell. At the same time, the singer's repeated exhortation suggests that the loved one is in that sleep from which one can never awaken.

The Pond also creates a sense of distance in time and in space. The "sound of a distant horn" is rendered literally by the hushed trumpet, the spatial features further emphasized by an echo of the tune in canon, a round. Thus, distance is represented not only in space but in time as the horn's tune is imitated by the flute a measure later. Ives wrote "Echo Piece" on one of his sketches. And in the echo there are two voices, only one of which is living.[6] At the close of the piece, the first notes of taps are heard in the distance.

Like other works by Ives, *The Pond* is a memorialization of George. The distance in both time and place suggests nostalgia. But a calm prevails, longing only hinted at in the disguised, austere rendering of the sentimental tune. A fantasy is expressed in auditory terms as we hear the sound of the instrument of the composer's father. And just as the sentimental tune speaks unabashedly of love, the final quoting of taps tells of mourning. Finally, the "echo" reminds us that two voices tell this story, one following the other at a pace in time.

That this was the way Charles followed George in life is something more than metaphor. For it is the thesis of this book that much of Ives's career in music was the result of an ongoing intrapsychic collaboration with his father. The endeavor of composition itself served this function, and from time to time elements of this underlying motive surfaced in the manifest content of the music. Accordingly, a true account of the life and work of Charles Ives cannot be rendered outside the context of the paired biographies of father and son and without consideration of both the nineteenth-century musical world of George and the creative life of Charles which spans the nineteenth and twentieth centuries.

Ives's first biographers, Henry and Sidney Cowell, knew Ives personally, as did John Kirkpatrick. But the Ives they knew and remembered was an old man who had outlived the composer within him. Vivian Perlis has recorded the recollections of others who had known Ives in *Charles Ives Remembered.*[7] A still broader picture may be drawn from Ives's own writings, all of which have an autobiographical (that is to say, self-revealing) side. An imagined equivalent—a *George Ives Remembered*—would be exclusively the product of one man, his son. It is the hidden biography-within-a-biography that is the subject of this book. When George died at age forty-nine, Charles had just turned twenty. Among the complex motivational elements of Charles's mental life is one that is intimately associated with remembrance—namely, mourning. The process engages every other mental function, including those subserving creativity. If the ordinary act of remembrance is an example of everyday creativity in its conjuring up of imagery, how much more potential for creativity is in the remembrances of a gifted person? Ives's mourning for his father was to give impetus and content to much of his creative life. The exploration of how this came about provides access to mental product as well as mental function—that is, to the music of Charles Ives. A collaboration between father and son began in life and persisted in mourning. Music was its medium and product. Indeed, the music of Charles Ives is the truest issue of their combined lives and is potentially the most reliable body of biographical documents available. Music itself may be the more intimately related to mourning and hence to acts of remembrance, since of all the arts it is, par excellence, the art of time.

The remembrance of *Remembrance* is rendered in time and in sound. In this "Echo Piece," to consider Charles the echo of George is to press metaphor toward actuality. For the lives of George and Charles Ives were not only parallel but overlapping, as occurs in the normal generational sequence. George was a father for twenty of his nearly fifty years. For Charles, the twenty years of life he shared with his father represented only one-fourth of his eventual lifespan; the rest was memory. The two decades from 1874, when Charles was born, to 1894, when George died, were also uniquely and decisively formative for the life of America.

George was a nineteenth-century man in all respects. In an age of practical invention, he was the Yankee tinker in music. But his endeavors were far from those that might lead to economic gain, at which the rest of the Ives family was adept. On the contrary, George was caught helplessly within the social and economic changes of his time. Charles averted this fate in his own later years by becoming a successful businessman, but he lived with its practical consequences during his first two decades as the son of the errant son, a gentle domestic deviant.

On the other hand, George carried within him the emblems as well as the scars of the single event that dominated the course of the country during those two decades—the Civil War, which had ended scarcely a decade before Charles's birth. In Charles's eyes, George was its living representation and a source of fierce pride. Of the two trends—historical and economic—in American life, George could be a hero in his son's eyes in at least one. Charles's early life ran parallel to the course of these historical and economic events which brought the country to the brink of the twentieth century. George, although the youngest of his siblings, did not live to see it.

A powerful identification with his father played a decisive role in the formation of Ives's character. It rendered him too in some measure a man of those earlier times. George was left behind, but incorporated in Charles's memory of him were the events and objects of nineteenth-century life. Prominent among these were the musical artifacts of the time—the hymns, popular tunes, and patriotic songs that became an intrinsic part of Ives's music. Thus were embedded in memory, traces not only of persons, things, and events, but also of ideals.

In both the business and the musical aspects of his double life, Charles Ives proved to be an innovator. Much of his music retains a distinctively "modern" quality despite its frequently disarming nineteenth-century features. In business, he was like the heir to a nineteenth-century enterprise in which his own father had never participated. It is the layering of the twentieth century upon the nineteenth, a frequently imperfect amalgamation and synthesis, that comprises one of the most distinctive characteristics of Ives's work. And at its core is Charles's relationship with George. Through this medium, George's Civil War became Charles's, and that Danbury of which Charles often spoke had the flavor of an earlier time, as if experienced through George's childhood. Thus, Ives

4

achieved his easy and heartfelt connection with an earlier period in America's history by experience, not by textbook, and its conduit was his father.

The combined life span of the two men—from George's birth in 1845 to Charles's death in 1954—exceeds a century. But an even broader expanse of personal and public history was accessible and usable for Charles. He sensed himself to be connected to the early years of the republic following the American Revolution, which remained deeply imbued in the history and daily life of Danbury. Few artists have been so situated in time and place, or among people. This singular position proved to be a critical element in Ives's art. It is revealed richly in his music, where it became a determinant of style. The style, like the man, is unique. Indeed, to study Ives at all is to study individuality in its extreme.

In the end, Charles's memory of George fused with historical memory to foster patriotism: his love for his father transformed itself into a love for his father's land. In the course of this process, and embedded in its content, George became his personal national hero. It is this George Ives we encounter in his son's fantasy and in his art.

BOOK ONE

GEORGE

ONE

THE IVESES OF DANBURY

Apru 27, 1854, was one of the great days in the history of Danbury, Connecticut. On that day a monument was dedicated to a hero of the Revolution, General David Wooster, long beloved by the town that had been the scene of his finest hours and of his death seventy-five years earlier. In its account of the event, the Danbury *Times* aptly called it "The Monumental Celebration."[1]

The citizens of Danbury met the day with a sense of solemnity mixed with restlessness and optimism, for the occasion was not only patriotic and historical but funereal as well. The recently completed Wooster Cemetery, where the monument to the fallen champion had been erected near his grave, was already a showplace of the town; however, if some of the five thousand or so Danbury residents were pondering whether this would be their own final resting place, there seemed little evidence of such melancholy. The town was secure and growing, and the future seemed as bright as the Thursday morning sunshine. The turnout was far greater than that for the militia training days of a decade earlier or even the Fourth of July festivals. The newly completed Danbury and Norwalk Railroad made it possible for people to travel to the celebration from every part of the state. The train pulling into the depot at the north end of Main Street brought many dignitaries: the governor and former governor of Connecticut, several generals, the editors of the state's leading newspapers (the *Palladium* and *Gazette* of Hartford), and the noted poet Mrs. Lydia Sigourney

(1791–1865), who distinguished the occasion with a commemorative poem. It was estimated that the swell of people who attended the event had effectively doubled the population of Danbury. It would long be remembered in the town as one of the finest and most important spectacles of the century.

Danbury, of course, made its own contribution to the color and dignity of the occasion. The growing American appetite for local organizations of every variety was in evidence throughout. The exercises of the day were organized and conducted principally by the masonic fraternity. Its exotic ritual commingled curiously with the patriotic fervor of the other participants, the simple Protestant ceremonial of the Congregational Church, where some of the speeches were heard, and the obligatory military exercises and parades. It was American eclecticism at its most vivid, yet on a scale appropriate to the small town.

It was a day for oratory and music. Danbury provided its own indoor variety of music in the Congregational Church, where following the procession and dedication of the monument those who were fortunate enough to find a place could hear an inspiring oration. However, the resources for outdoor band music were not yet developed on a scale for such an occasion and had to be bolstered by visiting groups.

The procession was dominated by officials and members of the numerous Danbury fraternal organizations. There were also, of course, clergymen, whose function was to anchor the occasion within a long New England tradition of linking the secular with the sacred and to remind the participants that there was, after all, a God. The handful of Revolutionary soldiers who attended, now in their seventies, were accorded an honorary position, marching immediately behind the highest officials. Pacing the parade were military organizations from every part of the state—the Hartford Light Guards, the New Haven Blues, and the German Rifle Company of Bridgeport—and from New York, with five marching bands interspersed among them. The new immigrants from Europe were also well represented, for the most part in the form of church and fraternal groups. The firemen of Danbury, including many Irish, marched along with those of Bridgeport and Norwalk. Danbury Fire Company Number 2 had thrown an ornate arch of evergreens and flowers across White Street in front of their engine house, under which the procession passed on its way to the cemetery. The rich regalia of the Odd Fellows competed with that of the Masons and the military while contrasting with the modest garb of the Sons of Temperance. In democracy made manifest, no group visible in town was omitted and even unaffiliated individuals could form ranks at the end of the parade to march with the "Citizens of Danbury, the Citizens of Fairfield County and Citizens of this and other States who desire to join in the Procession."

The lengthy procession assembled at Wooster House, an inn in the north part of Main Street, and wound through the town to Wooster Cemetery, where a thirty-foot platform had been erected. Following a prayer, Masonic ritual prevailed as the "chief stone" of the monument was laid by the Grand Master and the Master Architect under the honorary direction of Governor Pond. Before the sealing of the stone, a box was enclosed within the monument to preserve certain articles for future generations. These included copies of the Bible, the U.S. Constitution, and the Connecticut state constitution, American gold and silver coins, Continental bills, and a daguerreotype of General Wooster. Copies of the day's editions of the New York *Tribune, Herald,* and *Times* were included as well as of the Danbury *Times.*

Looking toward the future, the people of Danbury still keenly felt the past and revered it. At the same time, they hoped that future generations would come to respect them and their efforts of this day. The Revolutionary War had generated a musical legacy consisting largely of patriotic tunes, some of which were played on this day by the bands of the grand procession. But the Revolution had also produced heroes who had by now become an important part of American life. The unquestioned leader in national popularity was George Washington, but first in the hearts of his Danbury countrymen was General David Wooster, whose historical presence was nearly palpable to the boys and girls of Danbury in the first half of the century. The final object inserted into the memorial stone was the bullet that had been the cause of Wooster's death.

General David Wooster, a Yale graduate and a distinguished soldier, was sixty-eight when he was summoned to Danbury in April, 1777.[2] The preceding year, the village had had the misfortune of being designated a depository for Continental army supplies. Inevitably, it was attacked, sacked, and burned, but Wooster and his troops drove the British out. Wooster pursued them to nearby Ridgefield, where he was mortally wounded on April 27, 1779. In the late morning, as Wooster led the attack on the retreating British, he drew heavy fire. Rallying his troops, who were frightened by the grapeshot whistling through the air, Wooster turned in his saddle shouting, "Come on, my boys! Never mind such random shots!" At that moment, a musket ball, said to have been fired by a Tory, struck him obliquely in the back, splintering his spine and lodging in his stomach. He was brought back by carriage to Danbury, where he lay for several days in a House on South Street before he died. This house, at the foot of Main Street, was only a short distance from the point where the memorial procession began.

After the chief stone was laid at Wooster Cemetery, the procession continued to the Congregational church for the oration, a lengthy eulogy delivered by the Honorable Brother Henry C. Deming. Those who failed to participate in the church program, whether by choice or circumstance (it was quite crowded), might have found some solace at the Wooster House: on the green in front of the inn, a sumptuous banquet had been spread for all who wished to partake.

A prominent participant in Danbury's great day was George White Ives

(1798–1862), father of George Edward Ives (1845–1894) and grandfather of Charles Edward Ives (1874–1954). This occasion would not have been possible—at least not in this grand manner—were it not for Ives and several others of his generation who were developing, indeed transforming, the town. For these few and their families—Ives, Tweedy, White, Hoyt—public spirit and private benefit appeared to be inextricably entwined. Even in civic endeavors such as the advancement of the railroad line or the introduction of gas lighting, where motives of private profit might seem to predominate, there could be no question as to their salutary effect on the growth of Danbury in the 1850s. Other projects, like the organization and development of Wooster Cemetery, of which George White Ives was treasurer, were more traditionally in the line of community welfare. Romanticizing economics, this small cohort of contemporaries and neighbors saw themselves as a second wave of pioneers. The first wave, a group of eight men, had made their way from Norwalk along a Paquioque Indian path in 1684 and founded Danbury. Returning shortly thereafter with their families, they formed the rudiments of a settlement—homes, farms, a meeting place, a blacksmith's. The homesteads of the "original eight" occupied little more than a few hundred yards along Main Street (the old Indian trail) starting at what would become South Street and extending north.

A century and a half later, a new thrust was taking place, this time economic, not geographic. On the one hand, it reflected the times, the post-Jackson era of laissez-faire business expansion; on the other, Danbury's very survival depended on it. Although Danbury was a small town in the days of George White and George Edward Ives—and even, to a lesser degree, during Charles Ives's boyhood—it could not remain static. For industry had come to Danbury and committed it to progress, like it or not. A small inland town could not survive otherwise, and there was no going back. Despite the amenities of small-town life, the changes that would at length transform it were taking place even in its heyday. As was the case in many smaller communities, it was a handful of men who spearheaded change. Occasionally they made fortunes and great names for themselves, but more often the result was a degree of "being comfortable" and a respected name in town.

Ives had been such a name in Danbury since the days of Isaac Ives, George White Ives's father, who came to the town in the 1790s. His sojourn there was characteristic in some ways of many ambitious New Englanders of the time: the striving, the economic fits and starts, the ultimate success, and the comfortable establishment of self and family in tranquil retirement. Typical too were the social and family networks in which all this took place and the resultant family tradition. Isaac was the strong, singular root of the Danbury Iveses.[3] Born in 1764, he was an adolescent at the time of the Revolution. He went to Yale

College, the first of the Iveses to be associated with Yale, studied law there, and received the degree of bachelor of arts. According to one account, he came to Danbury via Morristown, New Jersey, where he may have tried his hand at teaching. Another suggests that he had rather limited success practicing law in Litchfield before moving to Danbury.[4]

Perhaps his best fortune there was to board with a member of an already prominent family, the Benedicts, who not only could claim both heroes and villains in the recently fought Revolutionary War but could trace their own Danbury origins to the original eight of 1685. Isaac married their daughter, whose death within two years climaxed a series of misfortunes: by then Isaac had failed in several business ventures. Left with a daughter, Jerusha, and again unsuccessful (this time in the tanning business), Isaac married again. His second wife was Sarah Amelia White, of another well-known Danbury family. Their son, George White Ives, was born in New York City in 1798.

Pressed by the need to support a growing family, Isaac attempted to set up business in New York, this time as a wholesale grocer in Pearl Street. The job eventually required travel to New England and the South. On one such trip Isaac wrote to Amelia, "How unpleasant, indeed how painful, to be absent and to not know conditions."[5] Further business failures ensued until Isaac finally went into the hat business with one of the Whites. This proved lucrative and led to a flourishing establishment at 152 Broadway, where Isaac remained until his retirement in 1829. Meanwhile, Sarah Amelia spent long periods of time with the Whites in Danbury. Even when she would return to Isaac in New York, she left George White with his grandparents in Danbury, where he received his education.

Maternal grandfather Joseph Moss White had graduated from Yale in 1766, following in the footsteps of his own father, the Reverend Ebeneezer White, the first of the Whites to settle in Danbury. The minister had been ordained somewhere on Long Island and given a parish in Danbury. In January 1735 or 1736, "Mr. Ebeneezer White was unanimously called by a town meeting to become the minister of the Danbury Church, on a salary of 200 pounds" and the use of the parsonage. He preached for more than twenty-six years, until a dispute developed among members of the congregation.[6] Ebeneezer is said to have lost his pulpit for refusing to preach the doctrine of original sin and infant damnation.

When he died in 1799, Ebeneezer White left three sons, one of whom, Joseph Moss White, was the father of Sarah Amelia, Isaac Ives's second wife. It was in Joseph's home that much of the family life carried on during the years that Isaac Ives spent in New York. Since Isaac was in business with members of the White family at various times, the two families were intimately entwined in many ways. As for their growing position in Danbury, it was said that the Iveses and the Whites were among the few families that *were* the town.[7]

In the 1790s, Thomas Tucker, a New York merchant, retired to Danbury and built a large house on Main Street in which he established a school for the children of friends in the community. Here George White Ives was enrolled while he lived with his grandfather Joseph Moss White. (Perhaps a family connection made this the likely place for his schooling, since Tucker had married a White.) However, Tucker seems not to have given up his mercantile interests completely in favor of pedagogy, for his card reads, "HOPS!" 250 weight of genuine well-cured Hops for sale." Only below this, in somewhat smaller type, is his school promoted.[8]

Later, George White was sent to a boarding school in Meriden, but he did not go on to college. Between the two schools, he evidently gained an educational background deemed sufficient to produce a successful nineteenth-century businessman.

When Isaac retired to Danbury in 1829, he purchased Tucker's house, which was to become the Ives family homestead for generations. It was here that George White Ives's five children—and his grandson Charlie—were born. With the purchase of the house, Isaac, then age sixty-five, and Amelia rooted the Ives family in the town for good. The house was the center of family life, and eventually it became one of the town's centers too. In the 1790s, it was situated toward the upper extension of Main Street, but even then there was a flurry of town life around it. Practically next door was James Seil's barber shop, and across Main Street was the drugstore of Eli Mygatt, a heavy-set gentleman well known for his idiosyncratic knee-britches. Uncle Eli, as he was called, also had in his shop the beginnings of a town library, a small circulating collection known as the Franklin Library.

In Danbury, then as now, no street crossed Main Street. Main Street grew from the life of the town and in turn confined the town's life within itself. When the original eight had followed the Indian path through a shallow valley between two north-south ridges, fir trees still covered the hills, and alders flourished along adjacent streams. At length, the valley opened into a broad plain, where the founding families settled. Four families built on one side of the path and four on the opposite side. As the village grew and the path extended north more than a mile, it was called, perhaps with more aspiration than accuracy, Towne Street. Eventually it came to span the length of the valley and acquired the name it retains today, Main Street.

After the generation of Isaac Ives, Main Street received a new and powerful impetus, this time not from the south, the direction of origin, but from the northern end of town. Following a brief but vigorously fought local political battle, the terminus of the Danbury and Norwalk Railroad was established in the northern part, within a few hundred yards of the Ives home. Indeed, George White Ives was one of a group that had been active and successful in this dispute, and he was one of the railroad's directors. He also happened to own property close to what would become the depot.

It was during the last decade of Isaac's life that the railroad was chartered and planned. By 1845, the year of Isaac's death, George White Ives was well into his forties, sharing the house at 210 Main Street with his parents, Isaac and Amelia, his wife, Sarah Hotchkiss Wilcox, whom he had married in 1831, and the first four of their children. The house itself was dear to the family. For the aging Isaac, it was the culmination of a mercantile life's work and the end of a journey. After purchasing it from the merchant-schoolmaster Tucker, he had it repaired, painted, and enlarged. He especially enjoyed cultivating its flower and vegetable gardens: "There were double Russian violets and loads of lily-of-the-valley and all around the border of the house little star-of-bethlehem flowers, and syringas over the side porch. The house always smelled of beeswax and fruit."[9] With an eye as much on progress as on sylvan tranquility, Isaac dammed up a nearby brook and piped the water to the house. "He had the first bathroom in Fairfield County. People came from miles around to see it."[10] To Isaac, as to so much of America, the pastoral ideal could readily accommodate the artifacts of the new technology.

For George White Ives, the house was a sign of his inheritance and establishment in the world. He had a curious romance with the building that had been his childhood school and later the home of his parents. From here he established his position in town—becoming, as his teacher had been, a deacon of the church—and here he reared his own children. George White's contribution to the heritage of the house, however, was not the cultivation of the gardens his father had so lovingly planted but the establishment of banks.

In 1845, Isaac died and the last of George White Ives's children, George Edward Ives, was born. Within the space of a few months, the forty-six-year-old businessman and his wife, Sarah, had completed their own family, and he had become its senior male member. He named this last son after himself, having already named a son born ten years earlier after his father. His mother, Sarah Amelia, was to remain alive for six more years.[11] The household also included George White's unmarried half-sister, Jerusha, from Isaac's first marriage. Isaac had taken great pains to provide for her in his will, and it was now George White's duty to accomplish his father's wishes.

At his death at the age of eighty-one, Isaac had come a long way from the chronic failure who first arrived in Danbury. His material legacies to wife and son were straightforward, only his detailed instructions for the welfare of Jerusha reveal the values that lay behind his achievement. In providing for her possible progeny—an unlikely occurrence by the time the will was probated—he set up a trust to be used for those practical rites of passage and sacraments that had been

15

close to his own life and characterized family values: "education, advancement, marriage and the setting out in life."[12]

George White Ives was at the height of his own career. His name was associated with most of the major events of the town between 1840 and 1860, such as the introduction of illuminating gas in 1857 (He was one of the incorporators of the gas company and later a director.) Perhaps his most distinguished achievement was organizing the Danbury Savings Bank in 1849. George White was elected treasurer, and the first advertisement in the Danbury *Times* records "the office (for the present) as the Residence of the Treasurer." No address was needed, of course; everybody knew where the Iveses lived. Thus the house on Main Street came to be Danbury's first savings bank. A chest was placed in the dining room, and the deposits for the first day amounted to $165. The dining room was open to the public from three to five o'clock on Saturday afternoons, but one could make a deposit just as readily during a casual meeting with George White anywhere in town or, in his absence, with Mrs. Ives.

The bank flourished, aided by the introduction of the cash system in the following year. Formerly, there had been a trade system by means of which "the workman, instead of receiving cash as a return for his labor, obtained an 'order' on some one of the merchants in its place . . . so there was not a merchant in Danbury but was in some measure concerned or interested in the hatting business, many of them taking payments in hats and shipping them to New York for sale." The cash system was said to have made "an entire revolution in the moneyed interest and financial operations of our village." This was no doubt reflected in the success of the bank, for at the end of the year total deposits exceeded twelve thousand dollars.[13]

Isaac had made his home a garden; George White turned it into a bank but found it equally beautiful. Three years later, he constructed the first bank building just south of the house and adjacent to it, on the site where, years before, the old barber shop had stood. The building reveals much about George White and the values of evolving Danbury. Reflecting a certain practicality, its dimensions were small, its scale perhaps appropriate to a town of some five thousand citizens. Its style, however, reflected grander aspirations, with its Greek revival pediment perched atop a building whose width was scarcely three times the size of its doorway. In all, it gave the impression of a fair-sized mausoleum rather than a financial institution, but it housed the bank until 1866, when a more ample structure was built next door.

The location of the tiny building, however, suggests something further. Isaac's gardens had been next to the house, which itself was set back from Main Street by a broad lawn in front. The flower garden with its little fountain had been in the rear, between the house and a barn that was later pressed into service as an auxiliary home for any family members who might need it. (This would be the boyhood home of Charles Ives.) All this meant privacy within a commodious suburban setting of some pastoral aspiration. At the same time, unscreened and unfenced, the house did not lack a sense of hospitality. The new bank, next to the house but jutting far in front of it, was right on Main Street. In fact, it now defined Main Street, and although the streets were as yet unpaved, it established the eventual location of sidewalk and thoroughfare, lending new meaning to the generous elm trees which by now lined the path.

Gardens gave way to commerce within the town. At its periphery, industry prospered, in particular the hatting industry, for which Danbury was famous. Machinery introduced between 1845 and 1850 began to make manufacturihg more efficient, and business progressed in spite of sporadic reversals and unemployment. There was other industry in town as well, including hat case manufacturing, paper milling, and, later, shoe manufacturing. Farms flourished nearby, and unemployed hatters frequently hired themselves out to farmers during haying season and harvest. But the rural features of the town itself were beginning to change. Country was beginning to be pushed out of town, although it remained readily accessible. Moreover, despite the inevitable transformations fostered by commerce, Danbury would always retain the small scale characteristic of New England towns. Its internal growth was taking place within the generally rural setting of Connecticut's Fairfield County, a land of hills, valleys, and small lakes.

Yet there was already a sense of loss for what was being transformed. Change and yearning were fast becoming partners in progress. Nowhere in the Danbury of the time could this be seen more clearly than in the planning for the rural cemetery, in which George White Ives was playing a leading role. In effect, he had not completely abandoned the garden; he had only shifted it to the outskirts of town and changed its functions from quotidian to ceremonial.

The Danbury historian, James M. Bailey, writes, "In extent and topography the grounds of the Wooster Cemetery are not excelled by any burial-place in Connecticut. There are eighty-three acres in the enclosure. It is rolling land, with a number of broad plateaux, is abundantly shaded, has attractive drives, and a lake dotted with verdant islands. . . . The shade trees are numerous and varied, the grass is green and thick, and everywhere are evidences of loving thought and care for those who have gone before. The pretty curving lake fills the place where once was a swamp thick with bogs and bushes, and the drive is shaded by trees, where the birds 'swing and sing' in the spring time."[14] The cemetery, in short, was the new garden, and the town treated it as such. It became one of the attractions of Danbury. Couples and families often strolled there of a summer afternoon, and people who came to stay for a few days (perhaps lodging in the

Wooster House, in which George had an interest) included it among the sites to be visited.

In the cemetery itself, George White Ives found his own memorial, since it was for this as much as for the bank that he was remembered. A memorial plaque in the chapel marks his contribution. Elsewhere, on one of the green knolls overlooking a pond, the "pretty curving lake," his monument presides over the members of the family.

TWO

A VILLAGE BOYHOOD

Eighteen-forty-five was neither the worst nor the best of years for the growing republic. An adolescent America advanced gawkily toward its first mid-century mark. Stretching, it extended itself to Mexico and Canada, pressured by an as yet untempered appetite to gobble Texas and huge territories of the Pacific Northwest. An entire nation, driven by a vast energy, burst forward while agitating inwardly in conflict over such issues as slavery which would soon threaten its integrity. It would rationalize its frequently uncoordinated motions as "manifest destiny."

The birth of George Edward Ives was not recorded in the weekly Danbury *Times*. (It was not yet the custom to do so, perhaps because the high death rate of children made the practice seem hardly worthwhile.) The youngest of the family's five children, George Edward was born when his father, at forty-seven, was well into middle age. His two brothers, Joseph Moss and Isaac Wilcox, were more than ten years his senior, and between them was a bossy older sister, Sarah Amelia, and still another sister, who died in childhood. After grandfather Isaac's death, his widow continued to live with her son George and his family in the house on Main Street.

At that time, George White Ives's activities and holdings were so widespread that his name appeared on the town records more often than that of any other man in Danbury. By the time George Edward was ready for school, his father had been appointed burgess at the annual borough meeting and had become treasurer of the new Danbury and Norwalk Railroad. That he lost the election for town treasurer was perhaps an unfortunate consequence of local politics: he ran on the Temperance ticket. Meanwhile, his personal fortune was increasing. As a result of the local "civil war" of 1851—a north-south controversy regarding the location of the railroad depot—his holdings in the north section of town became more valuable. He opened a carriage business there and became a founder of the new Wooster House Hotel on the corner of Main and White Streets, near the depot. Combining civic with paternal duty, a year after the birth of his youngest son he began to serve on the committee of the Danbury Academy, a private school. His oldest son, Joseph Moss, was sent there to prepare for Yale, the first Ives to aspire to that institution since grandfather Isaac had attended it seventy-five years earlier.

George Edward was five when Joseph went off to Yale. That Joseph did so at all was a reflection of his father's position and values, as a college education was hardly necessary for a career in business at the time. The second son, Isaac Wilcox, felt no need for higher education. In a sense, sending Joseph to Yale was a worthwhile investment for his father and yet another achievement beside his business and civic successes. Joe would probably study law, and lawyers were increasingly needed in Danbury by people like the Iveses. The law was a profession both utilitarian and honorable and was also a path to a position of civic leadership if not public office. As oldest son, Joseph was the bright hope of the family, and it was thought that he would continue the thrust of his father's life. But this was not to be.

At Yale, Joseph ran into trouble when he was caught in a prank and sent back to Danbury for two weeks. He and a group of his friends decided that six A.M. was too early to go to chapel and hence filled the chapel bell with plaster. The telltale remains were found in Joseph's room. He was "gated," sent home but not expelled.[1] His father, however, was disappointed and angry enough to decide that he should not return. Accordingly, the unhappy Joseph was sent to Boston to work in a branch of the family business—an unfortunate turn for him since he was said to be a lover of books and to have little talent for business. It was the next brother, Isaac, who had inherited their father's knack for business and was the more likely to follow in his footsteps. But Joseph's two-year exile in Boston was not without its own contributions to family tradition. George White set Joseph up in the hat business in Boston. Meanwhile, it was considered that brother Isaac had had about as much education as he required. In lieu of college, he was sent to New York to gain business experience in a Wall Street office.

In Boston, Joseph came to meet and admire the Cambridge group, in particular Ralph Waldo Emerson and James Russell Lowell. The depth and degree of their contact are not known, but there were several later results of these experiences. Books were added to the family library, one autographed by Emerson himself, and one of the Lowells subsequently visited Joseph and the family, staying at the house. Later, in 1857, after the Danbury Lyceum had been organized, Emerson came twice to give lectures. It is said that he stayed with the Iveses on those occasions, the house on Main Street being only a few steps from the Congregational Church, where the lectures were given. The Iveses were represented on the board of the Lyceum by the unacademic Isaac, naturally as treasurer. Thus it was that the actual life of the family was touched by the transcendentalists—through coincidence and a natural hospitality.

Returning to Danbury after his sojourn in Boston, Joseph proved to be neither as successful nor as visible as his younger brother Isaac, called Ike, would shortly become in Danbury's commercial and civic life. In 1856, Ike became the junior partner of the growing lumber company Stevens and Ives. The Danbury *Times*, in its fashion, acknowledged the paid advertisement of this event with a short news item noting that Isaac Ives "is possessed of the true spirit of go-a-head-ativeness—(unlike his 'sleepers,' he will always be found wide awake)." Taking the occasion to follow up with a brief item on "lumber", the local reporter shrewdly observed, "If any one wishes to see the material from which a good part of the rest of this town is to be built, they can do so by looking over the lumber yard of Isaac W. Ives in White Street."[2]

Ike's accomplishments were many, approaching although not surpassing those of his father. He initially eclipsed his elder brother, Joseph, by dint of his commercial ability. Meanwhile, George White himself had started a large business in which there was a place for Joseph, but a relative lack of Isaac's characteristic "go-a-head-ativeness" may have caused him to yield a portion of his birthright to Ike.[3] In any event, in the years immediately following the "Monumental Celebration" of 1854, both of George Edward's older brothers were well launched in business careers appropriate to the time and place, to their station in life, and, above all, to an evolving Ives tradition.

George Edward's mother, Sarah Wilcox Ives, was the domestic head of the varied and warm household which lent human support to the activities of husband and sons. The parents occupied the large bedroom over the south parlor. The bedroom had access to the back stairs, which led down to the kitchen. For a time, grandmother Amelia continued to occupy the master bedroom on the ground floor. There was also a large extended family living nearby, and many friends.

Sarah was involved in various charities, as might be expected of the wife of George W. Ives, in particular the Danbury Home for Destitute and Homeless Children, which she was responsible for saving from heavy indebtedness and making into a permanent charity in town. She also took part in the abolition movement and many years later maintained an interest in Negro welfare. She helped raise money for the Hampton Institute in Virginia after the Civil War.

In 1856, when George Edward turned eleven, Isaac started in the lumber yard, and Joseph returned from Boston, there was a new impetus to family social life. George White and Sarah sold a piece of land adjacent to the house to the First Congregational Church, of which they were members, for a new church building. It was considered "one of the finest localities of the village." The lumber for the wooden structure, of course, would have been purchased from Isaac. The work proceeded remarkably well with only one mishap, when the spire fell the summer it was being raised. Thereafter, the Ives house became something of a social center for friends and relatives on Sundays. As Amelia Van Wyck (née Amelia Merritt Ives, Joseph's daughter) later related, "After church (church got out at twelve o'clock, and Sunday School was from twelve to one) . . . people used to stop in . . . they used to call it having Sunday School over there. And they were the Hoyts and one set of Tweedys and the Houghs. And they discussed matters throughout the world, what was going on in the world, men and books and so forth, until it was time to pick up the children and go home to Sunday dinner."[4] The parcel of land that the Iveses had sold to the church had been grandfather Isaac's vegetable garden. So George White had wrought this final change on his domestic landscape. Now, in front of his home, he had his bank on one side and his church on the other.

This was the town and the family in which George Edward Ives grew up. That he could have a boyhood, as we have come to understand boyhood, was an accident of history and economic circumstance. For the mid-nineteenth century was a watershed period in ideas of child rearing and education in America. Earlier Puritan beliefs in the depravity of children and in their innate tendencies to wickedness still exerted a powerful influence, and it was only at about this time, in the years immediately preceding the Civil War, that more liberal ideas began to appear in the popular literature, notably in Horace Bushnell's *Views of Christian Nature* (1847). When they finally did, there seems to have been a groundswell: books on child rearing and education (in particular, moral education) had a wide readership. Actually, Bushnell did not completely abandon Puritan views in his revised ideas of pedagogy. *Nurture* was the key word—and proper nurture would counteract wicked tendencies at their weakest point, in early childhood. But weeding out sin, like cultivating a garden, required care and patience. This was the very issue the Reverend Ebeneezer White had addressed himself to seventy-five years earlier.

Until this period "the education of Americans was informal, unsystematic, and dependent on parental initiative and ability to pay."[5] The education of George White Ives was a perfect example of this state of affairs. Public schools of the day were mostly for the poor, and for those poor who were fortunate enough to be able to attend. Isaac could dispense with the youth's potential earning capacity for a time, a luxury that was beyond the reach of most families. Danbury was at heart a factory town, and proud of it. If the Iveses did not own the factories, they owned a large share of the supporting services, and the fates of the two were intermingled. But certainly, their children did not work in the factories as many a youth did in mid-century Danbury.

The movement for education reform, for free public education, and for improved schooling had penetrated to Connecticut and was closely associated with the issue of children's rights. By the time George Edward started school, the national ferment in education had begun to filter down to smaller towns such as Danbury. But Ike Ives was on the board of the local Danbury Academy, a private school. This is the school that George Edward probably attended.

The daily life of school and family was supplemented by the pleasures of play and enriched by special days. Everyday play encompassed the whole town: life was lived and pleasures found within a few square miles. Fishing could be done in any number of streams which were then scattered throughout the village, some providing power to local mills and other machinery. A few of the lakes could be "rafted" in summer; in the winter one could skate on them, and there was plenty of sleigh riding, both impromptu and organized. Kite flying and games with marbles were popular. Boys occasionally found their way to the more formal, even genteel activities of the town, often to make mischief. The local paper admonished boys and their parents alike, but not without humor. Aside from some complaints about the pilfering of fruit and produce, the youngsters of this generation seem not to have caused any problems worthy of note.

Special days were eagerly anticipated. Family days included not only Christmas (which, incidentally, was celebrated then without the elaborate gift giving of today) but also births and marriages. Even at funerals the guests could look forward at least to a lavish spread of refreshments. Sundays, however, remained dull for the restless. By the 1850s, circuses came to town three or four times a year. Although P. T. Barnum was a native of nearby Bethel and during George Edward's early years was regularly contributing a "Letter" to the Danbury *Times* describing his travels, his own spectacles seemed to have been confined to New York at that time. Bailey's Circus, with which Barnum's later merged, was a visitor, however. The circuses became increasingly elaborate and attracted children and adults of all ages. Brass bands gradually began to be a traditional and important feature of the circus, along with the usually well advertised solo cornet, who might be expected to give a dazzling display of virtuosity.

In Danbury of the 1840s, the Fourth of July was only beginning to become the holiday it was later to be. Its observance earlier had been erratic, and only gradually had the customs associated with it emerged—civic gatherings, patriotic speeches, family picnic, and, above all, fireworks and noise symbolic of victory in war. By now, it had become not only a patriotic holiday but a significant business and political event as well. Perhaps the Fourth of July as a symbolic celebration was late in coming to communities such as Danbury because the war it commemorated had been so real and vivid in the lives of many of the town; their grandparents had fought it and in many cases, older parents still had some recollections. There still remained a few veterans in town.

Since the end of the Revolutionary War, military preparedness had shifted from necessity to custom, and then to ritual and entertainment. Annual Training Days were held from the beginning of the century, when a stretch of common at a bow in lower Main Street was set aside for the two existing civil military organizations of the town, an artillery and a cavalry company, which met for drill. The artillery rendezvoused at a nearby tavern, which no doubt contributed much to the event; the cavalry traditionally met further north at what had been the home of the Revolutionary War major Starr. There was no lack of taverns in that quarter. A "training" was described as a "mighty event" in those days, "and the village would be full of visitors." By mid-century, this event was diminishing in popularity and was perhaps at that point supplanted by the Fourth of July celebration.[6]

One could see signs in America of the 1840s and 1850s that boyhood itself was emerging from individual life history as a definable, honorable, and, above all, lovable period of life. If something parallel was happening to girlhood, it was not immediately apparent; perhaps it took place with less visibility, within the home. Boys' activities tended to be noisy and exhibitionistic; when in competition, boys often were on the verge of a fight at any moment. Behind the wry complaints of adults about this boisterousness was a kind of pride. For despite attempts to confine this youthful energy through school and church, they saw in it the wellspring of a dynamic American manhood. Admiration, mixed with nostalgia for their own youth, fostered what amounted to a cult of boyhood. Already clear in local news items, by the end of the century it would culminate in a rich literature about boys, Tom Sawyer and Huckleberry Finn. Boyhood friendships and extended chains of friendship among groups fostered fraternity among men and provided the training ground for the adult fraternal and political organizations that were already popular in the large cities as well as the small towns of America.

Where would music, or any art, fit in such a vision of boyhood, and what might be the fate of a youngster who was born gifted in music? Traditionally, music had an honorable if constrained place in military life, which was by definition a man's place. In times of peace, the celebration of such patriotic events as the Fourth of

July, Washington's Birthday, and (following the Civil War) Decoration Day still required musical accompaniment. Accordingly, the nineteenth century saw the growth of the band in America, and Danbury, although a late starter, was no exception. By extension, all sorts of outdoor events, such as picnics, parades, political meetings, and other social gatherings, fostered participation in bands.

Indoor music—the music of church, parlor, and, later, concert hall—was something quite different. Unlike outdoor music, this area of musical experience was viewed as essentially passive. To the boy, it implied staying home and practicing piano, a sedentary activity deemed more appropriate for girls. In the community it was looked upon as unsuitable preparation for manhood.

One element that might move a family to encourage music in its children was a pretension to gentility. Music was largely held to be one of the finer things in life even if it was held, at times, at arm's length. Moreover, it was one of the things money could buy, and this feature might have helped counter the implication that the finer things ought to remain exclusively the woman's province. Besides, there appeared to be little danger that a boy reared in the early 1850s in Danbury would become a musician in any but a recreational sense. The models for a young man in commercial life were too compelling and the potential rewards too great. Indeed, not one of the very few men in town who attempted to make their living through music did so with any degree of comfort. All had many jobs both in and out of music. Moreover, none was a native of Danbury, and most appeared to fade from whatever musical scene there was after a few years.

George White and Sarah had given music lessons to all of their older children. But Joseph, Isaac, and Amelia found the lessons boring, and the parents came to consider them a waste of money, so they did not offer them at first to George Edward. Then, according to Amelia Van Wyck, "One day the family were going on a Fourth of July picnic, and they said, 'George, aren't you ready, don't you want to come?' and George said, 'Well, if you don't mind, I'd rather stay home and pick cherries to earn some money to buy a flute.' So they thought if George felt that way about it he should have music lessons."[7]

It soon became evident that George possessed perfect pitch and a refined sense of hearing in other respects as well. He proved himself adept on several musical instruments; in addition to the flute, he could play the piano, the violin, and the cornet, the last of which was to become his chief instrument. Musically gifted and motivated young people experience frustration in environments that do not encourage and nurture their talents. The existence of a growing, increasingly varied musical environment with at least a few role models would have been a source of comfort and nourishment for the young musician. Unfortunately, this was not the case in Danbury during George's early years.

The story of George's young life in music parallels the evolution of music in

Danbury and many small towns in mid-century New England. Although music was never devoid of a social context, concerts as a specific occasion to listen to music were rare events. On the other hand, the occasions for music were many, and accordingly there were some opportunities for teachers of music. A few came and went during George's youth, leaving behind a handful of more or less accomplished students, most of them young women. The teachers themselves, however, were men—Charles B. Hine, a hatter and a skilled amateur; Emile Gaebler, better trained, who remained for more than seven years; and later, in 1856, Charles Hazen. Some of them served as church organists as well. These men promoted the first concerts in Danbury and were influential in advancing what has come to be called the genteel tradition in American music.[8]

Thus, during the years from 1845 to 1860, those who were interested enough to venture out in the evening might be exposed to increasingly sophisticated music. At first, such evenings, often called "soirées musicales," were rare and consisted of local performers. Soon performers from outside Danbury, and eventually "artistes" from New York and elsewhere began to appear. Gradually, the well-known singing groups of the time came to Danbury—the Baker Family (as early as 1846), the American Vocalists (in 1851), and the most famous, the Hutchinson Family Singers (in 1855 and 1859).

The early Danbury musicians had to be musical jacks-of-all-trades. In addition to teaching and playing in church, they often tuned pianos for New York companies. At first they also sold pianos; Gaebler, for example, in 1853 placed the first advertisement of a musical instrument in the Danbury *Times*. But once Danbury businessmen saw the profit in that trade, they took it over. There was a struggling Danbury band at the time, a sincere but poorly organized and supported group. It was rare then for one of the "professors" to be involved, but Emile Gaebler was an exception and briefly led the band. Such musicians were more interested in promoting other musical events. Gaebler, for example, spent more than six months preparing a performance of Mendelssohn's *Saint Paul* in 1852, for which he engaged the Jenny Lind Orchestra in New York. The chorus of more than thirty singers came from Mr. Gaebler's own singing classes.

As was typical in the more ambitious musical projects of the time, a committee of local citizens lent its support to the concert, and the newspaper advertisement noted that tickets could be procured from them. Among these gentlemen we find the name of George W. Ives, a sign of the worth and respectability of the undertaking. Gaebler was no doubt the music teacher for the Ives family as he was for many in the town. His credentials appear to have been impeccable: he had formerly been a teacher at such locally respected schools as the Reverend J. W. Irwin's institute. When he first announced his presence in Danbury, he was supported by a panel of leaders from the best families in town: the Whites,

Hoyts, Tweedys, Wildmans, and, of course, the Iveses, the very group that supported all the town's progressive business endeavors.

When George Edward was picking cherries to purchase a flute in the proverbial family story, he probably intended to take lessons with Gaebler, who taught flute, among other instruments. If so, George was fortunate to have had as a model about as well trained a musician as one could expect to find in a community the size of Danbury. In addition to his teaching, Gaebler was organist of the Methodist church. Moreover, he was something of a composer: at least one of his works was published, an anthem dedicated to Mr. Hoyt, the pastor. But for George, perhaps most important of all was the example of an alternative path in life. George had grown up among the ablest businessmen and civic leaders of the community. What place was there in this environment for a boy who might have been viewed as doubly disadvantaged—first as a youth with no particular skill, ambition, or need for business, and second as a person endowed with a musical gift?

Another aspect of musical life in Danbury with which George was familiar was an offshoot of the church tradition: the camp meeting. Camp meetings were Methodist religious festivals consisting of prayer meetings, sermons, religious classes, and hymn sings, usually held at designated campgrounds in the countryside. They enjoyed enormous popularity from the early 1800s to the Civil War, reaching their high point in the 1840s, although they continued to flourish well after the war. The Danbury meetings generally took place for an entire week sometime in August at the campgrounds in nearby Redding. Methodism had especially strong roots in this area, for Redding had been the base of operations of the earliest circuit-riding preachers in America. Its appeal was in part its optimistic alternative to Puritan doctrine.

During George's time, they still took place in tents; later, a structure was erected to accommodate the vast crowd. After the railroad came to town, densely packed trains of up to sixteen cars made their way to the campgrounds. This permitted people to come and go with relative ease, although many adhered to the older custom of remaining at the meeting for the entire week, either boarding locally or sleeping on the grounds and taking meals in large communal kitchens. Sometimes the meetings would take place at a site convenient for several neighboring towns, and Danbury, Bridgeport, Bethel, Redding, and Norwalk would each have its own tent.

Although the Ives family was nominally Congregationalist and the camp meetings were a predominantly Methodist event, George seems to have attended them, drawn perhaps by the music. The camp meeting was a lively, outdoor community event of tremendous appeal. The chief and most characteristic music was the gospel hymn, with which George became familiar. It was not uncommon for a cornetist to join in these performances, as well as a choir (since no organ could be used). George found himself drawn more to this feelingful music than to the relatively austere and traditional church music, although his exercise book reveals that he was familiar with and skilled in church music too.

A popular aspect of folk tradition in George's youth was fiddling. Danbury could boast at least two fine, older fiddlers, Judge Homer Peters (an honorary title) and James W. Nichols. The tradition was continued by a contemporary of George's who later became a member of his band, John Starr. Although Judge Peters, a black man, was a fiddler in Danbury for more than forty years and was well known locally, it is in the nature of a folk tradition not to leave a written record. Except for the occasional observation in the Danbury newspaper that Peters had attended a party or a dance, we know little else of the circumstances of his performances, let alone the music.

Fortunately, James W. Nichols, who was also a local poet, left a diary. In his "Log Book of the Barque James W. Nichols Bound to 'That bourne whence no traveller returns,'" begun in 1846, he noted casually the frequent and informal occasions for fiddling.[9] At one wedding, Nichols deferred to Peters, who was also present: "Judge Homer Peters a finished professor of Music was now called on to conclude the festivities of the evening with a few scientific Cotillions." Elsewhere he noted, "When the honors of the table were over and the cloth removed, my fiddle was introduced and although I lacked the finished execution of Judge Peters, I must really take to myself the praise of giving our ladies an opportunity to display their charm and accomplishments in an infinite variety of jigs, waltzes, reels and cotillions." A country-town dance party could be a special occasion, marked by the spontaneity of its music and dancing long into the evening.

As for band music, its growth in Danbury closely paralleled George's life and development as a musician. A band in some form existed sometime before his birth, for in 1845 there is a report of a fair given by the ladies of the town for its benefit. The high point was the presentation of a splendid flag made by the women for the occasion. But we know little about the Danbury Band, and indeed other bands were engaged for major village events. Shaw's Bridgeport Band, for example, played at the Hatters' Ball of 1850 and at the New Year's Eve Ball the following year. At the Masonic Celebration of 1853, it shared the bandstand with another first-class band from New Haven. For less distinguished events, bands were brought in from elsewhere, as from nearby Ridgefield.

Of course, whenever the circus was in town, there was ample opportunity to hear a professional band, usually with a featured cornetist. The cornetist was to the small-town band what the concert pianist or violinist was to the orchestras of the world's capitals. It was not until shortly before the Civil War that the

Danbury area was able to muster and sustain a band of its own. This achievement was largely owing to such men as George Ives and to the public support they could attract. A decade after the war, the town boasted three bands.

By 1860, as George approached fifteen, it must have already been clear to the Iveses that he was not destined to follow any traditional family role model. He was still a boy in a family that now included three enterprising and successful men. Among them, they owned the largest lumber business in town and a store with an impressive array of home furnishings. Joseph and Ike were well established and George White, now in the last two years of his life, owned a considerable portion of the northern end of town near the railroad station. By now there was an Ives Street. Perhaps George White already had a sense that his youngest son was becoming the maverick, the black sheep; perhaps he felt that there would always be a place for the boy in one of the family's businesses should he need it. In any event, he agreed to George Edward's wish to advance his education in music.

A music professor, Charles Foepple, was found in New York, and George was sent to him for lessons. Foepple lived on a farm in Morrisania (now part of the Bronx) and later in downtown Manhattan, on Christie Street. Regrettably, about all we know of Foepple is that George considered himself fortunate to have been taught by so well grounded a musician. A neat and thorough notebook in George's hand is headed, "Lessons on Musical theory and thorough base Taken in the Winter of 1860–1 at New York, From Prof. Chas. A. Foepple by Geo. E. Ives." The lessons appear to have been drawn from a traditional European text of the time. Foepple had George write out the lessons from a translation or meticulously taught them himself. George's good training is clear from the lessons and associated exercises.[10]

So it was that growing up in semirural and commercial Danbury, George Ives, through his association with men like Gaebler and Foepple, was able to get a good classical background in music and some reinforcement in the possibilities of a style of life different from that of his father and brothers. His association with Foepple continued on and off until 1868, by which time he had already served in the Civil War and was trying to find his way back into Danbury life.

George left the Danbury of his boyhood to study in New York in August 1860; he had just reached his fifteenth birthday. In the fall, Abraham Lincoln was elected president. The Danbury-Charleston link of the hatting industry, established in the days of Isaac Ives, was becoming imperiled. Rumblings in the South were felt keenly in Connecticut through the loss of markets and the threat of war. The following April, Fort Sumter was fired upon, igniting the Civil War, and a year later, by the summer of 1862, the northern Army of the Potomac was in full retreat. Winter found the boys of 1845, now adolescents, tenting in despair in the Virginia mud. And thousands were soon impelled to join them, moved by President Lincoln's call for three hundred thousand volunteers, by a patriotism now long obsolete, by a song, *The Battle Cry of Freedom*, which infused spirit into a faltering nation, and by the inherent restlessness of youth. Among these boys and young men was the seventeen-year-old George Edward Ives.

THREE

AMONG THE CONNECTICUT "HEAVIES"

I n the spring of 1860, the Danbury Band appears to have received a new impetus, sparked perhaps by a new leader, a music teacher from New York named Merns. He was said to have roused the sleepy band of nearby New Canaan to new effectiveness. Merns himself excelled on the fife. George Edward, not yet fifteen, played at the band's first, sparsely attended concert. A reviewer noted, "Among the players we saw a young scion of George W. Ives Esq. who bids fair to become an adept with his instrument." The eclectic program included a local blackface minstrel, "a negro melodist and general delineator of ebony characteristics," and Judge Peters "with a well tried and faithful friend, his fiddle."[1]

The Danbury *Times* took this occasion to admonish the local citizens regarding their attitude toward the band: "The exercises were frequently applauded by the *slim* audience in attendance, and, considering everything, we have had many worse entertainments than that furnished by the Brass Band on Monday night." The article was dated April 12, 1860, exactly one year before the Confederates fired on Fort Sumter.[2]

Soon afterward, George left for New York and his studies with Charles Foepple, although he apparently moved back and forth, living for periods at home and continuing to participate in occasional performances in Danbury that year and the following two. Thus, all we know of George during the first two years of the Civil War is that he was in New York and a sometime student of Foepple's. In some ways, life in Danbury in 1860 proceeded at its accustomed pace. A characteristic note of optimism might be discerned in the expansion of the Hotel Pahquioque as summer approached, making Danbury's accommodations superior to any between there and New York, sixty-eight miles away. In advertisements its healthful location and appropriateness for a summer's holiday were emphasized along with its unique combination of the pleasures of town and country.

In the previous ten years alone, the population of Danbury proper had grown from 5,965 to 7,240, and this did not include adjoining Bethel. At the same time, it was becoming increasingly clear that both the rural tranquility and the growth of the town were in jeopardy as war became inevitable. Danbury was far from isolated from national events. Only days after its account of the debut of the Danbury Brass Band, the local press had more momentous news to report. At the Democratic party convention in Charleston, delegations from six southern states had withdrawn from the Union. By December, days before South Carolina seceded, President Buchanan, in his State of the Union address, publicly acknowledged what everyone already knew, that the "different sections of the Union are now arrayed against each other, and the time has arrived, so much dreaded by the Father of his Country, when hostile geographical parties have been formed." Danbury newsman James Montgomery Bailey, returning from a week's visit to New York and Brooklyn, was relieved "to get out of the political volcano, whose internal fires appear to be on the eve of uncapping." With more despair than hope, Buchanan called for a day of "national humiliation, fasting and prayer." Danbury, poised for the coming conflict, had already responded to events by planning such an occasion locally. It was held in the Hall of the Young Men's Christian Association and "attended by citizens representing almost every shade of religious and political opinion."[3]

By April 1861 and the firing on Fort Sumter, there was almost a sense of relief that the "volcano" of which Bailey had written had finally erupted. Governor William Buckingham issued a proclamation calling for volunteers to rendezvous at Hartford. In Danbury, citizens assembled at the courthouse and resolved that the administration must be supported in suppressing the rebellion. The local Wooster Guards received notice to march within hours and became the first unit to respond, the first to arrive at the rendezvous, and one of the first Connecticut regiments to be commissioned.

The departure of the Wooster Guards on April 19, 1861, marked the start of Danbury's involvement in the Civil War. A kind of optimism prevailed. The Wooster Guards had enlisted for only three months; no one in Danbury believed that the war would last four months, let alone four weary years. In fact, men responded eagerly, much concerned that the war might be over before they had an opportunity to get to the front. Everyone wished to participate in what promised to be one of the greatest historic events in the life of the town. The Guards, augmented by volunteers, numbered between sixty and seventy. A cavalcade led them to the concert hall, where a service was held. Elder E. E. Griswold, whose son-in-law was among those leaving, addressed the assemblage. All then marched north to the large square in the rear of the depot, where coaches of the Danbury and Norwalk awaited them behind an impatiently steaming engine. "Hundreds looked on from house-tops, balconies, and every point where a standingplace could be gained."[4]

Those in Danbury endeavored to keep in touch with their soldiers by letter and by extending the comforts of home. In addition to medicines, the regimental hospitals were provided with fruits, jellies, and wines for the anticipated convalescents. Knitting circles were formed to produce mittens and stockings for the Connecticut volunteers. At Thanksgiving, turkey and pumpkin pies were dispatched to the men in the field. The strong support of those at home and their concern for the everyday welfare of the local soldiers were reflected in Governor Buckingham's trip to see that the rations the boys received were what they should be. (Since they were near Washington by that time, it is conceivable that the governor had political as well as humanitarian motives.)

The July Fourth celebration in 1861 was without question the most spirited one in memory. It was far noisier than was customary, with small-arms and cannon fire announcing the day along with the ringing of the church bells. It was better attended too, with neighboring communities invited by Danbury to join in the festivities. The oration was delivered by Lyman D. Brewster, a prominent young Danbury lawyer who later (in 1868) married George White Ives's only surviving daughter, Amelia. The speaker's platform was in itself eloquent, with a bronze statue of George Washington cradled in folds of stars and stripes, above which the American eagle spread its wings.

Despite the intense heat of the day, the exercises in the concert hall received solemn attention. The audience was invited to exhibit its patriotism by joining in the singing of the *Star Spangled Banner*. The day ended with a splendid torchlight procession. The flags that lined the morning's procession were purposely kept in place for the night's activities and appeared brilliantly illuminated as the parade passed.

The only sour note in the celebration was revealed in a letter to the editor of the local newspaper. It had to do with the town's mixed feelings about its band. "Where," asks the writer, "was the Cornet Band? Our Band does credit to this place and is worthy of encouragement and what better could have been given them than good pay for a good day's work? . . . Every one who appreciates good music felt the loss of our Band on this occasion, and I sincerely hope on all occasions when music is needed that strains of victorious music may come floating from our own Band and no other. Long live the Cornet Band!"[5]

The Civil War exerted a profound effect on American music by pressing it into service. As a result, its character was defined, at least for those years, and its direction set for the future. This was the era of the brass band. The foundations of an orchestral tradition were being laid in some of the larger cities by musicians such as George's teacher, Foepple, and other German emigrants of his generation who were trained in the European tradition, in conjunction with American patrons. The need for bands provided a new and different stimulus to American music. Bands could be assembled rapidly since their artistic level did not need to be very high. Many regiments recruited their own bands and purchased their own instruments, under military order. This ferment of musical activity at length had an effect on the future: after the war, every hamlet had its band, bandstand, summer concerts, and parades as a matter of course.

In addition to being used in the field and elsewhere, bands were essential to the recruiting effort. Everywhere rallies were organized to encourage enlistments, and band music and oratory were powerful inducements. A regiment that had a good band and could present a smart appearance was in a better position to attract volunteers. Thus, at the beginning of the war there was considerable competition for good musicians, and advertisements like the following appeared in many newspapers: "The National Zouaves are well organized, but a Drum Major and Buglers are wanted for this Regiment."[6] Some regiments that were unable to form bands before departure would hire well-known bands for a professional and appropriate send-off. The Dodsworth Band of New York, for example, was hired by the Lincoln Cavalry for a parade to its point of embarkation.[7] The famous Gilmore Band of Boston was a frequent escort of local units to their training camps until Gilmore enlisted the entire group with the Twenty-fourth Massachusetts Volunteer Regiment.[8]

It is impossible to understand the spirit of the times without understanding the role music played. The Civil War may well be the most musical war in world history. We have already seen that even in the social life of a small American town, no event was complete without music, and certain civic events in particular required band music. Music was an essential ingredient in every peaceful assembly—so much taken for granted that mention of it might be omitted in an account of a day. In war, it was considered indispensable. The sheer number of musicians in the war was impressive: it has been estimated that if all vacancies had been filled, there would have been a total of 104,234 musicians in the Union army during the course of the war. In December 1861, the paymaster of the Union army reached the conclusion that if the bands (being "more ornamental than useful") were eliminated, the Union would save five million dollars annually. Actually, the sum would have been more than six and a half million.[9] Indeed, by the following year, the secretary of war Edwin M. Stanton, ordered the use of regimental bands limited, "[the] proportion of musicians now allowed by law being too great, and their usefulness not at all commensurate with their heavy expense."[10] Implementation of the order did cut expenses, but it hardly stopped the music.

In August, the Wooster Guards so brilliantly sent off three months earlier were returning, their tour of duty completed. By this time, there was no longer talk of a ninety-day war. Men who left for the front at this point had been recruited for three years, and the mood was quite different for their departure. There remained the cavalcade up Main Street and a fair assemblage of approving onlookers in addition to friends and family. But the speaker's stand had already become a fixture at the depot, and the exercises consisting of prayers, addresses, and the singing of the national anthem had become routine, far from exciting. Speeches, however florid, were approaching strings of clichés. And despite the clamor and bustle, these events were increasingly suffused with a sadness that would soon infiltrate everyday life in Danbury. At the beginning of 1862, the earliest reports of war deaths reached the country town. With the first, it became apparent that not all of the young martyrs would die heroes in battle. A young man of nearby Bethel died of measles and complications of typhoid fever. As the war went on, these diseases would claim the lives of many and prove far more pernicious than violence. In the Danbury of 1861, one-third of all local deaths occurred before the age of twenty. Now new risks threatened an entire generation of men. A few sick young men quietly rejoined the community since it was the custom to send men home for convalescence if they were not contagious.

Most of the new groups of three-year volunteers were funneled into the Fourth Infantry Regiment, which was eventually reshuffled in Washington to become the First Connecticut Volunteer Heavy Artillery, known popularly in Danbury as "the Heavies." This was the regiment in which George Ives would soon serve. A motley, ill-trained and easily disgruntled group at first, by the spring of 1862 the Heavies was considered an outstanding regiment. The adjutant general's report ranked it as "the best volunteer regiment of heavy artillery in the field . . . equal in all respects to any regiment of the same army in the regular service."[11]

The Heavies set out from the comfortable barracks of Fort Richardson, Virginia, where they had trained, to join the vast army under General George McClellan dedicated to capturing Richmond by way of the peninsula between the York and James rivers. Despite an absurd advantage in the number of soldiers (150,000 to 7,500), McClellan decided to lay siege to the city of Yorktown and the line of fortification across the peninsula. It took twenty-two days to position the heavy guns for this operation, which involved, among other things, conveying more than seventeen thousand projectiles weighing a total of more than four hundred thousand pounds. All this was carried out by the regiment working day and night with little relief. The operation was much admired, and the speed with which it was accomplished was compared favorably to the siege train by the English at Sevastopol. But it was to no avail. The rebels fell back, evacuating and regrouping. "Just as everything was ready," said a young volunteer, "the bird had flown."[12]

Nevertheless, the regiment did valuable service, often dispatched as infantry in several engagements. In one, pursuing the rebels in the raid on Jeb Stuart, they marched forty-two miles in thirty-seven hours. Miraculously, there were few casualties—three killed and four wounded. An order was issued directing that the following be emblazoned on the regimental colors: "Siege of Yorktown, Hanover Court House, Chicahominy, Gaines's Mill and Malvern."[13]

By the fall of 1862, the First Artillery had been pulled back to Arlington and was serving along a line of fortification protecting Washington. In October, Major Nelson White returned to Danbury on furlough. The mood of the town was increasingly sober, the people eager for news. In a well-attended lecture, White spoke admiringly of McClellan. Many who had been critical of the general came away from the lecture with a feeling of confidence. People listened raptly to White's descriptions of the war—the elaborate machinery required and handled by the Heavies, "the shock of arms and varied effect produced by the sight and presence of death upon the minds of the soldiers." White closed with an eloquent appeal to the young men of his town to join the Union army and in particular his own regiment.[14]

When White returned, he found that Colonel Robert O. Tyler, who had been responsible for training the Heavies, had been promoted to brigadier general and Henry L. Abbot to colonel. The men spent the winter drilling in both infantry and artillery. They remained in the Washington area throughout 1863, and even the regimental history had to acknowledge a "season of comparative inactivity" at Fort Richardson.

In December 1862, George White Ives died. The town mourned as all businesses on Main Street closed the day of the funeral. We know nothing specifically about the Iveses' participation in the war before this time, although it may be assumed that so prominent a family shared the prevailing public sentiment. Neither of George Edward's brothers served, although they were not too old to volunteer—Joseph was twenty-nine at the outbreak of the war and Isaac twenty-six. Their cousin Nelson White was fifty at the time. Meanwhile George Ives was still in New York, a sometime student and an occasional visitor in Danbury. It was during cousin Nelson's hortatory visit home in October that he spoke to young George Edward, now seventeen, about forming a band to be attached to his regiment.

It was after this encounter and the death of his father that George made the decision to join the Union army as bandmaster. Early in 1863 he recruited a band from among the musicians he had come to know in New York and Connecticut. The roster of the band bespeaks the origins of its members. Fetzer, Kopp, Lauterbach, Lorenz, Moslein, Oechner, Rudolph, Schleyer, and Schubert were all mustered into service on the same day, November 4, 1863. George himself was sworn in on June 16, 1863.

By the time George joined the army, the character of the war was beginning to change. Earlier, enthusiasm and patriotism had been the prevailing attitude. The cavalcades, parades, speeches, and music all buttressed an attitude of courage—at least publicly. But as the summer of 1863 approached, there was little cause for easy optimism. In early May, at the battle of Chancellorsville, the Union forces were routed. It was the third defeat in a year. Gettysburg followed during the first week in July. On this July Fourth, in sharp contrast to that extraordinary and joyous day two years earlier, Danbury had no heart for festivities. Most people by then had lost someone in the war or knew many who had. For every man who died on the battlefield, many more were claimed by disease and more still were crippled for life as a result of their wounds. Many familiar names were by this time on the rolls of the dead—Moore, Starr, Wheeler, Trowbridge, Hart, Barnum.

Bonfires, hitherto tolerated if not actually encouraged on such an occasion, were put out on the grounds that they were made with "illegal materials." There were even a few arrests for activities that in the past would be lightly passed off as "celebrating the Fourth."[15] It seemed as if at least for the moment certain forms of patriotism had gone out of style. On the battlefield, both armies were approaching the time when, to use Bruce Catton's term, glory was out of date.[16]

With the glory went the music. In the spring and summer of 1861, regimental bands consisted of twenty-two members including principal musicians plus a conductor. Competition among these musicians often fostered considerable artistry. After the musical retrenchment ordered by Secretary Stanton in July 1862, bands were cut to sixteen members (the number in George's band) and were permitted only at the brigade level. Moreover, musicians were increasingly pressed into other duties as well, such as service in ambulance corps and hospitals. Many were exposed to danger and some killed. Thus by 1863, being a musician in the army was far from the glorious position it had been earlier.

George reported for duty at Fort Richardson on July 29, 1863, only a few days after the battle of Gettysburg. The First Artillery remained encamped there until the following spring, through the first ten months of George's enlistment.

Although Nelson White had probably recruited him to lead a regimental band for the First Artillery, George was now to be the leader of the Band of the Third Brigade, manning defenses south of the Potomac. One month short of eighteen years of age, he was the youngest bandmaster in the Union army. The position of principal musician, George's title at his mustering in, was the equivalent of second lieutenant of infantry. The pay, established by Congress, would have amounted in George's case to about eighty-six dollars a month, a substantial amount for an eighteen-year-old; in addition, a servant was accorded him by law as one of the emoluments of rank.

What would George's life have been like during that "season of comparative inactivity"? Life was routine, often boring, yet could at times settle down in a kind of cozy camaraderie. Most of the soldiers—many still boys—were away from home for the first time, and off-duty activities had both a sense of adventure and a tendency toward the homely. While discipline could be firm for the troops, it was often less so for the musicians, who had much free time during such periods of military inactivity. Besides, in some sense the bandsmen themselves were agents of discipline—at least of order and ritual.

From the time of the Revolution, bands had assumed a role as guardians and performers of military ceremony, conferring a structure on it and providing it with musical commentary. Even the ordinary activities of the military day were codified and ritualized, announced and accompanied by music. A typical day started at daybreak with *First Call*, a tune well known through its later association with horse racing. A few minutes later, the band played a march as the morning gun was fired and the troops assembled in front of their barracks. *Reveille* was then sounded, followed by *Assembly*, after which the noncommissioned officers reported to the officer of the day. A half hour later, *Mess Call* was sounded. And so the progress of the day was marked, band and bugler serving as military clock and commander. Calls marked the hours and events of the day: *Tattoo* at 9:00 P.M., *Call to Quarters* at 10:45 P.M., and *Taps* at 11:00 P.M.[17]

In the field, these functions might well be performed by field musicians alone, a corps of bugle and drum, or bugler alone, as opposed to the full band. In such installations as Fort Richardson, the duties would be shared, the musicians amalgamated into one group under a leader. In addition, the band would officiate at drills, guard mounting, and parades. It would also be expected to perform for the same occasions that would require music in civilian life. Concerts in and around camp were one of the most popular entertainments of the soldiers. They were often given in friendly communities and, with less success, in occupied Confederate towns, as a gesture of reconciliation. Serenading, a carryover from civilian tradition, was also popular, the band playing, usually at night, to honor some visitor or favorite officer.

Like the clergy, the band attended all military rites of passage. It was present at all formal funerals, invariably playing Handel's *Dead March* from *Saul*. The tune was a memento mori; at times it was heard everywhere. Mary Chesnut wrote in her diary, "Now it seems we are never out of the sound of the Dead March in Saul. It comes and it comes until I feel inclined to close my ears and scream."[18]

Similarly, band and clergyman served as the fixtures of civilization in military executions. The band, playing the dirge, led the slow procession. After accompanying the condemned man to the site, they retreated only long enough for the riflemen and clergy to perform their part of the execution. The band then led a sprightly recessional to the tune of *The Girl I Left Behind Me*.[19]

At the time George enlisted, there were increasing numbers of assorted miscreants and, in particular, many bounty jumpers, men who signed up for the enlistment bounty and soon deserted. Some did this more than once before they were apprehended, and their punishment was death. One of the purposes of the ritualized public execution was deterrence: to caution those attending (usually the entire regiment) against high crimes such as desertion. For a lesser offense, "ceremonial disgrace" sufficed as punishment in the form of ritual discharge. Here a soldier who was unable to adjust to military life or who was convicted of thievery was publicly humiliated, drummed out of the regiment, and driven from camp as an undesirable. It was the most common punishment for a conviction of cowardice. The guilty party's head might be shaved and his cheeks branded, or he might be publicly whipped. Then he might be made to run the gauntlet of the entire brigade. And all this to the music of fife and drum or, if available, a band. The music for such occasions was prescribed: *The Rogues March*.[20]

Early in the war, it was not uncommon for the officer in charge to command one of the field musicians to administer a rawhide whipping. This had been a common practice in the regular army and may have associated musicians with these punitive rituals. Musicians were associated with suffering in another prominent way: they attended to the sick and dying and were routinely assigned as stretcher bearers in battle. When fighting became intense, their services were certainly seen as more expendable than those of the four to six fighting men it would take to carry away a fallen soldier. For the same reason, they were sometimes pressed into service on the battlefield as surgeon's assistants.[21]

George was well aware of these duties of a Union bandsman. But life at Fort Richardson was for the most part humdrum, and he had ample opportunity to practice his instruments. Rehearsal requirements for a band such as his in such an installation were far from demanding. Musicians had much spare time and usually spent it in whatever recreation could be devised. Reading and card playing were popular, as were, of course, the endless rumor and gossip ubiquitous in military life. Afternoons were often spent sleeping, as there was a long break between the midday meal and dress parade at 4:30.

Most of George's first year in the army passed in this way, until in May 1864 the regiment was suddenly mobilized for action which was to culminate in the battle of Petersburg on July 30. The regiment, seventeen hundred strong, was first deployed as infantry to reinforce temporarily a line of troops anticipating attack from the direction of Petersburg. After many months of routine service and training, the men were abruptly plunged into war. Immediately thereafter, they were shifted into the heavy artillery service for which they had been trained and fought "three sharp combats" within the space of a month, all before mid-June. Meanwhile, equipment arriving from Washington permitted the siege train, consisting of 127 guns and 73 mortars, to begin its way to Petersburg. The line of batteries was seventeen miles long, and more than twelve thousand tons of ammunition, hauled an average distance of seven miles by wagon, were to be fired during the siege itself. The depot for these operations was located at one of the pontoon crossings on the Appomattox River, called Broadway Landing. It was here that the Heavies and their band were stationed, in the midst of one of the most arduous campaigns of the war.[22]

From this point on, the exploits and further military achievements of the First Connecticut Heavy Artillery are well documented. All we have relating to George Ives's participation are a few military documents. The two sets of materials, however, are curiously at odds with each other. Colonel Henry L. Abbot, commander of the Heavies, was by July 11 satisfied with his success in organizing and deploying his men. Overseeing operations from a boat at one of his Broadway Landing wharves, he awaited further orders. Summarizing his position to the brigadier chief of artillery, he concluded, "Although my line is over thirteen miles in length, and my command over two thousand men, I find no difficulty and no confusion—so perfect is the working of the above system."[23] The Confederate line, thus far impregnable, was seven miles distant. At that moment, as a result of a puzzling turn of events, Abbot's bandmaster, George Ives, was being held under arrest.

Two weeks earlier, in the midst of preparations for the siege, George had left a letter at Colonel Abbot's headquarters addressed to his adjutant, Lieutenant B. P. Learned: "I respectfully request that I may be reduced to the ranks as a private sentinel either in the 1st Conn. Heavy Artillry Reg't or in any other Reg't that proper authority may direct."[24] On the same day that he wrote the letter, George destroyed his cornet.

There is no record of any response by Abbot to the request, and it seems unlikely that in the midst of the massive operation he was organizing, Lieutenant Learned would have drawn his attention to this unusual letter from his bandmas-

Letter from George Ives to his commanding officer requesting that he be relieved of band duties, June 29, 1864.

ter. George, however, would soon receive his answer. Breaking the instrument was a punishable offense and subject to court-martial. Meanwhile, George further complicated matters by being absent without official leave from his regular duty at guard mounting two days later, on July 1.

The garrison court-martial was convened swiftly on July 3. Its president was Lieutenant Colonel Nelson White, George's cousin. The charges were "neglect of duty" and "conduct prejudicial to good order and military discipline." The latter referred to the breaking of the instrument, which, the charge read, was done "with the intention of unfitting himself for duty as the Leader of the said Band." George pleaded guilty to both charges.

Punishments for such offenses were variable, and there existed a class of officers who believed that every violation of camp rules should be punished painfully.[25] Indeed, in the artillery, a favorite punishment was the lashing of the guilty party to the rear spare wheel of the caisson.[26] Later in the war, when breaches of discipline may have been more common and benignly tolerated, decisions and sentencing, on the other hand, could be summary. In general, noncommissioned officers were reduced to the ranks.[27] Considering the circumstances of the preparation for siege, the sentence of the court in George's case was extremely mild: forfeiture of one month's pay and close arrest for ten days.[28]

The siege operations of the regiment culminated in the battle of Petersburg Mine on July 30. Thereafter, the regiment continued to bombard the Confederate lines through February of 1865. In the final months of the war, units of the Heavies engaged successfully in action against the rebel fleet at Dutch Gap and the James River. The final battle in which they served, before Richmond, ended in victory. Before daylight on April 3, 1865, the enemy having evacuated his lines, the war was over for the First Connecticut Artillery. All that remained was the dismantling of the machinery of war. In mid-July the regiment was transferred to Washington. It was mustered out on September 25, and a week later given a reception in Hartford. Before they parted for good, they passed in review one final time before Governor Buckingham.

Where was George Ives in these final months of the war? Three related documents tell us his whereabouts on as many dates in February, March, and April 1865.[29] In fact, their purpose was to certify legally where he was. George had returned to Danbury on furlough some time before February 17, when the first document, a doctor's statement, was written. It avows that while on furlough, he had fallen on the ice and sustained an injury to the spine which required treatment and rendered him unable to return without danger of more serious injury. It was signed by E. R. Barecin, M.D., and attested by Roger Averill (serving as justice of the peace) to be "a physician in good standing and full practice." The following month, Dr. Barecin, now identifying himself as an examining surgeon for United States government pensions, stated that George Ives "has been quite ill [and] is improving. But still unable to report in person." A similar note, on April 15, declared that George was still under Dr. Barecin's care and that the doctor did not regard it as best for him to return at that time.

The news that very day in Danbury was the shooting of President Lincoln. In the South, George's regiment had already fought its last battle, and within a few weeks President Andrew Johnson declared that the armed resistance proclaimed by Lincoln on April 19, 1861, "may be regarded as virtually at an end." George finally did rejoin his regiment sometime before June 1865, during their last days in the South. He could not have been there more than a month or two before their return to Washington. During that time, he befriended a little boy who liked to listen to the band rehearse, the son of a woman who washed the men's clothes. He wrote home, "I've got a little Darkie working for me now. . . . I should like to bring him home if you could use him. He is a worker and honest."[30] The boy, Henry Anderson Brooks, was indeed brought to Danbury and maintained a relationship with the family for some time afterward. George was discharged along with the rest of the regiment on September 25, 1865, so it is likely that he returned with them to Hartford after mustering out in Washington, but he would probably not have led the band in its final review before Governor Buckingham.

We know nothing more about George's career with the Heavies or his involvement in the war. Did he have the stuff of heroes—spoiling to get into the action, frustrated by the ritual and ornamental duties of bandsman while others around him fought the war and, in doing so, were finding their manhood? Or was he a frightened and confused adolescent who, far from home, had reached the limit of his endurance? Military punishment for cowardice was public humiliation by being drummed out of camp to the *Rogue's March,* a ritual in which George and his band had participated. But, after all, both hero and coward may slip on the ice—a misfortune in one case, a blessing in the other.

As for any comment made by George himself about his experience in the Civil War, there remains only a fragment from an entry in his musical notebook written in 1868: "A space of three years servitude and one year sick."[31]

FOUR

DANBURY DAYS, FAMILY CIRCLES

It was autumn of 1865 when George Ives, now officially a veteran of the Grand Army of the Republic, returned to civilian life. But what was there for him to return to? Men settled in their careers and those with families, even younger men who had been apprentices, had a path to resume. And return where? George had spent much of his period of enlistment at home in Danbury. For many other young men, the war had been an excursion from the realities they would inevitably have to face. Returning to their hometowns, they were plunged headlong into a world that expected manhood from them.

Indeed, in many ways it had been a boys' war. Enemies had shared a common language and in some cases common acquaintances, even family. Moreover, there was a generational bond. Their interest in one another was betrayed in episodes of fraternizing which contrasted sharply with their mission to destroy one another. Above all, they shared the residual vulnerability of childhood and the attempts at mastery it elicited. Homesickness itself had been a common bond.

Now the boys of both sides had returned home. For some, the war may have served as a crucible for manhood, the participants emerging better prepared for the civilian conflicts they were about to encounter than they might have been otherwise; this is the fictive ideal expressed for all time by Stephen Crane in *The Red Badge of Courage*. For what were those boys of Danbury and elsewhere seeking who were anxious lest the war end without their having participated? Motivated by inner pressures of narcissism, the channeling of youthful aggression, and above all the appropriate leaving of the homes they dedicated themselves to preserve, the young men were responding every bit as much to the developmental requirements of adolescence as they were to Lincoln's call for three hundred thousand more troops.

Certainly George at twenty was far from mature. Essentially, he sat the war out either at Fort Richardson during a long, boring wait for deployment or in Danbury, "sick," according to his own comment. And one cannot fault him for lacking the kind of zeal that inspired the "patriotic gore" of song and story. George had little need for actual heroism to nurture his self-regard, nor did he need to express his aggression in actual combat. Such needs as he may have had were well satisfied by the ceremonial heroism of the job for which he was recruited. The leader of the band is perforce a leader of men. He marches at the head of a mass moving in space to the sound of martial music. The underlying shared fantasy of all participants, marchers and observers alike, is the going forth into battle. A hero may have his moment and may later receive public and ceremonial recognition. But the bandsman, particularly the leader, is the performer of the ritual itself, perpetually identified with the hero. In essence, this is what George signed up for when he joined the Union army. His being seventeen made him all the more the hero—the boy hero in a boys' war.

Dull as life could be at Fort Richardson, the practice of music and leadership was more or less in keeping with George's expectation. The reality of war as he began to experience it near Petersburg was another story. In the face of war, there was no honor and little glory in being a musician. On the contrary, ceremonial services were often deemed expendable and musicians were pressed into more necessary and sometimes highly distasteful, even gruesome, occupations. Above all, there was the ever-present danger of mutilation and death.

When Nelson White had suggested that George Edward organize the regimental band, it must have seemed a felicitous solution to the question of what he would do next. Although he had not been close to his father, the death of George White Ives changed the family structure for good. The younger George would never gain the esteem in which his father held his older brothers. George was isolated in youth, frozen in time as it were, while others went on with their lives. His brother Joe was officially his guardian. It is unclear whether George had been indulged or ignored. Certainly his father did not have the intense involvement with him that he had with Joe, his heir apparent in the community, or even with the go-getter, Ike, a more flamboyant version of himself. Nor could George find a father in either brother. Charles Foepple, his teacher, was the only man around with whom he could identify, but their contact was sporadic and limited. Nor did George use his father's death as the occasion to break away from his family. On the contrary, there appears to have been some unfinished business in Danbury, and he was far from ready to leave. The war was, for George as for many others of his generation, a timely occasion for a temporary solution.

The few documents we have concerning George's life at this time track the failure of his solution. One can only imagine the frustration and rage a musician must feel to destroy his or her instrument. To the degree that the instrument is a partial representation of oneself in mental life, this aggression is directed toward the self, and despair becomes manifest. In George's case, it was not only the despair of the occasion but also the frustration caused by the failure of a temporary solution—indeed, a sense of despair may have been latent even before George accepted Nelson's invitation. In this light, one cannot help wondering whether cousin Nelson was sensitive to George's uncertainty and floundering after his father's death and made the offer as much to help George out as for the glory of the regiment. After the war, when George looked back on these years and reflected in his notebook on his "one year sick," one wonders what sickness he was speaking of, the fall on the ice or the sickness of the soul. And might the latter condition, serving as mental background to his experience of the war, have made George especially susceptible to an accident at this time?

Nelson's presence at George's court-martial, let alone his leniency, is an intriguing detail of this period of George's life, confirming that in a sense he had never completely left home. Cousin Nelson had served as a symbolic presence, an influential and protective father. In fact, like many adolescents, George may have felt far more constrained in acting out frustration, rage, and fear had he not known that someone in the environment would tolerate, contain, and forgive the act. As it turned out, Nelson was in a position to do all of these, serving as guardian angel and forgiving father. Events in the years following the war reveal that George continued to be unprepared to leave home literally; events of later life suggest that he was never fully able to do so psychologically. To a degree, he always remained dependent on a family from which he was somewhat alienated and which regarded him as a beloved black sheep. The issue of leaving home reemerged many years later when his own son, Charlie, was about to do so. Indeed, a flood of reanimated feelings later had powerful consequences in both their lives.

George's own father's hand had not been firm. But had George perceived him as kindly and generous or as abandoning? George had certainly not had to oppose his father vigorously in choosing to steer away from the expectable family course in the world of business. On the contrary, George White Ives had helped his son find the best mentor he could within a limited field. But the question remains whether his yielding to his son's wish to pursue music as a career indicated respect for a talent he recognized in the boy or meant that he found the youngster in some way dispensable since his two older sons were already following in his footsteps.

The house at 210 Main Street was still home for the twenty-year-old George, and his ties to Danbury were profound. The family itself was reliable, stable, defined. Only George had not yet found his place. By now his mother had recovered from her husband's death three years earlier. Now, in addition to being nominal head of the household, Sarah continued and expanded the social and charitable activities that had defined her life earlier.

George's older brother, Joseph Moss, had by this time become heir to his father's position in the community. He was his father's executor along with Edgar Tweedy, another of that cohort of George White's generation who "were" the town. Their sons were gradually assuming their places. New developments in Danbury were still associated with the same families; only the Christian names differed. Joe's antics at Yale were long forgotten, eclipsed by more significant deeds. In the tradition of his father, he continued to be involved in projects that were not only remunerative but also civic-minded. His brother Ike, on the other hand, was frank about having his own fortune at heart even though he apparently did a measure of civic work as well.

Sarah Amelia, then in her late twenties, was as yet unmarried. A lively, intelligent, and attractive woman, Amelia did not lack for suitors, but she was picky. She was, after all, the only marriageable woman in a family whose name had been respected in Danbury since the 1790s. Moreover, her mother's family was, if possible, even more deeply rooted in Danbury than her father's. Her maternal grandmother, as a child, had been playing in South Street, a short distance down Main Street, within earshot of British cannon, when her father, Major Taylor, hurriedly bundled her off to safety. Amelia traced her heritage back to the original eight who had founded Danbury a century earlier. Amelia, far more than any of her brothers, saw herself as local royalty. Joe, in her view, would have been a pale reflection of their father, fundamentally a merchant, whereas George White Ives had been a patriarch, a benefactor of the entire community. No matter how successful Joe might be in the eyes of others, for Amelia her brother remained the potential spoiler of the family name.

If anyone in the family was sensitive to the unfortunate details of George's army career, it would have been Amelia, for already she was beginning to assume the twin roles of guardian of the family prestige and conduit for its traditions. That George was recruited for military service in such a visible position as bandmaster and that he served at all must have been sources of pride, especially since neither of the older boys had served. Moreover, both Joe and Ike had prospered during the war and were well positioned to develop their businesses immediately afterward. But George had the potential of being a family hero, promoting its good name and standing for ideals of leadership and community service which for Amelia were of the essence. However, his extended furlough in town during the critical final months of the war would have been troubling to her in spite of the medical proof of George's disability.

Amelia's relationship to George had a special quality rooted in childhood. The bond between them had been strengthened by the needs of each in a context of family circumstance. For George was born to a father who had entered his fifties, very much an older man by the standards of the time, and a mother already past forty. There had been another child born between Amelia and George, a girl named Sarane, who died in childhood. The details are not known, but it seems likely that they decided to have another child, despite their ages, to compensate for the loss. George, then, was both the replacement and the new baby. But he would have been Amelia's baby-in-fantasy, the special child for her to mother. From current knowledge about child development we might expect two elements of fantasy to have come into play for Amelia: that the new baby required special care (after all, the earlier one had died) and that the baby was a gift to her from an admired and admiring father who favored her over her mother. Especially beloved, the infant would be destined for great things.

Thus, to George, Amelia may have been a surrogate mother-in-fantasy and psychologically at the hub of the family. And Amelia may have felt particularly vulnerable to matters of family prestige during her marriageable twenties, given her aspirations: fundamentally, her requirement was to marry a man like her father, the idealized George White Ives. In this regard, she proved to be remarkably successful. She and Lyman Brewster, one of the most promising young men in the state, married in 1868, the year George finally returned to Danbury.

Picking up the thread of his life after the war, George appears to have shuttled between Danbury and New York attempting to find a direction in life, perhaps to make his way as a musician. What awaited him in Danbury was predictable and largely uncongenial. He did not fit in; he lacked the temperament and the skills for business and, more important, the energy and interest in it that his brothers had. Joe and Ike, by continuing a long-standing family tradition and successfully identifying with their father, had accrued a bonus: the comfort of establishment. There appeared to be nothing in their characters, styles, or interests to isolate them from their community. On the contrary, men such as these defined the community. It was a community, however, that George proved unable to embrace.

What if George had remained in Danbury and had permitted himself to drift into the role of town musician? In mid-century Danbury, only business itself was serious business; it defined status and was the standard against which all enterprise was judged. While music was pleasantly acceptable in some circumstances, even deemed necessary in others (such as at most religious and certain secular celebrations), its production was hardly considered men's work. Reinforcing this attitude was the prevalence and popularity of music making among women. A frivolous activity at best and suspiciously unmanly at worst, music making engendered well-defined and distinctly negative attitudes.

Danbury was certainly not the only community in which being a musician or an artist was associated with alcoholism and dereliction, and even worse. In the minds of many, in New York licentiousness, perversion, and prostitution were associated with life as an artist. Yet, as we have seen, the town musician could make magic, stir the spirit, and lend a sense of occasion to the progress of life in the community. The curious amalgam of respect and derision that characterized the community's attitude toward musicians is nowhere expressed better than in its calling them *Professor*.

However George may have perceived the attitudes of the community and his family, he had another element to contend with: his own internal reality. George, in all probability, was born with exceptional auditory acuity, which can be troubling during the course of development in that it calls for mastery of a potentially traumatic overstimulus of sound. Yet it leads to curiosity as well, and George's range of curiosity extended from the natural sounds of the country town to the relatively more cultivated musical sounds that could be heard in Taylor's opera house. Such efforts at mastery often lead to the development of skill in playing musical instruments. George already was a fine cornet player and could give an account of himself on other brass instruments. He almost certainly by now could play the piano, and at some point he learned to manage on the violin. This was an expectable course of events for a person with his endowment. Later, the drive to experience, harness, and master sound would continue. For proficiency on instruments, though gratifying and socially acceptable, is not the true goal of this activity. The need may persist, seeking new avenues of discharge and gratification and becoming a potential source of creativity. Thus, George would become fascinated with such naturally occurring sounds as echoes and other spatial phenomena, moving tones, sliding tones, and quarter tones.

George's particular musical endowment very likely enabled him to hear everyday sounds in a unique way. Similarly, he might perceive band music differently in different contexts. Even in the average listener the playing of the national anthem by a stationary band, for example, might induce spectators to share a sense of reverent patriotism. The moving band, on the other hand, is the vehicle for the march—organized movement, aggression at once harnessed and symbolized. Further, as pure sound, such musical events may have a completely different meaning. Masses of tone on the move in space may be highly interesting in themselves. What if two such masses approach, merge, and move away from one another? What may appear as a musical stunt to onlookers may spark the interest of someone like George Ives.

In another cultural environment, such endowments may lead to a completely different course. Had George been born in the Vienna of his time, he would have been exposed to a cultivated musical tradition that would have channeled the development of his gifts. Moreover, there would have been a supportive audience. In Europe of the 1860s, many provincial towns no larger than Danbury had a concert hall and an opera house, and the programs reflected an ongoing cultural tradition. Under such circumstances, George might have become like some of the musicians he had met in New York, refugees from the political upheavals of 1848 and thereafter. Many were highly gifted men, solidly trained, who had since won more or less accepted positions in their adopted communities. George had recruited some of these men for his band. They in turn influenced him, and through them George was able to have musical experiences which were little available in Danbury.

Thus, an accident of proximity—the Danbury–New York connection—played a constructive role in George's training that would necessarily influence his own students, including his son Charlie. This connection had long figured in the personal and business history of the Ives family. Now it was pivotal in George's private musical life.

The Danbury–New York connection had been enhanced in George White Ives's last days through investments shared by his two older sons. He left an estate of some fifty-four thousand dollars, quite a sum at the time. He provided a bequest of two thousand dollars each for George and Amelia in consideration of "advances" already made to Joe and Ike. For Amelia, this would serve as a handsome dowry. It is not clear to what use George put his inheritance. Very likely it sustained him during the ensuing years, in Danbury and New York, and perhaps the dwindling sum was a factor in his finally settling in Danbury.

The "advances" noted by George White in regard to Joe and Ike were, of course, investments in business ventures. Ike's commercial efforts led to the inception of a never-completed connection with New York, an extension of the Danbury and Norwalk Railroad to Harlem, known locally as the Danbury–New York Link.

Grandfather Isaac had struggled through several unsuccessful ventures in New York more than a hundred years earlier before establishing the hat business on which the family's fortune and reputation were based. And it was in New York that George White had been born, not far from Christie Street, where Charles Foepple was living when George Edward returned in 1865–66 to take a few lessons. George Edward may even have lived with him for a time. (Perhaps the fact that Mrs. Foepple had a greengrocer's shop at the same address reflected on his own teacher's potential for earning a living.) For the next three years, until George was in his mid-twenties, he appears to have spent a lot of time in New York, occasionally returning to Danbury (sometimes for a rare concert) but establishing himself in neither place.

Uptown from the Foepples' an active and exciting musical life flourished, and we can assume that George had opportunities to observe and participate in it. Although Boston was the center of the cultivated tradition in music,[1] New York City was without doubt the performance center. From the end of the Civil War, American music was dominated by the attitudes, ideals, and modes of expression of nineteenth-century Europe, particularly Austria and Germany, and George had ample exposure to this rich tradition through his contacts with emigre musicians.

That George witnessed another side of New York life as well is suggested by his purported acquaintance with Stephen Foster. If they had ever known each other, it could only have been either before George's enlistment in the Union army at eighteen or while he was on sick leave, for Foster, nearly twenty years older than George, died an alcoholic in New York's Bellevue Hospital in January 1864.[2]

By the time George came to New York, the city was said to have some seventy-five "concert saloons." Whether in the notorious hangouts of downtown Broadway, where most were situated, or the singular and exclusive uptown "Louvre," with its opulent appointments, music served the dual function of entertainment and euphemism. The invariable feature in such establishments was the presence of "pretty waiter girls" in the characteristic costume of low-cut bodice, very short skirt, and high, tasseled red boots. (Scarlet boots with tiny bells were the standard footgear for one well-known New York brothel.) A socialite at a costume ball dressed in this manner and called her presentation quite simply "music."[3]

New York provided musical opportunities for every taste. The Philharmonic Society was already offering a half dozen concerts a season, there were frequent performances of oratorios, and singers and instrumentalists could be heard almost daily during the season. Even before the war, George had attended Philharmonic concerts when he came to New York for lessons. He was on friendly terms with a number of the working musicians, and from what we know about his keen musical curiosity it seems likely that he sought out opportunities for musical experiences of every kind.

George did not break from his family, however. He began to participate in the growing musical life of Danbury. Concerts were gradually becoming freestanding events no longer associated with civic, church, or social functions. Some concerts were even held on weeknights. A degree of professionalism now suggested the possibility of a career in music that would involve greater challenges than teaching, working with local clubs, or playing in a band. But anyone seriously pursuing such a career at this time was likely to have one foot in New York—as did "Professor" H. G. Abbey, who was directing at least two choirs and running a singing school in Danbury.

About six months after his official return to civilian life, George was asked to play a cornet solo at one of Abbey's formal concerts, and it was well received. He played in several more concerts during this three-year period. At the time, George did not take any regular part in the growing musical life of the community, but it appears that he was a welcome addition as a home-grown and budding artist. In the summer of 1866, he was featured as the soloist in a "grand organ concert" to inaugurate a new instrument at the Baptist Church. The advertisement states, "Mr. Geo. E. Ives, the very fine cornet player, has been engaged for the occasion and will perform some of his choicest solos with an Organ accompaniment."[4] "A large audience," a later account noted, "expressed its delight with frequent demonstrations of applause with hands and feet."[5]

Despite his recent leadership of a regimental band, he was not especially involved in the increasing band activities of the town. During this period, band music was becoming increasingly important in most smaller communities in the United States, and Danbury was no exception. The chief impetus was the Civil War, which had fostered opportunities for performance as well as an expanding musical literature. The people of Danbury were experiencing a growing need for a band beyond recreational purposes, as an emblem of a cohesive and thriving community. However, Danbury's band could never quite get the ongoing community support it required, a fact that was deplored in letters to the local newspaper. A teacher serving as bandmaster must be paid, and any self-respecting band had to have uniforms. Beyond this was the question of whether its members should be paid, which involved such serious issues as when an amateur becomes a professional and who should support cultural institutions. An irate column in the Danbury *Times* in June 1867 went beyond the previous, mildly chiding letters of public-spirited citizens. The occasion was benign enough and typical: the Strawberry Festival, a fund-raising event that combined opportunities to hear the band and partake in the bumper crop of local strawberries. Yet in miniature it reveals much about basic issues that many more pretentious cultural institutions faced. Attendance was slim, although the charge was a modest forty cents. The mere fifty dollars that the band garnered seemed to intensify the local attitude that the band members were mercenary in trying to raise money for their own organization. Like clergy, teachers, and politicians, musicians were a ready target for gossip in which many heartily joined. The article comments on those gossips who actually "curse the band, its impudence and greed with fervor. The members of the band have been belittled and belied to the heart's content of those who haven't lost one cent by the Festival failure. . . They tell of the amount the Band made last fall, and distend their eyes in a manner to leave the impression that the organization has made itself opulent and to this day is reeking in filthy lucre. But the whole truth reveals the fact that every member is more or less out of pocket."[6]

Eventually, an attempt was made to establish a band once and for all. A two-day brass band festival netted $357, and the band was duly named the Wooster Band, joining the many other Danbury institutions named after the town's Revolutionary hero.[7] But after receiving a gift of two hundred dollars from Walker H. Bartram and Henry B. Fanton, owners of a prosperous hat-making company, the members of the band unanimously renamed the organization the Bartram and Fanton Cornet Band.[8] The band took care to recognize its benefactors in other ways too. For example, on the evening they serenaded E. B. Davis, reelected town warden, at his home, they passed Bartram's residence and made it a point to serenade him as well. On other occasions, they performed outside the company store. Thus, the band, like many grander institutions of the time, seemed to be moving in the direction of precariously supporting itself by paid performances and fund-raising from small contributors, with big business taking up the slack.

If some members of the public thought the arrangement "greedy"—arguing that musicians should be amateurs and music free—they nonetheless enjoyed having a regular band. The year was marked by eagerly anticipated events which required the services of a band, among them Decoration Day, the Fourth of July, and Election Day. By the summer of 1867, the band was decked out in uniforms for the first time. "They are," noted the Danbury *Times*, "of dark blue cloth, with red trimmings, and are very neat and tasty."[9] On July Fourth, the uniforms were displayed for the first time as the band paraded down Main Street. Businessmen helped finance the erecting of a bandstand in Elmwood Park for open-air concerts on summer evenings. A tradition of Tuesday and Friday concerts was initiated that lasted for many years. The band, however, continued to struggle.

Yet in some respects music was flourishing in Danbury in 1868. A variety of traveling attractions was beginning to come to the town—the Japanese Troupe, Buckley's Serenaders, Buchanan's Theatrical Troupe, Van Amburgh's Menagerie, the Ahwannetuks' Indian Troupe, Cotton and Sharpley's Minstrels, Blind Tom, the Continental Old Folks, and at least three different circuses each with a brass band—not to mention the numerous church and society festivals, concerts, and balls, all of which required music. In fact, it was estimated that in 1868 Danbury expended about sixty-five hundred dollars for amusements.[10]

Little is known of George Ives's activities during this period, but those of other family members are better documented because of their prominence and visibility in the small town. And it was to their kind of life that George finally returned for good in December 1868. However, he seemed to return with the same indecisiveness that had characterized his earlier years. It was not at all certain that there was a place for him in the musical life of Danbury, and in any event it was clearly at issue whether he could earn a living at it. George's initial activities are vague. He was not leading any band, although he played in one or more; occasionally, he performed as soloist. By the spring of 1869, he was in business with Joe.

Joseph Moss's hardware store in White Street had continued to prosper. At the same time, Joe continued to extend his interests elsewhere. In 1869, he became a director of the Danbury Savings Bank, the institution his father started when Joe was a boy. With George still unsettled and his inheritance dwindling, it seemed appropriate and prudent for him to enter the business. For although Joe was no longer officially guardian to George, who was now past twenty-one, as de facto head of the family Joe felt responsible for looking after his younger brother. Thus he renamed his business "Ives Bros., Dealers in Builders' Hardware." Most likely, George's title of manager was honorific. George worked in the store full time, leaving Joe free to drum up business and look into other ventures. In effect, Joe was George's boss.

In other references, George is noted as "serving" in the Ives Brothers business. An advertisement in the Danbury *Times* lists every imaginable material for building and maintaining house, farm, and garden, except lumber.[11] That was left to Ike, whose lumber business, also in White Street, was becoming the largest in the area. Ike's materials built the homes; Joe marketed just about everything that might go inside them. If Joseph was better respected, Isaac was better known, and as time went on, he was regarded with a certain awe. Ike had the knack of turning the most hare-brained schemes into cash. The best example of this is Moses Dames' Extract of Vegetation Wine of the Woods, a patent medicine which Ike developed and promoted with great success.[12] And this was merely a sideline to his several regular businesses. Isaac was an idea man, and the one element that seemed to characterize all his ventures was innovation. When he went into the hat business, for example, he came up with the idea of centralizing certain aspects of manufacture that had previously been done by several companies individually, hence more expensively. Even in the lumber business, Ike was a pioneer, shipping manufactured lumber directly by railroad to the Midwest, where previously only rough logs had been sent.

At the same time that George Ives was becoming involved in the Ives Brothers, he was also gradually becoming more involved in the musical life of the town. What amounts to his musical postwar debut was announced in June 1869, not long after his start in business: "At last Mr. Geo. E. Ives promises us a concert. It will come off about the 1st of July, and will undoubtedly prove the finest entertainment given to our public. His extensive acquaintance in the musical world, and his excellent knowledge of what is desired by the play going people of Danbury, will enable him to produce a programme that will be attractive in every feature."[13]

The concert was anticipated with some excitement, the newspaper touting it weeks in advance, noting the details of its planning. And the review of the concert was enthusiastic, particularly applauding "[A] Trip Across the Continent," concocted by George, who served as "engineer and conductor." He also played a cornet solo. "The grand entertainment closed with 'America' by the audience and orchestra."[14]

With this concert, George may be said to have come home and to have established a vocation for himself. By the summer of 1869, the outlines of the double life he would endeavor to lead are already in evidence. Having lacked the necessary talent, courage, capacity for work, and tolerance for deprivation to have left home for a musician's life in New York, George had nevertheless returned to Danbury as a well-trained and versatile musician who had some experience in the European tradition. He also had come into contact with something foreign enough to be of interest to his townsmen, and the contacts he retained were souvenirs of these experiences. Given the time, the limited opportunities, and the competition, George may have been wise to give up any aspirations of leading a life in music. Any genius for music would have been frustrated in a small town, but a modest gift could be cheerfully cultivated and serve as a source of self-esteem.

This compromise was made of material close at hand—George's own gift and the resources of his family. For the moment, the double life suited him well. His economic needs were not great as a single man, and his base in the store left him relatively free to spend time making music. By the following year, George appears to have become well established in both careers. If he was not as enthusiastic about business as about music, he seemed at least to be gaining competence. In the spring of 1870, Ives Brothers was grossing one hundred thousand dollars a year. George was beginning to take more initiative.

Increasingly, advertisements featured George's name as proprietor, although his income did not approach that of his brothers. The business was expanding, and a branch was planned for Brewster, New York. In March, an account of "Our Heavy Taxpayers" listed Joseph and Isaac among the highest. George was, of course, not mentioned.[15] Meanwhile, Ike's ingenuity was changing the appearance of White Street. He had the railroad extended directly to the lumberyard by laying 250 feet of branch track from the Danbury and Norwalk Railroad. This advance had been encouraged, if not financed, by one of his imaginative ventures that year; Ike had purchased twenty thousand feet of Georgia pine, which many predicted he would not be able to get rid of since it was material that had rarely been used in the area. He managed through advertising to create a demand for the lumber.

Soon George too was showing himself to be innovative in business by acting as agent for companies manufacturing various tools and gadgets new to Danbury. But he demonstrated his imagination best in music, where his "experiments" earned for him a reputation to some extent parallel to Ike's in business (without, of course, bringing him comparable esteem or money).

He soon became a regular in the musical life in the town and hence in its social institutions, such as its many churches and civic organizations. There was perhaps a single exception. In September 1870, the second annual reunion of the First Connecticut Heavy Artillery was held in West Haven.[16] Members assembled from all parts of the state. After disposing of the regimental business and determining the place of the next reunion, the veterans enjoyed a dinner which "presented a striking contrast to their old Virginia diet." Whereas "music, dancing and joyful return to the city" are recorded, there is no mention of the regimental band or any of its members, and it seems doubtful that George attended the event at all.[17]

In these years just before George's marriage in 1874, others of his generation were defining themselves and their place in life and in the community. Uncle Ike—restless, aggressive, a bit eccentric, and a true scion of grandfather Isaac—began to show those leadership qualities of his own father which had seemed earlier to have been the exclusive inheritance of Joseph Moss. Joe, meanwhile, quietly expanded his home furnishings store in 1872 by taking in a partner, a member of the Hoyt family. The store was now among the largest in the area, and the owners contemplated putting out a catalog to attract business. The implications of this development in the life of George, who up to this point was manager, remain obscure. Joe was a widower. He had married a second cousin, Amelia White Merritt, and lived in Boston until 1862, when his wife died giving birth to their son, Howard Merritt Ives, known as Howdie. Joe had returned to Danbury only to face the death of his father in December of that year. Amelia Merritt's brother Jacob died in 1871, and Joseph later married his widow.

Meanwhile, the courtship of Amelia Ives and Lyman Brewster had progressed to marriage in 1868, and now Lyman was establishing his own considerable role in the Ives family. He would eventually become the closest and most influential uncle to George's two children. Joe and Ike, while not without their influence on the next generation, would be, in a sense, sidetracked. Their influence would be felt more by George and his generation more as a standard of commercial success. But in Lyman—a professional, a sometime poet, a states-man-to-be—lay seeds of the future. Lyman joined his wife in carrying on an idealized version of the Ives tradition.

Lyman Brewster, born in 1832, was an exact contemporary of Joseph's. Whether they knew each other at Yale or whether Lyman was aware of Joe's dismissal is unclear. The son of Daniel Brewster of Salisbury and his second wife, Harriett Averill, Lyman had an older brother (a younger one died as a child) and two older half sisters by his father's first marriage. Although little is known of the wealth or social standing of the Brewsters, they were able to send young Lyman to Williams Academy in Stockbridge to prepare him for Yale. About one-third of his class became lawyers and a fourth became clergymen. Although Lyman was a serious student and was somewhat shy with women, he enjoyed his college days and made many lifelong friends. He corresponded with a number of his classmates for years afterward and remained active as an alumnus, serving on arrangements committees for reunions and other events. (Unlike many of his friends, he always brought his wife.)

He graduated in 1855 and on Presentation Day was named class poet. In addition to patrician good looks, Lyman had a way of expressing himself that was elegant and witty without being pompous. He wrote verse throughout his life. A chapbook of his verse, *Youth and Yale*, published by the Danbury *News* in 1900, included some of the poems he wrote as an undergraduate. Many of his efforts were urbane yet openly sentimental poems appropriate for such occasions as class reunions. But Lyman was earnest about his writing and in the early 1870s started work on a play based on the treason of Benedict Arnold. (He had written a poem on the subject as early as 1862). After Yale, Lyman spent two years of study with his uncle, Roger Averill, and prior to taking the bar exam embarked on a "grand tour" to England, Switzerland, and Italy.[18]

By the time he married Amelia in 1868, he was fast becoming a successful and highly respected lawyer. He had already been appointed probate judge and in 1870 was elected to the state house of representatives. By then he had been serving as a Danbury school visitor for a decade and was committed to organizing a fine library for the town, an institution that interested his brother-in-law Joseph as well. In 1870, Lyman wrote to a classmate, the Reverend Mulford of Salisbury, "Joseph Ives and I are busy during the out-of-court time in selecting a good readable Library for our town."

With Lyman Brewster, a new element came into the family. For one thing, the family finally acquired its lawyer—a necessity in a family of businessmen. And Brewster was a most distinguished and creative one at that, considered by some "the foremost member of his profession in Danbury in the last half-century." Lyman was an idealist in his profession as in all other things. A member of the elite who, because of family connections, did not have to struggle to become established in his profession, he nevertheless became widely known and respected through his own efforts. Although he was basically shy, at the same time he had an open nature that was especially revealed within the family. He brought to the Ives clan not only wisdom, wit, and a strong innovative bent in areas other than business but also a certain warmth and capacity for nurturing and developing its younger members. He had the look of a man who would make a good father, which almost certainly was a factor in Amelia's choice. Regrettably, they were unable to have children.

Lyman was thirty-six when he officially joined the family, although he had already been involved in their lives for several years. At the time of George's court-martial, subsequent illness, and extended furlough, Lyman had started a partnership in Danbury and was no longer working with his uncle, Roger Averill. Considering his close family and professional ties with his uncle Roger and his involvement with George and the Ives family, it seems likely that Lyman was in a good position to know a great deal about George, more no doubt than would ever be revealed outside the family circle. To him, as to Amelia, George was the errant younger brother—a dozen years his junior, almost a different generation. George was as unsettled as Lyman was settled, and Lyman assumed naturally the role of nurturing and authoritarian parent. Further, of all the members of the now-extending family, Lyman was in the best position to appreciate George's creativity as well as the energetic enthusiasm with which he practiced it. They were similar too in that both had experienced something of European culture— Lyman through his travels in Europe, George through his sojourn among European-trained New York musicians.

By the early 1870s George appeared competent, with the help of his brothers, to carry on the business of the store; but his heart was elsewhere. He certainly had no interest in the entrepreneurial activities of Ike and Joe. His only participation in the great sewing machine enterprise of 1871 was to drum up some interest for a Saturday evening public meeting by leading a brass band in a parade that afternoon with "a gong, several teams and a brace of men with throats of brass."[19] The closest he came to manufacturing was the sometime leadership of the Bartram and Fanton Manufacturing Company Band.

Another musical group was taking shape, however. It appeared for a time that there were going to be two bands in town. The Bartram and Fanton Manufacturing Company Band, with George as its occasional leader, boasted fourteen regular members and sometimes mustered as many as twenty. The second, which George also led, was beginning to be known as the Ives Cornet Band. A third group was performing as well—the Wildman Band, associated with the Wildman music store in town. George, then, was obviously not the only musician in town or even the best known, although he was making a place for himself through a variety of popular musical performances.

By now even the concert hall was inadequate, and a new opera house became the site of all major events. At a "Grand Concert" there on June 13, 1872, George led the twenty-piece Bartram and Fanton Band, assisted by a "large and efficient orchestra." The newspaper referred to him as "that moving and controlling spirit in our musical matters." George had also engaged and prepared a large chorus of singers from Danbury and neighboring towns. On the day of the concert, he led a parade through town and, just before the Grand Concert, offered a preliminary open-air concert. The hall was full, and many in the audience had traveled a long way to see and hear the event.[20]

The following year George tried something more innovative—a burlesque opera based on *Romeo and Juliet*. Although it was intended as a broadly humorous parody, a full orchestra was engaged. By now the Ives Cornet Band was increasingly to be found at local events ranging from the Anniversary Jubilee of the temperance Washingtonians to the Baptist Picnic. And, of course, the regular round of patriotic celebrations continued, each in its season. In addition, in the summer the band played on Saturday evenings on the bandstand at nearby Lake Kenosia and sometimes as far away as Brookfield, where several neighboring bands might participate.

At such events, people became aware of different qualities and styles of bands and the stunts and jokes band members played. One evening in 1873, for example, the band went up to Brookfield to play for dancing at Avery's Grove, together with a number of Danburyians who went along for the fun. They were soon joined by the Newtown Cornet Band, which had been spending the day at Hawleyville. About four hundred people dancing and singing enjoyed a typical band stunt of the time in which a passing band clashed with, and later joined, a stationary one. At length, "the two bands fused," according to reports, "and the music that vibrated among the halls of old Brookfield was of an inspiring nature."[21] The piece was *Hail Columbia*, led by George Ives.

That summer, George was courting Mary Elizabeth Parmelee, called Mollie. They made an exceptionally attractive couple, she petite and extremely pretty, he handsome in his trim new band uniform. Although George knew and was known by virtually everyone in Danbury, Mollie was a fairly recent arrival. About five years younger than George, she was born in nearby Redding, where her family had settled sometime in the late 1830s.

The Parmelees resembled the Iveses as they had been perhaps two generations earlier. Mollie's father, Noah David Parmelee, was born in Monroe, south of Newton, on July 1, 1808. He was living in Somers, New York, at the time of his marriage to Mary Ann Smith of Ridgefield on June 1, 1831. For some years he operated a general store in that town with William E. Morgan, who was married to Noah's sister, Maryetta. The business failed in 1836, probably as a result of the general depression that year. On August 2, 1837, in Danbury District Court, Noah and his brother-in-law presented a sad accounting of the $802.29 inventory in pleading bankruptcy. It was after this that Noah moved to Redding, where he worked as a tailor until his death.

Noah and Mary had six children in all. Mollie, the second youngest, was born on January 2, 1850. Noah died three years later, at the age of forty-five. By this time, some of the older children could help support the family. Perhaps that was an impetus for Mollie's brother Samuel to move to Danbury, where he worked as a clerk. There were other connections with Danbury as well, for Noah's former partner had also moved there when their business failed in order to work in the booming hat shops along River Street. A sister of Mollie's mother also lived on River Street, and Samuel boarded with her. This was probably the area in which Mollie and her mother lived when they came to Danbury.

By 1870, the entire Parmelee branch was living in Danbury except for the oldest son, David, who had moved to Louisville, Kentucky. River Street was a fair distance socially from Main Street. It was a gritty place with dozens of large smoky hat factories and the traffic of hundreds of workers. During the next few years, the remainder of Mollie's family—sister Lucy, younger by two years, and brother Jimmy, five years older—moved to a more middle-class neighborhood on Spring Street, an attractive area of one- and two-family homes that had been built shortly after the war. In the early fall of 1871, Jimmy, a warm and genial young man, was stricken with what was probably infantile paralysis. His suffering was said to be indescribable. He died six months later, in April 1872, just before the summer of Mollie's courtship with George, the summer of Kenosha Lake and Avery's Grove at Brookfield.

Noah David Parmelee, then, left a poorer legacy to his family than had George White to the Ives, although the Parmelees' genealogy was at least equal to the Iveses'. Descended from the noble Belgian house of Parmelie, founded in 1080, the Van Parmelies were well established in Holland by the sixteenth century. American descendants traced their ancestry to John Permely, one of the founders of Guilford, Connecticut, in 1639.[22]

After the marriage of George and Mollie on New Year's Day, 1874, their family life seemed to center around the Iveses. Samuel Parmelee and his family do not seem to have played an important role in their lives or in the lives of their children, although at least one of Samuel's children was close in age to Charlie. When, as an adolescent, Charlie was on the football team of the Danbury Academy and was playing against the team from Danbury Public High School, his opponent and counterpart as guard on the line was his cousin Samuel. But there is no evidence of an ongoing relationship with this cousin. In fact, it was the Ives cousins alone who gathered each summer at "Cousins' Beach" in Westbrook, Connecticut.

The only one of the Parmelees who maintained a close relationship with Mollie and eventually became accepted into the Ives family was Mollie's younger sister, Lucy. Mollie remained close to Lucy, and Lucy and Amelia Ives Brewster became friends. Lucy Cornelia Parmelee never married. She and Amelia were to share the common characteristic of longevity, which proved to be the ultimate family bond. After Charlie Ives's other aunts and uncles, his parents, and his brother had all passed away, only aunts Amelia and Lucy survived, one each from the Ives and Parmelee lines.

BOOK TWO

CHARLIE

FIVE

"Vox Humana":
A Composer's Childhood

Ives' Brass Band has included among its soloists an infantile performer on the *vox humana*."[1] Thus was Charles Edward Ives's entry into life on October 20, 1874, announced in the Danbury *News*. From the very beginning, Charlie was associated with his father and with music. George's stamp on his son went deeper than one could expect by the roll of genetic dice, although unquestionably, the infant entered the world with a predisposition toward music that affected the nature of his perception of reality. The most compelling element in his world was destined to be his father. Mollie, his mother, remains a shadowy figure in Ives's biography.

Charlie was born in the large bedroom over the south parlor of the Ives house, into which his parents had moved when they married; George and Mollie gave him his father's middle name, Edward, for his own. "Eddy" was the name by which the family sometimes called George. Charles would be "Charlie" from the beginning, but "Eddy" somehow crept in as an alternate family name. Although it did not persist, later, when Charlie used it in his writings, it was often unclear whether he was speaking of himself, his father, or some third figure—perhaps a merged mental image of the two of them. In a feisty mood later in life, Charlie wrote, "If he has a nice wife and some nice children, how can he let the children starve on his dissonances—answer that, Eddy!"[2]

The name Charles appears nowhere in the genealogy of either the Iveses or the Parmelees. Where one finds a rent in the fabric of convention, a parent's fantasy may glimmer through, as the choice of a name is one of the parents' first statements about their expectations, aspirations, and dreams for the child. The only person of that name who had any meaning in George's life was Charles Foepple, his music teacher. Charlie Ives was not named after Foepple in any formal sense, but the name must make us wonder about the continuing influence of George's experience with Foepple. For Foepple represented George's first contact with a tradition completely different from that of mercantile Danbury. Through Foepple, his adolescence had been deeply refreshed by New York, with its cultural and sexual excitement, and Europe, from which Foepple had emigrated. George had cherished and carefully preserved his lessons with Foepple and later used his notes as a basis for the music lessons he himself gave Charlie, who remembered them as rigorous and fundamental to his own education.

Charles Foepple had opened a new world of music for George, and it was while George was studying with Foepple that his father died, an event that may have intensified George's attachment to his teacher. In the naming of the child, George and Mollie connected him with an honorable past and expressed a wish for the future. It was thus that European-born Charles Foepple entered the Ives genealogical stream via George's fantasy—a fantasy to be shared by the child as he grew up. Foepple represented an unrealized dream of George, a path not taken, and an aspiration for his son.

At the time of Charlie's birth, George was in his prime and life was as stable for him as it ever would be. He appeared to be managing his business life with relatively little effort. It seems to have taken its place beside what he considered to be his main vocation at the time, music. These were happy years for George, full of activity and, given the mixed feelings of the community toward its "professor," of as much esteem as George was likely to achieve in his lifetime. Between his marriage on New Year's Day and the following October, when Charlie was born, George was engaged in a round of musical activity that was to be typical of the next few years. From time to time, the band would serenade its favorites by giving them a send-off at the depot—for example, J. M. Bailey, "The Danbury Newsman," the humorist who probably wrote the whimsical birth notice about Charlie. Sometimes it was the Ives Cornet Band that played and sometimes George's String Band, a more genteel group which performed for such refined social occasions as home parties and dances. At these and other events George was occasionally cornet soloist as well as leader.

There was another side to being a musician. A rare statement in George's own words appeared in the *News* on September 9, 1874:

FOR FUN

At present Danbury is "afflicted" with only one brass band. It seems necessary on the part of the band, to explain to a part of the public, how it is that they
can't always play "for fun!"

In the first place, it costs somebody almost one hundred dollars for the first
outfit (uniform and instrument) of each member. This amount is almost a dead
loss to the member and whenever he leaves the band, as anyone might know
who has even attempted to sell a second hand uniform or instrument.

. . . [T]he present Danbury Band have never asked or received any help
from the public, except as in pay for services rendered; yet it has survived for
quite a while by its own personal endeavors, kept up in the best shape it could,
and made the thing pay for itself after a fashion. Please remember that the
Band is not supported by any stock company or society, but by its own exertions
and by the friends that engage it or wish for it. So please talk up a good price
even if you don't pay it individually, and if we don't play as well as the prize
band of this world, don't help us downhill with your mouths and we'll endeavor
to deserve whatever praise or pay we may get.[3]

Here are reflected some of the economic realities of music in a small town and
the attitudes of its inhabitants. Making a living through music in Danbury was a
thankless struggle which rendered the musician helpless and angry. Rewards in
self-esteem were occasional and fleeting, and the paying public was fickle and
capricious. Early on, Charlie sensed George's relatively low status and economic
position within the family as well as in the outside world.

When George and Mollie married and went to live on Main Street, Sarah Ives
was sixty-six years old and still occupied the master bedroom over the dining
room, symbolizing her position as nominal head of the household. Stairs led from
her room to both the kitchen and the front of the house. Years later, Charlie's
first cousin, Amelia Van Wyck, remembered the house thus:

It was always a very open house. One night, a horse and buggy drove up with
two strangers in it. The woman came up and said that her husband was very
sick, and she couldn't take care of him, and they didn't know where to go. So
they stayed at the Iveses until the man was better and they could go back to
their farm. . . . Another time, the time of the wagon trains going through to the
West, one wagon train spent the night in Danbury. And a little girl in the train
was too sick to go on. They just left her with the Ives family until her other
friends could come along and pick her up. . . . And of course there were plenty of
friends and cousins who stayed off and on. It seemed to be an expandable
house.[4]

The house itself here assumes certain characteristics of the woman who ran it, for
they are maternal qualities. The house is portrayed as caring and nurturing: it
nurses the sick; it is trusting toward strangers and in turn is deemed trust-

worthy. It is a home for the homeless and center for the family. A sense of nostalgia prevails in this reminiscence. In fact, the house on Main Street had taken on several functions over the generations: great-grandfather Isaac, who built it, had made it his garden, and George White had made it his bank. But these functions were associated with men. Here it is the woman's house, the claustrum or womb in which children are nurtured and from which they issue. This was why George and Mollie were given the large, bright room in which Charlie was born. The women the house now represented were grandmother and mother, Sarah and Mollie Ives.

Living in the "expandable house"—in addition to the George Ives family, Sarah, and probably one or two servants—were George's brother Joe and Joe's twelve-year-old son, Howdie, who may have been away at school for a portion of the year. In 1875, when Charlie was one year old, Joe married his widowed sister-in-law, Sarah Merritt, and brought her, too, to live in the Ives homestead. This, then, was the human and nonhuman environment of Charlie's first years.

The most striking thing about Mollie Ives, Charlie's mother, is the lack of available information about her. Although we know that in his later life Charlie treated her with kindly respect, he barely acknowledges her in any of his biographical writings. Ives scholar John Kirkpatrick has observed that Charlie "wrote and talked so devotedly about his father that one tends hardly to notice his mother. Though unimaginative beyond household duties, she was a small but intense focus of energy and determination."[5] Kirkpatrick, in his exhaustive research, discovered only a single family anecdote about "Aunt Mollie": she once flagged down the train at Brewster, where it wasn't supposed to stop, when she wanted to go to New York.[6] Vivian Perlis's impressive collection of the personal reminiscences of Charlie's family, neighbors, and acquaintances provides little more about her—a curious finding in itself.[7]

Comments about Mollie indicate a conventional nurturing motherliness. Although Charlie never said anything about it, his nephews vividly remembered their grandmother Mollie as devoted and giving. It was their custom, for example, to take their lunches on school days with Grandmother Ives at the house on Main Street, and this became an important part of her life, too.[8] It was Mollie's lot to be remembered by her grandchildren in terms of this stereotype. Her own generation, however, appears to have demoted her from the status of mother. At times they referred to her as Aunt Mollie even when speaking to her sons.

George's unusualness in the small town gave him a degree of visibility, and one result was newspaper accounts of at least some aspects of his life. But domestic achievements are never acknowledged in this way. What is of prime interest here is the manner in which Charles Ives appeared to recall his parents and these influences. George was not merely remembered; he was revered, idealized, and vividly portrayed by his son-become-artist. By contrast, in Charles's writings Mollie is hardly mentioned. From an autobiographical point of view, she seems to have been virtually absent from his life, perhaps respectfully neglected.

Throughout his life, Ives similarly balanced mother against father. There may be as much to learn from the omission of Mollie as from the overwhelming presence of George. She must be sought beyond the larger-than-life image of the father that tends to obscure her, and sought in terms different from those aggressively biographical statements with which Ives promoted his father.

How can we account for this lack of recorded memory about one's mother in a man who was preoccupied with remembrance? The biographical absence of Mollie in the writings of Ives may well reflect a degree of stability and tranquillity that constituted a positive contribution to her son's early development.[9] If so, the contribution was made in the preverbal phase, and any memory trace must be sought in music, metaphor, and form. Autobiographical references to them may never be as explicit as those to the father. Further, there is no evidence in Charlie's early life that Mollie was anything but an excellent mother, and a few extant letters from later periods support a favorable view of her. Paradoxically, any potentially traumatic elements in his early life more likely stemmed from the revered father as well as biological endowment.

Charlie was born within ten months of his parents' marriage. He was fifteen and a half months old when his brother, Joseph Moss Ives, was born. Thus Moss, as he came to be called, was conceived when Charlie was about six months of age. In a sense, Charlie was never without his rival, for Moss's presence would have been felt, whether as potential or actual, in the developing consciousness of the older boy from six months on. He was his mother's *only* child, then, for a relatively short time. And although he would become his father's favorite, there too he was never without threatening rivals—not only Moss but his mother herself. For as Charlie's bond to George was developing, the fact that George had a stronger bond to his wife—indeed, a sexually compelling one—could be nothing but an insult to infantile narcissism. As for Moss, Charlie left little in writing about him. What remains suggests a shared storybook boyhood.

In any event, there was as much potential trauma inherent in the makeup of the first child as in the intrusion of rivals. That potential came from his exceptional auditory sensitivity. Every gift has a biological contribution that entails enhancements and perils, and Charlie's was no exception.[10] The sensitivity to the comforting crooning of a lullaby carries with it a potential for frightening, noxious auditory experiences. A child with this kind of inborn sensitivity can experience the world early on as a dangerous place. Visual stimuli, after all, can be shut off, and children soon learn to do so at will. But a child endowed with extraordinary auditory sensitivity is more vulnerable, and in the early psychological symbiosis of mother and child it becomes her task to hear the world with her child's ears and to provide a protective barrier that facilitates development until the child has the capacity to provide such a barrier for himself. What the mother, and later the child, "permits" to come through may subsequently be mastered more readily in its threatening sense, or organized in its developmental or even proto-creative sense. The alternative may be a degree of anxiety which, being overwhelming and not subject to mastery, may impede normal development. Unable to organize let alone symbolize sound, the infant may experience it as raw stimulus, intense and disturbing. Accordingly, "sensory mothering" may be comparable to such fundamental maternal tasks as feeding. The maternal contribution to the homeostasis of body and infant mind, the accomplishment of the "good mother," is often made more taxing by such individual characteristics of the child as extreme sensory sensitivity. Thus, in the case of Charlie, Mollie Ives may have provided unusually good mothering rather than the opposite.

If Mollie was a responsible and responsive early mother, might George, as perceived by the infant Charlie during the second half of his first year, have been the first human disturber of the peace in contrast to the beloved parent he would become in Ives's memory? The boisterous George of cornet and band, the George of warlike cacophonous sound, was the earliest image of father the infant would begin to discriminate in the outside world.

Charlie had been born into an unusual auditory environment by any standard, as well as into an environment in which his father was an extraordinarily strong presence. George did much of his work—practicing his music and preparing for musical stints—at home. The auditory environment at home comprised a veritable compendium of the music of the day—the genteel music of the cultivated tradition, ranging from classical music, adaptations of opera, parlor songs, religious music and the gospel song to frankly vernacular or patriotic music. This music was heard on all the instruments George played—cornet, violin, and piano—as well as the human voice. George had a very pleasant and distinctive voice, uninhibited in emotional expression and trained to bring out the fine nuances of song. He was also given to grunting the rhythms and miming the "tatas" and "doodles" of band instruments as he wrote arrangements. Only slightly beyond the confines of the house was the First Congregational Church, with its hand-pumped organ, which could be heard on Sundays along with the singing of hymns. And behind the house was a hill where on fine days in summer the Ives band would sometimes rehearse, offering the pleasure of incomplete but spontaneous concerts to passersby.

This myriad of audible, increasingly intelligible information was conveyed to the child's senses against a background which in its own way could be a discernible and even vivid auditory experience: silence. The level of ambient noise was lower in general in mid-nineteenth-century America than it is today. And just as each season had its music, so each season—even each time of day—had its distinctive sound.

Sounds differed not only in volume but in content. In Danbury, the evening indoor sounds were those of human transaction—voices against a background of the domestic noises of kitchen and table early in the evening, the sounds of the piano or melodeon later interspersed with quiet conversation. Agitation and activity were provided by the growing young—Charlie himself, Cousin Howdie, and, later, Moss. The evening was a time for slowing and quieting down. The general lowering of intensity was reinforced through other senses. Kerosene lamps, for example, gave far less light than does electrical lighting, and the house had many dark corners. After supper, the only sounds outside the house were of the occasional horse-drawn carriage in the gaslit streets. The house on Main Street drew itself in tightly at night, and no doubt the sounds of tenderness and moving bodies were clearly audible, for Charlie shared the parental bedroom in which he had been born. Here too, the child may have perceived the father as the disturber of the peace. Not only the birth of Moss but also parents turning toward each other must have threatened Charlie's wished-for union with mother and later with father. Bedroom sounds may thus have symbolized the loss of each, the potential for betrayal, and the anguish of rivalry. All could be represented in the world of sounds to which Charlie was drawn yet vulnerable, with George the source and master.

The father normally awakens the child to the outside world and to exciting new stimuli. He is Virgil to the infant, a guide to the new life. For the first experience of life, the child is born into a symbiotic union with the mother. Later he or she is ready, particularly as a result of a good experience, for the "love affair with the world."[11] It is father who will become the master of ceremonies, but he may tax his audience. Stimulation may threaten to become overstimulation, especially in a sphere of perception in which the child may be particularly sensitive. Where mother protects, maintaining peace and quiet, father may traumatize. Thus, the potential for a feared, destructive father, an overpowering rival, the ringmaster turned vicious as if in a bad dream—and all at an early moment in the child's life—can be symbolized in sound. On the other hand, the frightening, disagreeably overexciting sounds father brings may be compelling, even pleasurable, although at times frightening. For while anxiety threatens, compromise, in a fragile mastery, may induce thrilling experience.

From this vantage point, mother's contribution might be silence, symbolizing homeostasis achieved. Ives's *biographical* silence may mirror experience with mother, though in no simple way. It is not only a matter of some symbolic representation of peace and silence but ultimately of a relative lack of conflict. To

Ives the most meaningful birth was the psychological birth attended by his father. In Ives's writings, his mother never acquired such explicitly graphic verbal representation; she had been consigned to an earlier, preverbal life and to silence. Yet Mollie did achieve some form of representation in art. Like many representations of the earliest mother, she may be sought in images of nature, tranquil mental states, and utopias—all rendered in auditory terms in music.

In the end, the parent who was more visible, more influential, and indeed fundamentally more passionately loved was the parent of conflict, and the sources of conflict arose very early in life. This does not diminish Charlie's love for his father, his early admiration and later devotion to him. Rather, it suggests that the sources of both sides of ambivalence were complex, that the underlying bases lay in ever-shifting equilibrium all his life, and that the whole process began at the dawn of consciousness in the child.

Fatherhood was in the process of change during the latter part of the nineteenth century. In the Ives family, it had changed perceptibly since the days of great-grandfather Isaac Ives, when the Puritan heritage still flourished. Against a background of mutual love of a rather formal nature, father was at that earlier time progenitor, pedagogue, guidance counselor, and benefactor to his children. He was also moral overseer, expected to correct any excessive indulgence of the mother. The children appeared to be passed on to him from the breast, and fathers and sons maintained a particularly strong bond. The letters of a young man away from home were characteristically addressed to his father, with a formal request to be "remembered" to his mother. The father was an extension of a routinely functioning family unit, providing companionate leadership. By the nineteenth century, however, mother had become the primary parent, with the chief responsibility for appropriate child rearing. And as "mother's importance waxed, father's inexorably waned."[12]

Thus by the time of Charlie's birth, a new picture of fatherhood was emerging in Danbury consistent with the concerns and values of a middle-class, mercantile town. Earlier, providing had been only one of father's functions; now it became his central role. And he played it—or so it began to seem to children—in some unknown and mysterious way outside the home. Leaving home every morning, he had a new and revered place in it upon his return each evening, the reward for making his way in a world increasingly alien to domestic life. Throughout the nineteenth century, the Ives family had been forging that outer world from the small town; having made it, they negotiated it with ease and thereby earned esteem and status. This was certainly the case with Ike and Joe. With George, though, it was another story.

The pattern of George's daily life ran counter to that of the men around him. He did not keep what were considered to be normal working hours for a man of that time and place. His work—that is, his musical work, if the townspeople would allow that it was work—was performed evenings, weekends, and holidays, when most men were off. Home life seemed topsy-turvy. As manager of the builders' goods store, George was well grounded to be accepted as both a father and a man in the community; in his role as "professor" he was suspect, having veered from the main business of making money. The man who did not make money was not a man, especially if he assumed roles deemed more appropriate for women, and most particularly if he stayed at home, increasingly the woman's place. Added to this was, of course, the effeminacy associated with music. Musical instruments, including the human voice, were not the instruments of men, that is, not a means of action; machines and guns were.

George was in a sense more comfortable at home, with all its implications, than most men would be, and more comfortable in the nurturing role. Perhaps, as the youngest in the family, he had missed playing the elder to younger siblings, as his brothers and sister—especially Amelia—most certainly did toward him. His own father was already forty-seven at George's birth. George had never known him as a lively younger man, much less a companionate one. Moreover, his father had indeed been the prototypical American father of the time in that he provided amply, vigorously, and visibly and was accorded at home the appropriate respect for having done so.

Even during the war, George had not embraced any stereotyped masculine role. He had not been among those who could scarcely wait to be old enough to join the ranks. He had spent the last days of the war comfortably at home in Danbury, recovering somewhat lengthily from a fall on the ice. Similarly, he remained comfortable at home in fatherhood. And to the extent that fatherhood entails a degree of "mothering," George seemed comfortable with that as well. Involved with his son, he did not appear to be in the least embarrassed by what others might think of his behavior. Many years later, Amelia Van Wyck related a portion of the family history: "Charlie and Moss were born in the house. When Moss was coming, Mollie didn't want too much confusion, so George had to go up to the barn to practice the violin. Charlie, who was under two, was sent along where he sat happily in Uncle Joe's buggy playing with the whip while his father practiced. So Charlie's introduction to music began at an early age."[13]

During Mollie's pregnancy with Moss, Charlie grew from six to fifteen months old. If we take the anecdote literally—and there is no reason not to—it provides a picture of what were likely Charlie's earliest experiences. It is a picture of an infant at the brink of separation from the symbiotic union with mother and the very beginnings of his own individuation in the presence of a father who, while caring, was also opening a new world for the child. Charlie's perception of the world coincided with the development of the very apparatus that made it possible. For here is where the foundations are laid for symbolic function—language and other forms of cognition, including music—for movement patterns, for the generation and experiencing of affects, and for lifetime attachments to other human beings.

The child during this time speaks his first words, using them to engage autonomously in meaningful human interactions. At the same time, the foundations of memory are being established and the content of memory itself recorded. Like words, musical forms may be perceived and apprehended, preparing those appropriately equipped for the development of yet another form of cognition. If music has meaning that is in some way translatable into words, memory, and affect, this is the time and place in human development when all are fluid, all mutually translatable. And with the dawn of the first words came the first tunes. Soon he was able to recognize such frequently heard patriotic songs as *Marching through Georgia* and *The Battle Cry of Freedom*, hymns like *Bethany* ("Nearer my God to Thee . . ."), *Nettleton*, and *The Sweet Bye and Bye*, and parlor songs like *My Old Kentucky Home*. Sounding in the child's ear and turned over in mind, they became as if mental playthings representing in part their source, father.

This is the time in life, between six and sixteen months, when the father emerges for the child. Charlie must at first have sensed George as a twilight figure. Unlike other fathers, George was not someone associated with morning and evening and assuming full presence only on weekends. More important, his association with his manifold sounds, increasingly organized and cogent to the child, made him an extraordinary multisensory figure. In the auditory sphere alone, he could not only babble, talk, croon, and sing, as any parent would, but also produce, as the child heard it, a miraculous variety of fascinating sounds.

And the father now provided a new kind of play—not only the peekaboo redolent of the comings and goings of mother, with its potentially sad or fearful implications of separation and even abandonment, but a kind of play associated with new experiences and new affects like excitement, exhilaration, and joy. The upward sweep of movement when father tosses the child in the air imprints in the "up" of experience, the feeling of elation. And with the autonomous upright stance and locomotion itself, the child begins active exploration, a "love affair with the world."[14]

A distinctive feature of this particular human unfolding was the role music played in Ives's infancy. For example, as the one-year-old child who had recently learned to walk sought to exercise this newfound capacity, to push with his muscles and to explore space, the sounds of the march must have mirrored, organized, and symbolized experience. He further may have identified his own movement with that of his father and taken on the illusion of being very big and active. Thus, at this early age he already experienced an essential feature of one of the many musics George could make, that of men moving together—the march, with father as leader.

The image of George as larger-than-life hero, appearing early, was destined to be reinforced in the child's mind and, grandly embellished, became intrinsically associated with music. It remained an indelible impression in the growing storehouse of memory and fantasy. Father was first and foremost the master of sound. What was potentially frightening or overwhelming in the auditory sphere could become exciting and thrilling instead. When the band played, George was in front, the movements of his hands miraculously starting and stopping the din, and above it all, the martial sounds of his cornet.

By eighteen months, Charlie must have come to perceive, as every boy does, his similarity to his father in build and sexual apparatus. He could not yet know, however, of their similarity in specific cognitive and perceptual capabilities. For example, both had not only perfect pitch, the ability to discriminate tones absolutely, but an acute auditory sensitivity to the sounds around them. Such similar capacities fostered a bond that intensified during the next phases of Charlie's life. Music was the matrix in which this bond was cemented.

Captured within this matrix were unique features of development that at length determined the character of Charles Ives the individual as well as the character of his music. At the same time, early precursors to psychological vulnerability were establishing themselves. The child who is sensitive in the auditory sphere experiences intense excitement increasingly localized to the ears as orifices as well as to the vaguer inner space in which vibration enters the mental sphere. Loud musical sounds—especially the brass and percussion instruments of the brass band—produce vibrations in the tactile as well as audible range, stimulating and exciting skin and soft tissue on the entire surface of the body but particularly in the external ear and its canal, the portals of audition.

The male child's dawning perception of the organ he shares with the father facilitates the development of masculine identification. It too is in the process of becoming an intense focus of excitement. Thus, in the unique unfolding of this particular life, both organs—ear and genital—may have localized exciting experience and provided a pathway for mutual displacement. Through this pathway, Charlie may have experienced musical excitement and sexual excitement as interchangeable and as shared with and induced by the father. Through it, emerging father-son love gains its special homoerotic element.

At the earliest stage, this homoerotic element is free of conflict. Love for the father is as intense as every other aspect of the experience. With the boy's emerging fantasy, sexual excitement may be consciously displaced from the genital to a spatially superior and more conventionally visible organ, like the ear. Thus, the ear becomes the focus of stimulation, the orifice penetrated, the portal of entry. Accordingly, a potential for conflict is laid down against the day when such penetration will produce more anxiety than excitement as it comes to be associated with other mental events, a time when penetration will entail a fantasy of mutilation and castration. But the earliest layers of memory will persist forever; they will be retrievable and capable of achieving symbolization. In the case of Ives, the most likely available mode of symbolization was that intrinsic to the entire course of early experience: auditory symbolism, music.

As Charlie developed, so did the internalized mental image of his father. Where a parent shares an intense interest in an art with a child and is similarly endowed, many aspects of the child's development become more complex. For example, the father may not only stimulate but also demonstrate and later, as was the case with George, teach. To Charlie in the dawn of childhood, George not only introduced, shared, and played music; he *was* music

When Moss was born, it was father's felicitous availability that softened the blow of having been displaced. But soon it was Moss's turn to command George's attention; and Charlie became aware that George, in his work, belonged to other people—audiences and bandsmen—as well as to himself. Indeed, the very nature of George's work, which took him away from home, intimated and confirmed to the child the inevitability of separation and loss.

Within a day or two of Charlie's second birthday, in October 1876, George left Danbury to tour with a group called Lou Fenn's Alabama Minstrels.[15] The minstrel show first appeared in the 1820s and prospered during the two decades preceding the Civil War. By the 1870s, much to the dismay of those who held to the genteel tradition in music, it was a standard form of popular entertainment. There was a place in it for a musical jack-of-all-trades like George, who could sing and play a variety of instruments and was familiar with the repertory of latter-day minstrelsy. Since minstrel groups were small, in particular those touring the provinces, George may have appeared in costume and blackface.

The tour was brief, lasting a week or two at most, but it was the first of several during the ensuing two and a quarter years. For a child, two weeks can seem interminable. As the concept of time intrinsic to a musician's life was forming in the mind of the composer-to-be, he was already experiencing one of the variants of duration: endless time without the pleasurable daily punctuations of reunion with a familiar and beloved object, a sense of time that later may be revived during mourning.

Nor was George present for Charlie's third birthday the following year. A few weeks earlier, he had embarked on a five-month tour of Canada with Fortescue's Burlesque. He returned in late February 1878.[16] Later that year, after Charlie had turned four, George was on the road with the Swedish Ladies' Vocal Quartet for more than a month, a tour that took him to Albany, Detroit, and Hamilton in

Canada.[17] Thus, George was away for at least six months when Charlie was between the ages of three years and four years, four months. No doubt for Charlie this great loss was tinged with a sense of betrayal. It may be expected that Mollie was present to soften the blow, to soothe and pacify. Again, her contribution is characterized by silence.

But absence, too, may be symbolized by silence, for there was no music in the household when George was away from home. The person who was lost thereby served to organize the very experience of loss with its characteristic affects—not only sadness but also surprise, longing, nostalgia, anger, and guilt. With this first series of losses, the child was beginning to learn the vocabulary of feelings and to experience intimations of death, with its imperative of mourning.

Except for day trips in summer to Rockaway, which had started some years before, and frequent engagements in nearby communities, George seemed not to have toured extensively again. Between absences during those early years, experiences of the father's local performances could be vivid and unforgettable to the child. Certain musical events in Danbury during this period contained what were to become characteristic features of Ives's music. When George was home between tours during Charlie's third year, he bought himself a Distin light action cornet, made by a then-famous instrument manufacturer. Its effect was reported in the Danbury *News* in 1878:

> We had the pleasure, yesterday, of hearing Mr. George E. Ives play the new Distin light-action cornet, with their patent echo, and were pleased with the beautiful effect it produced, sounding as if another instrument were playing a great distance off and yet clear,—in fact, a perfect echo. This attachment is different from the mute, such as Mr. Arbuckle used here, in that the echo can be produced in any part of the piece, while the mute permits only the whole strain or piece being played with echo effect. Mr. Ives played us the "Sweet Bye and Bye," echoing each strain of the chorus instead of the chorus entirely, and this is what makes the delusion so complete. Mr. Ives will use this instrument in the Benefit Concert.[18]

That George's name appears in three other items of that week's issue suggests his popularity at the time.[19]

In September, only a few weeks before he was to leave on tour again, George repeated his echo performance on the Distin cornet at the First Congregational Church. He performed two echo choruses, *Softly the Night Is Sleeping* and *The Sweet Bye and Bye*, this time with organ accompaniment. These were so well received that he played *The Last Rose of Summer* as an encore. If the three-year-old Charlie did not hear this performance, he certainly heard George practice for it at home. But very likely, the child was taken to hear his father since the church was actually on the Iveses' property.

The Sweet Bye and Bye, a gospel hymn popular at the camp meetings at which George often performed in summer, was a favorite of George's. He frequently played it in concert, figuring that people would sing along if they wished. Charles Ives's idea that a song with words might as readily be expressed by an instrument as by a human voice stemmed from this earlier time. As for *The Sweet Bye and Bye*, it may have been the child's early musical *bye-bye*. The tune is quoted in a number of Ives's works.

As the seasons changed, so did the music. In the spring, the steamboat *Adelphi* began to ply the waters between Norwalk and Rockaway, with the Ives band supplying music for the trip. Within the space of a few months in 1879, George was asked to instruct and lead two other local bands: one was associated with Saint Peter's Catholic Church in Danbury, and the other was the Bethel Cornet Band. He was already leading the Bethel Citizens' Band. Meanwhile, the Ives Band and Orchestra flourished. One day that August they played four engagements. George was thirty-four years old and in his prime, doing about as well as any village musician could expect. By then, Charlie was approaching his fifth birthday.

In the summer of Charlie's fifth year, George was at the height of his popularity. His relationship to the Ives Company at this time is unclear. The store by now employed twenty-five people, and it is unlikely that he could have functioned effectively as manager. George's arrangement with his brother Joe probably remained very flexible.

The musical highlight of that summer was the reopening of Elmwood Park. The July evening was clear and pleasant,

> with no moon to dim the illumination and make the fireworks a mockery. . . . On the arrival of the evening train of the Danbury and Norwalk Railway there was quite a throng of people and teams in front of the station. The two Bethel bands came by this train and were met by St. Peters band. The three bands consolidated and passed through Ives Street . . . and appeared on Main Street playing a march from Boyer. In both volume and harmony the music was a success and the three bands moved down the street flanked by a throng of delighted people and followed by an army of teams. Approaching the Park the sight ahead was an inspiring one. The dark outline of the trees, the moving masses beneath the colored lanterns, the lights in the buildings and the spray from the fountain formed a spectacle that was very pretty and called forth involuntary exclamations of delight as it burst upon the vision.[20]

An estimated three thousand to four thousand people, said to be "the largest number in one body assembled in Danbury in years, excepting at the Fair season," attended the festivities. A joint concert was given by the three bands, all of which had been trained and were conducted by George Ives. In the middle of the third selection, strains of music could be heard from another band marching up Main Street, clashing with the music coming from the bandstand. The audience, bewildered, turned to one another wondering who it might be. As the band onstage resumed a waltz, the Ridgefield Band approached and promptly took its place with the other musicians on the bandstand, where the massed groups played a medley of popular airs. "The volume of sound was very great. There were nearly eighty players in the piece and the national airs were thus given with an enthusiasm never before heard here. The effect was remarkably fine."[21]

The evening ended with the universal favorite, *Home Sweet Home*, but the music was not quite over. The bands proceeded to the Turner House, where they had been invited to supper with the town dignitaries and other guests at tables set out on the lawn. The three bands then dispersed into the darkness of the streets. The muffled voices of the marchers and, from time to time, subdued band music could be heard here and there throughout the mile-square center of town. The Bethel bands were escorted by the Saint Peter's Band to the train station, where they struck up together a sprightly *My Educated Mary Ann*. En route, they stopped for several serenades.

Music seemed to be everywhere that night, on the bandstand and beyond—at times stationary, at times moving. It was destined to become one of those memories Charlie would never forget. Considerations of spatial orientation and the distribution of sound became part of his musical style, and more than once the acoustic image of clashing bands was evoked in Ives's music. The sound of eighty instruments must have been overwhelming to the child, and the experience an awesome one, the more so with his father harnessing the massed sound. For Ives, the very feeling of awe would come to be associated with George.

By the time Charlie was five years old, even before George began to give him more or less formal lessons, he had already experienced a wide range of music. In some sense, this personal, private education was to become as much the equipment of the composer as anything he was to learn in later childhood and adolescence from his teacher-father or, still later, from his professors in college. This spontaneous experiencing and self-teaching are the hallmark of the development of the artist. As the child attaches himself to the chief objects in his life—human objects, especially family members—he exercises the capacity to incorporate representations of these objects in his mental life and endow those representations with feeling. Such representations may extend to every aspect of the gifted child's environment—to nonhuman objects, nature, and, finally, the materials of art itself. Thus, long before formal education, the child becomes intensely involved with the language, geography, and algebra of art, with an interest in such raw materials as color, texture, and line in the visual arts or, in music, the nuances of tone-pitch, timbre, volume, orientation in space, and duration. All array themselves mentally in appropriate forms with which the child will become fascinated and which will in time serve as bases for the construction of new forms, the essential work of the artist. Thus, alternates to human beings become collectively invested.[22] Nor does this necessarily imply a withdrawal from persons close to the child in life; rather, it means a capacity for intense privacy and inner concentration. In fact, often a mental merging of the human object and the materials of art results in the making of forms whose *content* may suggest such persons—a portrait or reminiscence in art that might range from being purposely fashioned or to being inadvertently hidden from consciousness.

Thus, the music Charlie heard in his first years constituted his earliest musical education as well as his mental playthings. Moreover, by their intimate relation to George, they became for the child a part of the father. Through mental displacement, transactions with father could be accomplished through his surrogates in music. Tunes could serve as transitional objects—part of the child's mind, part of his father's essence; part real, part magic.[23] They might have provided solace during George's long absences. Once established in mind, the tunes would be hallucinated involuntarily and later at will. In this way, an exceptional fundamental capacity of the composer was being developed and exercised in the context of ordinary life. The tunes representing father could, in effect, bring him back to immediate experience. At the same time, affects associated with absence, sadness, and nostalgia exacted a toll on the living tune: forever it would be suffused in the child's mind of the adult with feelings of loss. Thus, musical phrases representing father could be brought to mind in a process that was an early variant of reminiscence. They could be transformed endlessly in mind into related or new musical ideas. Tunes associated with the "marching" George—vigorous, rhythmic, gay, triumphant—could thus assume formal characteristics representative of the person nostalgically recalled. In the child's mind, the workplace of the composer was becoming established and the raw materials of what would become a highly individual music were being assembled.

Ives's music is full of quoted tunes. Stylistically, its composer had, in John Kirkpatrick's words, "the habit of musical quotation." Kirkpatrick catalogued quotations from a total of 142 individual hymns and patriotic, military, popular, and college songs,[24] and since his work still more quotations have been found.[25] Virtually all of the quoted tunes were composed in the nineteenth century, and most were more characteristic of George's times than of Charlie's. They comprise, in effect, an anthology of a certain kind of nineteenth-century American music, specifically the everyday and holiday music of the American country town. This anthology became a part of Charlie's musical dictionary early in life. They came to have a complex history, multiple functions, and far-reaching importance in Ives's mental life and helped determine his individual style as a composer.

Early on, the tunes assumed a position not quite of the father or of the self exclusively but midway, as it were, transitional, part father, part the inner world of self. Long after young Charlie's inner musical mental life was developed and cultivated, he maintained access to this early variety of experience as a way of representing one or another aspect of George. The tunes came to serve as raw material for the refined, organized creation of musical form, but in early life they served other functions.[26] Obsessively replaying these tunes in his mind must have been a way of recalling his father during George's long absences. Thus, in a feat of creative adaptation, obsession ultimately became art.

Around the time Charlie was five, he came to experience losses of another kind. In identifying with a valued object, the loss of the object's esteem is experienced as the loss of one's own esteem. This is the toll of attachment. George's successes were dwarfed by the financial successes of other family members which garnered more esteem in the community. Uncle Joe's home-furnishing business was thriving, and Uncle Ike's money-making schemes were bringing him wealth.

The family was close; inevitably others too—most important, Aunt Amelia and Uncle Lyman—became models of identification for Charlie. Yet this close-ness may have been a source of some tension, because Charlie's love of them and the wish to be with them could have seemed to him a betrayal of the primary parent.

The Brewsters' dominance in the family life of the Iveses was a central element in Charlie's childhood. Their interest in and attachment to Charlie and Moss, while affectionate from the first, intensified as it became apparent that they themselves would remain childless. Clearly, Amelia needed to participate in motherhood. Mollie appeared to be willing to share, although she may have had little choice. The ascendancy of the Brewsters had opposite effects on the lives of Charlie and his father. George, long consigned to the role of little brother by his siblings, found himself entrenched there in the eyes of the family despite his own fatherhood. As for five-year-old Charlie, it was as if in Lyman Brewster he had acquired an auxiliary father.

Uncle Lyman, deprived of natural fatherhood, had all the makings of a caring and truly generative father. He was a natural teacher, and he loved to share his love of books, poetry, and games. He was a wonderful storyteller, and his breadth of knowledge and range of travel were far wider than those of anyone else in the family. As the only child of his father's second marriage, with two older half sisters, Lyman had not had the kind of extended family life that he seemed so much to enjoy through marriage into the Ives family.

It appears that even within the more extended family—that is, among the children of the other brothers—Charlie and Moss maintained a special position, perhaps because of the high esteem in which they were held by Aunt Amelia. In Charlie's childhood and boyhood, there is a sense that four adults share more or less interchangeably in parenting. But George always remained first for Charlie and later, with Charlie's increasing interest and competence in music, his involvement with George intensified. It was Moss, therefore, who became the Brewsters' favorite.

Ironically, Amelia and Lyman were responsible for the displacement of the boys and their parents from the Ives homestead. This was the price paid for the growing prominence of the Brewsters and the benefits of their reflected glory. The events that precipitated it were matters of family and local politics, circumstances far from the mind of a five-year-old boy. In spite of Lyman's devotion to the close family group into which he had married, the social and geographical range of his life was in no way parochial; nor was his later influence upon his son of fantasy, Charlie Ives.[27]

Almost from the beginning of his career, Lyman's reputation as a lawyer was statewide, owing perhaps to the influence of his maternal uncle, Roger Averill, who had been lieutenant governor of Connecticut during the Civil War. Lyman was considered by his peers to be an idealist in law, a position he acknowledged with characteristic humor by reporting in the Yale Class Book of 1865 that he was "keeping an office in Danbury for the prevention of litigation."[28] Local legend had it that he would as soon talk a prospective client out of a suit as accept the case, saying, "Now, a lawsuit is a good thing for me, but it isn't a good thing for you."[29] Nonetheless, he soon became known as an able trial lawyer. In time, he developed a national reputation; already in 1878, when Charlie was four, Lyman was a founding member of the American Bar Association.

As a Republican, Lyman was first elected to the state House of Representatives in 1870 and became deeply involved in politics, although he appeared to have misgivings about it as a career. He wrote of his concern to Simeon Baldwin early in 1878: "It makes one ashamed of human nature to see the selfishness and underhanded work that goes on. I wish we had a safe deliverance."[30] He apparently resolved his conflict regarding a life in politics only after a successful term as state senator, to which he was elected in 1879, the first Republican in fourteen years to achieve that position. Afterward, he appears to have lost interest in state politics and devoted himself to his law practice, legal scholarship, and a substantial role in establishing principles of law and ethics within the profession. Interestingly, he was elected senator largely on the strength of his call to abolish the manufacturing of hats in the state prison, a prime concern of both hat manufacturers and unions. The cause was dear to the people of Danbury, for hats were bread and butter to them. Lyman had always been held in high esteem, but he now became something of a local hero as well.

Lyman in his way was by now as much a part of the social fabric of the town as any Ives had ever been. His was a visible presence to all, and his influence spread far beyond the boundaries of Danbury, while he remained rooted in its institutions. His offices, occupying the second floor of the Savings Bank of Danbury, were an established part of Main Street.

George was not likely to have been among Lyman's boosters. Although he was increasingly concerned about making a living in order to raise and educate his two young sons, his real interests were elsewhere. By 1879, he had gone about as far as a village musician could in terms of esteem, but there were growing opportunities for new concerts and other productions. In fact, George was about to become something of a musical entrepreneur by bringing more opera and operetta to Danbury and neighboring towns. On the other hand, George's work took him in the opposite direction socially from Lyman. As Lyman cultivated contacts among the wealthier, more educated, and more influential citizens, George through his band work got involved with fraternal and religious groups of lower socioeconomic status. The Saint Peter's Band, for example, which had finished its first season playing Wednesday and Friday evenings at Elmwood Park, was sponsored by the local Roman Catholic church. Most of the congregants were from the working class and had settled in Danbury to work in various industries, particularly hatting. They were Irish and Italian and, for the most part, first- or second-generation Americans, in contrast to the Iveses and the forebears of Lyman Brewster. In a sense, it was their candidate who had been defeated in Lyman's election to office, for they tended to vote Democratic. These were the people to whom George was closest outside the family, and he measured their worth in terms of how well they played music, not how they voted. Although he regularly performed at the seasonal celebrations of other groups as well—for example, the temperance Washingtonians—he seems to have been more comfortable and more popular with the fraternal and ethnic groups than with the more traditional and quasi-civic groups.

Politics too had its music, which for Charlie was as likely to be associated with Uncle Lyman as with George. Large outdoor gatherings, in the past mainly patriotic events such as the Fourth of July or Union Army recruitment, were now often political rallies. Typically, they were held at night. For such events, the large calcium light, or limelight, used by the fire companies to illuminate nighttime fires, was pressed into service. The memory of the bright white light emerging from the darkness, together with the band music and the passing parade, engraved itself in the child's mind.

In the election of November 4, 1879, just two weeks after Charlie's fifth birthday, Lyman ran successfully for the Connecticut state Senate. In the months leading up to the election, it was becoming clear to Amelia that regardless of whether Lyman was elected to office, the house on Main Street was the only fitting place for the Brewsters to live, and that George Ives and his family would have to move out. Charlie had been born in that house, and it was the only world he knew. He and his parents had occupied the large bedroom over the south parlor in his first year. After Moss's birth, Charlie probably occupied one of the smaller rooms in the rear, looking out on Chapel Place. Its walls were papered with wondrous pictures of children in boats rowing among the rushes. What remained of great-grandfather Isaac's garden had been Charlie's playground, and the barn visible from the rear window was his concert hall. Now family pride took precedence, and Amelia Brewster, a strongly assertive woman, prevailed. As Amelia Van Wyck was to put it years later, "What Aunt Amelia wanted, she usually got."[31] George, the youngest and least powerful in the family, did not stand a chance, and Mollie was unlikely to complain.

In late 1879 or early 1880, the George Ives family vacated the house at 210 Main Street to make room for Lyman and Amelia. The move signified more than a change of locale for five-year-old Charlie. As the direct result not only of the Brewsters' influence and strength but also of George's relative weakness, it threatened the stability of the family and the child's perception of his world. This was one of the first times in Charlie's life when he had a glimmer of his normally idealized father as anything but the conqueror. There could be no doubt now that the nominal male leader of the family was Uncle Lyman. Any fantasy of father and mother as king and queen was being challenged by another image—the prince consort buttressed by the heiress to the throne.

Number 16 Stevens Street was only a few blocks away from the old Ives house. But it was in another part of the small town, and a strange one for Charlie. No amount of fixing up the house to make it a cheerful and comfortable place to live could make up for one fact: it was not on Main Street.

SIX

BOYHOOD AND ITS VENERATION

Ⅰn the Danbury of 1880, people still liked to think of themselves as dwelling in "the land of steady habits," though the term was more appropriate to their Puritan ancestors than to them. Danbury in the 1870s had been caught up in a flux of immigration, with new ethnic groups altering the makeup of the population virtually from year to year. The traditional institutions were growing, and new ones—religious, cultural, commercial, and fraternal—were springing up. A new opera house would soon be under construction. Protestant churches were losing their majority as Irish and Italian immigration strengthened the local Catholic church. And business itself was growing and changing. In addition to traditional industries like hatting, the furniture, carpet, and wallpaper industries were thriving.

Although the George E. Ives family had taken a temporary step down in its move from Main Street to Stevens Street, Danbury in general was spiraling upward. George's popularity was increasing to the point that he was mentioned in the newspaper at least as frequently as Joe and Ike—no mean achievement. But unlike George, when Joe and Ike made the news, it meant that they had made money. On the brink of the 1880s, for example, Joe's home-furnishing business had a work force of twenty-five. Now called the J. M. Ives Company, it was a corporation with stockholders. George continued at the old store, which sold mainly builders' hardware. Joe's new ventures were complex and demanding, requiring business skills and dedication. But George's musical activities were so varied and frequent that it would have been impossible for him to devote consistent attention to a regular job even if he had been inclined, let alone equipped, to do so. Later in the decade, he began to take on a series of part-time "accounting"—actually clerical—jobs as his need for income increased.

At the beginning of the decade, George was starting to lead a musical life that approached that of a professional musician anywhere. But the monetary rewards were meager, and what appears to be popularity may, from George's point of view, have been an attempt to piece together as much of an income as possible. Some days one or another combination of musicians drawn from his bands performed several times. The day he had four jobs, for example, playing on the boat to New York he split his musicians among a performance at the Opera House, the Germania dance, and a company party in Norwalk.[1] Thus, he too functioned at times as a contractor, although relatively rarely. The scale for a parade bandsman at the time was three dollars for a full day, two dollars for a half-day, and one dollar for an evening.[2] When George became popular as an "instructor" of bands later in the 1880s, his salary was paid by the bandsmen themselves. It did not amount to much. Some bandsmen were, like George, attempting to make a living from music. The popular fiddler John Starr, for example, for a time played in George's various combinations and sometimes took a group to play in one place while George and another group played elsewhere. But most of the bandsmen held regular jobs and played for recreation, attempting just to break even for whatever their pleasure cost.

In addition to his own Danbury Cornet Band, the Bethel Citizens Band, the Bethel Cornet Band, and the band associated with Saint Peter's Catholic Church, which performed for civic and religious occasions, the Norwalk Band engaged George as their instructor; he also coached the Danbury High School Band. The most important of these functions was directing the summer outdoor concerts at Elmwood Park, which had started in 1879.[3] The Danbury Cornet Band, incidentally, did not receive pay for this twice-weekly series, and at one point it could not meet its expenses. Even a last-minute cancellation of a band concert by its angry members did not do much to improve desultory support.

Nevertheless, there were compensations, and the bands had their moments of glory. They continued to be an important part of patriotic events. In fact, it was on such occasions that band and town were most in tune with each other, perhaps because the bands filled a real need. One such event occurred when Charlie was five and a half: the dedication of the soldiers' monument erected on the site of the old concert hall in May 1880.[4] The figure of a Union soldier holding the flag was perched on a column on whose base were inscribed the names of the major battles fought by Danbury men during the Civil War. The entire town was festooned with flags, including a large one "in front of Mr. Geo. W. Ives' homestead. A little son of G. E. Ives, dressed in national colors, sat in front and saluted the colors."[5] On that day, Charlie saw his father, in uniform, leading the band in a parade, and associated him with the war heroes. On such occasions, George appeared at his finest, and it would seem irrelevant that he might be earning only a dollar or two, if anything, that afternoon. He was a necessary celebrant for the patriotic occasion as far as the townspeople were concerned. For Charlie he would always remain the chief hero of the Civil War.

In some ways, the Stevens Street house was more an annex to the house on Main Street than an outpost. Amelia, by dint of character and because of her mother's growing age, was mistress of the homestead. Lyman, the male head of the house, still commanded the respectful title Judge Brewster, although he was now state senator. In contrast to the wealth of Joe and Ike and the eminence of the Brewsters, George and his young family were like poor relations. Both Charlie and Moss became the focus of the Brewsters' parenting, but in different ways. If Charlie was favored by his father, Moss inevitably felt himself to be the needier. He became, in effect, the Brewsters' boy, and Lyman was the chief figure of identification for him, as George was for Charlie. But Lyman's influence on Charlie's life should not be underestimated, and it was during this period that its basis was being established.

This was Charlie's world when "dressed in national colors" he stood on the porch of his grandmother's house, now the Brewsters'. From this point on, most of the letters that remain from Charlie's childhood and adolescence are either addressed to Amelia or Lyman or refer to them freely. In fact, Charlie's first letter, postmarked May 9, 1880, and written on Uncle Lyman's law-office stationery, was addressed to Amelia:

Aunt Millie
    I have wrote to you for hte fun fo it I have a sour toe. how is clams. I have nothing out of my garden. my name was in the newspaper for I worked for the school. my head aches for I mus leave you new.

goodby,
Charles Ives[6]

Charlie often wrote Amelia or Lyman when they were away at their beach house in Westbrook, close to the mouth of the Connecticut River on Long Island Sound. Even compared to a small town like Danbury, Westbrook was country. Amelia and Lyman bought a house there along with other members of the extended Ives family and other prominent Danbury families. Westbrook came to be known to the family as "Cousins' Beach." As Charlie grew up, he and Moss and frequently Mollie came to visit. There is no indication that George spent much time there, nor did the George Iveses ever own their own place at Cousins' Beach.

Charlie started at the New Street School in the spring of 1881. Danbury took pride in its six up-to-date district schools serving more than a thousand pupils. The New Street School boasted twelve rooms, one for each grade. Charlie was precocious in reading and writing and probably began in a more advanced class than Room 1, where the rudiments were taught. In the molding of an educational philosophy, reading was accorded a prominent position: "It is an extremely difficult matter to impress upon the scholar the advantage of knowing how to read, and yet everybody recognizes the charm of good reading. It is not a business qualification, but it is an important accomplishment."[7]

At home, George sometimes read to the boys. A collection of books in the old house had been assembled through the years by various family members, especially Joseph. And they were not just there for show; they had been read.[8]

At the New School graduation that year, it was noted that "the Chief novelty of the occasion was the excellent music given by the High School orchestra numbering eight pieces. These boys had associated themselves under the instruction of Geo. E. Ives for the practice of music."[9] The leader was Orrin S. Barnum, an older student of George's and a boy Charlie looked up to. George's involvement with the school seems natural enough. He was well known as an instructor by now and was engaged from time to time with his orchestra to play at graduations. However, his appearing as teacher the first year Charlie attended the New Street School suggests an ongoing involvement with Charlie's education. In subsequent years, Charlie always participated in the school orchestra under George, playing the drums and other instruments.

Soon Moss joined Charlie at school, and George's thoughts turned toward their future and, in particular, how he could keep them in school. Toward the end of 1882 George took the first of several jobs as a bookkeeper, this time in the hardware store of C. S. Andrews.[10] At the start of the new year, the newspaper noted that he had "taken charge of business of the Danbury Hat Case Company," a new venture of Ike's.[11]

In his *Memos*, Ives wrote that George began giving him music lessons when he was five years old. But he recalled differently in supplying biographical data to the Cowells:

> Young Charles was about eight years old when his father found him at the piano in the music room of the old family house on Danbury's Main Street, perched high on a green velvet stool and banging away earnestly all by himself in an attempt to play not a melody but the rhythms he had heard on the drums in the Danbury Band. "It's all right to do that, Charles," said his father, voicing a principle the boy was to hear expressed a thousand times during his later studies under his father's guidance. "It's all right to do that *if* you know what you're doing."[12]

He also remembered his father taking him down to the village barber shop, where he

> turned him over to the barber, an old German bandsman named Slier, who played the drum in Ives' Danbury Civil War Band. Old Mr. Slier gave the youngster an empty tub and a couple of drumsticks, and settled him on a stool just under the shelf that held the customer's shaving mug. There, between shaves and haircuts, he taught Charles the double roll and all the other things a good drummer was expected to know. By the time he was twelve, Charlie was confidently playing the snare drum in his father's band. [13]

Of the three memories, the second is the least plausible. The picture of Charlie "perched" on a stool attempting to play rhythms is not that of the eight-year-old who could already write a reasonably communicative letter to his aunt and uncle and had by now achieved the fifth grade at the New School but rather that of a much younger child—in fact, a child even younger than five. The conflicting stories about the start of music lessons probably indicates that there had been no distinct starting point, that teaching had progressed naturally out of the child's expression of interest and readiness and George's responsiveness to it.

The piano in the parlor at 210 Main Street no doubt was Charlie's first instrument. Children, in the course of exploring the family furniture, are often fascinated to find that a strange box or table opens up to reveal a shelf that makes sound when struck. In a sense, it might be less fruitful to document "when" Charlie started actual music lessons than to understand the developmental processes that were already making him a musician. It seems likely that George would have shown Charlie the way on this instrument, but it also seems possible that George might wonder how a child would approach the instrument on his own and what he might do with it. For George seemed to like to listen to what others did with music and, far from perceiving the result as odd, off tune, or out of rhythm, seemed to hear it as that person's individual music—even that of a child. In many anecdotes later cited by Charlie from his boyhood, it appears that age, station, and education made little difference to George in his appreciation of a person's music. If George did indeed *hear* and not prematurely *mold* the child's music making, he would have reinforced Charlie's earliest spontaneous attempts at motor discharge at the piano in the form of repetition of the familiar sounds of the marching band.

Ives set down all these recollections in his late fifties. Perhaps the "memory" from when he was eight is like a summary and substitution containing related memories of even earlier events and thus absorbing and eclipsing them. Such earlier memories are commonly preverbal, hence more likely to find symbolization and expression via a later, better organized experience. Here the memory Ives unconsciously depicts would be that of his first attempts to make music—the child reaching up and banging on the piano indiscriminately, with abandon, even enjoying the proud approval of the father. It would have been the very first instance of what Ives would call "piano drumming."

Later, after he took lessons and knew the "rules," he got tired of using the familiar cadential chords for rhythm in the bass and "got to trying out sets of notes to go with or take off the drums. . . . They had little to do with the harmony of the piece, and were used only as sound combinations as such. For the explosive notes or heavy accents . . . the fist or flat of the hand was sometimes used."[14]

With regard to the piano drumming, wrote Ives, "Father didn't object to all of this, if it was done with some musical sense—that is, if I would make some effort to find out what was going on, with some reason."[15] Here are the beginnings of artistic morality, the knowing of right from wrong in a creative context. And with George's loving flexibility there could be some compromise between the impulse and its containment. There was room for spontaneity, even aggression, if the close emotional attachment to father, the bearer of the rules, made it possible for the child to adhere to them more or less until they made good sense to him. The rules came to temper Charlie's inclination to experimentation and innovation, providing a framework that would somehow make the result more meaningful.

By age eleven, Charlie was working with his father on piano, violin, cornet, sight reading, harmony, counterpoint, and even rudimentary orchestration. Indeed, Charlie was acquiring the basis of an academic musical education from George. Besides learning much vernacular music from him—the patriotic, martial, ethnic, and religious music that later crop up as quotations in his work—Charlie also profited from George's vast knowledge of the fundamentals of the cultivated tradition. Charlie also began to study organ at this time. But George wisely shared responsibility for his son's musical education with others as the opportunities presented themselves. Ella Hollister, for example, who was becoming well known as a leader in the cultivated musical life of Danbury, had started a music school and became Charlie's piano teacher. By the time he was thirteen, Charlie was able to play Stephen Heller's *Tarantella* in a student recital at the West Street Church. Wallach notes that this "was the kind of flashy show piece which was used to demonstrate a music student's diligence in practicing, and is a model example of music in the cultivated tradition, since its primary function was to demonstrate cultivation."[16]

The one instrument Charlie took seriously with which George later appeared uncomfortable was the human voice, despite George's teaching vocal classes at the time.[17] Charlie had had some voice lessons and sang periodically in church, as on Easter Sunday, 1885, when he sang a duet with a friend and probably classmate in Sabbath school.[18]

Notwithstanding his father's encouragement, Charlie seems to have been following his own inclination in pursuing music. He was not being groomed for a musical career, but still he was something of a local prodigy. He was also on the honor roll of the New Street School. He seemed to possess inexhaustible energy.

Moss, just turning nine, was beginning to perceive himself as a writer, and his earliest attempts at writing are preserved in a diary which he kept irregularly during 1885. From it, we have further evidence of the family's involvement in church and music: "I went to church with papa and blowed the organ . . . I went to [chorus] meeting with papa and Charlie and blowed the organ for miss Ida Mcneal."[19]

At this time, George was involved in elaborate play with his sons, references to which are found in a few letters of the period, in Charlie's memories, later recorded in his *Memos*, and in Moss's diary. Innovative, imaginative play was an important part of family life for George and both boys. Ives recalled that the three of them would play an elaborate game of "train":

> The Ives Bros. R.R. under the clothes line . . . two barrels on the wash bench, an old stove pipe and the dinner bell . . . the cab was part of the chicken coop. . . . Father always entered into it seriously . . . and would just wave and never stop to talk while the train was going full blast. At that time I remember he was practicing the violin. . . . Father discovered that staccato passages and arpeggios could be made to sound like the clicking of the car wheels. . . . So he . . . rode in the rear passenger car for whole trips. . . . The noise of the wheels always stopped at the stations.[20]

Later, they all played "store," which they took so seriously that George had billheads printed up: "IVES BROS., Groceries, Main St. Danbury." The "store" was originally called Abbot Bros., "so that it would appear first in any directory starting with 'A'." In July 1886, Charlie, then approaching twelve, wrote to George from Westbrook that "Moss and I are going to change are firm. Instead of Cabotts Bros were are going to have it Ives Bros. Will you please take the sign down & letter it on the other side Ives Bros 165 & 167."[21] George attended to it promptly, for the following week Charlie thanked his father for lettering the sign.

George sent Charlie elsewhere for lessons on instruments, but he taught him the theoretical side of music himself, sharing what he had acquired from his own teacher, Charles Foepple. Charlie responded eagerly to these studies, the technical basis for composition, and he soon began to view himself as a composer. While he clearly identified with George, there is no evidence that he ever saw himself as a village bandmaster, and it is unlikely that George would have encouraged him in that direction. Aside from the drums and probably some passing knowledge of trumpet, Charlie did not favor band instruments. In his own way and even at this early point, Charlie strongly identified with George but was finding directions of his own and moving toward autonomy.

The principal area that father and son were beginning to share in Charlie's boyhood was the writing of music, whether as harmony exercises, musical arrangements, or the beginnings of composition. George was teacher, supervisor, and collaborator. But he had never been a composer; his writing consisted solely of arranging parts for various combinations of instruments. It was in this context that Charlie established his identity as a composer. Expectably, there were elements of play in the process as well as work. The writing of music became for the two of them a world of its own in which others—Moss, for example—could not participate. Here Charlie effectively asserted himself in the inevitable rivalry with his brother while otherwise maintaining a close relationship with him.

Mollie too was excluded from this world, although she was conscientious in helping Charlie make arrangements for any musical work he took on, such as playing in church, and saw to it that he met his obligations. On the other hand, she encouraged his interests outside music—for example, trips to Cousins' Beach. At this point, in a sense, she and George reversed earlier parenting roles. She was now calling Charlie's attention to a widening outer world, while George concentrated on the private and special inner world he shared with Charlie.

George still retained, from his days with Foepple, a hand-copied and thoroughly worked-through edition of the traditional Germanic harmony lessons. George shared it with Charlie, and there is evidence that Charlie mastered it, for he seemed to be reasonably well prepared for advanced studies when he entered Yale. The tangible souvenir of George Ives's studies with Foepple consisted of a few notebooks with comments on music theory (as well as on the German language). One copybook contained a series of graded harmony exercises, leading up to some original fugues. There were also some handwritten copies of baroque church music, whose chord progressions had been analyzed and identified by George. Finally, there were in the back of one notebook (and upside down) sketches of the melody line of popular band pieces—marches, polkas, quadrilles, waltzes. In all, the notebooks give a portrait of a unique musical world.

Charlie, in going over these exercises, was encouraged to share this world of his father's. The copybook had some blank pages following the fugue exercises that George had written for Foepple when he was fifteen or sixteen. Charlie filled these with his own exercises. George's working out of these assignments in the copybook show that he had no particular gift for sustained musical invention. Charlie soon revealed the opposite. Thus, in the earliest teacher-student relationship between father and son, it was already evident that Charlie might go far beyond his father in musical creativity. His realizing this potential depended greatly on George's encouragement and teaching. George's view of music, as well as his own training, left an imprint on Ives's musical style. The juxtaposition of the vernacular and the classical in George's copybook is but one example.

George once sketched an article on basic music theory, probably for the benefit of Charlie and of his pupils in the 1880s. Its outlines are traditional, but the result is far from mechanical; George reveals a freshness and individuality in approach and, above all, an acute ear for the sounds he was describing. About the seventh chord, for example, he writes: "This seventh note produces what all musicians call a dissonance—but sounds in some cases to me only like a partial dissonance and is used so much that we get used to it and treat it as if it were as much of a consonance as our other tones."[22] Traditional theory is peppered with an irrepressible liveliness of spirit. Suggesting to students that they play and listen to the dominant seventh of the key of C in a position in which F and G are adjacent in the bass, he exclaims: "Ain't they a little *too* tart?" But despite the occasional airy American informality, the article as well as the notebooks served an important function in the musical education of Charlie: they passed on a remarkably rich European tradition in a skilled and detailed manner. The fortuitous accidents of George's own adolescent experiences with Charles Foepple, his sojourn in New York before and after the war, and his close contact with the European-trained musicians who were recruited for the regimental band all came together in the musical training of his son.

Public music consisted of popular (vernacular) music and classical (cultivated) music. Vernacular music comprised the utilitarian band music and gospel hymn music at which Charlie's father excelled. What often passed for cultivated music was sentimental parlor songs and various adaptations of classical music. George engaged in both, making hardly a distinction between them.

Musical play and experiment were largely kept in the family. George certainly did not see himself as a composer. While he encouraged Charlie in composition and was even beginning to collaborate with him, he did not encourage experimental techniques of composition. On the other hand, George engaged in various musical and acoustical experiments, which were stimulated by his strong sense of curiosity. Here was George the scientist and naturalist (as Charlie saw him) fascinated by the phenomenon of sound.

In the *Memos*,[23] Charlie catalogued George's experiments:

1. The slide cornet, an instrument capable of playing any interval.
2. Musical glasses (filled with varying amounts of water and struck with a stick), for very small intervals.
3. A piano tuned in actual partials (individual frequencies which usually comprise complex tones acoustically); George doing the tuning himself, by ear.[24]
4. Glasses tuned in a scale without octaves—an alternative way of dividing up musical space.
5. Violin strings (a set of twenty-four) stretched over a clothes press and attached to weights. Charlie wrote, "He would pick out quarter-tone tunes and try to get the family to sing them."[25]

This list demonstrates George's curiosity and ingenuity as well as his interest in teaching. But it was Charlie who later channeled the energy behind these experiments into actual composition. There are social implications, too, in terms of how his Danbury neighbors might view these activities. Whereas the echo effect when George played *The Sweet Bye and Bye* on his Distin cornet could be meaningfully shared by the congregation of the Methodist church, violin strings stretched on a clothes press in the backyard were quite another thing. Such stunts as the one at Avery's Grove in 1873, when the passing Newtown Cornet Band "clashed" with the Ives Cornet Band, and at the reopening of Elmwood Park in 1879, when several bands all played at once, were fun for performers and listeners alike. But a parlor trick of musical glasses tuned to exotic scales raised eyebrows. In short, it did not take much for the musical experimenter to be viewed as a crank or a deviant. It must have been difficult for George to bear having his chosen profession viewed as trivial or effeminate, so it is understandable that he might have tried to avoid having it viewed as crazy as well.

And Charlie, in turn, must have recoiled at the idea that in the eyes of the townspeople, his father, whom he greatly admired, would be thus devalued. As adolescents seek self-definition, they are acutely sensitive to the judgments of others, often fiercely protective of family esteem while themselves being critical of family. Deviation from convention threatens shame. This was but one early source of conflict for Charlie—the tension generated from images of the valued father and the devalued father.

Another source of conflict was Charlie's musical gift. For Charlie was destined to surpass his father both as a performer and as a composer. Whereas earlier the relationship between son and father seemed to be relatively free of conflict, as George became more closely involved in Charlie's musical life, he came to be a potential rival as well.

To complicate matters further, it appeared as if Charlie, esteemed by the entire family and sure to be better educated and better prepared for life than his father, bid fair to win in any competition with George. Gradually, they were also becoming musical collaborators as George began to encourage Charlie to compose and Charlie began to seek his guidance in developing this talent. What resulted was a flourishing of musical creativity in all spheres, including the early establishment of Charlie's sense of identity as a composer. He remained eternally grateful for George's exceedingly rich contribution to this aspect of his life. But in addition, there was a latent sense of shame stemming from Charlie's perceptions of a devalued father. Moreover, he would begin to experience feelings of guilt for surpassing George. Such were the painful and unacceptable feelings Charlie needed to disavow. As a defense against experiencing them, he came to idealize his boyhood and his father's role in it.

In September 1886, when he was just reaching twelve years of age, Charlie first dared acknowledge thinking of himself as a composer. The extant title page to a piece now lost reads, "Schoolboy March: D & F Op. 1. Arr. Band. Sept. 1886 C. Ives." There was also a *Slow March*, based on *Adeste Fidelis*, which Charlie later said was played by the Danbury Band on Decoration Day, 1886, although there is no newspaper account of this particular event.[26] Through the good offices of George, the *Schoolboy March* was incorporated into the *Holiday Quickstep*, possibly the first piece by Charlie ever to be performed. The manuscript is mostly in George's hand, but some parts for violin may have been copied by Charlie. Although a march, it is not scored for band but is arranged for the odd combination of piano, violins, cornets, and piccolo. This arrangement suggests a "theatre orchestra" made up of whatever musicians happened to be available— no doubt George's orchestra. Two performances of the march were given, one at Taylor's Opera House and the other at the Methodist Sunday school. Charlie played the piano at these performances and Moss the piccolo. George, of course, pulled the whole thing together, simultaneously beating time and playing one of the cornet parts.[27] Thus Charlie's debut as composer was a family affair.

A short time thereafter, according to Charlie's recollection, George arranged the piece for the Cornet Band, for Charlie told the Cowells that *Holiday Quickstep* was played by the band in the Decoration Day parade the year that he turned thirteen. "Charlie was too overcome to appear in his usual place at the snare drum. Instead, when the band came marching down Main Street past the Ives house playing Charlie's piece full tilt, the boy was discovered nervously playing handball against the barn door, with his back to the parade."[28]

The anecdote, as recalled by Ives some forty years later, takes the form of an outsider's observation: "the boy was discovered . . ." Even if the anecdote is apocryphal or distorted, it nonetheless reveals a fundamental conflict that coexisted with Charlie's idealization of his boyhood days. The conflict reappears in signs of ambivalence toward George, the most loved and admired object in his life, and toward music. Joyful as the growing collaboration between father and son may have been, for Charlie it was clouded by a threat: to be a musician was to *not* be a true man. In the story, a beloved activity is avoided and replaced with a safer and manifestly more masculine occupation—hence the importance of the prop, the handball. In adolescence, sports served Charlie well as a temporary solution to this conflict.

A twelve-year-old boy's concern with his sexuality extends to any of the close objects in his life who might buttress or, for that matter, threaten his masculinity. Rossiter, who has written at length about the social background of music in Danbury at this time, demonstrates the degree to which it was dominated by women.[29] Charlie was aware of this association of music with women, and it

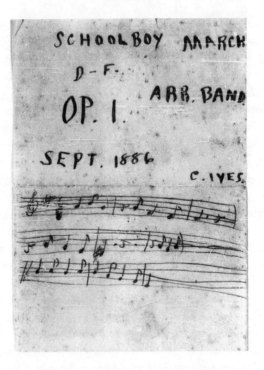

*Earliest surviving musical sketch in Charles Ives's
hand,* Schoolboy March in D–F, Op. 1, *September
1886, when he was twelve years old.*

colored his view of his father, whom he perceived as being used by women who devalued his efforts. Ives later wrote about this with some bitterness. In the *Memos,* for example, he wrote regarding a performance of Haydn's *Toy Symphony:* "I remember Father did all the work, rehearsing, arranging, etc. for this, and showed Miss Hollister how to conduct—as this was a ladies concert!" George received no acknowledgment for his efforts.[30]

At this time, Charlie was discovering the pleasures of baseball—the company of men, the assertion of leadership, the discharge of aggression, and the exercise of aptitude. And as Charlie's interest in the game was developing, he was also becoming increasingly involved in music and beginning to establish his identity as musician and composer. The two activities were apparently polar, competing for time and dedicated practice. On a deeper level, sports provided an avenue for both the discharge of aggression against men as rivals and the expression of love toward them as teammates. In accomplishing these, the exercise of sports could exert a liberating and enabling effect on the practice of music. George could hardly be in a position to appreciate this. Before long, Charlie's involvement in sports became a source of open friction between father and son.

The anecdote about the *Holiday Quickstep* is the only indication we have of Charlie's turning away from his father. In doing so, he was also turning away from his own music. Indeed, another piece written that same year suggests, to the contrary, a growing closeness and collaboration. This was the *Polonaise in C* for two cornets and piano—doubtless, in Charlie's musical imagination, a duet for father and son. It probably represents Charlie's growing competence on his father's primary instrument. Curiously, it takes the form of a piece in the cultivated tradition; indeed, it incorporates a quotation from the sextet from Donizetti's *Lucia di Lammermoor*. The manuscript, which exists in incomplete form, is in ink and in George's hand.[31]

George also assisted Charlie in his first efforts in church music. Basically simple harmony exercises with a rather limited vocabulary, these awkward pieces are rather elaborately entitled "Hymn & Chant Op. 2, Arr. Organ and Voices." Charlie later penned a memo to it: "none of these any good just for curiosity."[32] George probably helped him polish some of the more awkward progressions. Certainly he was involved with Charlie's ambitious setting of Psalm 42 in the form of a short church anthem. In a list of his works written many years later (on the back of an Ives and Myrick promotional calendar), Charlie noted, "Anthems, Hymns, etc. 'As Pants the Hart' 1885 (fathers help)."[33]

And "fathers help" was, in fact, the reasoned and disciplined help of a mature teacher serving to keep Charlie on the straight and narrow in music. There was no question of any experimentation in public music, be it vernacular or culti-vated, for band or church. But might not the teacher's gratification clash in some way with his envy of his pupil? Charlie appeared to have so much that George did not, including the love of a unique father and a promising future. George, on the other hand, had just passed his own fortieth birthday and was entering a not very promising middle age. The doodles in George's notebook seem aimless.[34] By contrast, Charlie's earliest titles, giving opus numbers, reveal the dream and intent to become a composer. George could not have harbored such aspirations in his own adolescence, for he lacked the drive and creative talent, as well as an appropriate model and encouragement.

That George was companion to Charlie as well as teacher is clear. A mutuality arose during Charlie's childhood that at times blurred the distinction between generation and role. Through Charlie, George participated in a kind of childhood he himself never had. In a sense, then, Charlie was as much the companionate father to George as George was to Charlie. The bond this engendered was vital and gratifying to both. It was to remain an enduring part of Charlie's mental life, persisting in an idealized image of George.

Writing of his father in later years, Charlie not only reminisced about their experiences together but placed them side by side in the act of experiencing: "As I remember some of these [barn] dances as a boy and also from father's descrip-

tion . . ." "It came over me at that time (as it had come over father) . . ."[35]
The mental image of George as companion and collaborator in music continued throughout Charlie's life. So eager was he to credit George in this collaboration that when John Tasker Howard sent a questionnaire to prominent American composers in 1930, Charlie wrote as much about his father as he did about himself, in response to a question about "early musical background, education, home influences, etc.":

> My father was a musician and a teacher (in Danbury and neighboring villages) of the violin, piano, (brass and wood instruments), harmony, sight reading, (and ear training), etc. He played in and taught the brass band (and orchestra), led the church choirs, the music at the Camp Meetings, and the local Choral Society. He had a reverence, a devotion, and a talent for music which was unusual. His interest lay not only in what had been done but in what might be done. His study of acoustics led him to many experiments into the character of musical instruments and of tonal combinations, and even into the divisions of the tone.
>
> He had a belief that everyone was born with at least one germ of musical talent and that an early application of great music (and not trivial music) would help it grow. He started all the children of the family—and most of the children of the town for that matter—on Bach and Stephen Foster. (Quite shortly after they were born—always regardless of whether [they] had, would have, or wouldn't have any musical gifts or sense, etc.—) he put a love of music into the heart of many a boy who might have gone without it but for him.
>
> (I feel that, if I have done anything that is good in music, I owe it almost entirely to him and his influence.)[36]

Yet for all the admiration, respect, and idealization of his father expressed in Ives's writings, one cannot help but wonder whether the perceptive child knew more about his father than he dared acknowledge even to himself. It seems unlikely that Charlie—sensitive to nuances of sound and its content, alert and responsive in human relationships—would not know more about his father. Many in the small town knew that George's Civil War career was not as glorious as Charlie persisted in viewing it. Nor was it the court-martial alone that was important but what it represented and portended: the element of shame. And Charlie had to contend with his own conflict regarding feelings of shame toward the person he loved most.

That as a boy Charlie did not, or could not, permit himself to know about his father's tarnished war record is not remarkable, but his avoidance and perhaps suppression of that knowledge later in life is. If anything, his positive feelings toward George intensified, giving rise to the idealized version of boyhood that became the core of his autobiography. In his reminiscences he stressed the shared musical experiences with George that were at the heart of his boyhood. With the years, memories of his boyhood father became more vivid and George became more revered. There is not the slightest suggestion in Charlie's writing about his boyhood that George was anything but perfect, sensitive, flexible, and admirable in every way. There is not a hint that George was on the lowest branch of the family tree, that the esteem in which the community held him was occasional and uncertain, or that as he was getting older, he increasingly appeared to be a failure in life. Denying any such perception throughout his life, Charlie cultivated the image of his father as hero.

The image of father as hero, which emerged from conflict, was itself drawn into conflict with respect to a second father. Charlie liked and admired Uncle Lyman, intuitively recognizing in him a quality of fatherhood different from what he experienced with George. Literate and well-educated, Lyman was universally respected and, unlike George, was frequently in a powerful position in public and private life. It is hard for a boy to sustain two such loyalties, especially when the first is a fierce one, stoked by a need to deny the perceived shortcomings of the person with whom one most identifies. As the boy loves his father, he is hurt by these perceptions; as he is competitive with and hostile toward his father, such knowledge can only intensify anger and reinforce contempt. Denial, however, is merciful. At the time, the image of George as the beloved hero was sufficient. Later, other solutions had to be found.

Ives's sentimental images of the past—complex, refined, preserved as if in amber—convey his own preferred version of boyhood, and it is a loving and reverent one. Nearly always these images occur in the context of musical experiences, yet one may extract elements of his love and admiration and gratitude for George. Only occasionally are these feelings stated plainly:

> What my father did for me was not only in his teaching, on the technical side, etc., but in his influence, his personality, character and open-mindedness, and his remarkable understanding of the ways of a boy's heart and mind. He had a remarkable talent for music and for the nature of music and sound, and also a philosophy of music that was unusual. Besides starting my music lessons when I was five years old, and keeping me at music in many ways until he died, with the best teaching that a boy could have, Father knew (and filled me up with) Bach and the best of the classical music, and the study of harmony and counterpoint, etc., and musical history. Above all this, he kept my interest and encouraged open-mindedness in all matters that needed it in any way.[37]

Looking back at his boyhood, Ives maintained the conviction that "if I have done anything good in music, it was, first because of my father, and second, because of my wife."[38] Father came first.

An image of George the beloved hero emerges not only in the anecdotes but also in asides and such proud phrases as, "When Father was in the Civil War . . ." Indeed, Ives construed a connection of George with both General Grant and

Abraham Lincoln in citing an anecdote in which Lincoln was supposed to have said, "That's a good band," with regard to George's First Connecticut Heavy Artillery Band, and Grant, "It's the best band in the army they tell me." Ives, extrapolating with apparent confidence to a time before his birth, goes on: "The things he played then (during the war) were mostly the things that most bands played, but he put something in them that most band leaders didn't—ask Mr. Lincoln or Mr. Grant."[39] Thus, in his fantasy, even the most ordinary tune was magically transformed by George's touch: "Father had a gift for playing. He'd take a familiar piece and play it to make it mean more than something just usual."[40]

Some of the most fervent memories of George from Charlie's childhood relate to camp meetings. A religious revival was just under way in the Danbury area around the time of Charlie's birth and continued throughout his boyhood. George was much involved through his role in the Methodist church, for it was the Methodist and Baptist denominations, which drew their membership largely from the lower classes, that initiated the revivals. George and Mollie had been married in the Methodist-Episcopal Church, one of the churches with which George was then most closely associated. By the time Charlie was four, the meetings were being held in Brookside Park, in Redding. Indeed, local interest seemed to have peaked; by 1878 it was said that more than three thousand people, mostly from Danbury, attended the meetings, where the Methodist church had a large tent. Charlie wrote in his *Memos*:

> I remember, when I was a boy—at the outdoor Camp Meeting services in Redding, all the farmers, their families and field hands, for miles around, would come afoot or in their farm wagons. I remember how the great waves of sound used to come through the trees—when things like *Beulah Land, Woodworth, Nearer My God To Thee, The Shining Shore, Nettleton, In The Sweet Bye and Bye* and the like were sung by thousands of "let out" souls. The music notes and words on paper were about as much like what they "were" (at those moments) as the monogram on a man's necktie may be like his face. Father, who led the singing, sometimes with his cornet or his voice, sometimes with both voice and arms, and sometimes in the quieter hymns with a French horn or violin, would always encourage the people to sing their own way. Most of them knew the words and music (theirs) by heart, and sang it that way. If they threw the poet or the composer around a bit, so much the better for the poetry and the music. There was power and exaltation in these great conclaves of sound from humanity.[41]

Such memories are suffused with strong affect, feelings not only about father but about father's beloved music and his times as well. The music itself was the vehicle of those feelings. The gospel hymn predominated. Elsewhere Charlie elaborated on his father's accompaniment on the cornet: "The fervor of the feeling would at times, especially on reaching the chorus of many of these hymns, throw the key higher, sometimes a whole note up—though Father used to say it [was] more often about a quarter tone. . . . Father had a sliding cornet made so that he could rise with them and not keep them down."[42]

It is a curious amalgam of memories. For by 1878 Danbury was no longer a predominantly rural country town. Farmers may indeed have come to the meetings by horse and buggy and by foot, but many more people came from increasingly industrialized Danbury on one of the frequent excursions to Brookside provided by the now-flourishing Danbury and Norwalk Railroad. The excursions reflected an increase in leisure time. The "let-out" souls also included recent immigrants, characteristically more emotionally effusive than the staid New Englanders. So Charlie's recollection of the 1878 revival or those immediately thereafter seems to include elements of earlier revivals he did not attend. These details of rural New England life are more characteristic of George's time and had doubtless been told to Charlie by George. Hence Charlie's memory incorporates George's memory. Moreover, as those memories were tied to acute perceptions of music, Charlie came to hear such emotion-laden music his father's way. Eventually, memory and perception not only became integrated into personal characteristics but endowed his musical style as well.

An example of such shared perceptions and feelings comes from an anecdote in which "a nice young man" once asked George, "How can you stand it to hear old John Bell [the best stonemason in town] sing?" George answered, "He is a supreme musician." And the young man retorted, "Why, he sings off the key, the wrong notes and everything—and that horrible raucous voice—and he bellows and hits notes no one else does—it's awful!" Charlie relates his father's final comment: "Watch him closely and reverently, look into his face and hear the music of the ages. Don't pay too much attention to the sounds—for, if you do, you may miss the music. You won't get a wild, heroic ride to heaven on pretty little sounds."[43]

Throughout his writings, Ives the man reveals the pleasure of the boy Charlie, adoring and receptive at his father's side. Indeed, the pleasure is thereby revived. This account of his early life is a celebration of Charlie's boyhood, his father's, and boyhood in general. He seemed to have been well informed about his father's boyhood, as if through a shared nostalgia as much as fact, a sentimental knowledge. Although his rendering of it was distinctly selective, it had become an intrinsic part of his own prehistory and mental life.

In his *Essays*, Charlie wrote, "Thoughts and memories of childhood are too tender and some of them too sacred, to be worn light only on the sleeve."[44] But they could be expressed instead in music. For Charlie, composing became an autobiographical act, incorporating much of George's biography: "There is a difference in the arts themselves; for example, a composer may not shrink from having the public hear his 'love letter in tones.'"[45] Charlie's "love letter in tones" was music intimately related to his father.

Yet some things could not be expressed at all, either in words or in tones. These comprised the dark side of Charlie's feelings toward George and, indeed, what he may have considered the dark side of his father's life. These feelings as well were too tender, in another way. They were the feelings of shame, anger, and guilt that led to the idealization of George. They operated outside of conscious life, generating a need in the man to repair that which the child was not supposed to know. Further, repair and the avoidance of shameful feelings proved to be motivating elements in Ives's double professional life as composer and businessman.

There is not a trace of anger toward his father in any of Ives's writings, not even a hint of ambivalence. Rather, father was eternally revered. Elsewhere, and particularly in Ives's later years, anger—even rage—abounds, and there were times when it threatened his reason. Yet Ives, as apologist, insulated the enduring image of father from this anger. Thus, Charlie's idealization of George became the conscious and unconscious mission of his life. The past was realigned and biography (his own and his father's) written more according to the heart's desire than to reality. In the process, repair was accomplished, George was rescued from shame, if not oblivion, and boyhood itself was rendered holy.

SEVEN

COLLABORATIONS

In the final years of the 1880s, childhood itself was beginning to draw to an end. Charlie was in the process of becoming a competent musician and, more important, a professional one. By the time he was fifteen, following a period of intensive study on the organ, he already held two posts as church organist, the "youngest in the state."[1]

George's childhood was also coming to an end, both his own prolonged youth and that which he had shared with Charlie. Although the band was still a big part of his life, its importance in Danbury was diminishing with the town's changing needs. Greater sophistication and professionalism resulted in changes in the local cultural institutions. With Charlie's growing sophistication and competence, George's various roles in his son's life began to change as well; not only father and guide, he was now manager and agent too. Above all, he became the secret sharer of his son's composing.

George's own musical activities were decreasing as he began taking various bookkeeping jobs to pay for his sons' education. Yale University soon came to loom large as a goal toward which both father and son would devote themselves—Charlie with study, George with financial support. Yet George must also have dreaded Yale as the barrier that would inexorably part them, not only geographically, but also by dint of education, social standing, and career. Each would come to know the pain of separation; but Charlie was at the beginning of a musical journey, whereas George was already nearing the end, beginning to give up music. For him, the separation would be a prelude to death.

Significantly, Charlie's first song, written around this time, was about death and separation. He composed *Slow March* in the summer of 1887 or 1888, in collaboration with "the family and L. D. Brewster."[2] The occasion was the death of the family cat, Chin-Chin, and the place was probably Cousins' Beach. Lyman supplied the words:

> One evening just at sunset
>   We laid him in the grave;
> Although a humble animal
>   His heart was true and brave.
> All the family joined us,
>   In solemn march and slow,
> From the garden place beneath the trees
>   And where the sunflowers grow.

George provided some ideas for the music, and Mollie ("Mamma Ives") and Grandmother ("S. H. Ives") also made contributions.[3] A dedication appears beneath the title, "Inscribed to the Children's Faithful Friend." A sketch of the piece was put in George's copybook.

The simple hymn-like setting incorporates a prelude and postlude, which are a musical quotation of Handel's *Dead March* from the oratorio *Saul.* The young composer had written in his father's copybook, "D.M. Sual."[4] This is the music that George had regularly performed at the funerals of fallen Union soldiers, and Charlie doubtless associated it with George's stories of Civil War days. In *Slow March*, we already find the kernels of stylistic features that would mark Ives's most characteristic music: quotation (in the music) and citation (in the dedication), an atmosphere of mourning and nostalgia, direct reference to a biographical context as well as a context of collaboration.[5]

The social backdrop against which events in Danbury were unfolding was in flux, for the town's youth too was coming to a close. What had been a large, flourishing village until about the time of George's birth was in the process of becoming "a city of no small importance."[6] The village had achieved borough status in 1822, but by now its complex needs could no longer be served by a skeletal government and volunteer services. Danbury eventually became a city, in April 1894, and was moving toward the goal. Throughout, Lyman maintained his position as the leading Republican of Danbury.

As for music, the vernacular tradition of band music was men's domain, whereas the cultivated tradition of classical music remained in the hands of women.[7] Two women in particular, Ella Hollister and Belle Fayerweather, were central figures in advancing the cultivated tradition of music in Danbury and upholding gentility against the encroaching vulgarity of the vernacular. In mid-September 1887 they opened the Danbury School of Music, serving as co-directors. Fayerweather, a native of Danbury and choirmaster of the Episcopal church, was already well known in the community. Her father was a hatter and, like Mollie Ives, she grew up on River Street. Her pleasant contralto voice made her a great favorite at concerts. Hollister, organist at the Disciples church, who came from a more well-to-do background, appeared to have been involved in a wider range of musical activities. On occasion she served as entrepreneur for the kind of entertainment that George Ives had been involved with a decade earlier, promoting and popularizing music by engaging artists from outside Danbury.

By the late 1880s George's own musical interests focused on the band, which now straddled the genteel and vernacular traditions. The music at Elmwood Park, for example, was frequently of the genteel concert-hall variety, although it was full of marches, opera selections, and medleys of popular or patriotic tunes. George's involvement with the Methodist church, reinforced in 1885 when he was named chorister, also appeared to engage his interest. This increasingly connected him to the kind of vernacular music heard at camp meetings, for it was the same Methodist influence that had spawned the revival of camp meetings in western Connecticut earlier in the century. While it continued now in less robust form, George led the singing that Ives recalled. (In Ives's later writings, these events were almost certainly distorted in the direction of earlier times as related by George.)

George still occasionally performed in musical entertainments and engaged in stunts, and takeoffs. That, in fact, was exactly what he was doing in some of the musical "experiments" that Ives later attributed to him. The Humanophone, for example, "was an idea of Father's [in which] songs of wide leaps were to be sung [with the] different notes by different voices—not a duet, quartet, etc.—but one voice taking a high note, a middle voice, and another man taking [a] low note, etc."[8] This was an actual performance Charlie was remembering, given in City Hall in November 1888 at a benefit for the Methodist church. George appeared as performer on a human "organ" consisting of a dozen "notes," people costumed as organ pipes. Other acts included a boy orchestra, a recitation of "Barbara Freitchie" (accompanied by occasional "thrilling" music), and a nod to gentility in the form of a "finely executed" violin solo whose title was not mentioned—in all, a typical entertainment of the time and place. George's act was placed among the last on the program in order to heighten the suspense:

The disclosing of the mysterious humanophone was awaited with impatience. . . . Finally the curtain arose and the mystery was a mystery no longer. Herr Schwergeblassen (George Ives), the manufacturer and importer, stepped forward, and a liberal amount of amusement and laughter was afforded during the whole exhibition. . . . The first thought when the curtain was raised was that of an organ of which only the monstrous pipes were visible. It soon appeared though when the exhibitor drew the stop that each pipe concealed a human form, the back of which was only visible when the withdrawing of this stop raised a small curtain arranged in each pipe. Then the beauties of the humanophone unveiled for a dozen faces to as many pipes appeared. The kazoo and chestnut bell stops were great "take offs."[9]

Charlie was somehow able to turn the embarrassment of his father's exhibitionism into pride in his father. As apologist, he later dignified the City Hall performance by calling it one of George's "experiments in music": "Father had a kind of natural interest in sounds of every kind, everywhere, known or unknown." But it seems that he could not quite dispel his keen sense of humiliation even years later, for he added, "and this led him into positions or situations . . . that made some of the townspeople call him a crank whenever he appeared in public with one of his contraptions. But as I and (better) my aunts and some of the older people remember, this was not often."[10] Certainly, Aunt Amelia would have hoped not! And if years afterward she assured Charlie that such episodes were few and far between, it could only have been to bolster her view of the family and ease the discomfort of her nephew. Neither the matriarch nor the sensitive adolescent could have appreciated the cavorting of Herr Schwergeblassen. It would have been Amelia's style to ignore the event publicly while deploring the continuing disgrace of the problem brother privately to Lyman. Charlie would defend against the sense of shame and the threatened devaluation of his father in his own mind through denial and idealization: George was *not* a "crank"; he was a visionary and innovator, a scientist in music. There would come a time when Charlie would prove it: in a feat of identification, he would compose his father's music.[11]

If George had not been able to enter either the economic or the musical mainstream of the town, Charlie in adolescence was showing promise of entering both. He had already established himself as a gifted student within an increasingly well-defined, cultivated musical tradition, and plans were being made for further education to prepare him for a career in the professions or commerce. Yale, a university which at that time had only casual facilities for the study of music, had been spoken of, probably by the Brewsters. Despite Charlie's personal commitment to music and the proud dream of becoming a composer, it seemed to have been expected that Charlie's future lay elsewhere at Yale. The Iveses liked to think of Yale as the natural continuation of a tradition harking back to the Danbury progenitor Isaac Ives or to great-grandfather Joseph Moss White. But in the most recent generation, Uncle Joe had been expelled from Yale, and Uncle Lyman became the standard-bearer. That seemed appropriate since Amelia valued the tradition more than any of her brothers. In addition, both Charlie and Moss viewed Lyman as a far closer relation than any of their blood uncles.

As an adult, Charlie would have to come to terms with the inherent conflict engendered by his close relationship with both Uncle Lyman and his father. Without question, he was being groomed to follow Lyman's example, but there would always remain a secret compartment in Charlie's mental life for sharing music with George. During adolescence this area was becoming defined. Charlie's activities as a classical instrumentalist and as a competent and maturing organist moved him toward autonomy. As a composer, however, his collaboration with his father increased. The two paths, though related, were ultimately divergent. Another compartment of endeavor, commerce, owed much to the influence of Lyman Brewster. Through the competing demands of business and music the actual tensions between Lyman and George were becoming internalized and intensified within the mind of Charlie. One of his principal tasks in approaching adulthood was to adapt to these inner pressures—a near-impossible charge. Not only the sources of conflict, but the groundwork for resolution as well, were in the process of being established during these years of adolescence.

The young composer of the *Holiday Quickstep* was fortunate in having the music he completed around Christmas, 1887, performed twice before the next year was out. Charlie worked hard at school and made the honor roll.[12] At the same time, he began to study organ in earnest. In the space of two years, he progressed from moderately skilled amateur organist to competent church organist to accomplished performer. At the beginning of 1888, for example, Charlie was assigned Bach's *Toccata, Adagio, and Fugue in C Major,* a virtuoso piece particularly with regard to the use of the pedals; by May he could give an acceptable performance.[13] By summer of that year, Charlie was able to serve as "supply" organist, that is, fill in for a vacationing church organist. Soon thereafter, at age fourteen, he became a regular church organist. The *Evening News* noted, "Charles Ives, a young son of George E. Ives, is to take charge of the organ of the West Street Church . . . Charlie has inherited a generous supply of his father's musical genius."[14]

The appointment spurred Charlie on toward greater accomplishment. He immediately started taking two lessons a week from a gifted organist, J. R. Hall, who held a brief tenure at the First Congregational Church, close by the homestead on Main Street. By the time Hall left, Charlie had moved on to a better post at the Baptist church, where he was regular organist until he went to New Haven. He could now afford the $1.50 for lessons with yet another teacher, Alexander Gibson. He gave an impressive account of himself at his first service, on October 20, 1889, which was also his fifteenth birthday.[15]

With his growing commitment to the organ, Charlie was entering a different musical world from that of his father. He had long been drawn to indoor instruments—first, tentatively, to the violin, then to the piano, and now to the organ.

Indeed, the piano and the organ are played seated; they were the instruments of parlor and church, the province of women. Band music, by contrast, had its historical as well as psychological roots in aggression, and it was the province of men. But Charlie's focus on the organ at this point in his life was more complex. The church provided him with a psychological space separate from the real world of Danbury and the musical world he shared with George—a space in which he could grow independently of and apart from his father.

At fifteen, Charlie was handling the standard repertory of a professional organist. He was competent not only in planning, selecting, and performing music for church services but in improvising and composing. He also came to know vast portions of musical literature from Bach to modern French masters and those popular American and European works that were part of the standard repertory of the time.[16]

The year 1889 was pivotal for Charlie, his family, and Danbury. By the time Charlie turned fifteen and Danbury had been officially incorporated as a city, the George Ives family had made another major move—this time back to the house on Main Street, nearer to the Brewsters. It had been Grandmother Sarah Ives's idea. They did not move into the house itself, however; rather, Sarah Ives had the large barn behind the house on Chapel Place converted into living quarters, Amelia supervising the renovation. The move only reaffirmed the growing ties between the Brewsters and the George Ives family. It was here that the final episodes of lively and imaginative play between George and the boys took place.

As the city became more modern and the lives of others moved on with it, George seemed to remain static, already appearing to be an old-fashioned bandmaster. Further, Charlie was progressing beyond his father's sphere—toward an educated and genteel world in which George could be only at the periphery, and toward the traditional world of the Iveses, a world that George had abandoned in his own adolescence and that as he approached middle age seemed to be abandoning him. The move to Chapel Place was, in a sense, more of a coming home for him than for his father.

In summer the family went regularly to Cousins' Beach, except for George, who was only an occasional visitor. The adults at Westbrook were formidable. Lyman and, in her own way, Amelia were distinguished people. Grandmother Sarah, widow of George White Ives, certainly retained more of his reflected glory than did their son, George. Others included George's brothers' families and first cousins, many of whom were well established. Westbrook was an uncomfortable place for George, eliciting a degree of resentment and a sense of reduced esteem. He might have rationalized his absence from Cousins' Beach as a need to remain in Danbury in order to work. If so, a sense of distance between George and Charlie developed for the first time. The father inevitably resented the son for turning toward others, and perhaps envied him as well. Before long, he felt a need to control him in order to preserve that which they shared and which had earlier been so gratifying for both of them. What is more, Westbrook would have revived for George an earlier situation in his life, as he would inevitably be cast as the little brother to the eternally bossy older sister.

Mollie was perhaps more at ease in Westbrook, accepting her place and role in the family of attending to the children. By now, Amelia's "arrangements" had become a family institution. But it was Mollie who wrote George from Westbrook in August 1889, in her characteristically breathless style:

> Dear Papa,
>
> Aunt Milly wants to have you come down and stay over Sunday and come home with us Monday . . . Charlie wrote to you this afternoon but did not say all he wanted to. He wanted very much to stay over Sunday . . . if it is necessary for him to come home to be there Sunday you can telegraph to us & we can come Saturday but I guess they will be able to get along without him Sunday tell Nell to write to me we would like to have you come down and spend Sunday if you can & feel like it is very late & time to go to bed . . .
>
> With love,
Mollie[17]

Mollie too was concerned with arrangements. Here they centered around Charlie's commitments as church organist while at the same time she revealed her support for his desire to go off on his own. She appears to have been sensitive to Charlie's difficulty in letting George know that he wanted to stay at the seashore an extra day—away from George and from music.

Mollie here was able to empathize with those tensions of her son that were the result of increasing inner conflict with George. Although she was concerned with his proper attention to responsibilities, she perhaps sensed that, connected as they were to the duties related to music, they may have screened the inner requirements of duty to father. From this point on, if anyone is having trouble with the adolescent's need to distinguish himself and separate from family, it is father, not mother. The sensitive and soothing Mollie was more comfortable with this aspect of her son's development: she accepted that he would soon leave home. But her ability to let go is nevertheless remarkable. Her own father had died early, when she herself was only three, and a beloved brother died just before she met George.

George, on the other hand, was beginning to clash with Charlie. He was becoming demanding, even petulant. Beneath the surface appearance of a cohesive extended family lay old rifts and rivalries. A portion of Charlie's identification was now with those toward whom George was ambivalent. Charlie was beloved by them, and he in turn responded with affection and respect. George might well have been jealous, the more so in view of the sacrifices he was now making in giving up many of his own musical activities for more economically rewarding if frustrating work. The blend of feelings of anger and fear of losing his son to others and to a kind of success he never had resulted in a subtle tugging and clinging that only served to make Charlie feel anger, anxiety, and guilt.

George did not seem to appreciate "a boy's fooling" quite as much as he had before. The sense of seriousness that pervaded his own life was reflected in concern about Charlie's future. This feeling lent a certain rigidity to his formerly flexible and easygoing outlook. This characteristic would become more marked within a couple of years as George anticipated Charlie's departure from home. At this point, however, it seemed to be associated with changes in his own career. George's musical activities were by now taking up less of his time, but it is not completely clear what he was doing instead. He no longer seemed to be involved in the hardware store or any other of Joe's businesses and certainly not in any of Ike's enterprises. At some point, he took an office job in the hat-manufacturing business of Charles H. Merritt.

Merritt was the maternal uncle of Howard Merritt Ives, Joe's son. Cousin Howdie had been a member of the Ives household on Main Street during Charlie's early years. Now in his late twenties, he held an important position in his uncle's business as head bookkeeper. As business flourished, he hired paternal uncle George to help out as assistant and clerk. George was remembered vividly by Philip Sunderland, a younger coworker in the Merritt office: "Mr. Merritt was always looking after everything. They were building a bridge across the stream, and George Ives looked out one morning and saw Mr. Merritt out there. George said, 'There you are, you damned old monopolist, you have to tell them how to build a bridge!' Now that's the kind of fellow he was—talking under his breath in this office, which would be heresy if anybody heard it."[18] Here George comes across as a peppery Yankee. "George Ives was a kind of original creature," notes Sunderland.[19] But the anecdote also betrays a certain bitterness toward successful contemporaries. What Lyman had achieved in the professional and civic sphere, Charles Merritt had in the world of commerce. Merritt had become a wealthy man while George remained a clerk.

What is more, working for Merritt must have been an embarrassment for George, and the association a source of troubled conscience. Merritt was a notorious anti-union activist who later led a two-month lockout of four thousand men and women in 1893.[20] By then, George had another job. His loyalties and affiliations had always been with the working people, whom Merritt was trying to suppress.

This new, "regular" work seemed to represent to George a giving up. Depression in George expressed itself in rigidity, withdrawal, pessimism, and the erosion of a usually spontaneous humor. Its onset was insidious, its course gradual, and the signs subtle. The pivotal period appears to have been 1889–90, around the time George's family moved back to the center of Ives family activities. In a photograph taken a short time later, a much subdued George Ives had lost the alert, prickly appearance of earlier pictures. He was beginning to look like a prematurely old man.

In the midst of these events, a striking polarity was developing in the relationship of father and son—a continuing closeness yet an emerging pulling away. The closeness centered in musical composition as distinct from other aspects of Charlie's involvement with music.

The pair were drawn together in an intimacy of creative endeavor. The unfolding of a gift for music and a genuine capacity for invention in Charlie must have been the most fascinating musical phenomenon George had ever known. His bond with the boy, rooted in love and later charged with ambivalence, was strengthened by their mutual compelling interest in the possibilities of music. From the time of "Opus 1" and Charlie's declaration to himself that he was a composer, what had started in play now turned into increasingly shared musical activity.

In Charlie there existed a wondrous instrument. Threatening his growth was the danger that George might use the child as his personal instrument, causing a loss of boundaries. Alternatively, there was the potential for the parent to help the child develop it and claim it for himself. Had George been a more controlling person, the combination of his fascination with music, awareness of his own limitations and failures in life, and latent depression might have led him to use the boy and his talents primarily for his own gratification—the destructive use of the child as instrument. But in fact George was respectful and nonintrusive both as a parent and as a teacher. Only in the last few years of his life did this attitude begin to change as Charlie began to separate from his parents.

An unconscious shared fantasy of collaboration in composition—joint authorship in music—was generated by father and adolescent son. In one sense, it suggests that George was the secret sharer of Charlie's gift; at a deeper level, the composer was represented by some merged image of parts of both men. Nor is such a fantasy static, especially one shared and operating through the vicissitudes of two lifetimes. At the beginning, collaboration hewed closely to the conventions of instruction. If during this phase Charlie was George's "humanophone" in fantasy, it was not manifest in the conventional behavior of teacher and student. But later, particularly after George's death, the fantasy is enacted by Charlie through the creation of music. Sidney Cowell realized this intuitively when she observed of Ives that "the son has written his father's music for him."[21]

The period of youthful collaboration spanned roughly eight years, from 1886 to 1894. It began in the days of the *Holiday Quickstep*, which dates to 1886, when Charlie was twelve years old and George forty-one. It was at about that time that Charlie also started to write choral music. The collaboration continued unabated until September 1894, when Charlie entered Yale. Two months later, George died.

The period may be divided broadly into two parts. The first, to about the end of 1890, yielded twenty-seven works, eleven of which fall into the category of sacred choral music. There were three organ pieces; the remainder of the works were for band, piano, and voice. Charlie was sixteen when this initial phase came to a close. Although Charlie later called these his "early works," some were little more than exercises, others youthful pretensions. But a thrust and direction were present that both Charlie and George addressed with the utmost seriousness. They were rewarded by the increased compositional competence that Charlie developed and displayed. For example, Charlie's *Variations on "Jerusalem the Golden"* of 1888–89 foreshadows the *America Variations* of 1891–92, which is in many respects the culminating work of the first half of the period.[22]

During these eight years, Charlie not only moved from the position of an aspiring student to one of impressive competence in the management of musical materials but also developed in an increasingly imaginative and innovative direction. Both trends, as well as the balance between them, reveal George's subtle influence, and many of the human transactions upon which it was built were nonverbal. It was certainly not a simple matter of Charlie's receiving George's endorsement for each creative act. And by the end of this time Charlie had acquired a degree of autonomy that shielded him from George's influence, enabling him to transfer creative attachments elsewhere—to other teachers—as it also permitted him to proceed independently. But by 1894 a fantasy of the *conditions* for writing music was well established in Charlie's mind and would forever be related to collaboration with George.

Pivotal in this period was the year 1889, when the family moved to 10 Chapel Street, around the time George went to work for cousin Howdie. George was in the process of giving up music and was becoming depressed. What George was giving up, Charlie was now taking up. Both may have seen George's sacrifice as making Charlie's ascendancy and development in music possible. At the same time, whatever energy George customarily expended in his multiple musical interests was increasingly deflected toward Charlie. Charlie's pleasure and profit in being the beneficiary, with all its artistic as well as family implications, was tempered by guilt. Both guilt and gratification increased the bond, at the center of which was the shared endeavor of composition.

Early in 1890 or 1891, Charlie produced a piece that illustrates par excellence the working relationship of father and son.[23] It was probably on January 8, 1891, that the sixteen-year-old Charlie sketched out portions of a nine-part *Communion Service*, his most ambitious choral work to date, a complete service in the form of an Episcopal mass.[24] Charlie wrote it in pencil in the notebook George had kept from his own student days. George, in turn, made copies in ink of the voice parts of several sections (*Kyrie* in D, *Sursum corda*, *Sanctus* in C minor and C major, and *Benedictus* in F).[25] This music was performed the following November in the Saint James Episcopal Church, with George directing. Manifestly, its purpose was practical and utilitarian: the music was written (composed) by Charlie and rewritten (copied) by George for a specific use during a service around Thanksgiving. This in itself reversed the customary relationship of teacher and student. But the music lived on as a mental phenomenon in the mind of Charlie, forever associated with the conditions of its origin and changing with the accrual of later experiences.

If the tie to George is implicit in the sixteen-year-old's management of his *Communion Service*, so are elements of aspiration and even rebellion. These may be sought in the social implications of the music. Charlie held the post of organist at the Danbury Baptist Church from October 1889 until early 1893, shortly before he went to New Haven to prepare himself for the entrance exams at Yale. The congregation consisted of solid, middle-class businessmen as well as affluent farmers. Although George too was associated with this church, his chief musical involvement had been with Saint Peter's Catholic Church, with its largely immigrant congregation of Irish and Italian descent, mostly from working-class or lower-middle-class families.

Within the Ives family itself, there were various gradations of social class. At one extreme, Amelia and Lyman Brewster, better educated and socially aspiring, tended to attach themselves to the upper classes that attended the Episcopal Church, where *Communion Service* was first performed. It was to this faction that Charlie aspired at the time.

Religious works predominated during the earlier period of collaboration, when Charlie held an apprenticeship as church organist. Musically, they served as a springboard to secular music, of which the most important example is the *Variations on "America"*. A turning point in the forging of a style, it reveals Charlie's musical equipment on the brink of his departure from home. The patriotic hymn that serves as its subject had the status of a national anthem before there was an official anthem. Thus, like all music played in Danbury at the time, whether in the cultivated or the vernacular tradition, it had a fundamentally utilitarian purpose. Charlie had already tried his hand at the variation form, probably sometime early in 1889, when he was fourteen. A clean copy of his *Variations on "Jerusalem the Golden"* exists, written in George's hand, which is thought to be some version of what Charlie actually would have performed.[26] There was probably a band version of this piece as well, a paraphrase recalled later as a *Fantasia on "Jerusalem the Golden"*.[27] Thus George was involved on more than one level in this anticipatory piece to the *America Variations*. For not only was his band the one that performed it, but *Jerusalem* was one of the gospel hymns that was popular at camp meetings where George led the singing.[28]

In addition, shared experiences at once more ostentatious and more subtle may have influenced Charlie in the selection of the theme for *America Variations*. For example, at the close of the ceremonies for civic celebrations and patriotic holidays, the band frequently played *America*. Following a concert of airs and marches or an exciting day of events, the performance had a soothing, religious quality that helped bind the community. At times, too, the performance could be quite spectacular, with massed bands and fireworks.[29] Such experiences repeated throughout Charlie's childhood lent rich associations to the tune *America*, which had been one of the earliest building blocks of his musical vocabulary.[30]

Variations on "America" reveals considerable mastery of a traditional organ-pedagogical style of composition on the part of the seventeen-year-old composer. It also contains many imaginative, innovative passages. The piece is not, however, without signs of Charlie's inexperience, and on the manuscript George pointed out some typical student errors. Formally, the piece consists of the theme and five variations framed by a prelude and postlude of equal length; it includes two important interludes, after the second variation and before the fifth. These interludes are important not only for technical reasons of transition and tonality but also because Charlie used the musical space and occasion they provided for the composition of brief polytonal passages using multiple keys simultaneously. These polytonal interludes were penciled in an ink manuscript, crammed into available staves. They probably reflect passages that were actually played or meant to be played but omitted from the copied score because George had hopes of publishing the *America Variations*, and polytonal interludes would just not do for the prospective buyer of organ music.[31]

Charlie had this to say about his *America Variations*:

> . . . an organ fantasia played in 1891–92 in organ recitals in Danbury and Brewster, N.Y. One variation was the theme in canon, put in three keys together, Bb-Eb-Ab and backwards Ab-Eb-Bb (but this was not played in church concerts, as it made the boys laugh and noisy).[32]

Charlie perceived George as somehow granting him permission to experiment, even if his father was reticent to expose the result in public performance. He notes elsewhere, "He even let me try out 'two keys to once,' [*sic*] as an Interlude in an organ piece, Variations on America, but didn't let me do it much, as it made the boys laugh." The last passage comes up in a part of the *Memo* describing George as a teacher:

> I couldn't have been over ten years old when he would occasionally have us sing, for instance, a tune like *The Swanee River* in the key of E♭, but play the accompaniment in the key of C. This was to stretch our ears and strengthen our musical minds, so that they could learn to use and translate things that might be used and translated (in the art of music) more than they had been. In this instance, I don't think he had the possibility of polytonality in composition in mind, as much as to encourage the use of ears—and for them and the mind to think for themselves and be more independent—in other words, not to be too dependent upon customs and habits.[33]

Charlie played the *America Variations* in Brewster, New York, on February 17, 1892. His recollection of the performance years later is almost certainly distorted. For although it was only later that he composed and notated the polytonal interludes as they would remain in the score, he recalled having performed them that way. (He may actually have played a more diluted version.) But what is more, in the distortions of memory "the boys" do not merely laugh; in Charlie's imagination, they are caught up in its spirit, much as the boy Charlie must have been in George's performances. Indeed, they acclaim the music and participate in it spontaneously. In Charlie's enthusiasm in fantasy, the boys break into a march, even producing small flags![34]

This imagined "march" relates to the fifth variation and those final measures that serve to balance the introduction. Here the organ pedals carry an accompanying figure marked "Allegro—as fast as the pedals can go." In the final measures, the eighth-note figure breaks into sixteenth notes at what the score calls "full organ." It is no wonder that on one of the older manuscripts Charlie wrote, "This passage was often played by the pedals while the left hand hung on to the bench."[35]

The final work of the period of youthful collaboration, a setting of Psalm 67, indicated Charlie's vast musical development during the second four years as well as George's participation.[36] There is some question about the actual date of composition—estimates range from 1894 to 1898—but Charlie makes clear in his own writings the nature and degree of George's involvement. (Since these notes were written many years later, however, they also have a commemorative function and hence may be distorted.) This unique piece, scored for "Full Chorus of Mixed Voices, a cappella," is an example of Charlie's interest in and experimentation with polytonality. Here two keys are frankly employed: the female parts (soprano and first and second alto) are in the key of C whereas the male parts (first and second tenor and bass) are in G minor. In the first and third sections, the voices proceed rhythmically in homophony, canticle-style, singing

115

the opening verse of the psalm: "God be merciful unto us, and bless us; and cause his face to shine upon us." The middle section starts in strict canon, the bitonal idea briefly giving way before returning in the final section to the canticle style.

Charlie later wrote at length of his collaboration with George on *Psalm 67*.[37] It came under the heading of "a boy's fooling" as he wrote admiringly about the human background to his use of such musical devices as polytonality. Their sources were in play and in George's attitude toward musical play as well as his own playful experiments.[38] In a remarkable passage, Charlie both idealizes and memorializes George as teacher and collaborator. In tribute, he delineates certain specific human qualities of the teacher which tend to favor originality and innovation in the responsive student—flexibility, openness, and respect for tradition as well as for the person.

Charlie was not in a position to absorb such new devices and trends as polytonality from European tradition. In the early 1890s, such innovations were still untapped by American composers, and in any event, the European tradition with which Charlie was familiar came from George's training in the 1860s. While his use of innovative devices may resemble that of other composers, Charlie came upon these privately, isolated from ongoing tradition, and in the context of a relationship with his most important teacher. Their relationship was the foundry of Charlie's musical style.

The musical workshop was a mental space they shared; its most palpable feature was George's copybook, in which Charlie wrote exercises. The copybook is referred to twice in the memorializing passage cited from Charlie's *Memos*: Breaking the rules of music could normally be done only playfully, in jest, in a pretend manner. But inscribing an innovative musical passage—"a boy's fooling"—in Father's copybook gives it authority. Father's approval, respect, and seriousness with regard to such matters cultivated a freedom that became imbued with near-manic intensity. But experimentation and musical transgressions, as well as feelings of excitement associated with them, were not permitted to get out of control. A moderating father/teacher saw to that. He was "willing . . . within reason" to permit the "wrong way" in the service of independence, to have "the boys think for themselves," but "he somehow kept us in good balance." "Even in some of the old psalms for choir," one did not have to fear chaos if "two or even three keys were tried out, or at least thrown in together. *Father let me do it*" (italics mine).

Moreover, having broken the rules and pursued the full implications of play, Charlie was urged by father "not to stop when it got hard." The permissive father displays a strong hand only in insisting that you know how to do it "right" before you are permitted to do it "wrong" and that, having been adventurous ("roam for fun"), you not retreat fearfully but "stick it to the end." He makes it clear that all this is in the service of something beyond play—namely, the musical idea: there had to be "some sense behind it." What the student sought did not have to be conventional or thought out at the outset ("maybe not very much or too good a sense, but something more than just thoughtless fooling"). Above all, he had not to accept rules blindly. The conditions for innovation were created by George for Charlie, an ideally responsive student. Permission, play, and perseverance were important elements.

Charlie's natural endowment flourished within the relationship and led to a unique artistic morality. An unrestricted, creative superego was the chief artistic developmental accomplishment of his adolescence. It remained the psychological residue of the collaboration between teacher and student, father and son. The capacity for innovation that it fostered became the hallmark of Ives's music.

EIGHT

AT PARTING

Charlie's boundless energy as an adolescent was evident in the range of activities he undertook, his devotion to each, and the degree of excellence he was able to achieve. He carried on his regular professional work as organist and with the money he earned continued music lessons privately. Composing was more than an occasional activity. The thinking and forming of music was becoming an established, ongoing function of Charlie's mental life. A musical idea was always in a state of becoming and might never be completely realized in a single notated piece of music.

Activity of this kind can be so absorbing that it leaves time for little else. This was hardly the case with Charlie. His relationships with others were rich and involved. What may have suffered was his attention to conventional schooling; he was only an average student. Charlie was also shy with girls, but perhaps no more so than were other young men of the period. In any event, Charlie had two other passions in adolescence. Music continued to be the first; the other was sports.

A story about young Charlie has it that someone who heard he was a musician asked him what he played. His answer was, "Shortstop."[1] And many times in humorous remarks or figures of speech, music was juxtaposed with sports. He once said that he enjoyed playing the last variation of the *America Variations* nearly as much as he liked playing baseball. (The analogy has some literal, motor basis, the feet fairly running over the pedals as fast as they can, especially in the

118

sixteenth-note figure.) Charlie's avid interest in baseball seems to have reached its height in 1889, when he was one of a group of boys who organized a team called the *Alerts*.

Charlie's brother, Moss, was not among them, and despite his being only two years younger it appears that the brothers by now had parted ways in certain respects. Moss was clearly headed in the direction of scholarship and some sort of professional future modeled on that of Lyman Brewster. He was beginning to see himself as a writer and had started the *New Street Weekly*, a one-sheet mimeographed newspaper. Later, he was editor of the Danbury High School *Chronicle*.[2]

Charlie also became interested in football—a considerably rougher sport then than it is now. At Danbury High as well as Danbury Academy, to which he switched in 1891, he excelled in both football and baseball. By 1892, he was also captain of a football team comprised of the combined forces of the high school and the academy.

Sports served as a counterweight to music, balancing active and passive, masculine and feminine, outdoor and indoor activity. It also provided an alternative source of self-esteem and self-confidence. Sports not only allowed him to channel his considerable energy and aggression but also to show that he could do what other boys did as well or better than they and thereby assert his manhood. For his love of music carried with it a degree of embarrassment because of its association with effeminacy: "As a boy [I was] partially ashamed of it—an entirely wrong attitude, but it was strong—most boys in American country towns, I think, felt the same. When other boys, Monday A.M. on vacation, were out driving grocery carts, or doing chores, or playing ball, I felt all wrong to stay in and play piano."[3]

Perhaps most telling is his feeling "all wrong," an experience related to a fantasy of being the "wrong" sex. Music might reinforce this feeling in several ways. The need to "stay in" to practice evokes the image of home, the province of women. Confinement is also at issue in contrast to the out-of-doors activities of the other boys. Moreover, practicing the piano is a sessile activity and as such may be perceived as passive. Music itself may be divided into a more masculine, active, erect, and outdoor aspect and a feminine, passive, indoor one. The epitome of the former is the march, of the latter the parlor song.

A further way in which music might be seen to reinforce the sense of femininity is revealed in another of Charlie's memos:

> Father felt that a man could keep his music-interest stronger, cleaner, bigger, and freer, if he didn't try to make a living out of it. Assuming a man lived by himself and with no dependents, no one to feed but himself, and [was] willing to live as simply as Thoreau—[he] might write music that no one would play,

publish, listen to, or buy. *But*—if he has a nice wife and some nice children, how can he let the children starve on his dissonances—answer that, Eddy! So he has to weaken (and as a man he should weaken for his children), but his music (some of it) more than weakens—it goes "ta ta" for money—bad for him, bad for music, but good for his boys!!4

This passage touches on several emotionally laden issues. To weaken and submit for money is like prostitution—a fantasy related to a specific image of woman as used.

Elements such as these in conscious and unconscious mental life buttressed a paradoxical trend of Charlie's attitude toward music: the man who loves art must hate it as well. The passage in his *Memos* ends somewhat illogically—"I sort of hate all music."5 The hating of music has another source as well, relevant to this period of Charlie's life: namely, a keen perception of George's position, the specter of shame, empathy with it, and associated guilt as one of "his boys" for whose good George has submitted.

Charlie's avid pursuit of sports in the midst of his involvement with music provided an answer to the gnawing question of whether he was truly a man. At the same time, he could enjoy the company of men—particularly men he respected. Although the roots of this gratification lay in his relationship with his father and represented an identification with George and George's involvement with groups of men, it enabled Charlie to move away from his father. At this juncture, it was becoming imperative for Charlie to do so in the service of avoiding in his own mind the twin dangers of engulfment and emasculation. As a result, sports, like education, served as a wedge separating Charlie from his father. But unlike education, it was hardly an endeavor George endorsed for his son, perceiving correctly in it Charlie's beginning attempts to move away from him. As Charlie's shift toward sports became clear, an element of apology intruded in his relationship with George, as if this new interest were a betrayal of things they shared.

It was assumed that both Charlie and Moss would enter Yale and carry on a family tradition. Yet that tradition was a tattered one. Nor did any such tradition seem compelling to the other Ives children of that generation. George Ives directed Charlie's musical education, but the deans of his secular education were the Brewsters. It seems likely that the chief booster for Yale was Uncle Lyman and that the only Ives to whom Yale meant a great deal was Aunt Amelia. Within her sphere, Charlie's mother, Mollie, was responsive and responsible. But she did not have the leadership abilities of Amelia, to whom she habitually deferred. They spent much time together, especially in the summers, when both Lyman and George remained in Danbury. Besides a substantial difference in age (twelve years), a class distinction between the two women persisted. But if Amelia had the family background, it was Mollie who had the family, which Amelia undertook to share. Like a conscientious godmother who considers religious education her duty, Amelia felt herself responsible for the boys' secular guidance; she almost certainly would have been more sensitive to the social implications of education than Mollie.

It is unclear where George fit into the family, except that he was expected to pay the bills, a task for which he was ill prepared by his own education. Nevertheless, once it became apparent that both Charlie and Moss would advance to college, George started working as a bookkeeper and clerk. George did indeed go "ta ta" for money whenever possible, but even so he could not have made a living from music. What later troubled Charlie was that, as he saw it, his father gave up music to go "ta ta" for the business world. In 1892, in anticipation of Charlie's going to Yale, George took yet another job that carried the potential for humiliation: he became a clerk at the Danbury Savings Bank, the bank founded by his own father. Insofar as the sacrifice was made out of love for his boys, it was no doubt acceptable to George; insofar as George was caught up in the aspirations and values of others in the family, he could only have felt ambivalence, confusion, and some sense of entrapment. From his correspondence it becomes clear that he did not want Charlie to follow his path in life. Thus Charlie's separation from his father in some respects had George's eager consent and even anxious encouragement.

Education in Danbury had been utilitarian; its terminal goals were literacy, competence in the three Rs, and preparation for life in the community. Even so, Charlie's grades had not been sterling. In March 1892, Charlie transferred from the public high school of Danbury to the private Danbury Academy. A year later, in February 1893, at age eighteen, Charlie left Danbury to attend the Hopkins Academy in New Haven, a preparatory school well known for placing students in Yale. This was the first time Charlie had ever left home; he would never again return to live in Danbury.

Soon after Charlie enrolled in the Hopkins Academy, he began to look into a possible post as church organist, contacting Charles Bonney, choirmaster at Saint Thomas's Episcopal Church in New Haven. He was accepted pending parental consent. On March 1, George sent Bonney his approval, and a day or two later Bonney sent Charlie the music from the organist's cabinet.

News of Charlie's first Sunday at Saint Thomas's was eagerly awaited at home. He seemed by now to have developed the habit of writing about some things more or less interchangeably to his parents and the Brewsters. However, details of musical matters were shared with George alone. Charlie wrote to Lyman the following day about how the service went; on Tuesday he wrote

George about the details of the music and the technical problems he had with it. Charlie was proceeding at his usual pace; he had promptly arranged for private music lessons and immediately joined the Hopkins baseball team.[6]

The Brewsters were responsible for finding Charlie a room in a boarding house owned by a Miss Porter, probably an acquaintance of Aunt Amelia's. Miss Porter had a reputation for tutoring and counseling Hopkins boys seeking admission to Yale. The school itself was virtually at Yale's gate, on the corner of Wall and High streets, and Miss Porter's place was a few blocks away.

After Charlie had been at Hopkins for several weeks, Miss Porter told the Brewsters (who happened to be visiting New Haven) that in her judgment he needed more time to prepare for the entrance examinations. Charlie kept putting off writing to George, anticipating his disappointment.[7] George had hoped that Charlie by now would be well on his way to college. He blamed sports for the delay rather than the difficulties of the undertaking and Charlie's conscientious attention to church work, which was doubly demanding because of Bonney's rigidity: "He was a drillmaster."[8]

No sooner had the decision to postpone the examinations been made when George himself proposed an alternative plan for the late summer and early fall, which would probably delay Charlie's further preparations. He wrote to Charlie that Uncle Lyman

> has been appointed Commissioner on Equalization of Laws & is to be paid expenses to attend a convention in Milwaukee the first week in Sept. He could get a secretary's expense & thought if you could go. He would like to go to Chicago the last week in August (for the World Fair) & back to Milwaukee for the first week in Sept. In that case you couldn't get back until one day before the second Sunday in Sept. so I think it would be necessary to get a substitute for the two Sundays in Sept., if you could get one at all, which I doubt. But there is a possible chance & Lyman is anxious to have you go. If you hear of an organist any time this month that would satisfy Mr. Bonney, shouldn't think two weeks taken from study would necessarily be any detriment. LDB thinks you might get enough practise on typewriter the first three weeks in August.[9]

There could be no doubt that the opportunity would be a fine one for Charlie. He would be stepping into the secular world of Lyman, who by now had a national reputation in the field of the equalization of laws among the states. Although George made some attempt at casualness ("If you hear of an organist . . ."), it is he rather than Lyman who appears anxious to give Charlie the boost. At once he proposed the scheme, gave it his approval, and directed Charlie with regard to arrangements. He appears to have taken it for granted that the already overburdened Charlie could master typing in three weeks. But to do so, of course, Charlie would have to give up sports. He was already a star on the Hopkins baseball team, and George knew that the trip would pull him away at the height of the season.

George seemed to take for granted Charlie's ability to learn to type and serve as Lyman's secretary, although Charlie had already given clear indication that he was ill prepared for the kind of academic study that was to be his ticket in life. If George had not pushed his son into a career in music, he now seemed eager to arrange his future in business. There certainly seemed to be little room left for "a boy's fooling." George himself had definitively put away the toys of childhood, and he appeared to expect Charlie to do the same. At the same time, at the Chicago Exposition there would doubtless be exceptional opportunities for Charlie to hear music of a kind he had never heard before. There is something self-effacing in the letter in George's deference to the wishes and opinions of Lyman. If George had mixed feelings because these experiences would be shared with Lyman, he did not reveal them. Increasingly, Lyman and Amelia appear as parents, interchangeable with George and Mollie and accepted by them.

Charlie responded to his father's letter by return mail. He had already spoken to Bonney and was trying to arrange for a replacement at Sunday services. He only worried about finding time for the typewriter as he would have to be studying on the trip as well. But go he did. On August 22, Charlie wrote George from Chicago, where he and Lyman had heard Theodore Thomas's orchestra, the Chicago Symphony, now in its third year. This was the first time Charlie had heard an orchestra of such stature, although Thomas himself did not conduct on this occasion. He was looking forward to hearing the French organist Alexandre Guilmant later in the week, one of the finest organists of his time.[10]

On the trip, Lyman wrote to Amelia at Westbrook, "Your good long letter & Aunt M's came last night and as we have now finished up the business of both the Am. Bar Assoc. & the Convention of Conferences . . . we can stop to write a little & look round this beautiful city."[11] The "Aunt M" Lyman refers to is of course Mollie. As the couples assume joint parenting of both young men, this form of address creeps in, suggesting some fantasy of the childless Brewsters that the sons are theirs and that George and Mollie are the more distant relations. At the very least, the Brewsters were like benign grandparents who desired to pass to their children's children that which the younger couple could not give. The pleasure Lyman took in Charlie is evident, and he was also pleased to share with him the privileges of his life.

Lyman Brewster had a strong interest in literature, and he wrote verse all his life. His primary effort was a verse play entitled *Major John Andre*, about an incident at the start of the Revolutionary War in which Andre was arrested, convicted of treason, and executed.[12] At some point, possibly on this trip together, Lyman shared the text of the play with Charlie, who referred to it as

Benedict Arnold.[13] The two were considering collaborating on an opera; it would have been their first collaboration since Lyman helped write the words for Charlie's first song, *Slow March.* The beginnings of Charlie's later *1776 Overture* may have been in this time, the incipit of a proposed overture to an opera that never progressed further: "*Overture* to Judge Lyman D. Brewster's play, '*Major John Andre.*'" In its several subsequent transformations in Charlie's work, this piece was always associated with the Revolutionary War. Through it, Lyman himself came to be associated in Charlie's mind with that phase of American history, just as George was associated with the Civil War.

On his return to New Haven in September 1893 Charlie moved from Miss Porter's to the home of a Hopkins classmate, Tom MacIntyre, in order to save money. The year 1893 was an arduous one for Charlie and George, and by that fall, when Charlie had just managed to be accepted for admission to Yale, something had changed between them. As the academic year began, the Danbury *News* picked up the following big-city item since it mentioned a local boy:

> The New Haven *Register* in its account of the football game between Hopkins Grammar School and the Bridgeport High School, in New Haven, Saturday says "it was a rough game. . . . Cheney started the game brilliantly and his loss was a serious one for Hopkins. Ives was placed in charge of the Hopkins team and in the 2nd half he had his nose broken and also had to give up the game." Ives is Charles Ives, the well-known young organist of this city and son of George E. Ives.[14]

When George saw the item, he immediately sent off two telegrams—the second probably to Mrs. MacIntyre *in loco parentis.* Charlie answered the following afternoon with the maddening nonchalance of youth (he had just turned nineteen in October):

> Dear Father
> We received your telegrams last evening and answered both. I suppose you thought I was nearly killed as all the papers here had accounts of horrible accidents & how we had to be carried off the field etc etc. . . . Cheney . . . broke his collar bone, but I just bruised the cartillage of the lower part of the nose. It pains a good deal but Dr. Cheney says it will be all right in a week or so and will not leave any scar or deformity.[15]

Charlie took the occasion to inform George of the doctor's bill and to cite Mrs. MacIntyre's kindness in having him take his meals with her now, adding, "She says that she would always let you know if anything serious has ever happened." Beneath the signature, Charlie offered some compensation by adding, "There was a choral service yesterday & they said that it went better than *any* service went before."[16]

No doubt his parents experienced the enraged and frustrated relief at this news. Details of physical welfare had always been a topic in their letters, representing in part the continuing infantile bond of childhood. In attempting to handle the situation himself, the adolescent Charlie asserted his independence, at the same time inflaming his father by not informing him about an event George was sure to learn about. Charlie had been carried off the field, a certified football hero, now with the stigmatic emblem of a broken nose. In earlier photographs of the Hopkins baseball team, the young man scowled to disguise his regular youthful features. This was no longer necessary; Charlie would bear the twist and bump of the broken nose for the rest of his life.

The tone of Charlie's letters through the rest of the autumn is restrained and conciliatory, with more than a hint of expiation. With football over for the season, Charlie turned to tennis in the daytime; in the evenings he worked out with Indian clubs, a popular body-building sport. In his letters, he associates particular parental figures with specific aspects of his life—Uncle Lyman with books and study ("Tell Uncle Lyman to send books for the bookcase"), Mollie with clothes and laundry, George with music. Charlie solicits his father's advice about additional lessons to prepare for anticipated recitals but is sensitive to their cost in a rather elaborately self-denying manner. As winter comes, he writes that he "might get by without a new overcoat if the buttons on the old one could be set over." He also suggested purchasing a suit midway in size between Moss and himself so that either could use it.[17] Moss, meanwhile, now seventeen, was making arrangements to attend the University of Pennsylvania the following fall and apparently looking for work in order to contribute money toward his education. Money was a constant concern. Charlie soon found himself between jobs as organist, and in a letter he lamented, "I wish I was doing something for my expenses; tho I hope I will be again next year."[18]

Charlie had returned home only overnight on Thanksgiving (he had to play at a service at Saint Thomas's Thursday morning, and the normal choir rehearsal was held on Friday), but the family was reunited for Christmas in Danbury. Charlie would remember this as the last Christmas with his father. With the new year, an increased element of tension wove its way into their correspondence. Charlie was pulling away, attempting to put the physical distance to psychological use. He was not merely avoiding being with his parents—all four of them— but was also finding his own world in New Haven. He was, after all, not very far from Danbury, but he somehow managed to stay away for at least three months and was constantly making excuses to the family for his absence. His church duties, which required him to be in New Haven on weekends and religious holidays, served this purpose admirably. But they did not cover secular holidays, such as Washington's Birthday. Charlie procrastinated elaborately.[19] He managed not to get home for Easter and, further, in a slip of memory, neglected to mail a letter in which he ostensibly had stated his plans to remain in New Haven—and likely offered excuses. A telegram arrived from Danbury as the Easter weekend approached. Charlie answered Mollie at the last minute:

"School vacation begins today [Holy Thursday] and lasts until next Thurs 29. I would have come home this week but there is svc [service] in the church good Friday and for that reason it wouldn't give me as much time as I could have next if I cut a day or two at school. . . . I wrote a letter Sunday and thought that I had mailed it until, having rec'd the telegram, I looked and found it in the pocket of my coat."[20] On the eve of Easter Sunday, Charlie received two letters from George, which must have been insistent, for Charlie responded, "will try to get to D. Easter Sunday evening if there is a train if not, the first one I can get Monday."

As the school year drew to a close with the Yale decision imminent, George appeared to be quite anxious about appearances and impressions. Tensions resurfaced, again related to sports. Charlie wrote:

"I saw Miss Porter last evening the first chance I got, and she said that I ought to come out all right at Hopkins, that she will speak to Mr. Fox [the headmaster]. He seemed to be all right today, and asked how my arm was for baseball (I think maybe that is one of the reasons he wants me to come back). I don't quite see what you mean by the "appearances" it would make. It would be a means of regular outdoor exercise and don't take much time as I won't have to practise with the rest. Unless someone else comes I feel as if I was needed to pitch—Of course if you decidedly think it would hurt me very much, why I don't."[21]

Charlie was no longer responding to George as the easygoing, playful, nurturing father idealized in the *Memos*. George's involvement with Charlie seems to have been as intense as ever but was now tinged with the anxiety of loss of control over Charlie's life. For George, Charlie's increasing independence was tantamount to losing him. In wanting the best for Charlie, George became far more concerned with appearances for his son than he ever was for himself. Baseball was time-consuming and frivolous; the only serious preparation for life was study. George appears to have worried about the headmaster's motivation. Was he more interested in the Hopkins baseball team or in getting Charlie into Yale? The silent figure in the background is Lyman Brewster, the man whose genuine and visible accomplishments had made him the most estimable person in the family but who nevertheless was committed to appearances.

Although Charlie tried to satisfy George's demands as well as ward them off, at base he was confused about them: what did his father want? Nor can we assume that George himself was less confused about the goals of his own life than he had ever been, or for that matter that his goals for Charlie were completely clear. He wanted Charlie to be successful and to avoid the humiliation and sacrifice his own choices (or lack of them) had brought. He wanted Charlie to be like Lyman, a "Yale man," and thus in some way to satisfy Lyman and Amelia, to justify his own position with them and the clan they represented. At the same time, some continuation of the gratifying father-son collaboration would have been seductive to George, compelling perhaps. With the waning of other musical interests, it appeared as if Charlie were all that remained, and that in him lay the promise of the future. At this time the two of them were still seeking to publish the *Variations on "America."* Beneath it all, he did not wish to lose Charlie; he could not let go.

Confused and hurt, Charlie wrote to George, "Why don't you think I don't understand your letters? Maybe I don't write as though I did but I think I understand what you have advised what I have got to do. You know after first of May which is nearly here I can come over Sundays. Of course if your writing won't do until then, I could come up some afternoon and you might come down."[22] The tension between father and son was mounting and becoming murky and complex, betraying the inner conflicts of each of them. We now find Charlie and George reversing positions in an incident concerning appearances of masculine behavior.

In early May 1894, Charlie expressed a wish to take voice lessons. He had a good tenor voice extending into a fairly high range as well as an acceptable lower register. The intimate musical potential of his own body won out over any inhibition that the associations of singing with effeminacy might foster. The opposite seemed to be the case with George, who now appeared to be embarrassed by Charlie's desire to sing. George had uncharacteristically indicated to Charlie that he preferred that the rest of the family not know about his voice lessons. Charlie, confused about George's attitude, confronted him: "I can't think of anything in my last letter that wouldn't do for the family to hear. Don't they know I'm taking singing lessons, and if they don't don't you want them to know?"[23] George might also have been concerned that Amelia and Lyman would censure him for permitting Charlie to dilute his efforts as well as spend scarce money on something that would not help get him into Yale.

In a long letter, Charlie attempted to gain George's approval for two independent interests, singing and baseball, both of which now met with his father's disapproval as George feared they might be reproved by the rest of the family. Charlie allowed himself a burst of protest at George's harping on baseball. At the same time, he responded to some explicit or tacit demand on George's part that he communicate with Lyman, whom George seemed eager to reassure.

During this period, the only respite from strain between Charlie and George was when they seemed to resume a sharing of music, although in a new way. This was initiated by George when he sent Charlie a newspaper announcement of a performance of Wagner's *Die Gotterdammerung* at the Metropolitan Opera. So eager was Charlie to attend that he managed to get down to New York for the performance on two days' notice. The young critic eagerly shared his observations with his father. His comments to George show both a sophisticated, if pristine, ear and naive concreteness—a combination of art and artlessness.

With the term at Hopkins over, it remained for Charlie to keep his nose to the grindstone until Yale entrance exams the last week in September. Charlie now applied himself to his studies with the help of tutors. In Westbrook, Lyman coached him, while George sent anxious queries from home. Charlie reassured him in a note written hurriedly in order to make the six P.M. mail: "Uncle Lyman has just arrived and says you want me to write about the studies. As Mr. Hume [a tutor] said I am taking more time down here with the things Uncle Lyman can hear as English and Latin. Have also done quite a deal of German but have kept to the hours of the schedule except for 2 or 3 days. . . . I can usually get in about 4 or 5 hrs. of study, mornings."[24]

Thus passed the summer. There was, however, one unfortunate interruption. On September 1, cousin Howdie died suddenly. If David Wooldridge is correct, Charlie "lingered absently by the grave long after the funeral party had left. His brother Moss had to come back three times to fetch him."[25] Howard, the son of George's brother Joseph and the oldest of Charlie's generation, was the first of either generation to die. It may have seemed strange to Charlie that Howdie's life had ended as he himself was on the brink of a new life.

Both Charlie and George had changed in the past year. Charlie, approaching twenty, had proved that as a professional musician he could handle anything he was asked to do as church organist. And he could do it away from home and without regular coaching. In his church job, he had survived in an unfamiliar setting with a difficult superior—a martinet, some said—with whom he now enjoyed a mutually respectful relationship. At the end of his term, he had secured another position, in part on the basis of reputation. He had managed to live in another city. For a short time, traveling with Lyman, he had seen other parts of the country and met people of far different background and aspiration than those of his immediate family. If he made it to Yale—and he was close to doing so—his opportunities in new directions both socially and musically would be great. He *looked* different, not only more serious but more manly: vigorous exercise had made him muscular, his broken nose made him appear more masculine, and sports had given him the opportunity for leadership among his peers.

George, on the other hand, seemed to have lost more than he gained. He had become more anxious, even quarrelsome, and rarely showed his accustomed sense of humor. He was likewise far less flexible than he had been, as a person and as a family member. Perhaps he associated some of these personality changes with the businesslike, serious behavior required in his job at the Danbury Savings Bank, attributing them to external circumstances. Change of occupation had certainly been pivotal in his life, and he had some reason to feel that he had made a sacrifice. He was proud of Charlie and Moss, but somewhere there was a sense of bitterness at what he might have felt to be the personal cost of parental duty. Rewards in terms of commensurate filial devotion could not be expected. Charlie was now often elusive and did not seem to have the time for his father he once did, nor the unquestioning admiration. If George was not conscious of this, he was certainly aware of the feeling of depression that had gradually set in. Sometimes it took the form of a physical complaint, sometimes of concern for the health of others, together with an unaccustomed pessimism.

Charlie knew that George, however changed, was not a sick man. Indeed, in some ways George remained vigorous, and father and son could still look forward to sharing much in music. Charlie continued to respect George, but now he also felt stifled by him and angry at him. He came to experience his father as demanding, clinging, and restrictive. He had been glad to be free of him, and wishes to be rid of him for good were not far from consciousness. He had begun a painful separation. With the events of the past year, could Charlie have wondered at cousin Howdie's funeral what the final separation from his father would be like?

Charlie had by now written a number of songs, some of which had been performed. One of the most recent was called *At Parting*. Charlie had written an earlier version of it in 1888, when he was fourteen: "The sweetest flow'r that blows, I give you as we part / For you it is a rose, for me it is my heart."[26] In September 1894, before his acceptance to Yale and following Howdie's death, Charlie returned to this song introducing a verse in the middle (possibly resetting a verse that is now lost): "The fragrance it exhales, Ah! if you but only knew, / Where but in dying, dying fails, it is my love for you."[27] These new words contain the gist of the poem's meaning: eternal love, not the death of Donne's poem ("Deathe, thou shalt die") but the failure of death ("in dying, dying fails"). This romantic conceit is in fact a denial of death. But the setting of this new section some five or six years later belies the complacency of the verse. The earlier simple diatonic harmonic structure yields to one that is intricately chromatic, almost Wagnerian, and the harmonic voice leading in both vocal and piano parts suggests quarter tones in the way the notes are "spelled."[28] The line, "dying, dying," descends in graphic representation of dying, only to ascend in a more sprightly if still dissonant manner in the optimistic measure that follows— ". . . is my love, my love for you."

Clearly, ideas related to love and death, as condensed in images of parting or separation and the affects associated with them, had their place in Charlie's mental life during 1894. These find expression in this small song that is both conventional and radical, obedient and iconoclastic. But the radical elements were not exclusively Charlie's province: George had long been interested in quarter tones and, as Charlie noted, "as a boy I had heard and become somewhat familiar with tone-divisions other than the half-tone."[29] So the notation may emulate as much as it rebels.

In this setting, Charlie employs the interval of the tritone (B-E♯) in a remarkable and unanticipated way. He knew from his lessons with George that the tritone (the augmented fourth or diminished fifth) was a "forbidden" interval in traditional harmony. Could he have known too that historically it was called *diabolus in musica*, the devil in music? Although Charlie was not the first composer to utilize the tritone in representing death, at nineteen he may have been among the youngest. Charlie was preoccupied with the song for months. It was one of the first pieces of music he showed to his music professor, Horatio Parker. It represented the feelings Charlie was experiencing at the psychological parting of ways with his father. The death of cousin Howdie and the funeral at Wooster Cemetery on September 1, 1894, lent poignancy as well as portent to the experience. All the Iveses present knew that someday there would be a place for them there as well. Perhaps as Charlie lingered, he was thinking of George.

Sarah Amelia White Ives (1773–1851).

Isaac Ives (1764–1845).

Sarah Hotchkiss Wilcox Ives (1808–99).

George White Ives (1798–1862).

Mary Elizabeth Parmelee Ives, "Mollie" (1849–1929).

George Edward Ives (1845–94), at age forty.

Lyman Denison Brewster (1832–1904). Danbury Scott-Fanton Museum and Historical Society.

Sarah Amelia Ives Brewster, "Aunt Amelia" (1837–1918). Danbury Scott-Fanton Museum and Historical Society.

George Ives in Union army uniform, 1863.

George Ives in bandmaster uniform, ca. 1892.

Detail from Augustus Saint-Gaudens's Memorial to Robert Gould Shaw and His Soldiers, *the inspiration for Ives's* The "St. Gaudens" in Boston Common.
Photo: Eakins Press Foundation.

Charles Ives and Joseph Moss Ives, ca. 1876.

The Danbury "Alerts." Charles Ives, captain, is seated in the middle row, far left. July 1890.

Charles Ives at eighteen, 1892.

The fifteen members of the Yale senior society Wolf's Head, 1898. Charles Ives is in the top row, second from the right.

Horatio William Parker (1863–1919).

John Cornelius Griggs (1865–1932).

George Ives in the last year of his life, ca. 1893–94.

NINE

AT YALE: MUSIC AND MUSICIANS

Charlie sat for the Yale College entrance examinations in September 1894 and was accepted into the class of 1898. He telegraphed George immediately upon hearing the news. George replied by return mail:

> Dear Charles,
>   Was glad to rec've Telegram. Want to know particulars but suppose you've been too busy to give details. . . . I am to stay in Bank all day which will be the first day I have done so since last week Thursday. I feel awfully weak & shaky, but besides that & a cold & a cough, am about well I hope. Your Mother & Moss each have colds. Mother has another new Nurse, quite a young girl but starts off well. Rest are as usual. [Am sending] Draft for $5 as you must need that much at least by this time.
>
> Love from all
Father[1]

George, burdened with work and physical complaints, wrote in a pessimistic tone that Charlie henceforth ignored. The mystery of Mollie continues in the reference to a "new nurse," suggesting some illness more than a "cold." Such a further burden on George may account for the letter's weary and depressed tone. There had always been domestic help in the house on Main Street. It was different around the corner on Chapel Place, where the George Ives family lived. If George had to hire a nurse for Mollie in his current financial circumstances, there must have been a pressing need. There is no record in the existing correspondence of Charlie's inquiring about the nurse or his mother's health. Nor is there any comment in his later writings. In the ensuing correspondence, however, he dutifully and enthusiastically—even exhaustively—provided the details George had asked for. He was proud of his new home and, despite many requests to the family for furnishings, jealous of it: "Don't have anybody come down, we want to fix the room all ourselves."[2]

Charlie's roommate was Mandeville Mullally. The two young men would share a room at 76 South Middle for the next four years. Charlie began to describe the other young men he was meeting, including many from outside his social realm at home and with connections to the finest and oldest families in Danbury: "Began to eat at Commons today. I happened to get at tables with Ned Tweedy." And, "There is a fellow who sits at my table at the Commons, he asked me the other day if I knew Mr. Henry Hoyt in Danbury that he was in his father's class '33 & had heard his father speak of him often. His name is Birmingham of Honolulu, Sandwich Is."[3]

Money was a continuing problem. Although few letters remain from this period, finances are a recurrent theme. As far as is known, George paid Charlie's tuition at Yale, just as he paid for Hopkins and the summer tutoring. But Charlie was expected to bring in some regular income as a church organist. Money was needed immediately just to be admitted to the Commons ("$10 security"), and even heating had to be paid for ("steam $12/yr."). Charlie started his new job at Center Church on Sunday, September 30, and that would surely be a help. "Seemed to go very well," he wrote to George; "Am going to see Mr. Bonney tomorrow and also get my music from St. Thomas to Centre." Charlie was beginning to enjoy his independence from family and newfound prestige as a Yale man. He was sensitive, however, to what appeared to be the herculean academic efforts required of him to get into Yale. He wrote a few days earlier, "Rec'd. Moss' papers [no doubt the *New Street Weekly*, which Moss continued to put out and which evidently had some news about Charlie's admission]. To read it, it would appear that I didn't often pass a successful examination (which is about right I would guess)."[4]

He continued to be tentative about the issue of sports and approached George about it with a combination of submissiveness and tact. "Ned [Tweedy, of Danbury] is trying for the football team. Some of the fellows want to have me try, but of course have given up hope of that. They sometimes put fellows together later in the season and play scrub games just for the fun of it, Sat. afternoons, would like to play then if I get to it and will you send me my football things."[5]

The wistful reference to sports was not only for George's benefit. At this point, Charlie probably expected that academic demands would be at least as heavy at Yale as they had been at Hopkins and would leave little time for sports.

Moreover, he had to maintain his church job, and it was his hope to continue in music in some other manner while at Yale, perhaps by taking private organ lessons or auditing a course. The curriculum at the time did not allow for electives until the third year.

As Henry Seidel Canby, who was first a student and then a teacher at Yale, pointed out, "two colleges and two systems of education . . . existed side by side in the 1890s. One was the official Yale of the catalogue and classroom. The other was the unofficial Yale of 'college life'—a system of athletics, extracurricular activities, and styles of living that had become highly elaborated and was the educative force in the life of the great majority of the students."[6] In fact, Yale was out of step with the time and was in transition. President Noah Porter, who had been a minister, represented a two-hundred-year-old tradition which stressed "moral and social training" through "a communal experience that was organized and balanced." There was a "proper order" to instruction. The curriculum aimed to inculcate "the discipline of having to do hard and unpleasant work," which "taught self-sacrifice and gave a man readiness and power."[7] Porter opposed the elective system then being advanced by Charles William Eliot of Harvard. At Yale, the curriculum had been inflexible, and it remained so during the tenure of Timothy Dwight, who succeeded Porter in 1886. Although President Dwight in principle favored the more liberal "University concept," in which various schools, including professional schools, were part of the larger university, concentration in a particular area of study was not yet provided and indeed was looked askance upon. Yale's tenets were typical of the older ideal of a "Christian institution whose purpose was to bring together a small body of men in isolation from the outside world, mold their characters by a common and all-embracing discipline, and send them out for altruistic service in a Christian commonwealth."[8] Such a system was outmoded by the 1890s, when the entering class had grown to three hundred or more young men, many of whom were anticipating going into business instead of the clergy, the law, or other of the "older professions."[9]

The second Yale, the Yale of college life, was another institution entirely. It was, as Canby put it, "at least 90% of our felt experience, and therefore 90% of the college as we knew it. . . . Intense extra-curricular competitions for personal prestige in such spheres as sports or the *Yale Daily News* were rationalized as 'loyalty' or 'doing something for Yale.'"[10] The entire enterprise was from the very beginning tinged with strong anticipatory nostalgia.

Charlie was excited, elated, and not a little bewildered by the flux of new experiences and new people in his life. It was a relief that, since he had achieved the goal of admission to Yale, pressure from all four parental figures greatly diminished. Indeed, he was now more than ever a family celebrity. There was relief too from the guilt toward his father that had so often plagued him during the preparatory year, revealed in his letters to George. In addition, as a result of his acceptance, he had gained at least a measure of independence. The stimuli of new people and experiences, reports of which filled his letters, resulted in a displacement of energy formerly invested in his family. As the intensity of ancient ties diminished, particularly that to his father, Charlie underwent a further degree of psychological separation, not merely social independence. But as always, a further source of guilt was latent in his moving away. For the moment, however, having found an interim home, he was leaving home.

Whatever psychological equilibrium Charlie achieved with regard to his father was short-lived. George died suddenly of a stroke shortly before midnight on Sunday, November 4, 1894. Charlie was summoned back to Danbury, and on Tuesday George was buried in Wooster Cemetery. Despite Charlie's expansive writings about George's life, there is virtually no explicit mention of his death, an event from which Charlie never quite recovered. What comment there is is displaced to certain remarks on the writings of Thoreau, which proved to be a comfort to Charlie, as in the haze of bereavement he cast his father in Thoreau's image, with a flute at the edge of Walden Pond on an autumn day.[11]

Only a few weeks before George's death, a significant event of another kind occurred: Charlie's first meeting with Horatio William Parker, professor of music at Yale. The two events became fused in memory. Much else about the meeting was distorted retrospectively by Charlie so as to suggest the mixed feelings he had about the occasion and about Parker in general. For example, he wrote that as a freshman he took courses with Parker; but Yale did not allow electives until junior year.[12] Charlie probably wished to audit one of Parker's courses, and Parker would naturally have asked the unknown young man who identified himself as a composer to bring in his work for routine purposes of placement and assignment.

As with so many issues related to music, when Charlie attempted to recall the event years later, he could not leave George out. Kirkpatrick correctly notes that Charlie's wording "suggests that his work with Parker was more important in his memory than his strong filial sense liked to admit."[13] Charlie wrote:

When I went to New Haven, and took the courses with Professor Horatio W. Parker, in connection with the regular academic courses in Freshman year, I felt more and more what a remarkable background and start Father had given me in music. Parker was a composer and widely known, and Father was not a composer and little known—but from every other standpoint I should say that Father was by far the greater man. Parker was a bright man, a good technician, but apparently willing to be limited by what Rheinberger et al and the German tradition had taught him. After the first two or three weeks in Freshman year,

I didn't bother him with any of the experimental ideas that Father had been willing for me to think about, discuss, and try out. Father died in October 1894, during my Freshman year.[14]

Charlie's erroneous dating of George's death places it even closer to his first encounters with Parker. The meeting with Parker is associated in Charlie's mind with George's death, just as the entire enterprise of Yale represented his separation from George. Although Parker emerges as an influential figure in Charlie's life, here he is recalled in contrast to George. In unfavorably comparing Parker to George, an example of that "strong filial sense" born of duty and guilt, Charlie singled out one piece of music from among those he showed Parker at that first meeting: *At Parting*. In citing it, Charlie incorporates in this memory a musical memorial, the song itself as well as the encouraging circumstances of its composition:

> An instance shows the difference between Father's and Parker's ways of thinking. . . . Parker asked me [to] bring him whatever manuscripts I had written (pieces, etc.). Among them a song, *At Parting*—in it, some unresolved dissonances, one ending on a [high] E♭ [in the] key [of] G major), and stops there unresolved. Parker said, "There's no excuse for that—an E♭ way up there and stopping, and the nearest D way down two octaves."—etc. I told Father what Parker said, and Father said, "Tell Parker that every dissonance doesn't have to resolve, if it doesn't happen to feel like it, any more than every horse should have to have its tail bobbed just because it's the prevailing fashion."[15]

This passage is remarkable for its joining of psychological associations with the details of music. The issue of parting had been the principal one with which both Charlie and George had been painfully struggling the previous year. As Ives recalled the meeting with Parker in which he included George spiritually, perhaps the words of the song echoed: "If you but only knew, where but in dying, dying fails, it is my love for you." More than the note of music remained unresolved at George's death, and perhaps this is what Charlie represented in the music. If George could not have accepted a lack of resolution in the emotional tensions between them, he assuredly could accept this musically, even endorse it. Charlie took comfort and encouragement from this as he idealized his father. What "Father said" in this passage amounted to his last words as Charlie construed them. He never forgot them.

The misdating of George's death is associated with a pair of other circumstances that October. The first was Charlie's twentieth birthday. The second was his avid exercise of his newfound independence in his appetite for new people and new experiences. His last surviving letter to George reflects this. Dated October 30, it would have been received by George a few days before his death and was probably Charlie's last communication with him. It was a breezy letter full of news of college life. Charlie apologized for not having been able to find another letter, which he had started four days earlier but left unfinished because he had had exams to prepare for. He promised "to get them [the letters] off on Sunday after this."[16] The Sunday letter would have been especially meaningful to George since in it Charlie would have reported on that morning's service.

As if prophetically, the excuse Charlie gave for not having got off a letter a previous Sunday was that "Mullahy had wanted to go to Dwight Hall to hear the Reverend Dr. Twichell of Hartford." Joseph Twichell would in time become Charlie's father-in-law. And in a letter to Twichell some years later Charlie wrote: "Father died just at the time I needed him most."[17]

In fact, George died not when Charlie needed him most but when he needed him least. Rather, it was a time when George, in his son's mind, needed Charlie most. In moving away from George physically, socially, and emotionally, Charlie saw himself as abandoning his father. Their final letters to each other were emblematic of this state of affairs. In these letters, Charlie is lively, optimistic, George pessimistic, depressed. Charlie is healthy, George sick. Charlie is moving forward in a life of expanding possibilities; George's life has become constricted and stagnant, his choices limited. Charlie found himself apologizing for not writing and making excuses. He appeared to find it unacceptable that a part of him wished to be rid of his father and to be on his own. Hence his father's sudden death represented the fulfillment of his most despised wishes and initiated a state of mourning which is necessarily complex. For his most beloved opponent had been rendered so completely helpless as to make the struggle meaningless. Worse was the enduring self-suspicion of mortal responsibility. Thus was loss burdened with guilt.

At the extremes of the mourning which must now be accomplished lay the freedom born of resolution or chronic despair; the eventual compromise was ongoing guilt. These were the issues activated at George's death. They became the psychological backdrop to Charlie's years at Yale. This is apparent in Charlie's retrospective account of his first weeks at Yale and in his prompt conclusion, following his meeting with Horatio Parker, that "Father was by far the greater man." This encounter, as so many others would be, was mentally suffused with the presence of George. Years later, when John Tasker Howard asked Ives for an autobiographical entry to include in his book, *Our American Music*, the composer started with a biographical statement about his father, which concluded with the homage: "I feel that, if I have done anything that is good in music, I owe it almost entirely to him [my father] and his influence."[18] But Charlie also acknowledged Horatio Parker in his response: "I had and have the greatest respect and admiration for Parker and most of his music. (It was seldom trivial—his choral works have a dignity and depth that many of [his] contemporaries, especially in the religious and choral composition, did not have. Parker had ideals that carried him higher than the popular) but he was governed too much by the German rule, and in some ways was somewhat hard-boiled."[19]

Charlie was ambivalent in his attitude toward Parker. Had it been otherwise—if, for example, he had turned to Parker as a model for identification and a substitute for George—his music without doubt would have been very different. Nonetheless, Parker left his stamp on Charlie as artist and person far more than Charlie would have liked anyone to think.

Parker was considered one of the most important American composers of his time as well as an influential educator.[20] He was a musical jack-of-all-trades—choirmaster, organist, conductor, lecturer, and writer on musical subjects. Hardworking and idealistic, he was able to earn a living for himself and his family through music without compromising his principles. Throughout Charlie's four years at Yale, Parker served as church organist in Boston's prestigious Trinity Church, where Phillips Brooks preached. It was no doubt Parker's ethical as well as musical qualifications that led the Yale Corporation to appoint him Battell Professor of Music Theory in May 1893. In short, he was the exemplary musician of his time.

Parker was of the generation between Charlie and George—eighteen years younger than George, eleven years older than Charlie. He was born on September 15, 1863, in Auburndale, Massachusetts, then a village much smaller than the Danbury of that time but sharing many of its rural characteristics. He was the oldest of his mother's four children and clearly her favorite.

Both Charlie and his teacher were the oldest child and the favorite of a gifted parent. Parker's mother, Isabella Jennings Parker, was the daughter of a local minister. Educated at the Lasell Female Seminary in Auburndale, she remained there after graduation as an instructor in English and music. Isabella was a fine musician and something of a poet. She appears to have been as much a collaborator with her son in his artistic endeavors as George was with Charlie. She was responsible for the texts of nearly every one of Parker's major choral works until her death in 1904.[21]

The close relationship between mother and son rendered Horatio's father a shadowy figure. Charles Edward Parker, an architect, was about a dozen years his bride's senior. Hardly the companionate father, the role he played in Horatio's life consisted of religious guidance and was irrelevant to the main direction of his son's life. Nevertheless, Parker's most successful work, the oratorio *Hora Novissima* (1893), was written after his father's death and is dedicated to him.

Parker's musical training was as effective as it could be for an American of his time. Boston offered the greatest opportunities for hearing, performing, and studying music. Parker was strongly influenced by George Chadwick, a Massachusetts-born composer just returned from Leipzig. He studied with Chadwick for less than two years before going to Munich to study with Joseph Rheinberger, Chadwick's teacher, at the Königliche Musikhochschule.

Parker's study in Europe was eagerly supported by Isabella, who understood that "a native-born American musician could compete most successfully for positions in this country by going to Europe and mastering the same training as the immigrant European musicians had acquired."[22] Within five years of his return, Parker was well established as a major New York church musician. He taught at the new National Conservatory of Music in 1892–93, the first year Antonín Dvořák was director. Dvořák was also judge of a competition in composition in which Parker took first prize.

Parker had written *Hora Novissima* under a cloud of personal loss. A year after returning to America he married Anna Ploessel, who had been a piano student at the Leipzig Conservatory. Unlike Isabella, she did not pursue a career, choosing instead the more traditional course of making a home, raising a family, and providing an atmosphere in which her husband could compose. Of four children, the last, William, born in March 1891, lived only a few months. A period of private tragedy and despair had begun with the death of the composer's father the previous October and was reinforced by the death of his younger sister, Mary, in the spring of 1891, around the time of William's birth. It was in this atmosphere of loss that *Hora Novissima* was conceived and written.

Parker selected a rather esoteric text for his oratorio. *Hora Novissima* is a section from a medieval Latin poem, *De Contemptu Mundi*, a diatribe on worldly sinfulness and "a vision of eternal life in the celestial city." Thus, Parker chose a text whose poetic idea suggests a fantasy of heavenly reunion with recently deceased loved ones. The work was given a meticulously prepared premiere on May 3, 1893, with Parker conducting. The critical response was enthusiastic; Philip Hale, the critic of the Boston *Journal*, acclaimed it as a work of distinctly American genius.[23]

By the time of its first performance, Parker had already accepted the position of organist and choirmaster at Trinity Church the following fall. In a sense, Parker had never left his mother, Isabella, and never did subsequently, remaining devoted to her until her death. Nor (as William Kay Kearns points out) had he ever left Boston in attitude or outlook: He was and remained the "proper Bostonian."[24]

At their first meeting, on October 10, 1894, Parker observed that Ives's Christian names, Charles Edward, were the same as Parker's father's. Although he may have recognized Charlie's competence as a church musician, it is unlikely that he took a favorable view of Charlie's composing. From Parker's perspective, much of it lacked seriousness in both content and intent. At best, it seemed playful or frivolous. Parker responded to Charlie's music with his characteristic humor, which ran from gentle joshing to open sarcasm. Parker was known to be capable of frankly sadistic classroom behavior. John Tasker Howard observed, "His brusque manner frightened the timid, and he despised those who were afraid of him. In this he was somewhat of a bully; he would often willfully confuse his pupils in class, and then scoff at their confusion. But for those who stood on their two feet and talked back to him, he had the profoundest admiration."[25] Charlie, however, found him to be "seldom mean."[26]

Charlie himself, as Frank Rossiter correctly points out, was shy and therefore unlikely to have "talked back" to Parker.[27] But in virtually all shy people, much talking back goes on in the private reaches of the mind, in an attempt at narcissistic repair—salving fantasied psychic wounds sustained in real encounters. This would be the worse for particular wishes Charlie undoubtedly harbored with regard to Parker, which intensified following George's death within weeks of their meeting: "I went around looking and looking for some man to sort of help fill up that awful vacuum I was carrying with me. . . . [I had] a kind of idea that Parker might—but he didn't. I think he made it worse—his mind and his heart were never around together." George, he said, had "filled [him] up" with Bach, and the fantasy of being psychologically filled by his father had long been an underlying feature of their collaboration.[28] The wish now to be "filled up" by Parker was not without conflict. For to replace George was to betray him intrapsychically. Moreover, he would be replacing him with someone who was everything George was not and could never have been.

While consciously avowing his father "the greater man," how would Charlie have evaluated his father with respect to Parker? The access to European tradition passed on to Charlie from George's studies with Foepple, previously so precious, must have seemed paltry, makeshift, and somehow homespun in comparison with Parker's elegant and thorough training. Nevertheless, the points of contact were a source of pride: Charlie had already been through the exercises in Jadassohn's harmony textbook, which was the one Parker used. However, Parker was clearly more skillful and demanding than George Ives as a teacher. He drew more out of Charlie than Charlie liked to credit him for. Kirkpatrick points out, "The surviving counterpoint exercises show clearly that those for Parker maintain a more exigent level than those for his father."[29]

Parker had done what must have seemed to be everything possible in music. He had many advantages George lacked, of course, chief among them a guiding parent who was sensitive to inborn potential and was in a position to encourage it. He also had the good fortune of locale—the value of Auburndale's proximity to Boston was inestimable. He had become as thorough an artist as possible for his time, place, and talent. Yet despite all this, Charlie concluded gratuitously that "Father was by far the greater man."

George had joined the Brewsters in pressing Charlie to go to Yale—demanding, in effect, that Charlie encounter his own betters in music and otherwise, and indeed go further than he had. In this not-uncommon domestic drama, Charlie appeared to have submitted fully to parental demands regardless of whether they dovetailed with his own inclinations. In their communications as Charlie began college, George encouraged his son's fantasy of renunciation and self-sacrifice, thereby complicating and intensifying the untimeliness of his death for Charlie.

Charlie was receiving contradictory messages from his father: "Be like me" now sometimes turned into "Don't be like me." In such circumstances, the son who has successfully identified with the father feels betrayed, confused, and angry, and his ability to feel good about himself is shaken. Moreover, the invitation or even imperative to surpass may be taken as license to aggress, the father presenting himself, in the mind of the child, as the passive, helpless object. For a boy like Charlie, who had both the talent and the opportunity to surpass his father, a move in any direction—prevailing or renouncing—would invite conflict, including resentment toward the father for having put him in that position. This ambivalence was a critical element in the unique solutions Charlie devised for himself as his life progressed.

Charlie was more like Parker, his teacher at Yale, than he cared to admit and received more from him than he was ever able to acknowledge. Charlie could not fully admit Parker's helpfulness lest it reflect badly on his first teacher, his father, by contrast. And Parker seemed unreceptive to and unappreciative of Charlie's ideas, whereas Charlie was accustomed to being the teacher's favorite and had come to expect that his productions, however strange, would be loved as his father had loved them. This, of course, was unrealistic from any point of view. Imagine, for example, Parker's response to Charlie's showing him "a couple of fugues with the theme in four different keys, C-G-D-A—and, in another, C-F-B♭-E♭. It results, when all got going, in the most dissonant sounding counterpoint."[30] It would be wishful thinking to expect a man like Parker to perceive this as anything but a gimmick. "Parker took it as a joke (he was seldom mean), and I didn't bother him but occasionally after the first few months. He would just look at a measure or so, and hand it back with a smile, or joke about hogging all the keys at one meal and then talk about something else."[31]

In the few anecdotes Charlie left in which Parker criticizes his music, there is often a "good" critic present who saves the day, softening the narcissistic blow and perhaps even showing Parker up for what he missed. In November 1897, during his junior year, Charlie played his *Prelude and Postlude for a Thanksgiv-*

ing Service at the Center Church.[32] Looking back on it, he said it was "the first piece that seems to me to be much or any good now. Parker made some fairly funny cracks about it."[33] But Charlie's friend John Griggs, the choirmaster and baritone soloist at Center Church, said that it "had something of the Puritan character, a stern but outdoors strength, and something of the pioneering feeling. He liked it as such and told Parker so. Parker just smiled and took him over to Heubleins for [a beer]."[34] Retrospectively, Charlie would fault Parker for failing to perceive not only the masculine in him but the "pioneer" as well.

The most telling of such events involves Parker's own teacher and close friend, George Whitefield Chadwick. While in New Haven in March 1898 for a performance of his *Melpomene Overture* by the New Haven Symphony (with Parker conducting), Chadwick visited Parker's Music 4, the class in "strict composition" in which Charlie, by then in his final year, was a regular student. When Chadwick arrived, Parker was criticizing a song of Charlie's, *Summerfields*, objecting that there were "too many keys in the middle." But Chadwick praised the piece: "In its way [it's] almost as good as Brahms! He winked at H.W.P. and said, 'That's as good a song as you could write.'"[35]

Charlie commemorated the event in his accustomed manner—by making a note directly on the manuscript of the music. In this instance, he not only recorded the incident but commented on the practice: "[This was] written on the sides of the ms. of this and [of] the *Summerfields* sketch copy after I got back [to] 76 S[outh] M[iddle], after class in Tr[umbull]—carefully on the margin, as at that time (1897–8) Chadwick was the big celebrated man of American music."[36] He was beginning, in effect, to use the manuscripts as if they were pages in a journal or diary. Further, he would make entries from time to time on earlier manuscripts, a practice that became more frequent later. Many times the pieces that had autobiographical significance would be coupled with a frankly personal diaristic entry. The music might stand on its own merits, but from the point of view of biography, the boundaries of music and comment began increasingly to blur.

The anecdote about *Summerfields* reads like a musical competition. Judge and jury are George Chadwick, Parker's father in music, who also bore the name of Charlie's father. Parker was unquestionably Chadwick's favorite and most successful student, and the relationship that had started thus soon deepened to friendship. Charlie, accustomed to being the favorite, could not but have felt hurt by not achieving this same status with his own teacher, and Charlie never quite forgave Parker for this. The wish to be the musical heir of Chadwick and Parker must have been compelling under the circumstances.

Nonetheless, Charlie owed Parker a debt of gratitude which was only modestly and somewhat begrudgingly repaid. Parker was able to connect Charlie with the European tradition in a far richer and more rigorous manner than

George ever could. He imparted the ethos, if not the best example, of romantic ideals in music, which legitimized Charlie's pursuit of personal expression. Charlie came to admire Parker's considerable personal qualities. Parker was a man of ideals. He believed in the traditional virtues of duty, sacrifice, and service. Strongly individualistic, Parker was a proponent of self-reliance and self-improvement. He had a conviction about the necessity of progress in music and believed in its spiritual and moral force. He preferred a "strong" music, much as Ives would.[37] With regard to principles and ideals, Parker held a parallel position in Charlie's mind to Lyman Brewster. In his writings Charlie gives the impression that the entire course of his life was influenced by one person exclusively. Yet through his ideals Parker entered the mainstream of Charlie's mental life forever just as had Lyman Brewster and even George. Parker translated these into the expressive aspect of Charlie's inner life—his music. Without Parker, Charlie would not have come to write his music in the way he eventually did, nor would the aesthetic behind it have been quite the same.

The notion that Charlie was introduced to transcendentalism by Parker, as some have suggested, seems unfounded. More likely, similarities in background and character rendered both men subject to influence by this current of thought, which remained vital and ubiquitous in late nineteenth-century America. Charlie knew family stories of Uncle Joe's literary interests in Boston a generation earlier, as well as that Ralph Waldo Emerson had stayed at the Ives homestead when he lectured in Danbury. If any teacher promoted Charlie's interest in the transcendentalists, it would have been William Lyons Phelps, who in Charlie's freshman year was an instructor in English literature. Phelps exerted an influence on Charlie that endured throughout his creative lifetime, although Charlie never experienced it with either the intensity or the ambivalence he had for Parker. Charlie later recalled him with loving nostalgia, in strong contrast to the terse and self-consciously fair comments he reserved for Parker.[38] In years to come, many of the poems Charlie set to music were those to which he had been introduced in Phelps's classes.

In senior year Charlie took Phelps's course, "American Literature of the Past Hundred Years." Burkholder suggests that the contribution of this course to Charlie's fascination with the Transcendentalists may not have been so great as one might infer. For one thing, Phelps's favorite was Robert Browning; for another, his assessment of the Concord group differs from Charlie's. Charlie wrote an essay on Emerson and always remained a great admirer of Emerson's *Essays*. Phelps, by contrast, considered Emerson's greatest achievement to be his poems. There is no suggestion that Phelps held Thoreau in the passionate esteem that Charlie did. Although this feeling grew during Charlie's Yale years, its source was idiosyncratic and deeply personal. Thoreau was associated with the comfort his writings provided for the pain of bereavement. Charlie wrote of "my Thoreau—that reassuring and true friend, who stood by me one 'low' day, when the sun had gone down, long, long before sunset." The ensuing lines, referring to "an autumn day of Indian summer,"[39] confirm that the "low day" was November 4, 1894, the day George Ives died. This "apparent allusion"—as Howard Boatwright, the editor of Ives's writings, puts it—is the only more or less specific reference to George's death Ives made. It may be that a latent and casual interest in the Transcendentalists was given sudden impetus by George's death, focused in a fantasied figure of George as Thoreauvian father. Later, the fantasy thus organized would enlarge and encompass aspects of each of the Transcendentalists of Ives's *Concord*.

But Thoreau was of the spirit; the twenty-year-old Charlie needed someone with more substance to help him through the period of painful longing following George's death. He found this person in John Cornelius Griggs, to whom he would later address these reminiscences:

> I don't know as you remember, but when I came to Centre Church under and with you, my father had just died. I went around looking and looking for some man to sort of help fill up that awful vacuum I was carrying around with me— the men among my classmates—the tutors program, etc.—and a kind of idea that Parker might—but he didn't—I think he made it worse—his mind and heart were never around together. You didn't superimpose any law on me, or admonish me, or advise me, or boss me, or say very much—but there you were, and there you are now. I didn't show you how or what I felt—I never seem to know how—except some[times] when I get sort of mad. I long to see you again.[40]

Griggs was of Parker's generation. He had arrived in New Haven in the summer or fall of 1894, Charlie's freshman year, to assume the post of choir-master at Center Church, in addition to serving as baritone soloist. A graduate of Yale with the class of 1889, he had been a student when Gustav J. Stoekel, the college organist, offered instruction to students (music was not part of the curriculum at the time). Griggs had a varied interest in music and a lively mind. An undergraduate essay on the literary works of Richard Wagner had earned him the position of editor of the *Yale Literary Magazine*. Although he followed the classical curriculum, with special interest in modern history, physics, and philosophy, he independently pursued musical studies, traveling to New York for voice lessons at the Metropolitan School of Music on Fourteenth Street. At Yale, he sang in both the College Choir and the Glee Club.

Griggs was the son of the pastor of the Home Missionary Church of Spring Valley, Minnesota, where he was born in 1865. Early in his life, the family moved to Terryville, Connecticut, a small village not far from Hartford, where Griggs later attended high school. His religious and missionary background helped focus his multiple musical interests on church music and influenced his assuming an academic post in China much later. Upon graduation from Yale he married, and with his wife he left for the University of Leipzig, a popular center for study abroad, to pursue his scholarly interests. Unlike Parker, he did not have a gift for composition; his interests were in theory and musicology, which as a discipline was flourishing in Germany in the late nineteenth century. He received his doctorate in 1893, graduating magna cum laude.

Griggs combined the method and style gained in his training with content close to his heart in his dissertation, "Studien über die Musik in Amerika," published by Breitkopf & Härtel in 1894. His study reveals a thoughtful even-handedness in considering various points of view about American music of the time, a spirit of eclecticism, and faith in the idea of progress in the development of music in America. In its conclusion he considers the dilemma of the American composer—namely, that "this very breadth of outlook [traditions and "impulses" received from various countries], and the lack of any musical history of importance, are the two great reasons why American music cannot for the present, have any distinctive national character."[41] Nevertheless, Griggs appeared to have been highly sympathetic to individual American composers.

The year after his graduation, Griggs accepted the post at Center Church which brought him to New Haven. His presence there was Charlie's extraordinary good fortune. Griggs was not only a fine musician and a well-educated person but also was informed about and interested in American composers. Like Parker, he shared Charlie's New England background. And like Parker, he was something of a jack-of-all-trades in music although firmly identifying himself as a teacher. The Center Church Choir was to him what the New Haven Symphony was to Parker. During the period when he and Charlie were both in New Haven, Griggs lectured on church music at the Yale Divinity School, with Charlie performing the musical examples on the organ.

Charlie's unambivalent tributes to Griggs, scattered throughout his *Memos*, are second only to those to his father. "After father's death," he writes, "Dr. Griggs (Choirmaster and baritone at Centre Church, New Haven—we were together four years there in the choirloft) was the only musician friend of mine that showed any interest, toleration, or tried to understand the way I felt (or what might be felt) about some things in music. . . . He didn't like all the things I wrote by any means, but he was always willing to listen and discuss anything seriously. He had his own way of looking at things."[42]

Charlie appreciated and loved Griggs's characteristic respect, modesty, and open-mindedness. The give and take they had was as close as he would come to his exchanges with George years earlier, before the tensions in their relationship had developed, and the time they spent "together . . . in the choirloft" was the closest equivalent to the ideal world Charlie and George had shared. As in Charlie's comments regarding Parker, George was brought in for comparison. Charlie noted that Griggs "had a better sense of intervals than he thought" and that, accordingly, "he did better than most singers with difficult songs." Griggs is compared with George, who, "with a slide cornet could strike any interval (containing even less than a half-tone)." Charlie intended high praise of Griggs by the comparison, at the same time idealizing George, who certainly could not have had Griggs's skill or experience.

Charlie chose Griggs to become the secret sharer of his music. Intense need on Charlie's part, as well as personal characteristics of Griggs—especially those he perceived to resemble traits of George—sealed the bond. Further, Griggs's natural philosophical bent, influenced by a New England transcendentalist background, combined with his training in musicology in Leipzig to give him some unique views on the philosophy of music. These evidently played a role in early discussions between them and were later to serve as a strong influence in Charlie's life and his writings.

The vacuum of which Charlie wrote and which could not be filled by Parker was to a degree filled by Griggs. "Parker at the beginning of the freshman year asked me not to bring any more things like these into the classroom, and I kept pretty steadily to the regular classroom work, occasionally trying things on the side, sometimes with the Hyperion Theater Orchestra, and in organ works, and sometimes in church services, as, for instance, the *Thanksgiving Prelude and Postlude*."[43] The last is a reference to the Thanksgiving performance of 1897. The music is now lost, or perhaps the few sketches that remain are all that ever existed. Griggs again understood and approved of the dissonances Charlie used, which employed elements of atonality and polytonality: "I think these are Dr. Griggs's words partly—but I agreed with him (Parker didn't) 'Our forefathers were stronger men than can be represented by 'triads' only—these are too easy sounding.' "[44]

Thus, the spark of creativity and innovation was kept alive during those years in Charlie's relationship with Griggs. At the center of it was Center Church, a pun that Charlie was later to enjoy making. And Thanksgiving or Forefathers' Day had special meaning to Charlie, not only for its general reference to forbears but because it was celebrated near the time of George's death. During those initial Thanksgiving periods, when Charlie performed the service at Center Church, Griggs was a stabilizing influence to whom Charlie turned. Neither Griggs nor Charlie's experiences with him were ever forgotten—as indeed nothing musical appears to have been. A reminiscence was later reworked into the fabric of the *Holidays Symphony*.

In the *Thanksgiving Prelude and Postlude* of 1897, as in all later versions and derivations, Charlie probably quoted from other works of music. Yet unlike in his earliest pieces, he now incorporated quotations into the substance of the music as formal material in their own right. (In *America Variations*, the "quotation" itself is developed and explored, but not in a new context.) Ultimately, the borrowed material served to establish "the high degree of structural organization prevailing in Ives's larger works."[45] Of course, Charlie was not yet ready for larger works of concentrated integration. But the groundwork for them was being laid in his conservative studies with Parker, while the creative, innovative element was being cultivated in a strongly felt relationship with Griggs. The combination was more fruitful than Charlie acknowledged. Parker constrained him; Griggs, like George, "let" him: both features are characteristic of a creatively operating artistic superego. Charlie, in his grief over his father's death, was more fortunate than he realized.

Griggs's affectionate, accepting, and hands-on personal style was compelling. He endorsed Charlie's work by performing some of the pieces himself. For example, he probably attempted Charlie's *Psalm 150* and *Psalm 54* (both 1896), continuations in style of the radical *Psalm 67*, with the choir, and possibly later settings of Psalms 23, 90, and 100 (written or conceived in 1898). Charlie would then have had a unique opportunity to hear his own technical experiments quite early in his career. At Center Church on various occasions Griggs sang *The Light That Is Felt*, *Abide with Me*, and *All Enduring*. At a concert at Yale, he performed *At Parting*, the very piece Parker had criticized.[46]

At Yale, Charlie continued his interest in organ music and, as Wallach points out, made significant advances. His output from 1894 to 1898 includes lost preludes and postludes written for services at the Center Church, which served as prototypes for some of his earliest important chamber and orchestral works, including the last two movements of the *First String Quartet* (1896) and the two halves of *Thanksgiving*. An organ sonata from 1896 provided the initial impetus for the *Second Symphony*, having been transformed into part of a first movement. Even more innovative, perhaps, is the short *Adeste Fidelis* prelude of 1897 or 1898.[47]

By contrast, his orchestral works of the period are associated with the classroom. The most important of these was the *First Symphony*, Charlie's senior thesis written under Parker's supervision. Charlie later noted, "The better and more exactly you imitate the Joneses, the surer you are to get a degree."[48] Similarly, virtually all of the forty new songs written during this period were in conventional style, and about a quarter had German texts. In fact, during these years there appeared to be a split between classroom work and more adventurous composition. Parker represented one side, Griggs the other.

Charlie worked on two symphonies during his Yale years. It is difficult to imagine how in that hectic freshman year he found time to write the *First Symphony*. Charlie started it in conjunction with the composition class he was auditing. (He was taking courses in Greek, Latin, German, mathematics, and English literature at the time.) Charlie wrote on the manuscript of the full score of the first movement, "Finished 76 So. Middle, Yale . . . May 29–1895."[49] In his junior year he worked on the other movements and as a senior, now officially taking the course with Parker, he submitted the entire work (which was accepted) as part of a graduation requirement in June 1898. Charlie later had this to say about the piece:

> The *First Symphony* was written while in college. The first movement was changed. It (that is, the symphony) was supposed to be in D minor, but the first subject went through six or eight different keys, so Parker made me write another first movement. But it seemed no good to me, and I told him that I would much prefer to use the first draft. He smiled and let me do it, saying "But you must promise to end in D minor."[50]

The *First Symphony* is ultimately an amalgam of many elements, in effect an elaborate compromise along the way to artistic individuation. If Charlie struggled to preserve the freedom in the disposition of keys granted by his first teacher, he was at the same time most certainly influenced by the second. Although Parker's legendary connection with Dvořák was in fact only slight—briefly social and ceremonial—Charlie's *First Symphony*, especially the first movement, appears to be strongly influenced by the Czech composer, whom he no doubt associated with Parker. That this work proved "acceptable" and accessible because of that influence was a source of chagrin for Charlie. "Accepted" as an academic requirement was one thing, but for one's music to be acceptable because it was easy to listen to enraged him after he had produced music of more complex interest. Therefore, Charlie both liked and disliked this work at the time he wrote it. Later, he came to appreciate its virtues while still deploring the fact that others found it appealing because of its comfortable familiarity. Given his own mixed feelings, he could hardly credit Parker for his contribution: workmanship.

The content of the *Second Symphony* began to relate to themes that would occupy him throughout his composing career: it incorporated the act of remembering. Yet Charlie did not altogether forget Parker. The only other major work he undertook at Yale, *The Celestial Country*, was in many ways an homage to Parker. Charlie dated his *Second Symphony* to a period spanning his college and post-college years. He called it "finished" about 1901 or 1902. By then, his work with Parker had enabled him to cast a symphonic form in a manner that utilized traditional means. It served as a solid basis for the composition of his later major symphonic works.

The *First Symphony* is, above all, a romantic symphony. Ives reveals an extraordinary mastery of the idiom and its means. By the last decade of the nineteenth century, the symphony "had become a bastion of the orthodox world of music," firmly rooted in the Germanic tradition.[51] Tradition played a leading role in the life and mind of the developing composer. For Charlie was and would remain a man of the nineteenth century, although the century was rapidly drawing to a close.

The Germanic tradition was very much alive in the late nineteenth century in such institutions as Yale and Harvard. By the 1870s German was a required course for all juniors, and in Charlie's time it had been moved up to the freshman year. Charlie had studied German in preparing for entrance exams, and by the end of his first year he was familiar enough with the language to put it to use musically. He did so by taking texts already set by the great composers of lieder and setting them to his own music, a common pedagogical practice.[52] The songs, like the *First Symphony*, represented a compartment of musical practice in which, by emulating models, Charlie acquired the techniques and aesthetic that he would later integrate into his unique style. The later inclusion of these songs in Ives's *114 Songs* constitutes another diaristic entry: This is where I came from and this is what I did.[53] It is an homage to Parker and the Germanic tradition he inculcated.

The desire to absorb and emulate, born of admiration and need, harbors the wish to surpass, which stems from a sense of rivalry. Charlie, for example, appreciated Chadwick's chastising his former student Parker since he himself had an inclination to outdo Parker someday. Similarly, some crotchety comments he made later about Dvořák suggest a curious rivalry with that master—one Charlie very likely would have vigorously disavowed. Yet the style of the *First Symphony* betrays the influence. And later, in writing about his *Second Symphony* (already germinating in his mind during the Yale years), Charlie noted:

> Some nice people, whenever they hear the words "Gospel Hymns" or "Stephen Foster," say "Mercy Me!" and a little high-brow smile creeps over their brow— "Can't you get something better than that in a symphony?" The same nice people, when they go to a properly dressed symphony concert under proper auspices, led by a name with foreign hair, and hear Dvorak's *New World Symphony*, in which they are told this famous passage was from a negro spiritual, then think that it must be quite proper, even artistic, and say, "Ain't it awful!"—"You don't really mean that!"—"Why, only to think!"—"Do tell!"— "I tell you, you don't ever hear Gospel Hymns even mentioned up there to the New England Conservatory."[54]

Among Charlie's most tender, nostalgic, and idealized memories of George were of gospel hymns. These memories were represented in his music through musical quotation, and hymns comprise the largest category of quoted material. Most of these tunes were part of Charlie's earliest musical vocabulary, harking back to the preverbal period of his life, when the child experienced tunes as a form of human communication associated with his father's music. Charlie's tirade late in life against Dvořák's use of gospel hymns reveals the fierce pride of the possessor in the face of the poacher. Charlie identified with his father as an uncouth purveyor of the vernacular who was turned away while others flourished. It was enough to move Charlie to extravagances of vernacular New England speech, which might well be quotations from an embittered George, in his very voice.

Nevertheless, Charlie had heard the symphonic music of Dvořák, and there is little question that it impressed him. In some ways, the initial hearing of the *Largo* from the *New World Symphony* may have given Charlie a shock of recognition of his own potential, barely formulated let alone realized. It served perhaps as symphonic stimulant and permission to incorporate nonliteral vernacular music in a symphonic setting, toward the end of making a musical statement of far greater complexity than the tune itself. Already in his *Second Symphony* Charlie was experimenting along these lines. Thus he placed himself in the dual role of emulator and rival of Dvořák—the relation of son to father. Musical materials were now available for this endeavor, the result of considerable musical experience both formal and informal. In this way, the *Second Symphony* reflects the influence of the nationalistic Dvořák in his "American" period, whereas the *First* reflects the Dvořák of the Germanic symphonic tradition.

During his three years (1892–95) as head of the National Conservatory in New York, Dvořák wrote his "American" works under conditions of homesickness, a longing for the past and the thrall in which memory holds the present. These would shortly become precisely the mental circumstances under which Charlie would compose once he had forged his style. Thus a musical influence may be transmitted not in technical terms but in terms of the underlying human context that informs music.[55] This fundamental humanism is universal, and so it is all the more interesting that Ives, after he had formulated his ideas on transcendentalism, did not include the art of Dvořák in its all-encompassing embrace. Dvořák was more of a participant in his transcendental aesthetic than Ives could ever have realized. Instead, Charlie came to view him as a rival and a musical carpetbagger. He disavowed the emotion he must have felt upon hearing such un-American yet "American" music as Dvořák's, so expressive of some potential within himself.

The *Second Symphony*, in fact, represented a major development in Charlie's mental life. Although he began work on it as a student, it occupied him during the first postgraduate years and served as a bridge to musical maturity. It integrated many musical experiences of the past, even as it looked to the future. A major aesthetic, stylistic, and psychological difference between the *First* and *Second* symphonies lies in the extensive use of musical quotation which characterizes the *Second:* treasures of memory and vanished days are invoked in wordless, musical fragments. While there is much of George Ives in it, it also shows Parker's contribution to Charlie's training at a level his father could not have provided.

Although Charlie spoke for his father in bitterness toward the musical establishment, he was able to digest the considerable nourishment it had to offer and expel what proved to be alien to him. As a result, he always remained at the edge of that establishment, aspiring at times to be a part of it despite his disclaimers. The artistic potential explored in the *Second Symphony* existed in a mental compartment quite separate from the world of the *First Symphony*, which was Parker's world as well as Dvořák's, the musical world of German tradition. Other musical worlds, too, were compartmentalized, like the world Charlie shared with John Cornelius Griggs. The energy with which he engaged in each of these relationships, and the endeavors with which they were associated, is impressive; it is the energy available to emerging genius and essential to its development. Throughout his life Charlie retained mixed feelings about Parker; for Griggs, though, he had nothing but affection. But he drew upon each in forging his own style. And his relationship with George provided him with the personal characteristics that made it possible to do so, just as his father's death provided the occasion and the necessity.

TEN

76 South Middle

Even for Charlie, there was more to Yale than music. Freshman year at Yale started with "rush." Invitations were issued to all freshmen to participate in this first class exercise, a mass formation on the Hopkins Grammar School lot one evening in September. The event was nostalgically recalled by an alumnus: "Each class was in the most perfect sardine formation. The members did not hold each others' arms; they put their arms around each others' bodies. They backed each other up so perfectly that the different files not only stepped together, but had to breathe together. . . It was called a 'push rush.'"[1]

And so began the rites, rituals, customs, and ceremonies that forged the "Yale man" of the time. The contribution of such exercises to the students' sense of membership was inestimable. "For God and Yale" on the athletic field and the fields of war was a youthful sentiment scoffed at by some but keenly and earnestly felt by most. It was as much expected that the Yale man would acquire such values as it was that he would enter into college life with the boundless energy that was essential for success there and hence in life. Athletics was life not merely in miniature but distilled and concentrated, a field like the battlefield where young men proved their valor and devotion to cause and principle.

Henry Seidel Canby, who entered Yale in 1899, the year after Charlie graduated, wrote of the "tense activity behind the romantic facade":

> The cry in our undergraduate world was always "do something," "what does he *do*?" Freshmen hurried up and down entry stairs seeking news for the college

paper; athletes, often with drawn, worried faces, struggled daily to get or hold places on the teams; boys with the rudiments of business ability were managers of magazines, orchestras, teams or co-operative pants-pressing companies. Those who had a voice sang, not for sweet music's sake, but to "make" the glee club. . . . Some voice always seemed to be saying, "Work for the night is coming." The toil was supposed to be fun, but the rewards were serious. No one that I remember did anything that was regarded as doing for its own sake. No, the goal was prestige, social preferment, a senior society which would be the springboard to Success in Life. And all gilded, made into illusion, by the theory that in such strenuosity we demonstrated loyalty to our society, which was the college; that thus the selfish man transcended his egoistic self-seekings, and "did" something for Harvard, or Amherst, or Yale.[2]

Acceptance by the principals of the new world, the "big men" of college, was paramount. And in the initial social reshuffling and the establishment of one's new identity, there was the promise of being dealt a new hand. George's death released Charlie to devote his energies not only to music but also to the pursuit of other, new goals in life, of which social success in college was precursor. Psychologically, Charlie was walking a tightrope. As gratifying as personal achievement in music might be, it could threaten prestige and position in college life from two directions: to be either too effeminate or too crazy would invite social ostracism. One had to be "just so." Indeed, a certain degree of deviance was applauded so long as it was exercised within established institutions such as glee club and fraternities.

At twenty, Charlie was well equipped to be an organist; for many, this could be a career. Meager income could be supplemented by teaching. Nevertheless, although it lacked the potential to bring money and power inherent in other careers, it was respectable and genteel. But Charlie had already experienced alternatives. Uncle Lyman, the "other" father, lived on not only in the reality of Danbury but in a now shared college life, as Charlie tended to address academic details to the Brewsters in his letters. In addition, Lyman was a part of the available past of Charlie's mental life which enriched the sources of identification. Similarly, the potentials for choice were informed by Charlie's awareness that he was, after all, an Ives—the scion of men of distinction, capability, and achievement—above all, businessmen. His great-grandfather Isaac had walked the identical paths at Yale that Charlie now did. He was at once continuing a tradition and closing the gap left by George, although in doing so he would inevitably reveal the generational fault.

At Yale, Charlie soon found new friends and models. These were for the most part descendants of families of distinction. Perhaps the most distinguished was that of his future father-in-law, the Reverend Joseph Hopkins Twichell, who was the father of his classmate and close friend David C. Twichell. The Reverend Mr.

Twichell was himself a member of the class of 1859 and still retained close ties to the college. "Twichell of Hartford" was often a "Sunday night talker" at the Young Men's Christian Association in Dwight Hall: "He has rowed for Yale and fought for Yale in the old days when the town ever threatened the Gown. He was a fighting chaplain of the Civil War, and has rejoiced to live and see the day when there is neither North nor South. He has his army story always, and his college story; but more, the personal magnetism of an orator, who quickly makes that audience feel his affection for them."[3] During the last week of September 1894, with so much happening in his life, Charlie somehow found time to attend the "Freshmen's First Sunday" in Dwight Hall, where the reverend was speaking.

Above all, there was music in different forms—academic, student vernacular and that which would provide some small income. Already at Yale Charlie learned to split his endeavors, serving two masters at once—even more if necessary. Along with the split between the musical worlds of Parker, the exemplary musician, and Griggs, the secret sharer, a further split in Charlie's musical world was becoming manifest—this time with his classmates serving as both sharers of the process and auditors. Once again, he turned an opportunity born of necessity to creative use. Early compositions incorporating the vernacular automatically become acceptable to his classmates by being dubbed "stunts" or "take-offs." But they provided a space for Charlie's active musical imagination to range and develop further. Throughout the Yale years and beyond, however, he remained concerned about how such work would be received by his friends, and his later *Memos* record endorsements and words of encouragement from classmates, fraternity brothers, roommates, and others who could not have had the slightest idea what Charlie was doing musically.

Thus, at Yale Charlie was coming to develop not only a personal style of finding solutions to the contradictory demands of life from within and without, but also the elements of his eclectic artistic style. If his psychological compromises were elaborate, they served their purpose—providing sufficient inner tranquility to carry on gratifying relationships with others and a successful creative life. In young adulthood, cohesion of the self often hangs on the coattails of group cohesion. In Charlie's case, there were other sources of integration as well; for forming the materials of art into a cohesive whole has a reciprocal effect on the one who forms, engendering a feeling of wholeness. Charlie's continuing private life of music, carried out in association with Parker and Griggs, served this personally integrative function admirably, as did the composition of music written in the social context of student life, which incorporated a strong vernacular element.

This vernacular compartment of music is important not only in itself and for Charlie's continued cultivation of a tradition practiced by George but also in its felicitous application to the problem of social acceptance. The vernacular practice of music—musical jokes, takeoffs, barbershop quartets, and marches—was part of what Charlie *did* as an undergraduate, and it gained him the esteem and acceptance of his fellows. These, as Rossiter shrewdly observed, "were not the scholars, the poets, the lovers of fine music, the alienated. His friends were the big men, and it was these friends from both prep school and college who secured for him an honored position among Yale's elite." The shared music was the vernacular music. Charlie "was not above composing potboilers in order to increase good fellowship."[4]

From his first days in New Haven, Charlie aspired to the elite. The vernacular music of this period tracks the process. While the personal style may reflect that of George Ives in the social context of fun and fellowship, the fellows themselves were more like Lyman, members of an educated social class in which money, influence, leadership, and tradition counted. The real world outside Yale was reflected in such formal and informal institutions of college life as the fraternity, the glee club, and the selection of friends and a roommate. Since his days at the Hopkins School, even the Danbury boys Charlie encountered were from the most prominent families. In his first letters to his father from Yale, casual mention of tony classmates like the Hoyts seemed aimed at flaunting his association with those from a world to which George had never belonged.

Charlie became a fraternity man at Yale. He was elected to Delta Kappa Epsilon in May 1896 during his junior year. Hence the composer of sacred music in the form of organ preludes and art music in the form of symphonies now added to his musical accomplishments such vernacular efforts as *Hells Bells* and *Pass the Can Along*.[5] The former was original music for a play given on Initiation Day the following year. One of its authors, Sidney Robinson Kennedy, president of the Banjo Club, later, like Charlie, became an insurance company executive; he was kindly remembered years afterward for quite another reason, which related to the music stunts and takeoffs that Charlie improvised for his fraternity brothers:

> When other similar things (half in fun, half serious) were tried, as I remember, there were usually one or two, either among the players or the listening students, who would be sort of interested and ask to have it played again. And in playing the songs in D.K.E., I used to play off-beats on black keys, etc., and often men would ask to have those "stunts" put in. Some said—one was Sid Kennedy—that it made the music stronger and better, after he had got used to it. Now this may not be good evidence, but it shows what the ears can handle, when they have to, and [with] practice—not that the things then were worth much—but the ears have to be on their own.[6]

Charlie had a habit of crowding each scrap of music paper with sketches of various works in progress. On the same manuscript page as *Pass the Can*

Along—manifestly a drinking song despite its excretory allusions ("Fill, fill, fill. O fill the flowing Bowl . . .")—are sketches for the third movement of the *Second Symphony*, which Charlie had tried out on the organ in Center Church as a prelude. This is the section that quotes *The Missionary Chant*, and the date of the performance, according to Kirkpatrick, was probably November 2, 1897.[7] The tune and the date are significant in Charlie's mental life, for it was on Missionary Sunday three years earlier that George had died. The event inspires and informs the music, and no doubt its special meaning led Charlie years later to note on this same manuscript fragment, "This was the one played in Center Ch. When scored later, it was made better and spoiled (by advice HWP[arker]). This was scored as below on long score paper but lost. . . . P said—a movement in Key of F should start in key of F so change and weaken it!!!!!!!!!"[8] Looking back over his college years, Charlie often seemed to be more grateful for his comrades' receptivity to his music than for his professor's criticism.

In many ways, initiation into fraternity life was a turning point for Charlie. Election to a fraternity was a further step up the narrowing pyramid of social acceptance. And with it the potential for future directions life might take were being laid out. Charlie would never return home to live in Danbury again. Lyman had returned a generation earlier, but two related elements made it unlikely that Charlie would even follow in Lyman's footsteps. First was the inevitable rivalry that Charlie must have felt with his brother, Moss, about which we have few details. Moss, at the very time of Charlie's election to the fraternity, was a student in the Yale Law School. Interestingly, the brothers were on the same campus for two years, between 1896 (when Moss entered) and 1898 (when Charlie graduated), but there is no extant reference of contact between them. Rather, it appears as if they led separate lives and pursued different goals. Charlie sought brothers elsewhere, in the big men of the campus, members of the fraternities and elite secret societies. These were the men who, in Rossiter's words, "showed solid organizational achievements in the college's managerial, athletic, religious, journalistic, and musical activities."[9] They also held the power to carry along with them acceptable, likable, and useful friends who were themselves less prominent. The second set of circumstances that made a return to Danbury unlikely was Charlie's growing ambition, stimulated by the highly competitive society that was Yale. If he was not one of the big men, he was remarkably successful in his own way. Charlie always sought channels for his considerable aggression. A short time before, it had found an outlet in sports. Now other avenues for it were sought, more social forms of competition. Later still, it would be expressed in the world of business. And throughout Charlie's life, this aggression showed itself in his music, in the forms he devised and the massed forces required to realize them in sound.

For Delta Kappa Epsilon, Charlie composed humorous pieces (*The Circus*

Band), sentimental love ballads (*For You and Me*), and college songs (*Battell Chimes*) as well as the music for Delta's shows. This activity served him well in fostering bonds with contemporaries in the Yale community whose friendship he desired and who might be of help to him. Early in his freshman year, he had participated only in the freshman glee club. By senior year, he was both well known and well liked on campus. Off campus he identified with the college owing to the adoption of *Battell Chimes* (also known as *The Bells of Yale*) as a regular presentation by the glee club both locally and on its western tours during Christmas vacation.[10]

Somehow, George Ives continued to haunt these works. Charlie's original copy of *The Bells of Yale* was written on a manuscript page from George's original copybook—the page on which George himself had copied a portion of Charlie's *Communion Service*, among their earliest collaborations, sometime in 1890 or 1891. Charlie seemed to have felt some explanation was in order for using George's manuscript and lamely cited the "heavy expense" of music paper.[11]

The activities of clubs and fraternities were entirely self-supporting, and it was expected that participation would involve some financial contribution. Charlie was among the minority of Yale students who could not rely on family for their pocket money, and he had to fund his social life at least in part by his own earnings. The cost of Yale social events could be astounding.The Junior Promenade, for example, a three-day event usually held in January or February, ran to forty or fifty thousand dollars by some estimates.[12]

This, then, was a world far apart from the penny-pinching Yankee tradition Charlie cleaved to in his note about saving paper. Here, too, he was able to accommodate both realms. The habit of saving paper had several determinants. One was a sense of guilt for present privileges and future successes. Another was an adherence to tradition, the New England "use it up, eat it up, do without" of his ancestors. The habit revealed as well a growing notion about the nature of composition: everything was part of the same thing, and every musical element could be associated with every other in a unifying coexistence. Later, Ives refined this notion into a highly personal transcendental definition: "the fabric of life weaves itself whole."[13]

The need for more money may well have been responsible for the few attempts at writing popular music for publication that Charlie made during his college years. Three pieces were published commercially in 1896: a march for band, the *Intercollegiate*;[14] a kind of barbershop quartet, *For You and Me*; and a song for the presidential campaign of William McKinley, *William Will*.[15] The march is a version of one Charlie wrote four years earlier, which George had performed with the Danbury Band in October 1892. It demonstrates that quotation was already becoming a regular stylistic feature of his music, for the middle section consisted of an extended passage from the song *Annie Lisle*. The tune (perhaps best known in its version as the Cornell *Alma Mater*) was later quoted in another of Charlie's works, the song *Old Home Day* (originally *Old Home Town Day*), to which Charlie himself wrote the words.[16] The latter song is a re-creation of George's band, including a musical portrait of its Irish members "march[ing] along down Main Street."

William Will ("A Republican Campaign Song") points in the opposite direction from the Danbury of George Ives and the working-class ethnic groups whose members served as bandsmen. If anyone was popularly viewed as representing those "old monopolists" George disdained, it was William McKinley (introduced to the Republican Convention as the "advance agent of prosperity"), a curious hero for the young Charles Ives. McKinley's Republican party was the party of Danbury business and of Lyman Brewster. A rousing populist-type campaign song for McKinley was something of a contradiction in terms, for unlike his opponent, William Jennings Bryan, McKinley remained somewhat aloof from the campaign.

The designation "Yale '98" would henceforth be a part of Charlie's identity. College class determined companions—often lifelong ties—and linked forever a generation of students. They studied, worshiped, loafed, and played sports by classes. Equally important, "They break into secret societies by classes."[17] In time, many would marry by classes as well.

By the summer of 1896, Charlie had developed a close relationship with a classmate, David Cushman Twichell. In August, he was invited to spend part of his summer vacation with the Twichells at Keene Valley, in the Adirondacks. There Charlie got to know the rest of the family, including David's younger sister, Harmony. They may have encountered each other before since Harmony had often visited the New Haven home of her roommate from Miss Porter's school, Sally Whitney. Harmony must have heard Charlie play then, for the Whitney family regularly attended Center Church. In any event, through David each was well aware of the existence of the other. In 1896, Harmony, at twenty, was already an impressive person, hardly merely David's "little sister." She was an attractive, tall, full-figured young woman who was intelligent and articulate. More than likely, Charlie was awed by her and characteristically shy and uneasy in her presence. Having had a close and mutually admiring relationship with her father and accustomed to the company of his friends, Harmony was as comfortable in the presence of men as Charlie was uncomfortable with women. Superficially, Harmony was as different from Mollie Ives as could be imagined—poised, well educated, and of impeccable background. If either harbored a fantasy of marriage at the time, it was obscured by the tasks ahead of them.

A symbol of Charlie's success in integrating and balancing the many pressures on him during this period was his election to a secret student society in his junior and senior years. This reflected the social acceptance of a young man whose rich creative life could well have alienated him from his peers. To the contrary, he had managed to achieve social goals without compromising his continued creative development. The young composer was mentally incubating a second symphony even as he was tapped for elevation to the elite of Yale.

Charlie's election to the senior secret-society system, the ultimate honor, called by the *Yale Graduate* the "peculiar institution," had been prepared the year before by acceptance into a junior society, Delta Kappa Epsilon, which was more like a traditional fraternity. This in itself was a distinction since the three junior societies at Yale each accepted only twenty-five of the three hundred sophomore men. Each society had its own distinctive building on campus; Delta Kappa Epsilon's was a Moorish temple on York Street. Elections of new members to the junior societies were held a week before Senior Tap Day, in a ceremony replete with pseudo-medieval pageantry. The occasion delineated provisional boundaries of social lines during the course of junior year in anticipation of the climactic last year of Yale. The final establishment was accomplished during senior year with the elections of the elite secret societies.

On the day of the junior societies' elections, members of each society robed themselves in their official colors: Delta Kappa Epsilon in red, Psi Upsilon in white, and Alpha Delta Phi in green. After dark, a procession formed. Hundreds gathered on the campus to watch the groups, each lustily singing its fraternity songs, converging, intersecting, and at length aligning behind a large calcium light, marching two abreast, each man supplied with sparklers and other hand-held fireworks to add to the spectacle. Each group attempted to out-sing the others. Before joining the central procession, small groups from each fraternity proceeded to the dormitory rooms where the new juniors were waiting to find out who would be invited into their ranks. Thus was Charlie chosen for Delta Kappa Epsilon, an event significant enough for him to incorporate it later into a complex musical memoir, *Calcium Light Night*.

When Charlie was tapped the following year for the senior society Wolf's Head, the atmosphere was far more tense, and the grim social economics of who was in and who was out were far less tempered in pageantry. One Thursday afternoon in late May, 1897, Charlie waited with his classmates in front of Durfee Hall for the hour and a half during which selections were made. Other observers crowded the windows of the surrounding dormitories and even perched on the roof of Dwight Hall to see members of the secret societies entering the campus from their respective society halls and approaching the massed juniors. Each of the fifteen seniors in each of the three societies had been delegated to tap one junior. Working his way into the crowd to find his happy and relieved target, the senior slapped the nominee on the back and sent him to his room. There the official election was solemnly announced, and the elector then withdrew from the room and the campus. Meanwhile, the man elected returned to his classmates by the junior fence (the gathering place on Old Campus) to receive the unstinting acclaim required by the mores of good fellowship. Clearly, lines for the future had been drawn between the elected and the rejected which would extend far beyond the single year to come.[18]

Charlie had two sponsors from the senior class in Wolf's Head, James Lineaweaver, a former classmate at Hopkins Academy, and Ebeneezer Hill, Jr., another Hopkins alumnus. A novel of the period, *Stover at Yale*, bitterly classifies the men who were chosen as "big men" or "lame ducks," the latter being those who were selected at the former's pleasure.[19] The bitterness is not without foundation, since election was the culmination of social ambitions held openly or privately for three years, and more than 85 percent of the men would have their hopes dashed, as only forty-five were selected each year.

Tap Day was avidly anticipated by the students, and a student publication, *The Horoscope*, had suggested that Charlie might be a candidate for the most prestigious of the societies, Skull and Bones, although he was "not a sure man." The student prophet commented that "he has much to recommend him . . . [he] has put himself through college very creditably by acting as organist at Centre Church, and always acts with becoming independence." However, "he is not a big man in any way and the chances are a trifle against him."[20] Charlie was in fact a lame duck. Certainly, membership was never a reward for scholarship—more frequently pure scholarship was a hindrance—and a student who was as dedicated to academics as Charlie was to serious composition was less likely to be socially successful. A case in point was Charlie's classmate David Stanley Smith, who had committed himself to a career in academic music, was a favorite of Horatio Parker's, and later became Parker's successor as chairman of the music department. Smith was not tapped, nor were the few other serious musicians in the class. Such men might be socially suspect because it was clear that they would never, through their own endeavors, achieve the proper if unstated goals of the Yale graduate—to be prosperous, content, and well liked.[21]

As for wealth, at this stage of their lives these men were unlikely to acknowledge placing the acquisition of money and power above artistic interests. In fact, any serious interest in music, it was felt, should properly be confined to adolescence and youth. Later, however, after marriage, such inclinations should be satisfied by way of membership in the appropriate social institutions associated with music, the opera and the symphony orchestra. When the class astrologer acknowledged that Charlie as a candidate was neither a "sure man" nor a "big man," he utilized the beloved slang of the undergraduate adolescent boy of the time, deeply concerned with masculine performance in a world in which women were kept safely outside the gates. Eventually, economic performance would distinguish the truly successful alumni. Among the rewards would be the most attractive women, who served as judges as well as prizes. Against that day of reckoning, the men would honorifically designate their own "men."

Virtually anything that could be construed as mitigating potency doomed the "man" to being considered something less than a man. At the same time, students bonded themselves into a community of men in which the love of men that motivated the bonding must never be revealed in its physical dimension. For the specter of homosexuality carried with it the threat of the loss of potency, and ultimately fantasies of castration. Certain forms of sentimentality, however, were permitted and even favored. Music and musicians had their proper place. The two essential genres were the college or fraternity song and the sentimental love song, the first apparently a representation of sexually laundered fraternal love and the second of romantic, heterosexual love. But in both cases the performers were perforce men: the male barbershop quartet and the banjo player.

An example of the acceptable, even celebrated musician who could minister properly to this company of men was Charlie's friend Sid Kennedy, president of the Yale Banjo Club and the acknowledged "class musician." In a review of the musical activities of the class of '98, only one reference is made to Charlie: "Charles Ives composed 'Chapel Chimes,' which has been sweetly sung under several aliases."[22] Sid, on the other hand, was every bit the exemplary college musician, as Parker was the exemplary professional. Writing to Charlie many years later, Sid, himself a member of a senior society, told how his tenure as president of the Banjo Club "had been a fine preparation for his life in business."[23]

If election to a senior society was as much a sign of success in college activities as a predictor of future success, what was it that Charlie had managed to achieve? Again, operating within one compartment of his emotional life, isolated from others progressing simultaneously (such as those that the creative worlds of the *First* and *Second* symphonies suggest), Charlie pursued a communal life with men which nourished him—the legacy of his relationship with George. Unlike his father, and perhaps owing to his sense of George's experience, Charlie knew what to reveal and what to conceal, what to highlight and what to keep private. Paying one's way through college was an admirable, self-reliant, American thing to do even as a church organist in a women-dominated institution. He could have worked as the house pianist at New Haven's vaudeville theater, Poli's, where a noncollege acquaintance, George Felsburg, performed, but perhaps he saw that job as too demanding of his time and less regular in income. Charlie did try some of his experimental pieces in the acceptable form of musical stunts at Poli's, and on one such occasion Sid commented that what were essentially polytonality and polyrhythms "made the music stronger and better."[24] With such endorsements, Charlie's music was not considered deviant or downright crazy but just fun, and accordingly it was held in high esteem. Most of the *composer's* inner world germinating within his mind, however, was kept to himself. Charlie was already establishing and practicing a pattern of creative privacy in the context of multiple lives.

In strong contrast to his father, Charlie was ambitious. He was hardly unaware of the kind of business career that Yale promised, nor was he blind to the fact that the best preparation for it was the kind of social success in college that election to the senior society signified. Thus, a degree of opportunism intermingled with other motivations. Possessed of a marked capacity for aggression, which revealed itself now as boundless energy, Charlie always remained uneasy about its possible destructive or exploitative facets. (Only in later life did it become more manifest.) The mature Charlie developed a clear distinction between visions of America as a land of opportunity and as a land of opportunism. At Yale, Charlie, although apparently shy, somehow managed to know and to be liked by those who could help him. His own long-standing capacity and need to love men played no small role in the bargain.

A feature of Charlie's composing that was already established was a tendency toward autobiographical reference. As time went on, this trend continued with more complexity and subtlety. In good measure, this was conscious and deliberate, as in Charlie's practice of making biographical notes or "memos" on sheets of music. One of his final works, the collection *114 Songs*, is nothing less than an American diary in music. But no one can be in complete control of symbolic representation; layers of unconsciously derived autobiographical material inevitably find representation in the work of the artist. More than this, elements of memory *seek* representation; memory traces of experiences that have gone into the formation of the psyche in the past are regularly revived. Outside of consciousness, such memories constantly participate in the ongoing sense of identity. This constitutes a background flux of remembering which is a regular part of the mental milieu. It is against this background that ordinary, everyday thinking and remembering occur, which may include the need to remember, as in mourning and memorialization, or the need to forget or repress. What is impossible is to remember a *single* thing. All experiences exist within a network of associations.

In 1907, nine years after graduating from Yale, during a period of innovative and experimental composition, Charlie wrote a piece of music with manifest reference to the experiences and events surrounding selection into the societies. *Calcium Light Night* is a short piece for a chamber orchestra that in instrumentation suggests a marching band: piccolo, oboe, clarinet, bassoon, trumpet or cornet, trombone, snare and bass drums, and piano—the last used largely as a percussion instrument.[25]

A number of the experimental pieces Charlie was writing by then incorporated musical quotations, by now a constant stylistic feature, and contained other elements that showed these works to be acts of memory. But they were more than that as well: they were innovative essays and explorations of one or another aspect of musical form. The musical quotations in *Calcium Light Night* richly suggest the events of Tap Day and its more colorful antecedent, the procession associated with the selection to the junior fraternities. The three most prominently quoted tunes are fraternity songs, two from Delta Kappa Epsilon, to which Charlie belonged, and one from Psi Upsilon. At the time, he had written on a fragment of manuscript paper, "for On the Campus—Calcium Light Night."[26] Charlie vividly recalled the scene of the junior procession as well as the songs that accompanied it, when many years later he wrote out the words, along with the tunes, in a shaky hand:[27]

> 1) Psi U—Marching Song
> And again we sing thy praises ψ v, ψ v,
> And again we sing thy praises ψ Upsilon.
> We don't give a damn for D.K.E. ψ v, ψ v.
> We don't give a damn for D.K.E. ψ Upsilon.
> 2) When in after years we take our children on our knee
> We'll teach them that the alphabet begins with D.K.E.
> For we always are so jolly-o, jolly-o, jolly-o,
> For we always are so jolly-o D.K.E., etc.
> 3) DKE Marching Song
> A band of brothers in D.K.E. we march along tonight.
> 2 by 2 with arms locked close & tight.

In writing *Calcium Light Night*, Charlie reveals nostalgia for his college days and for an earlier time as well. Past memories abide in a context that informs and enriches the more recent ones. Indeed, the deep emotional background that Charlie brought to his college experiences lent them rich significance and caused them to endure in mind.

Tap Day was hardly the first time Charlie had witnessed a parade illuminated by calcium light. In the decades following the Civil War, torchlight parades were popular, especially around election time. Born of practicality and enhanced by tradition, they were also favored because of the sheer excitement they lent to the events. George and his band often performed at such occasions, and various sources of illumination were pressed into service, in particular the calcium light—otherwise known as limelight and commonly used in theaters. Such lamps, large in size and on portable mountings, were popular with fire companies, and so they found their way into nighttime parades of fire brigades. The local fire companies in Danbury, typical of the time, were also fraternal organizations, which frequently held celebrations, usually employing the local band; in Danbury, this meant George Ives. There were many such celebrations during Charlie's boyhood, especially in the 1880s: for example, an "advertisement" sponsored by the Kohanza Fire Company on August 29, 1883, reported in the Danbury *News*, "The advertising of an organization's picnic by music and fireworks the night before is a new feature, and one worthy of this great picnic year. The display made by Kohanza boys was very fine. . . . The fireworks went off without accident or delay, and in the flaming red light the elegant carriage showed up admirably. The company preceded by the band marched down to the Park. Back of them a calcium light, mounted in a wagon, gave the procession the appearance of an enormous comet."[28]

Thus, *Calcium Light Night* superimposes two memories. The more recent is the fraternity processional, the more distant a parade led by the composer's father, both representations of memory in music. But like every re-creation of memory, there is more to be sought—distortions of many kinds, including revisions and accruals from earlier times as well as associated affects. Music, being nonverbal, is fundamentally more ambiguous than the literary arts, but it may nevertheless subserve representation of a more subtle (if less readily decipherable) variety. The work aims toward as much symmetry as taste and judgment will allow. Its several sections are performed serially, leading up to a climactic turning point. Then each is repeated in retrograde fashion. The effect on the listener is that of a band approaching from a distance, passing in review, and fading away in the opposite direction. The volume is thus imitated quite literally while the tempo is distorted from its literal representation.[29] The approach and departure of the band in *Calcium* is a representation of presence and separation. Nor is this some spurious connection: it is enriched with associated affects. The excitement of anticipation is enhanced musically by a gradual quickening in tempo and increasing in volume of sound (*accelerando* and *crescendo*). The presence (actualized out of darkness) of the passing parade is rendered triple-*forte*, while a fading into the distance is highlighted by a gradual slowing and decrease in volume (*ritardando* and *diminuendo*). The music fades into a silence which is in itself an important musical element, starting and finishing the piece.

Marching bands, so important in Ives's auditory environment, are of course not actually perceived in this way. The volume of sound changes, but the tempo is constant. What may distort a tempo in actual performance has to do with an emotional element on the part of the performer. This may be seen in the child who, in the early stages of learning music, may become excited as a passage gets louder and so plays it faster as well. This device in *Calcium* may then relate to a yet earlier stage of Charlie's life and musical experience. At the same time, it draws our attention to the excitement he associated with his father and music. Conversely, as the band fades, it gets slower; distance is associated with slow time and quieter, if not sadder, affects. The piece, marked "slow march time," never quite decelerates into a dirge.

The title of the piece is strongly evocative of those visual elements that might enhance the excitement of such an experience. The light too is perceived at a distance and gradually reaches its fullest, glaring intensity before fading into darkness. Further, its climax of the piece may foster a loss of boundaries between sight and sound, a synesthesia in which the data of one perceptual modality are experienced in terms of another.[30]

In *Calcium Light Night* the erotic element is modified and displaced. The musical quotations are specifically not those regularly used in works of Ives associated with his father and his father's music; there is none of the sentimental, religious, or patriotic tunes that would become characteristic. Rather, the quotations are apparently from another era of Charlie's life—his Yale years, for they recall fraternity songs of the 1890s. Yet there is a matrix in mental life from which love of the father becomes a determinant of love of other men and their ideals. Charlie was more than opportunistic in his relationship with fraternity brothers. He embraced not only fraternity life but also the very ideal of fraternity with the utmost earnestness. *Calcium Light Night*, written when Ives was thirty, reveals a nostalgia for two earlier times, that of fraternity life in Yale and that in which the mental representation of Charlie's father was associated with groups of other men—the fraternal and quasi-fraternal groups of Danbury and, above all, George's own bandsmen. The very form in which the piece is cast, the march, represents the idea as well as the experience of men moving together. This was an experience dear to Charlie, associated at one extreme with the feeling of being a part of a corpus of men—whether the Yale "push rush" or the Danbury Cornet Band—and at the other with the ideals of patriotism, the love of his father's land.

Anticipating graduation in 1898, Charlie planned to go to New York. Although he had little idea of what he wished to do eventually, music continued to be important. First he secured a job as church organist—a post he had held continuously since he was fifteen—across the Hudson at the First Presbyterian Church in Bloomfield, New Jersey. The job served, among other things, as a familiar bridge to the past while he looked for a regular job and a permanent place to live. Meanwhile, he stayed at the Yale Club. If Charlie had any awareness of retracing his father's steps in a sojourn in New York, he never revealed it. But again it was a member of the White family who came forward with a job. Charlie contacted George's second cousin, Dr. Granville White, who was a medical examiner for the Mutual Life Insurance Company in New York, and White got Charlie a job in the actuarial department.

On June 26, 1898, the twenty-three-year-old organist Charles Ives played his first service at the First Presbyterian Church. That afternoon, he returned to New Haven, where Class Day, commencement, and other graduation festivities took place over the next few days. The class book of 1898 lists four nicknames for Charlie in a remarkable characterization of several aspects of his complex personality (the glosses are by Henry Cowell): "Dasher (the spontaneous and explosive Ives); Lemuel (the Ascetic New Englander); Quigg (the crotchety Quixote); and Sam (the punster and joker addicted to paradoxes)."[31] Significantly, nothing in the mix refers to anything musical. Later that summer, Charlie started to work at Mutual Life. By fall he was fortunate enough to find a place in a fourth-floor, cold-water walk-up on the West Side—one of two flats in the building shared by a group of Yale graduates. With companionate roommates, a piano in the other apartment, and what seemed to Charlie to be plenty of time to compose in the evenings and on weekends, all was in place for the next phase of his life.

BOOK THREE

THE RECONCILING YEARS

ELEVEN

POVERTY FLAT

T he uncertainties that clouded the first years after Ives's graduation from Yale are obscured by an engaging myth relating to the group of young men among whom Ives lived soon after he came to New York. The actual men and places changed from time to time, but the institution became known as Poverty Flat. Virtually none of the young men who occupied the movable premises was destined for poverty. Poverty Flat was understood to be a stepping stone to some great success in life (the modest institution had been founded a few years earlier by a group of Yale graduates attending the College of Physicians and Surgeons at Columbia University). But in the meantime one could enjoy the illusion of living *la vie de bohème*.[1]

The apartment at 317 West Fifty-eighth Street, to which Ives moved in September 1898, became an extension of his life at Yale and a base of operations from which to take his first steps in the outside world. The pressing question, however, was, In what direction? Far from settled at the outset, and characteristically juggling multiple elements, Ives continued to pursue all the endeavors he had cultivated at Yale.

Thus, for example, he kept his regular position as organist–choir director of the First Presbyterian Church in Bloomfield until he secured a more advantageous position in New York at the Central Presbyterian Church in April 1900. During these first New York years he continued to compose, and musical evidence suggests that he was considering a path not unlike that of his teacher,

Horatio Parker. For from 1898 to 1902 he wrote mostly pieces for organ and choir, among them settings of Psalms 14, 25, 100, and 135[2] and the *Three Harvest Home Chorales*.[3] Parker's continued influence can be seen in the ten or twelve songs Ives wrote, of which half were in French or German.[4] It is also evident in a major work of this period, Ives's cantata *The Celestial Country* (1898–99),[5] which demonstrates how Parker's life, work, and teaching were reverberating in every aspect of his student's life.

He did not ignore vernacular music, however. Ives wrote *The Yale-Princeton Football Game*[6] after attending the 1899 game with David Twichell. David had left Yale early in 1898 to volunteer in the Spanish-American War. He was graduated in absentia and remained in the army a year after the war. Returning in time to enroll in the College of Physicians and Surgeons in the fall, he moved into Poverty Flat. The full score of the *Yale-Princeton Game* (if it ever existed) is lost, but the surviving sketch reveals Ives's attempt to depict the game somewhat literally in music. Throughout the piece, the progress of the game is noted: "Fat guards pushing and grunting" (over bassoons), "dodging halfback" (under oboe), "1st down" (over piccolo trill), and "when Trumpet (= Running Half Back) (Charleyn Desaulles) reaches this meas. every other instrument must make a hell of a noise and stop." Appropriate cheers are also indicated. There is even a musical representation of the wedge formation! Charlie put the piece to use to keep in touch with classmates in other cities by sending them copies. Later, he also noted a housemate's approval on the sketch: "OK by Dick Schweppe 318 W 59 Nov. 1900". A reminiscence of still older days is included, a memo on the next-to-last staff: "Reeves 2nd Reg. Quickstep—always played by Brass Band at Games and reunions etc."

The brass band was, of course, George Ives's, and the Reeves March was the favorite of both Iveses. Despite Charlie's focus on music of the Parker variety during this period, a posthumous relationship with George persisted in his mental life and, as always, was reflected in the music he composed. For Ives concurrently worked on the *Second Symphony*, parts of which even date back in sketch to 1889, the heyday of his living collaboration with George. Declared finished in 1902, it was one of the two major works of this period, along with *The Celestial Country*. The musical style of both was basically conservative, with the form cast along the line of European nineteenth-century models. But in the *Second Symphony*, a distinctive voice emerges in the quotations of tunes associated with George Ives and with rural life in George's boyhood. *The Missionary Chant, Materna*, and, above all, *Bringing in the Sheaves* are associated with church and gospel music; *Camptown Races* and *Massa's in the Cold, Cold Ground* with Stephen Foster; *Reveille* and *The Red, White and Blue* with the Civil War. Additional elements are borrowed from European art music and at least one from Charlie's college experience (*Where, O Where Are the Verdant Freshmen*).[7]

Parker's influence can be seen principally in the form and George's in the content and associated affect of nostalgia. Ives himself felt that among all his works there was something distinctive about the *Second Symphony*. Very late in life, Ives once indicated to the Cowells that if he were ever to go out to hear his music, it would be if the *Second Symphony* were performed in Carnegie Hall, so full was it of nostalgic references to music of the period when his father was still alive.[8]

The Celestial Country suggests a different line of thinking. A cantata for organ, chorus, and orchestra with soloists, it was cast in the image of Parker's *Hora Novissima*, and Ives was not reticent in identifying himself to the newspapers as Parker's student when the work was performed. Moreover, he was indebted to Parker not only for the formal aspects of the cantata but for its ideational content and affective components as well. Ives chose as his text an English rendering of Henry Alford's Latin hymn *Forward! Be Our Watchword* (which he erroneously believed was derived from Bernard of Cluny, the author of Parker's Latin text).[9] As a student, Ives had resented exercises requiring strict modeling on the examples of established composers, although he did them for class and even included songs written under these circumstances in the *114 Songs*. He had certainly been unhappy about the "corrections" along traditional lines that Parker had urged in the *First Symphony*. Yet in *The Celestial Country* Ives probably came closer to this procedure than in any of his later major works. He emulated Parker here not only in text and music but even in the fundamental poetic idea, essentially a fantasy, of eternal life in the shining celestial city. The text of Parker's *Hora Novissima*, for example, ends with *Urbs Syon Inclyta*: "Thou city great and high, / Towering beyond the sky, / Storms reach thee never: / I seek thee, long for thee."[10] Ives's *Celestial Country* begins, "Far, far, far o'er yon horizon / Rise towers, rise city towers / Where our God our God abideth / That fair home is ours."[11] The music is similarly and uncharacteristically derivative. If the *Second Symphony* already had Ives's distinctive voice, the voice of the contemporaneous *Celestial Country* was Parker's.

Ives was testing out a potential direction both professionally and musically: the fantasy and the wish to be like Parker, to enjoy his success, and perhaps even to surpass him in kind. Music had become for Ives a mode of thinking, a mental workshop in which musical ideas were tried out and articulated with mental content in other forms—daydreams and wishes, for example. Thus, the imitation of Parker here is not mere regression; it serves a more complex psychological function. And incongruous as it may seem, *The Celestial Country*, which represents an identification with Parker and a host of related fantasies and strivings, may be compared to *The Yale-Princeton Game*, representing a memorialization of college days, a striving to be accepted among men, and the assertion of masculinity (and fear of its opposite) that sports had always meant to Ives.

Perhaps more to the point would be to compare the emotional factors that relate to *The Celestial Country* and the *Second Symphony*, the one representing Parker and the other the George Ives of the past. Psychologically speaking, Ives had more than one master to serve; the *Second Symphony* and *The Celestial Country* reveal them in different ways. Elements of compromise can be seen in the conception and realization of *The Celestial Country*. Parker had dedicated *Hora Novissima* to his own father, and the text reveals a fantasy of union and reunion. These were elements that doubtless appealed to Ives in his selection of a text whose author, he believed, was the same as Parker's. The text Ives chose, however, is more homespun and redolent with personal association, as in the accompanied quartet (no. 3): "Seek the things before us, / Not a look behind; / Burns the fiery pillar / At our army's head. / Who shall dream of shrinking / By our Captain led. / Forward through the desert, / forward through the toil and fight, / Jordan flows before us, / Zion beams with light. / Forward when in childhood / Buds the infant mind; / All through youth and manhood, / not a thought behind: / Speed through realms of nature, / Climbs the paths of grace; / till in glory / Gleams our Father's face."[12]

If Parker's Latin text aspires to High Episcopal, Ives's veers in the direction of Baptist. Even in this brief excerpt, ideas can be observed that Ives developed richly later. The flowing Jordan will appear in quotation in the *Fourth Violin Sonata* and ultimately, in excerpt in *114 Songs, At The River*.[13] The "Captain" was always Abraham Lincoln to Ives, with his associations to George.[14] The reference to father as spirit subsumes the temporal father. Equally important to the associations of text, however, is the realization of ideas and affect inherent in the text, in the music. Already we find the germ of a musical idea that Ives repeated time and again: an upwardly striving tonal figure associated with textual elements of optimism or utopian ideals.

Thus Ives brought to his identification with Parker distinctive elements of his own mental life. At the same time, the composition of *The Celestial Country* involved an element of submission to the master, at least in terms of adherence to his rules. The exemplary musician of his time had been rewarded with a classically successful career. *Hora Novissima* had at first been hailed as an inspired work of contemporary music by an American, although it very rapidly became unfashionable. Within a year, Parker's reputation had grown to the extent that he was awarded a Yale professorship. Ives very likely harbored such a fantasy of success for himself.[15] If so, it related to a wish to be favored not only by the fates but by Parker. Yet Parker had already designated his favorite, David Stanley

Smith (Yale, 1900). Smith sometimes came by Poverty Flat, so Ives was in a position to follow his career. Ives himself, this once in any event, was testing out doing the "right thing" in the composition of *The Celestial Country*.

But this represents only one facet of creative work. Ives composed a few smaller pieces; more important, the seeds of the *First Piano Sonata* and even the *Third Symphony* were already germinating in his mind. Yet this represented only the musical side of his life. At the same time, he was also testing out a business career. In fact, for a time, starting the year after graduation from Yale, Ives was studying law in the evenings. His brother, Moss, had received his LL.B. after a year's study at Yale in 1888–89 and had just been admitted to the Connecticut bar. Ives was uncertain enough about his own direction to test out this avenue as well.

By early 1902, Ives was well enough established at the Central Presbyterian Church to arrange for the first performance of *The Celestial Country*. Preparation for the April 18 performance involved no small effort. Although Ives was already hedging his bets by pursuing a business career and was in any event ambivalent about following Parker's example, he could hardly suppress the wish that this premiere might be the gateway to a respectable career in music. The Kaltenborn Quartet was engaged as well as fourteen soloists to perform the vocal parts and support the church choir. Ives himself conducted from the organ.

That he could not quite yield to the realistic requirements of his own fantasy or at least felt compelled to express spontaneously a degree of individuality is evident from a later reminiscence of the event. In looking over the score, Ives found it "hard to realize that anybody could have found anything very unusual or original in it. . . . But, come to think [of it, I] do remember that, in playing the first and last choruses of [the cantata, I] would throw in 7ths on top of the triad in right hand, and a sharp 4th against a Doh-Soh-Doh in the left hand. . . . This would give a dissonant tinge to the whole, that the Musical Courier man was not quite used to, and so to him it seemed unusual."[16] Kirkpatrick genially relates the use of the dissonant tritone that Ives describes (C-F♯) to the piano-drumming chords he later devised.[17] It might also be viewed as a form of nose-thumbing, a musical Bronx cheer.[18] (A third possibility might be Ives's later tendency to add dissonances after the fact—here, in fantasy and over thirty years later.) Neither the piece as written nor Ives's sly additions seem to have made an enormous impression on the reviewers from the New York *Times* or the *Musical Courier*, both of whom noted that Ives was a student of Horatio Parker. The *Courier*'s reviewer responded rather positively. He wrote, "The work shows undoubted earnestness in study, and talent for composition. . . . Beginning with a prelude, trio and chorus, with soft, long-drawn chords of mysterious meaning . . . the music swells to a fine climax. . . . Throughout the work there is homogeneity, coming from the interweaving of appropriate themes etc." The critic acknowledged "some original ideas" and even suggested that one of the movements, the intermezzo for strings, might be performed as a concert piece by the Kaltenborn Quartet.[19]

Certainly many composers have fared far less well at a first New York performance. From all evidence, however, Ives appears to have been deeply discouraged by the response to the performance. It was not just the passing letdown following great effort. He was dejected and preoccupied, a state of mind which heralded a major decision. Immediately after this incident Ives, as he put it, "gave up music": he resigned his position at Central Presbyterian within a week after the performance and gave his last Sunday service six weeks later, on June 1, 1902. Thereafter Ives never held any professional position related to music, nor did he earn a penny from music. And his works received no performances of any significance for the next fourteen years.[20]

Ives's response to the performance appears to be out of proportion to the events. What might he have been expecting? The reception was not completely without promise. And if he had wished to follow Parker's path, this was hardly a signal that his way would be blocked. Ives was generally inclined not to make hasty decisions, and if anything he strove to maintain all options. It seems likely that his decision to "give up music"—that is, give up a career in music—was already made and that the act itself was ceremonial. He had delayed action, gambling on the performance—a magical shot in the dark to provide fate with the opportunity to favor him richly. What may not have been tolerable was the merely modest success he could at best anticipate, which he would construe as failure. His ambivalence may have been revealed in the self-sabotage of the dissonant improvisation in the performance. If a sense of low esteem prevailed after the performance and depression settled in—not for the last time in his life—this had less to do with outer events than with these ambivalent requirements of inner life. For even if the performance had been successful in Parker's terms, Ives would have viewed it as giving in—submitting to Parker and giving up an individuality which he valued and cultivated and had shared earlier with his father. Equally important, success in music, especially the prospect of earning as comfortable a living as Parker did, would declare Charlie once and for all superior to George, the failed village bandmaster.

Intrapsychically, unconsciously, Ives had made a compromise: giving up music. Resigning from the minor position of church organist signaled a deeper resignation. He would no longer compete or strive in the direction of Parker, for neither winning nor losing could entail happy consequences. Instead, a new phase of creative life beckoned, one in which he would continue composing in what appeared to be artistic isolation. In fantasy, it was an isolation previously shared with his father. Thus, the compromise involved not only resignation but also surrender, a yielding to the needs and demands of the past which required restitution, reunion, and rescue. Paradoxically, while this was part of a process of prolonged mourning, George still could not be put to rest. The compromise, however, constituted a turning point in Ives's life and marked a new phase in his collaboration with George. He was now poised to write the best of his music and, in fantasy, his father's music as well. The occasion of the concert had brought this about. Now only a catalyst was required to set it in motion. And that catalyst would soon appear in the person of Harmony Twichell.

The spring of 1902 marked four years since Ives's college graduation. His business career, while not completely without promise, was still uncertain. Meanwhile, life was progressing for others. Moss was well established in law practice, as Uncle Lyman's partner in the Danbury firm of Brewster, Davis, and Ives. In addition, he had assumed some of Lyman's commitments and was secretary to the National Conference on Uniform State Laws. A year earlier, he had been designated corporation counsel of Danbury. More indicative of life moving on, Moss had married Minnie Goodman of Danbury in December 1900, and in February 1902, Richard, their first child, was born. George had been twenty-nine when Charlie was born. Ives, now approaching his twenty-eighth birthday, was far from marriage and family. He was accustomed to being the star of the family; the circumstances of life were creating a far different picture.

It was also in 1902 that Ives completed the *Second Symphony*—at least for the moment. Short works such as the *Ragtime Pieces* of 1902 and 1904[21] and the *Country Band March* of 1902[22] seem to be written from a new perspective. The apparent prominence of the vernacular is deceptive. Burkholder observes that such works "are no longer simply vernacular pieces but are concert pieces that are 'about' vernacular styles and vernacular performance, quoting tunes, using familiar ragtime rhythms, and evoking the spirit and atmosphere of performances by amateur musicians."[23] He calls such pieces *fictional music.*[24] I suggest that *autobiographical music* might be a more apt term because it is more specific. What the music was about was experiences in Ives's life, of which music was a part. He was able to symbolize elements of complex events in terms of significant musical form. Ives seems to have practiced and refined this technique throughout the period.

Ives began work concurrently on his next symphony, the *Third*. The dates he gives it are 1901–12, but by 1904, the first and third of the three movements were fully scored.[25] It is a pivotal work in many respects. Two of its movements, Ives later pointed out, were revised and scored from organ pieces written in 1901, while he was at Central Presbyterian. (At some point he had used them in the church service.) Ives himself later wondered about this crossroads in his life. "I quite often think of and wonder about [it]. . . . The last time I looked at the *Third Symphony*, it was brought back to my mind . . . it's a kind of crossway between the older ways and the newer ways. . . . And I sometimes feel that something like the following accounted for it. I seemed to have worked with more natural freedom when I knew that the music was not going to be played before the public, or rather before people who couldn't get out from under, as is the case in a church congregation." With regard to "religious matters, not until I got to work on the *Fourth Symphony* did I feel justified in writing quite as I wanted to."26

The *Third Symphony* was subtitled *The Camp Meeting*, with three movements called *Old Folks Gathering*, *Children's Day*, and *Communion*. The affective sense of the piece is deeply religious, owing in part to the fact that virtually every borrowed tune is from a hymn. The series of musical tableaux has an intense, concentrated effect that reflects the means by which it is achieved. The chamber orchestra for which it was written is a tightly organized group consisting only of strings, four winds, three brass, and bells. If the *Second Symphony* cannot be said to be "exclusively American,"27 the *Third Symphony* can in terms of form and content, as well as the means of rendering both. It contains an evolving and original voice not heard previously. The classical features and European allusions so important in the *Second Symphony* are no longer called upon, and other solutions are found for technical problems.

After 1902, Ives wrote no further music of the kind he had written for church choir or organ solo up to that point. Burkholder is correct in asserting that Ives "was leaving behind not just a position, but also the genres and purposes for music associated with it."28 Ives may have given up any aspiration to lead a life like Parker's, but he clearly retained Parker's influence in terms of genre.29 At the same time, he utilized media and procedures in his own way, developing new forms. Burkholder discerns two directions. One is purely experimental; the other, characteristic of the concert music written throughout this period (about 1902–08), he describes as a "cumulative form that develops motives from a borrowed theme, usually a hymn tune, and often presents important countermelodies over the course of a movement before the theme itself is presented in full."30 This latter development is clear in the *Third Symphony*. Accordingly, the musical universe rendered is no longer reminiscent of Dvořák's "New World" in any way. It is Ives's personal world of Danbury newly discovered.

The "natural freedom" Ives mentions twice as characteristic of this period of composition was exercised in privacy and isolation. The statement that he became a "weekend composer" falls short of taking into account the human process involved in composing. This is important to the understanding of how Ives's music became autobiography. In composing, musical problem solving overlaps other kinds of mental activity. The primary work of the composer—the invention of musical form—articulates with all other aspects of mental life. Ideas symbolized in one medium or sphere of experience must somewhere be translatable into another. An idea, for example, may be represented in visual or auditory terms. Similarly, affects may be experienced or represented multiply. Fundamentally, ideas and affects are infinitely displaceable in mental life. It is thus that the ideational and affective aspects of experience and memory may find representation in auditory form in music. This is the mode in which Ives's music became autobiographical.

As in the *Second* and *Third* symphonies, there is much in Charles Ives's music that suggests aspects of George Ives. The trend continued in other works of the period. For example, Ives's earliest attempt at a violin sonata, later called the *Pre-First*, sketched between 1901 and 1903, is full of quotations and evocations of the past.[31] In thus tracing Ives's continued intrapsychic relationship with his father, one can follow the process and progress of mourning as well as its failures. In this regard, if 1902 represented a milestone, it also marked a shift from random reminiscence to a more organized and enacted form, the beginning of a posthumous intrapsychic collaboration that took up where the actual one had faltered in the year or so before George's death and ceased completely on November 4, 1894. Thus "giving up music" in 1902 was Ives's characteristically paradoxical way of indicating a beginning.

Now music all the more pervaded Ives's mental life, and from this point on, his external life would be organized to accommodate it. This is not to say that Ives failed to be conscientious in his business tasks, only that they did not demand his all, that music was more compelling, and that he had the mental capacity to manage both at the same time. In all likelihood, the business demands on his energy at this point were not great, although the demands on his time may have been more exacting.

Composing is a mental activity requiring concentrated inner listening to a near-hallucinatory flow of virtual sound with endless exploration of possibilities. The actual notation is a relatively mechanical task that may be discharged at any time after choices have been made and the results fixed in mind. There can be no question about the competence and capacity of Ives's musical mind. However unconventional the melody or complex the rhythms, Ives could "hear" and reproduce what he heard mentally, either physically in performance or graphically on the manuscript page. His creative instrument was with him constantly, and during these years he was probably using it much of the time when he was apparently engaged in other activities. The evidence consists, first, in his large output considering that he could "write" music only in the evenings, on weekends, and during vacations. Second, Ives at this time began a practice that was to continue throughout his creative lifetime: he notated rapidly in barely legible sketches as quickly as possible, planning to revise them later. Even before he could comfortably afford to do so, he began to engage copyists; as early as 1901, he had music copied at the William Tams Copying Bureau.

Meanwhile, Ives was diligently trying to find and establish a business career for himself. In fact, had it not been for his church positions and the single performance, few people would have had any inkling of Ives's ongoing involvement with music. After 1902, Ives's double life became entrenched. It involved greater isolation musically. Although Ives was never a hustler in business or outgoing in business relationships, he did maintain a public facade in commerce that stood in strong contrast to the privacy of his creative life. He had cultivated this stance in relationships at college, in which he often had a quality of standing at a respectful distance while strongly desiring admiration and acceptance. Now these qualities came into play in the business world.

Ives always did his best in a partnership, as in his musical collaboration with George. In business life, too, Ives needed a partner, and he managed to find one in the unlikely person of Julian Myrick.

Julian Southall Myrick, called Mike, was born in Murfreesboro, North Carolina. His father, Charles, a horse breeder, moved his family to Virginia when Mike was three and then to Dobbs Ferry, New York, when he was twelve. Four and a half years younger than Ives, Mike had dropped out of the Trinity School in New York at seventeen over an argument with his family about which college he should attend. Mike got a job with a friend, which involved wiring electrical signs to steel frames perched on tall buildings. The signs would sometimes sway high above traffic. When his parents learned of his dangerous pursuit, they persuaded him to quit and go to business school—at that time, the last honorable refuge of the academic failure. Mike lasted three months, after which his father got him a job with an agency of the Mutual Life Insurance Company, the Charles H. Raymond Agency in New York, where he and Ives met.[32]

Mike Myrick was a plucky, energetic young man—bright, outgoing, likable, and with a charming Southern manner. Restless and athletically inclined, he was far from ideally suited for the position of applications clerk at the Raymond Agency. Before long, he took a leave of absence.

Meanwhile, Ives was working as an actuarial clerk at the parent company, a position he had got with the help of George's second cousin, Dr. Granville White. As poorly suited for this job as Myrick was for his, and further handicapped by his unreadable handwriting, Ives also had barely escaped being fired. Instead, he was transferred to the Raymond Agency, through which Mutual did most of its business; there he was to replace Myrick while he was away. Eventually, Myrick returned, and somehow the scarcely competent pair managed to keep their jobs with the agency for a half dozen years.

It is unclear what either of them did during that period.[33] Neither actually sold insurance. If Ives was involved with agents in the field, it was surely not in a supervisory position, although it appears that Myrick supervised clerical work.[34] The two young men may have been kept on at first through outside influence. Nepotism was rife, and both Ives and Myrick had gotten their jobs through family. They were not paid much (Myrick started at fifty dollars a month), and, consistent with the disorder in the insurance industry at the time, there was probably a fair amount of administrative inefficiency. But meanwhile, the pair had an opportunity to learn the business from the inside. Each was good material in his own way. A combination of charm, common sense, and good salesmanship would ultimately earn Myrick the title "Mr. Life Insurance." Ives, as Rossiter observes, had the "'proper' ethnic and social background, his Yale diploma and his social contacts." Thus he was considered "an excellent prospect for an executive position." And after six years at Mutual, both men could roughly fill the role of junior executive.[35]

What undoubtedly kept them going was the prospect of a great deal of money. Ives and Myrick were watching and learning. It could not have escaped their notice that some people were earning vast amounts in the fledgling industry. Robert Grannis, for example, Mutual's vice president and a distant cousin of Ives, was earning $200,000 a year. Mutual's president, Richard A. McCurdy, drew a salary of $300,000, and his son Robert, executive head of the Raymond Agency, a salary of $30,000 plus commissions totaling over $100,000. As it turned out, Raymond got virtually all of Mutual's business. In fact, it was exactly such nepotistic practices that led Senator William W. Armstrong to launch an investigation in 1905.

The life insurance industry in America is largely a nineteenth-century phenomenon. Mutual Life of New York, incorporated in 1842, was one of the two oldest commercial insurers. By the last quarter of the century, practices and disregard of the duties of trusteeship were epidemic. Insolvencies by insurers were occurring as frequently as one a month, leaving policyholders helpless to collect on their claims.[36]

Corruption was widespread, and among other excesses were lucrative commissions given to favored local agents out of first-year premiums, which were supposedly held in trust, as well as the exertion of undue political influence.[37] Commissions and salaries were extravagant and nepotism widespread; some insurers were also in banking, which they naturally favored. Public resentment had led the New York legislature to appoint the Armstrong Committee, with Charles Evans Hughes as its chief counsel. Although Hughes made it clear that it was not the institution of life insurance that was on trial but its excesses, there was a wave of panic in the industry.

The end result of the Armstrong investigation was the regulation of the industry established in the New York Insurance Code of 1906. It is generally felt that the housecleaning paved the way for the development of the life insurance industry in America.[38] Shortly before, Mutual did some housecleaning of its own, purging itself of some of its more unscrupulous executives. In the shuffle, the Charles Raymond Agency was closed, its owner, Colonel Raymond, having been involved in questionable dealings with the dismissed executives.

There is no evidence to suggest that either Ives or Myrick had participated in the practices exposed by the Armstrong investigation or that they were even in a position to do so. But they would certainly have been aware of these practices, which were not illegal at the time. One may speculate that they narrowly escaped being a part of, or at least associated with, the corrupt old guard of the field whose roles they were aspiring to fill. With the inevitable reorganization, in which established companies and executives disappeared from the scene, opportunities for new people and companies were created. Ives and Myrick thus became beneficiaries rather than victims of the Armstrong investigation; again they were in the right place at the right time. They became good friends.

The Armstrong Committee was relentless, and the general stress in the industry reached all of its workers. To those who were not involved in the lucrative and soon-to-be illegal practices, their livelihood and future were at stake. Ives, now thirty-two years old, had made an investment of eight years for an uncertain reward. Men whom he may once have viewed as models were being exposed as corrupt, and a sense of shame by association prevailed.

If Ives had viewed the events of 1902 as signaling a failure in music, a few years later, in 1905, failure threatened in his second pursuit, business. In the background was his father, the beloved failure. The dream of earning anything close to cousin Robert Grannis's annual $200,000 served to reconnect the George Ives family to the old Iveses of Danbury and their now affluent progeny.

On February 14, 1904, a year before the Armstrong investigation, Lyman Brewster died at the age of seventy-one. He had revised his will a month earlier with a final gesture of admiration for Amelia, "because it is chiefly owing to her forethought and economy that I have anything to will." He left his law library to Moss and named both Moss and Charlie as his heirs after Amelia, designating them joint executors of his will.

Ives returned to Danbury for Lyman's funeral. Although he continued to make regular visits, as time went on he derived less and less pleasure from them. The disparity between the country town of his memory and increasingly urbanized Danbury grated on him. He much preferred the fantasied, mythologized Danbury of his own private invention, which he could reexperience in his autobiographical compositions, which were infused with the feeling of loss and nostalgia. Current losses had a way of reevoking earlier losses and eliciting feelings associated with them. In this way, the death of Lyman, his second father, gave additional impetus to the chronic process of mourning that Ives was engaged in for his first. But he mourned his uncle, too—as usual, through music and with a degree of guilt.

Between Ives and his uncle there was an unfinished collaboration on an opera based on Lyman's play *Major John Andre*. The idea may have dated from 1893, but over the years Ives had not written a note specifically devoted to the work. In the summer of 1903, Lyman was suffering from his final illness. Ives began a piece for chamber orchestra, *Overture and March: 1776*,[39] writing that at the time "we were talking about making it into an opera."[40] He was responding to an impulse to both memorialize Lyman and discharge an obligation. The piece was also a companion to *Country Band March*, written the year before.[41] But in the earlier piece, tunes associated with George Ives and the Civil War were richly quoted—*Marching through Georgia, The Battle Cry of Freedom*, and others. In *1776*, Ives borrowed tunes related to the Revolutionary War—*Hail Columbia* and *The British Grenadiers*—a war that Ives had always associated with his uncle.[42]

In December 1903, back in Danbury for Christmas, Ives started to score *1776*, noting under the title, "for Uncle Lyman's Opera as such." It was no doubt his hope to finish it before Lyman died and so to please the old man and make good on an old promise. This was not to be; Ives failed to complete the manuscript over the holidays, although he may well have thought it out. Lyman's death in February would have rekindled Ives's feelings about his father in any event, the more so by repeating a situation of parting amid unfinished business. The funeral at the family plot in Wooster Cemetery was the first since George's death. In the midst of composing the other works of the ensuing year, Ives found time to complete *1776* in Danbury the following summer. He inscribed the manuscript, "Pine Mt.—July–1904. Danbury ct."[43]

Pine Mountain, about three miles southwest of Danbury, was a piece of property owned by the family, probably the Brewsters. The summer when Ives started *1776*, he, along with a friend from Poverty Flat, had managed to erect a "shanty" there, making "a good young camp," according to Ives. He noted, however, that "[we] did it unbenowed [sic] to Aunt Amelia fearing adverse suggestions."[44] It was one of the outdoor locales Ives loved best, a precursor to later favorite places in the Adirondacks and to the house and pond at Redding, where he finally settled. At Pine Mountain in the autumn of 1904, probably around the anniversary of George's death, Ives had an idea for a piece he called "An Autumn Landscape from Pine Mt. 1904. Strings, woodwind, Cornet (muted) is heard from Ridgebury."[45] Although Ives put the work on one of his several lists of compositions, no music has ever been found. The idea of the sound of a muted cornet wafting through the air from westerly Ridgebury suggests that this was an early version of *The Pond* (1906),[46] which became *Remembrance* in the *114 Songs*.[47] The melancholy references in word and tone reveal Ives's mood. Distance and separation are represented in both time and space. The imagined muted cornet tones come from the west—the direction of the setting sun, a symbol of death.

Although events of a personal nature may have given impetus to the music Ives was writing at this time and endowed it with layers of meaning, the music thus produced was increasingly sophisticated and innovative. Its roots may have been similar to those that produced Lyman's stilted, amateurish, sentimental play, but the result was quite different. Perhaps it was Ives's awareness of this— ultimately his musical judgment and taste—that made it impossible for him ever to set *Major Andre* to music. Thus *1776* was a kind of compromise as well as an example of Ives's representational skill in music. Here Ives incorporated one of his finest and most characteristic takeoffs, a musical imitation of the amateur country band he knew from childhood, with melodies played off key, drummers losing the beat, and cornetists failing to insert the detachable shank that produces the correct key. On the manuscript score, Ives wrote by way of direction and explanation, "2 cornets—B [flat] A shanks get mixed up—with small orchestra better to have Clar. play some of A shank as wrong notes." A complex wrong-beat rhythm is achieved by the instruction, "Just drop 1-eight beat every 4 measures."[48]

Here is autobiographical music at its best, a refreshing fabricated reminiscence but sophisticated and interesting musically in its own right. Similarly, when Ives developed the idea of having the sound of his father's muted cornet waft over the autumnal landscape—the mountain space transformed into the pond—he created a musical idea of uncommon auditory interest from a simple, sentimental tune. Part of the interest derives from the idea and representation of space in music, part from the arrest of time in the slowness of the tune. Regardless of psychological background, then, works such as these stand on their own musically, although a sense of their human source may lend them special appeal.

Sometime during this period Ives began to notice David Twichell's sister, Harmony. He viewed her as formidable from the first. His feeling that so able and attractive a young woman, successful in all she undertook, would not have accepted him may even have contributed to his melancholy and sense of loss in the autumn of 1904, when he learned from David that Harmony had become engaged to the Reverend Walter Lowrie, the son of a family friend and neighbor from the Twichells' summer community in the Adirondacks. The engagement proved to be a brief one. Kirkpatrick suggests that it was "early in 1905 that she met Charlie again."[49] If so, a separation occurred at the beginning of their renewed relationship, when Harmony went off to Europe for two months as companion to Mrs. Dean Sage, a friend of her father's.

While business life became increasingly stressful around the time of the Armstrong investigation in 1905 and the period immediately preceding it, composition was taking a physical toll. Music filled Ives's nonbusiness hours. He began to sleep less. Although at times his output may have flagged, composing had become an autonomous daily activity throughout the period. Ives tended to be working on several pieces at the same time, keeping them all in his head and beginning to notate ideas on scraps of paper or on blank portions of other manuscripts. There seemed to be a period of integration during which Ives incorporated earlier experimental ideas into apparently traditional forms. Before and during 1905, he continued to work on the *Third Symphony*, the *Trio* for violin, cello, and piano,[50] the *First Piano Sonata*,[51] and the first of the violin sonatas.[52] With a single exception (the scherzo of the *Trio*), experiments, humor, and takeoffs seemed to be in abeyance, possibly reflecting Ives's mood. He spoke of a composer's "slump,"[53] which occurred from time to time, during which he would revert to conventional styles of composition. The term also served to acknowledge a periodic and generalized sense of depression.

The "slump" of 1905 was likely to have been frank depression. It followed a period of fervent creative activity and was precipitated by exhaustion as well as realistic concerns stemming from the Armstrong investigation. It was associated with a low sense of esteem and dread of what the future might bring. The pattern of a periodic disturbance of mood—cyclothymia—was becoming apparent in the thirty-year-old Ives. There is insufficient evidence to suggest a clear manic-depressive (or bipolar) illness, but the disturbance of 1905 appears to go beyond the moodiness of the "Dasher" and "Quigg" of the 1898 Yale yearbook. From this time on, mood swings—whether gradual over a period of weeks or months or rapid within hours or days—became ever more apparent in Ives.

Meanwhile, Ives's classmates, brother Moss, and some of the original men of Poverty Flat were becoming established and leaving. David Twichell, a relative latecomer, had graduated from the College of Physicians and Surgeons in 1903 and was practicing at Edward Livingston Trudeau's tuberculosis sanatorium on Saranac Lake. He was rapidly becoming a specialist in the field and was already preparing papers for publication. David was home in Hartford in the early spring, and Ives made what seems to have been an urgent visit to see him. Aunt Amelia, alarmed, later revealed her concern about the likelihood of a "nervous collapse."[54]

David invited Ives to spend a few weeks with him at the family retreat at Robert's Camp in the Adirondacks. Ives not only accepted but even stayed longer than planned, which meant that an anticipated visit to Danbury had to be postponed. Aunt Amelia, who was demanding of Ives's attention after Lyman's death, was evidently worried enough about his health to yield to his greater need, however grudgingly. Characteristically, she proffered guidance: "I should not wish you to stay your 'welcome' out but if you should think best to stay in the Mountains (now you are there) that is, spend most of the month and only give us a day or two . . . We want you to get the *most good* possible out of your time and while you know we are always glad to have you home, your health is of the first importance and we wish you to do what is best."[55]

At Saranac, Ives's flagging energy seemed to revive as his depression lifted for the moment. He made sketches for a piece for horn and strings which was destined to become an important element in the *Fourth Symphony*. As Ives noted on the sketch, it was done "at the suggestion of DCT—Saranac Lake 1905."[56] He also began another piece, which he noted "started as Cornet & Violins Qu piece 1905 (with Dave CT at Saranac Aug 1905 . . .)."[57] This became the third movement of the *Fourth Violin Sonata*, called *Children's Day at the Camp Meeting*. It was an unusual setting of the hymn *Beautiful River*, a particular favorite of David's. What David had suggested for the horn piece was another hymn, *Watchman Tell Us of the Night*, the hymn that haunts the beginning of the *Fourth Symphony*.

Thus David Twichell briefly became Ives's collaborator, and in effect his healer, during the weeks at Saranac. This healing, however, was not the physical healing Twichell sought for his patients; it was spiritual. Wooldridge suggests that the two attended a camp meeting at Saranac,[58] which may have reevoked for Ives the tender memories of camp meetings he went to with his father. The words to the hymn *Beautiful River* form a question and an answer:

> Shall we gather by the river
> Where bright angel feet have trod
> With its crystal tide forever
> flowing by the throne of God?
>
> Yes, we'll gather by the river
> The beautiful, the beautiful river
> Yes, we'll gather at the river
> that flows by the throne of God.

Ives was shortly to become interested in philosophical and musical questions and answers, as demonstrated by one of his best-known works, *The Unanswered Question* (1906). *Watchman* too is about a question and answer:

Watchman, tell us of the night,
What its signs of promise are:
Traveler, o'er yon mountain's height,
See that glory beaming star.

Watchman, does its beauteous ray
Aught of joy or hope foretell?
Traveler, yes; it brings the day,
Promised day of Israel.

The "question" that was beginning to preoccupy Ives was the question of death, and the pieces reflected his manner of thinking about it. Another person might ruminate; Ives composed. The fantasy of a hopeful answer, the hymn's comforting promise, is that of reunion. Ives transformed the "shining city" of *Hora Novissima* and *The Celestial Country* into something closer to home in his renderings of familiar hymn tunes. In his preoccupation, Ives was finding those philosophical and musical ideas that would come to determine the direction and shape of his music, influencing the many choices involved in the forging of musical form. When *Beautiful River*, for example, was turned into the third movement of the violin sonata, *Children's Day*, the entire movement took on the form of a question.[59] The theme is not *given;* it is *sought* and eventually makes its full appearance. The movement and the sonata conclude with a repeat of the first phrase of the hymn, sung to the verse "Shall we gather at the river?" But no answer follows—no resolution, no ending; silence prevails. And the silence of that unresolved phrase carries the unsung affirmation, "Yes, we'll gather by the river."

By the time the *Fourth Symphony* was eventually assembled in 1916, Ives had developed its first movement richly from the germinal idea noted during the summer of 1905 at Saranac. The morbid preoccupations of a discouraged and depressed young man mired in an unresolved state of mourning had by then been transformed symbolically into a vast artistic statement of hope, redemption, and reunion. But for the moment, the healing friendship with David Twichell helped Ives through a difficult time. David did, in fact, arrange an actual reunion for Ives with Harmony. She had planned to visit Saranac early in September, and David encouraged Ives to remain for a few days. Toward the end of the visit to Saranac, in a burst of activity, Ives wrote a piano piece which, as he sketched it in pencil, filled three manuscript pages. In a sassy mood, he noted at a repeat sign: "back to 1st theme—all nice sonatas must have 1st theme." He was feeling better. The piece received its name, *Three-Page Sonata*, from Ives's note at the end: "End of '3 page Sonata' Fine at Saranac L. NY with Dave—Aug '05."[60]

The reunion with Harmony was equally restoring. She later wrote, "That day we went up to Saranac seems almost a miracle—I remember saying then, as we looked across the lake to the mountains at sunset that I didn't think Paradise could be any more beautiful; nor do I.[61] Amelia herself had to acknowledge, with relief, the effect of this vacation, revealing at the same time the depth of her concern: "It is not strange that men in business circles break down—for many of them are working to the very *limit*—in ordinary times and then when additional strain comes . . . there is no reserve strength to meet the emergency—I hope this has quieted down for *good* and that *all* may have rest."[62]

TWELVE

QUESTIONINGS

Ives's "giving up" of music in 1902 had paradoxically brought about a greater commitment to it. But by 1905, the vigorous and innovative thrust of the music seemed spent, a symptom of the depression Ives rationalized as composer's "slump." When the creative spirit broke through once again the following year, it required an exhausting effort for Ives to organize. Ideas for experimental works bubbled over and were realized in brief, highly unique works which had to be sketched in a hurry. Nor was this creative activity necessarily a result of a complete lifting of Ives's bleak mood; equally, it was a part of its persistence. Aunt Amelia's hope that his troubled state had quieted down for good had not come to pass. By year's end, in December 1906, Ives suffered what was considered a physical breakdown of some indeterminate kind. It was later referred to as a heart attack, but there is no evidence of any cardiac symptoms. Ives spent Christmas recuperating at a spa at Old Point Comfort, Virginia, accompanied by Julian Myrick.

Although standard biographical materials are mute with regard to 1906, Ives's creative output tells a story of its own. He wrote in his *Scrapbook*:

Around this time, running say from 1906 (from the time of Poverty Flat days) up to about 1912–14 or so, things like *All the Way Around and Back, The Gong on the Hook and Ladder, Over the Pavements, Tone Roads, The Unanswered Question,* etc., were made. Some of them were played or better tried out usually ending in a fight or hiss. . . . I must say that many of those things were started as kinds of studies, or rather trying out sounds, beats, etc., usually by

187

what is called politely "improvisation on the keyboard"—what classmates in the flat called "resident disturbances."[1]

All the pieces to which Ives refers here were highly individual and experimental. Most were composed in 1906 or at least had their inception in that year. Others were part of a trend characteristic of this period. These pieces had their forerunners in the musical jokes and takeoffs of earlier years and in certain recent works that were unfinished, only conceptualized, adapted for something else later, or simply lost. Among these forerunners were the two pieces Ives had worked on with David Twichell the previous summer at Lake Saranac, one for horn and one for cornet, in which hymn tunes were prominent.

All these experimental works are richly associated with Ives's continuing inner relationship with his father. Another precursor, what Ives called "An Autumn Landscape," had been an anniversary meditation on George's death. Unscored as far as is known, it may have existed only in the musical imagination of its composer. And if so, as conceptual music, it was harbinger to the later *Universe Symphony*. Ives's continuing meditations through this extraordinarily productive period may be traced in the *Piece for Small Orchestra and Organ*, written some time after the summer of 1905.[2] It was scored for the kind of unusual combination Ives had begun to experiment with—here organ, trumpet, trombone, clarinet, flute, and strings. He called the piece "a kind of brass band outdoors organ indoors" and arranged it for violin and piano, hoping to get a performance of it from the Kaltenborn Quartet, which had performed his *Celestial Country*. Later, the piece was adapted to become one of Ives's most remarkably condensed and sophisticated representations of nostalgic reminiscence in song, *The Things Our Fathers Loved*.

The quotations and borrowings already present in the *Piece for Small Orchestra and Organ* serve as a not quite subliminal backdrop to the words of the later song: *In the Sweet Bye and Bye, The Battle Cry of Freedom, On the Banks of the Wabash, My Old Kentucky Home, Dixie*, and the hymn *Nettleton*. The associations of these tunes in Ives's early life were rich. *Nettleton*, for example, Ives remembered vividly from the Redding camp meetings.[3] But the ongoing influence of George is revealed in more than musical content. First, all these works are written for a motley group of instruments typical of pickup theater orchestras such as George led. Ives heard many such unusual combinations in his youth, and now, in some of his works, he developed personal variations of this idea. Second, these are among his most experimental works, continuing a private exploration of musical materials in accordance with what he came to construe as his father's musical principles. George, the experimenter, not only remains alive through Ives's identification and idealization. He becomes exaggerated and, in some respects, invented.

The nature of the experimentation was both playful and serious, capturing what Ives loved best in his father's character. Ives occasionally disavowed the seriousness of his own endeavors. In the *Trio* for violin, cello, and piano, for example, the second movement, which incorporates *In the Sweet Bye and Bye*, *Marching through Georgia*, *Old Kentucky Home*, and *The Fountain*, is entitled "TSIAJ," standing for "This scherzo is a joke." Ives began the trio at his sixth Yale class reunion in 1904 and worked on it over the following years. He had written a memo in the score by way of title: "Trio . . . Yalensia & Americana Fancy Names Real name: Yankee jaws—at Mr. (or Eli) Yale's School for nice bad boys!!"[4] The scherzo is anything but a joke musically. It incorporates large segments of well-known tunes in a complex rhythmic and harmonic matrix in which the breathtaking pace is set off by reflective, reverent slow sections. One wonders whether Ives's comments stem from a continued need to be accepted by his male companions and not viewed as effete while clandestinely pursuing his musical explorations.

Humor is a feature of other works of 1906. Ives wrote *Halloween* in a weekend in 1906 at Pine Mountain, and the manuscript is dated "on the 1st of April!"—a reference to an April Fool's joke.[5] Ives described it as "a take-off of a Halloween party and bonfire!—the elfishness of the little boys throwing wood on the fire, etc., etc.—it may not be a good joke [but] the joke is: if it isn't a joke, it isn't anything."[6] However, Ives was well aware that the opposite was the case: his jokes were in dead earnest. In this instance, he provided a rare example of musical analysis in which the subjective programmatic element blends into the technical.[7]

The creative events from April 1906 to the end of the year were of the utmost seriousness and resulted in some of Ives's most innovative works. Most were written for theater orchestra. The mixed instrumentation, as if the pieces were composed for some fantasied pickup band, reflected George Ives's continued presence in his son's private musical life. *Scherzo: Over the Pavements*, dated May 30, 1906, was scored for piccolo, clarinet, bassoon, trumpet, three trombones, cymbal, drum, and piano.[8] The scoring conjures the image of a miniature marching band with the three trombones leading the way—not down the cobbled Main Street of Ives's boyhood memory or the dirt-packed country road of George's time, but down Central Park West. A note in the margin of the score contains a reminiscence: "2 Bands! C.P.W. 'D.D.' May 1906."[9] "D.D." stands for Decoration Day, 1906. Although the holiday had been known as Memorial Day since 1873, the year before Ives's birth, many continued to refer to it by its original name; in 1906 it still served as a day of remembrance of Civil War dead, an occasion for decorating their graves. Although their numbers dwindled each year, sizable groups of veterans still marched in the parade, especially in large cities like New York.

Characteristically, this scherzo was derived in part from a sketch with a baseball reference, "Rube trying to walk 2 to 3," about which Ives noted, "written as a joke, and sounds like one! Watty McCormick only one to see it! and Harry Farrar! at 2.45 A.M."[10] Ives was still living at Poverty Flat, by then located at 65 Central Park West, and he involved some of his housemates in humorous fantasied collaboration. If they accepted Ives as the crazy good fellow who banged at the piano late into the night and on weekends, his continued residence at the flat provided him with the place and the community to carry on serious creative work. References to this context appear repeatedly on the manuscripts of this period. One housemate, Tony Maloney, dubbed "Tony Bill," called him the "disturber of the peace." He is duly mentioned in a note on the scherzo: "Storm and distress to 'Tony Bill' not to Dolan or to 'Disturber.'"[11] Such citations also call attention to Ives's continued and often intense need to be accepted and loved by his men friends. If playing the clown was the means by which this could be achieved, it was more than acceptable to him.

Joking and clowning served a double purpose, one directed toward the immediate outer life of Poverty Flat and the men Ives lived with, another toward his inner life, the continuing intrapsychic relationship with George. Many of the compositions manifestly reveal the fantasied hand of George—the music Ives imagined his father would have written, with the musical combinations and even quotations woven into increasingly sophisticated wholes. The artistic direction, however, was toward autonomy; and if Ives had permitted himself to perceive the difference between his father and himself in the strongest light, it would have been the difference between musical tinkerer and creative genius. The issue of surpassing his father was hardly a theoretical matter at this point in Ives's life. He was beginning to think of marriage. In fact, three critical issues of Ives's life—music, vocation, and love—hung in the balance at this time, each related to his failure thus far to come to terms with his father, living and dead.

In his pursuit of a career, his struggle for artistic identity, and his erotic life, Ives had to deal with the wish, capacity, and even imperative to surpass his father. Playing the fool is an effective retreat from the conflict inherent in this triad of issues. Through it a person seeks to deny that the game is played for keeps, that surpassing the father entails not only the fantasy of losing him and his love forever, but that of being responsible for the loss. The sense of guilt is formidable.

Decoration Day, 1906, marked the start of a melancholy and ruminative summer. In June, Ives wrote *In the Night*,[12] for bells, harps ad lib, horn, piano, and strings. It eventually became one of the three movements of the *Set for Theatre Orchestra*. Another movement of the set, *In the Cage*,[13] was written the following month, and the third, *In the Inn*,[14] around the same time. All had, in

Ives's mind, heavy associations with the past. Two were of the musical character heralded in the *Autumn Landscape* and most effectively stated in *The Pond*. The summer culminated in the two "contemplations," *Central Park in the Dark* and *The Unanswered Question*,[15] perhaps Ives's most characteristic and innovative work to date.

The writing of *In the Night* incorporated a fantasy that Ives described freely years later. In fact, in a remarkable passage in his *Scrapbook*, he writes of the aesthetic effect he was seeking, the technical means by which he achieved it, the conscious fantasy which served as background, and the biographical context in which he wrote and tried out portions of the brief piece, which took four years to bring more or less to its final form.[16] The biographical element harked back to a time four years earlier, in May 1902, "when I resigned as a nice organist and gave up music." It was then that he tried to substitute three very different chords for the tiresome three fundamental triads in an accompaniment to *Abide with Me*. Two years later, in June 1904, he arranged it for theater orchestra for the Yale Sexennial Reunion. Now, in 1906, he added more material, including an old minstrel song (*I Hear the Owl A-Hootin*) and the *Down in the Cornfield* tune from Foster's *Massa's in the Cold, Cold Ground*. "What I had in mind," he wrote, "was a general sounding tonal effect, and the technical plan was but a ways and means." The technical plan he put simply: "All there is to it is this:—three chords used over and over again, two rhythms (a three and a four) used over and over again in each of two measures, and a melody in each of three keys . . . and in the accompaniment the first two measures are repeated practically the same throughout." With regard to the fantasy, Ives wrote, "Behind the music is a simpler picture—the heart of an old man, dying alone in the night, sad, low in heart—then God comes to help him—bring him to his loved ones. This is the main line, the substance. All around, the rest of the music is but the silence and the sounds of the night—bells tolling in the far distance, etc."[17]

In the Night, then, refers to dying and to reunion with loved ones, with *Abide with Me* serving as cantus firmus. The work is a gentle, melancholy, and homespun *Death and Transfiguration*. Years later, when Ives was approaching sixty, he wrote to a friend, "It is a quiet piece—a sort of Reverie of an old man who has lost everything but his faith—and memories."[18] But writing the music at thirty-two, in the summer of 1906, the image was that of George Ives. It was George who had died "in the night," that "one low day, when the sun had gone down, long, long before sunset." In the summer of 1906, an alternative to loss is suggested in the fantasy of the old man—that of reunion in afterlife. It was not the first time this image had found representation in Ives's music. The previous year, at Saranac with David Twichell, Ives had started the cornet piece that eventually became the third movement of the *Fourth Violin Sonata: Children's*

Day at the Camp Meeting, with its "Shall we gather by the river that flows by the throne of God." Nor would it be the last, although references to the other world would become increasingly refined, abstract, and sublimated in Ives's tonal thinking. By the end of the summer, the achievement of *The Unanswered Question* reflects this progression of musical thought.

The other two movements of the *Set for Theatre Orchestra* are also rich in extramusical association and in innovative technical ideas. Ives calls attention to both in his comments on *In the Cage,* the "result of taking a walk one hot summer afternoon in Central Park with Bart Yung (one-half Oriental) and George Lewis (non-Oriental)," both residents of Poverty Flat. "Sitting on a bench near the menagerie, watching the leopard's cage and a little boy (who had apparently been a long time watching the leopard)—this aroused Bart (an Oriental fatalism)— hence the text in the score."[19] The text, added later, reads, "A leopard went around his cage from one side back to the other side; he stopped only when the keeper came around with meat; a boy who had been there three hours began to wonder, 'Is life anything like this?'"[20] "The principal thing in this movement," Ives later wrote, "is to show that a song does not necessarily have to be in any one key to make musical sense. To make music in no particular key has a nice name nowadays—'atonality'"[21]

The presence of Bart Yung enabled Ives to substitute some notion of Oriental philosophy for plain human depression and despair. In the imagery, the animal aggression of the leopard has been crushed and confined. *In the Cage* suggests an American *Hamlet*—melancholy and indecisive. From a technical musical point of view, however, Ives employed atonality in seeking a musical representation of idea and mood, inventing it for himself, as it were, independently of any particular stylistic trend of the time. Increasingly during this period, small pieces with strong biographical reference become important technical studies, private workshops in style.

In the Inn of June 1906 was a ragtime piece, again for mixed chamber orchestra (clarinet, bassoon, tympani, piano, violin, viola, and cello). It became the second movement of the *Set for Theatre Orchestra* as well as having (in Ives's words) "been used in whole or in part in several things," according to Ives's habit.[22] One of these "things" was the scherzo of the *First Piano Sonata,* which was derived in part from *In the Inn.*

In reminiscing about *In the Inn,* Ives was brought back to "George Felsberg's reign in 'Poli's.'" Poli's was a vaudeville theater in New Haven where Felsberg was the pianist. Among other entertainments were minstrel shows, which were still presented in New Haven during Ives's college years. Later, Felsberg played background music for the silent films shown there. Ives had had a strong feeling of affection for Felsberg, who made his living performing vernacular music, as routine a secular task as that of his counterparts among New Haven's church organists. He was well known to generations of Yale men and commemorated in *Stover at Yale* as "the sleepy pianist pounding out his accompaniments while accomplishing the marvelous feat of reading a newspaper." Ives wrote that "George could read a newspaper and play the piano better than some pianists could play the piano without any newspaper at all."[23] He was lavish in his praise of this natural musician, who was leading the kind of life George Ives may well have had if he had not come home to Danbury after the war. Shadows of Stephen Foster, George Ives's "friend," flicker at the edges of Ives's associations to both minstrel shows and alcoholism: "When I was in college, I used to go down there [to Poli's] and 'spell him' a little if he wanted to go out for five minutes and get a glass of beer, or a dozen glasses. There were black-faced comedians then, ragging their songs."[24]

In the Inn stems from about a dozen ragtime dances Ives wrote during the first decade of the century. Some are related thematically or rhythmically, developments of the same line of musical thinking. Three found their way into the *First Piano Sonata*. Musical ideas inherent in ragtime fascinated Ives because of the rhythmic possibilities, which he later developed from these early "studies" into massive polyrhythmic musical structures. The psychological roots go deep—not only to ragtime music but to earlier minstrel music associated with George's time and even to band music. Ives noted that "even in the old brass-band days, there was a swinging into off-beats, shifted accents, etc.—and these ragtime pieces written from about that time . . . were but working out different combinations or rhythms that these began to suggest."

Even before 1906, Ives was prone to depression. The autumn melancholy of 1904 was perhaps related to Harmony's engagement to Walter Lowrie, although Ives was hardly ready to approach her himself. At that time, Ives had devised *Autumn Landscape*, shortly to be transformed into *The Pond*. In the following year, he was troubled enough to alarm the family—probably with a combination of anxiety and depression, a state that led to the healing vacation with David Twichell at Saranac and a reunion with Harmony. Now, in the summer of 1906, symptoms surfaced again.

Two products of that summer are in sharp contrast, revealing attempts at a psychological solution which were each very different in nature. The unconscious preoccupation with George produced the complex reminiscence of *The Pond*, in which, among other things, the actual auditory presence of the father is recreated. In its original form of 1906 as a "song without words" for chamber orchestra, words are written beneath the leadline, scored for trumpet or basset horn—both instruments that George played: "A sound of the distant horn / O'er shadowed lake is borne—my father's song." Later, Ives reclaimed the composition for himself by including it in the *114 Songs* and renaming it *Remembrance*. On the page, a line of Wordsworth stands in lieu of a title: "The music in my heart I bore / Long after it was heard no more."[25]

Just as in everyday mental life unconscious conflict and its reflection in conscious preoccupation will ultimately exert pressures that may result in a dream, something was similarly driven toward representation in the composition of *The Pond*. In one sense, it is a wish in purest, most elementary, and earliest form. Father is more than idealized; he is actualized in "my father's song." Ives's conscious wish, frequently experienced even in later life as "How I long to see Father again," is unshakably bonded to its earliest occurrences, at least as far back as Ives's third year of life when George had been absent from Danbury for as much as six months in an eighteen-month period. Already by that time, the father's music had come to represent George in the child's mind, and music could subserve reminiscence during absence, a childhood accomplishment reflected in the Wordsworth lines. The same condition prevailed in the mind of the adult composer: music could bring George back to life in an act of remembrance and magic.

At the same time, in the very act of creating these musical forms Ives invented for himself the foundations of musical ideas that henceforth he elaborated in major musical works. Complex and intricate manipulations of musical time and space became a hallmark of his work, their psychological origins obliterated in the kind of sublimation that comes to be called aesthetic judgment and taste. In Ives's life, they go back not only as far as the ruminations of 1906 but further, to George's "experiments" in music. The stationing of groups of band members in different locations in the square, the passing of "clashing" bands, are examples of this. And going back to the deepest recesses of Ives's memory were images of his father's playing *In the Sweet Bye and Bye* on his Distin trumpet with its built-in echo effect. Such memories stem from the third year of life, when, in the child's mind, the mysterious echo itself would have magically fused with the father who was there and not there.

In the summer of 1906, rumination gave rise to contemplation as Ives composed two short pieces which were among his most original to date. They were scored for separate combinations of instruments, each a variation on the theater orchestra. On a postface, Ives gave them the following titles:

I   "A Contemplation of a Serious Matter"
    or "The Unanswered Perennial Question"
II "A Contemplation of Nothing Serious"
    or "Central Park in the Dark in 'The Good
    Old Summer Time.' "[26]

His comments regarding the two were of a very different nature. Ives still lived at Poverty Flat, and the first sketch of *Central Park in the Dark* bears the note, "return C. E. Ives 65 Cent. Pk. W." Indeed, the second sketch mentions his continued sharing of his music with the men of the flat, and Ives scribbled on the manuscript, "heard at 65 CPW July–Dec . . . 1906, with JSM."[27] This was, of course, Julian Myrick, who also lived there by now. *Central Park* was a piece as rooted in the present as the park bench Ives mentions in his commentary. At the same time, it contains a reverie of the same spot thirty years earlier, as if he were sitting there and contemplating the past. He wrote:

> This piece purports to be a picture in sounds of the sounds of nature and of happenings that men would hear some thirty or so years ago (before the combustion engine and radio monopolized the earth and air) when sitting on a bench in Central Park on a hot summer night. The strings represent the night sounds and silent darkness-interrupted by sounds from the Casino over the pond—of street singers coming up from the Circle singing—in spots—the tunes of those days—of some "night owls" from Healy's whistling the latest or the Freshman March—the "occasional elevated," a street parade or a "break-down" in the distance—of newsboys crying "uxtries"—of pianolas having a ragtime war in the apartment house "over the garden wall," a street car and a street band join in the chorus—a fire engine, a cab horse runs away, lands, "over the fence and out," the wayfarers shout—again the darkness is heard— an echo over the pond—and we walk home.[28]

Present and past commingle in the hot, dreamy darkness of the summer night. The passage relates a rapid series of purely auditory impressions that perhaps say as much about how Ives heard as about how he composed. (At the end, darkness itself "is heard".) While the present is explicit in such references as to the apartment-house music of Central Park West and Healy's, a favorite restaurant a block away on Columbus Avenue, "thirty or so years ago" suggests a time when things would have sounded different. Ives draws us to the first two "or so" years of his own life, the impressionable years of first experiences with his father's music. Beyond this lies a layer of personal prehistory in what Ives might have heard about George's sojourn in New York when he was only slightly younger than Charles was at the point of composing the piece. In George's New York, Central Park was nearing completion, extending from its Fifty-ninth Street border at the outskirts of town to its northern reach in suburban Harlem. Beyond this were farms and country houses. The summer-night nostalgia of Ives's *Central Park* has a rural quality, relating more to what lay beyond the city and to images of Danbury. And mention of the pond once again makes us wonder about Ives's associations to it. The pond in Central Park was close at hand at the time, but two other ponds in Ives's mental life had long been significant. The first was Walden Pond, made famous by Thoreau, whom Ives had long admired and who would later inspire a major section of the *Concord Sonata*. The second was the pond in Wooster Cemetery, across from the knoll where George was buried.

The other "Contemplation," that of *The Unanswered Question*, contrasted strongly in style and idea. Like *Autumn Landscape*, which may have served as inspiration for *The Pond*, this too was a landscape. Ives called it *A Cosmic Sometime Landscape*. Scored for the unusual combination of four flutes (two of which could be replaced with oboe and clarinet), trumpet, and strings, it is as otherworldly and timeless as its companion piece is of this world and of times present and past. Ives provided elaborate stage directions for its performance in which matters of space and time are considered, both literally and in a highly abstract manner. The muted trumpet intones "The Question," answered by the flutes, "The Fighting Answerers." Question and answer occupy different sections of the same space. Elsewhere, "if possible . . . off stage," the strings put forth a timeless background music. Ives wrote:

> They are to represent—"The Silences of the Druids—who Know, See, and Hear Nothing." The trumpet intones—"The Perennial Question of Existence," and states it in the same tone of voice each time. But the hunt becomes gradually more active, faster and louder through an animando to a con fuoco. . . . The "Fighting Answerer's" [*sic*] as time goes on, and after a "secret conference," seem to realize a futility, and begin to mock "The Question"—the strife is over for the moment. After they disappear, "The Question" is asked for the last time, and the "Silences" are heard beyond in "Undisturbed Solitude."[29]

The trumpet theme, identified by Ives as "the Perennial Question of Existence," in fact incorporates question *and* answer in the detail of musical motif—cosmos in musical microcosmos.[30] The phonetic inflection of a question comes through in the disposition of the notes of this motif. At the same time, it is as close to a graphic representation of a question mark as might be notated on music paper. The disposition of offstage strings and the layering of discrete musical groups constitute spatial effects in this countertemporal context. These innovative musical elements were already becoming characteristic of Ives's music.[31]

The remarkable achievement of *The Unanswered Question* was not merely a by-product of the inner, often confused questioning of the conflicted thirty-year-old composer. It was part of the manner in which he questioned, a manner that can only be called musical. The formal musical solutions he achieved were a satisfying result even if they were of limited value in the solution of inner problems, let alone the conduct of life. Nevertheless, some shift in inner life is reflected in this and later musical works. The shift from temporal to timeless, from specific to abstract, the autobiographical transformation of personal into formal, all reflect a growing capacity for sublimation. Not content alone—for

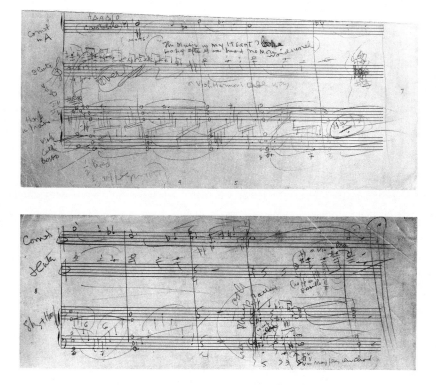

A manuscript page from The Pond, *ca. 1906.*

example, musical quotation from the composer's flowing memory—but the increasingly skillful forging of form makes the music distinctive and of universal interest.

What were the underlying fantasies that gave rise to musical and nonmusical "questions"? Perhaps the best point of entry is not the sound but the silences, which are intrinsic to the musical form of both "contemplations." After all, night sounds subside in *Central Park:* "again the darkness is heard—an echo over the pond—and we walk home." And after the final question, "the silences are heard beyond in 'Undisturbed Solitude.'" A similar carefully contrived silence ends *The Pond.* There, according to Ives's sketch, the small voice of the piccolo should be heard in the distance playing the opening of *Taps.*[32] Silence, in this context associated with darkness and sleep, is a representation of death, the fundamental theme of Ives's ruminations and contemplations of 1906.

Thus in 1906 the young Ives was attempting to come to terms with certain universal human conditions. His contemplations, prompted by the challenges of object love and loss, turned into preoccupation with his own life and death. That is the pivotal point where contemplation turns to rumination and depression supervenes. Rumination had already been represented in Ives's *In the Cage*—as the pacing of the leopard and as the question, "Is life anything like this?" Indeed, ruminations in the form of questions had appeared in his music several times—for example, in the question and answer of *Beautiful River*. Although art cannot cure, it can organize, externalize, and conceptualize conflict in unique terms. Thus the process of composing may have helped Ives maintain psychological equilibrium, at least for a time.

Meanwhile, during the summer of 1906, Harmony Twichell, although far from forgotten, did not seem to be in the forefront of Ives's mind. Occupied at his job, preoccupied with the past, and deeply engaged in composition (he spent evenings putting musical ideas on paper), Ives seemed to lead a life quite separate from Harmony. Yet they saw each other from time to time. Harmony already knew from the previous autumn's reunion in Saranac that she was in love with him. In his mental state and financial position, Ives may not have been able to view himself as suitor to so accomplished and attractive a young woman. This was hardly a period of high self-esteem for him, despite recent creative accomplishments. But Ives's vulnerability drew Harmony to him. Quite early, she seemed sensitive and responsive to his moods. She later wrote to him about a day they had spent with friends from Poverty Flat on Long Island, "You were feeling very quiet to say the least—I used to be so anxious to *do* something for you and the only thing I *could* do was to say nothing about how you felt or how I felt about it."[33]

On July 15 Ives was in Hartford, this time to visit Harmony, not David. Both later recalled a "walk over Prospect Hill Sunday evening . . . midsummer eve" as a turning point. Did they privately exchange vows on this walk on the wooded road to Farmington? In August a letter from Harmony, serving as nurse companion to Mrs. Dean Sage in Albany, expresses the warm concern that was characteristic of her: "Lovely here and we have been having the most wonderful run of weather for a week or so. I've been quite distressed imagining you in all this heat and hope it is well over."[34] The caring and forthcoming quality of this and other notes should have been reassuring to Ives.

But Ives was at a low point as the end of 1906 approached. He had by then consulted the doctors at Mutual's medical department several times. The medical records are no longer available, but according to Kirkpatrick, "Ives's heart had been cause for anxiety."[35] For reasons that I shall take up later it seems unlikely that there was any physical problem at the time. Probably Ives was suffering from a combination of anxiety and continuing depression, the result of stress whose origins were internal as much as external. At some point the doctors recommended he take a rest and suggested that Julian Myrick accompany him. The pair spent about a week at Old Point Comfort, Virginia, around Christmas, 1906.

Julian and Charlie probably stayed at the Hotel Chamberlain, a spa which boasted that no European "cure" surpassed its own. The program included "a very valuable, natural medicinal water, flowing free. . . . "Others get well by using Nature's remedies alone—the Sun, the Sea, the Salt Sands." The resort was situated near Fort Monroe, a site of great strategic importance to the Union during the Civil War. Among the advertised "pleasures of getting well" was the proximity to "the pomp and circumstance of war." Coincidentally, Fort Monroe was literally next door to indoor and outdoor medicinal baths. Army drills and parades were part of a social life in which "the Army, the Navy, and Society mingle as nowhere else on this continent." The area was rich in Civil War lore: the battle between the *Monitor* and the *Merrimack* had taken place in Chesapeake Bay within view of the fortress ramparts, and from there the Army of the Potomac had launched a campaign north of Richmond with a fleet of vessels extending up the James River. The site was within miles of the locale where George Ives had seen service.[36]

It is doubtful that the "cure" did much for a physical condition that was questionable in the first place. On the other hand, it was probably as helpful for Ives as it is for many others who attend such sanitoria for vague psychosomatic problems that are symptomatic of an underlying depression. Being pampered in a scenic place and pleasant climate away from the site of his immediate woes may have helped raise his mood. At the same time, the vacation accomplished something quite different. The young friends, realizing that they were on the brink of a new era in their chosen profession, decided to leave Mutual and go into business for themselves. January 1, 1907, was the day when the new Armstrong Laws regulating the industry were to go into effect. Mutual had already reorganized. To Ives and Julian, it seemed just possible under the circumstances to finance themselves with borrowed money and, by using business contacts well established after eight years, to start their own agency. Ives returned to New York hopeful about the future. He had acquired a new business partner in Myrick and would shortly acquire another partner by initiating the courtship that would lead to the happiest and most creative period of his life.

THIRTEEN

HARMONY

Ives returned from Old Point Comfort with a sense of optimism. The ruminations of 1906 had found some semblance of a resting place, not far from those places his father knew as a youth. Beyond the rest cure, a pilgrimage had been made and a small piece of mourning accomplished. The new year started with the opening of Ives and Company. Ives felt renewed, and his symptoms had abated. It would be a dozen years before he had any further physical complaints regarding his heart.

With the start of 1907, the affair of the heart that increasingly dominated Ives's life was his relationship with Harmony Twichell. Harmony was in Albany with Mrs. Sage when Ives returned in January. Although she was thinking of Ives a great deal, she did not yet even know his telephone number in New York, and the few letters from her that remain through the spring are signed, "Yours as ever sincerely." She too was experiencing a crisis of sorts in her own life, if a more normal and expectable one than Ives's. To commit herself to him entailed a psychological departure from a father to whom she was closely attached. And not only was the person of the Reverend Twichell involved but also his ideals. Harmony had pursued these in her choice of career as surely as her brother, David, had done in his. That summer, Harmony took a position as a nurse at the Henry Street Settlement in New York. For the first time, she and Ives had regular dates.

Harmony Twichell was born in Hartford, Connecticut, on June 4, 1876, to

Harmony Cushman Twichell and Joseph Hopkins Twichell.[1] Her father was at that time minister of the Asylum Hill Congregational Church, on the western limit of the city. But Harmony was born into a much larger community. She was also a child of Nook Farm, Mark Twain's circle in Hartford, and of a tradition that included Yale University and the ecclesiastical teachings of Horace Bushnell, particularly as her father applied them in his ministry. Twichell's ministry was rooted in service and friendship and, full of good humor, did not take itself too seriously.

The Reverend Twichell was destined to be remembered as a friend of Mark Twain's, enshrined in *A Tramp Abroad* as Mr. Harris. The two men shared a similar wit and personal style. Harmony Cushman had been an able teacher who maintained her interest in the profession well into her marriage to Joseph Twichell. Harmony Twichell was their fifth child and third daughter, the most middle of middle children in this family of nine. Named after her mother, she remained a special favorite of her father, who liked to call her Meg. Against the background of a warm identification with her mother, the most powerful influence on Harmony's life was her father.

Whatever Joseph Twichell's capacity for love, friendship, and Christian ministry, his paternal affection and approval were sparsely distributed among the nine children. In addition to his church duties, he seems to have spent a great deal of time among friends, particularly Twain. During Harmony's early life, he frequently took vacations with Uncle Mark, leaving the family behind. From his children's point of view one had to *be* something and *do* something to get that which he appeared so capable of giving others.

Joseph Hopkins Twichell, himself the oldest of nine children,[2] was born in 1838 in Southampton, Connecticut. His father, Edward, was a businessman. His mother died when he was ten. Among his earliest memories was of being taken by his father, a deacon of the church, to hear Horace Bushnell preach, an important experience that years later exerted its influence in Twichell's choice of career and ecclesiastical perspective.

At Yale he made and inspired lifelong friendships, but his academic distinctions were, in truth, few. Following graduation in the fall of 1859, he enrolled in Union Seminary in New York. In 1861, with the outbreak of the war, the twenty-three-year-old Twichell enlisted for three years. He served at Gettysburg in July 1863.

After being mustered out in the spring of 1864, Twichell returned to divinity school, and in 1865 he completed his studies, married, and assumed his lifetime post at the Asylum Street Congregational Church in Hartford. In the summer of 1868 the first of the Twichell children was born; he was named Edward Carrington, for a Yale classmate, but later was known as Deac.

Of Joseph Twichell's offspring, the two that most surely carried their father's healing touch were David and Harmony. As they grew to adulthood, David, the doctor, eventually served as conduit for those strivings of Harmony that stemmed from her identification with her father. In another age, Harmony might have become a physician or a minister. She and David were both idealists, perhaps to an even greater degree than their father. In both, idealism led to a life of service. However, Harmony was too ready for deep attachments to men themselves to make this her sole purpose in life, a consequence of her attachment to her father whose favorite she very likely was.

While David was living in Poverty Flat, a number of elements came to confluence in his life—a maturing scientific interest in tuberculosis, a dedication to service, and a love for that combination of wilderness and homey civilization that Saranac had come to represent for him. An alumnus of the College of Physicians and Surgeons, Dr. Edward Livingston Trudeau, had in the course of the 1880s raised money for a project called "the Adirondack cottage cure" and was developing a sanatorium at Saranac.[3] Not quite the Magic Mountain of Davos, neither was it Lambaréné. But in an atmosphere somewhat withdrawn from the world, the physician enjoyed a respected position while as a scientist he carried out his researches. David took a position with Trudeau at Saranac and made the battle against tuberculosis his professional life. This became David's world, and under his influence Harmony, for one brief moment, considered entering it. But she decided instead to marry Ives.

Harmony was far from the average girl at Hartford High School. She was the minister's daughter and heiress to a tradition that included the literati of Nook Farm, who were her father's parishioners, and Horace Bushnell, who had been the greatest influence on him. She was sophisticated beyond her seventeen years, in part owing to the benefits of Twichell's influence and friendships. A two-week trip to the Chicago Exposition in 1893 was a gift from Joseph Twichell's Yale classmate and lifelong friend Albert Sprague, the wealthy Chicago businessman and philanthropist. (By coincidence, Ives had visited the exposition at the same time that year, as secretary to his Uncle Lyman.) Harmony knew Sprague as Uncle Albert, and the visit was one of several turning points of her young life. It was Albert who subsequently paid her tuition at Miss Porter's School in Farmington, which she attended on her return.

Miss Porter's, a finishing school for young women, certainly did not settle her in the expected manner. Graduating in 1896, Harmony was restless. She lived at home for the next two years, studying painting with a local artist, Charles H. Flagg. During this period she served as her father's companion, joining him frequently at his speaking engagements. In her early twenties she was known for her beauty in Hartford, and according to conventional thinking this was the ideal time to marry the appropriate man. Instead, in the fall of 1898, she entered the Hartford Hospital Training School for Nurses and, two years later, received her degree as a registered nurse. Her graduation gift from her father and yet another of his friends and her "uncles," Cornelius Dunham, was a two-month tour of Italy with Twichell, visiting Genoa, Milan, Venice, Bologna, Florence, Rome, and Naples.

At Harmony's graduation, she read a short valedictory, which she called *The Nurse's Gain*. In a fervently optimistic tone, Harmony spoke of the gratification in what some perceive as renunciation or even sacrifice in the nurse's calling. She deemed being "forced into alleviating pain" as "really a great piece of good luck . . . for it is proved that the fullest development means in the end the greatest usefulness and happiness."[4] Unselfish endeavor was first but other "gains" included the chance to increase one's knowledge, to earn a living, and to learn "most interestingly and intimately" about people. Her ideal was Florence Nightingale.

Following graduation, Harmony went to Chicago to work with the Visiting Nurses' Association in the slums. Meanwhile, David was not having an easy time of it at Columbia, and in the spring of 1903 he left medical school for a month's rest. Harmony was delegated to accompany him to Summerville, South Carolina, as companion and nurse. This was the first time she was called to serve as private nurse to family members and family friends. Shortly thereafter, Cornelius Dunham's sister required similar care, and Harmony obliged for the summer of 1903. By then, David was working at the Trudeau Sanatorium, and Harmony joined him at Saranac, where she worked as a Visiting Nurse for nearly the whole of 1904. During this period her brief engagement to the Reverend Walter Lowrie was announced and soon broken.

She had ample opportunity that year to observe the work at Trudeau's, which by now had become an established institution. Despite appealing accommodations, it was not quite so easy for Trudeau to attract workers to the daily demands of attending to the chronically ill. The situation appealed to Harmony, and she seriously considered taking a regular position with Trudeau.

Instead, another of Twichell's friends required a companion, and Harmony responded. She remained employed by Mrs. Dean Sage or her family for more than two years. Her service started with a trip to Europe in the spring of 1905. Upon her return that summer, Harmony briefly went back to nursing, working at the Henry Street Settlement in New York. She did so again in the summer of 1907. In the interim, she attended to Mrs. Sage in Albany, except for visits to the family in Hartford and Saranac.

It was during such intervals that she met Ives again in Hartford in January and July of 1905, and at Saranac in September. Whatever understanding resulted from their midsummer walk led to a long courtship. Harmony said that "we were very formal in those days."[5] Very likely, neither Harmony nor Ives was certain of commitment as they moved toward 1907. In the interim, Harmony turned thirty.

Ives, returning from Old Point Comfort, spent the last of his holiday in Hartford. Harmony's interest and concern were evident as the New Year started. In a letter the following week from Albany she wrote, "I want to know awfully how you are—what you are doing and all—please tell me."[6] Holiday dreams lingered into the following spring in a poem Harmony wrote on a sheet of Mrs. Sage's notepaper:

> Sweet music of the Christmastide
> My heart can hear it still
> The music that the angels say
> Above the shepherd's hill . . .

On the verso of the notepaper, Harmony wrote the lyric for a song—verse and chorus—"For long I wandered happily / Far out on the world's highway."[7]

She sent it to Ives, who responded to the love letter in verse by setting it to music. It was their first collaboration. True to form, Ives put it to music he had written some time earlier, although Harmony did not know that at the time. Harmony had a sweet voice and had acquired some voice training at Miss Porter's. She learned to sing this song—the only one of Ives's that she attempted to sing. It remained a favorite of theirs, and Ives later included it among his *114 Songs*.[8]

Collaboration through music was the way to Ives's heart, and perhaps Harmony knew this intuitively. She surely by now knew something of his family, and it is likely that the image of George she was beginning to glimpse through Ives was an idealized and legendary one. It is clear that she had fallen in love with Ives and was thinking of settling down, which for her meant giving up the pursuit of greater ambitions in a wider world.

Harmony's rival among the Ives women for Charlie's affection was not so much his mother as his Aunt Amelia. Mollie, for reasons still obscure, was respected while devalued. It was Amelia, not the mother of record but the mother *de facto*, with whom Harmony would have to contend. But beyond both current mothers loomed the image of an earlier and enduring love in Ives's attachment to his dead father. George was her most serious rival, and the ongoing intrapsychic collaboration between father and son, showing in Ives's intense involvement with music, was the true obstacle to the burgeoning relationship between her and Ives. Thus it is significant that the first thing they made together was a song. Before long, their life together was to have many shared

elements, cherished and duly recorded in the black leather journal, *Our Book.*
And inevitably, they would each, for privately preordained reasons, desire to
make a child together. Ives's fantasy would be one of restitution; Harmony's is
manifest in her "world's highway," where there is a "blessed call" to that small
private place where things grow, the garden.

And what were the creative antecedents of Ives's contribution to their first
issue, the song? We know only that the tune of *The World's Highway* bears an
additional, earlier date—1893, the year before George's death, and musical
elements of the tune recall the sentimental parlor music of the time.[9] (Indeed, in
the *114 Songs*, it is bracketed among "a group of 'Sentimental Ballads.'")

That spring or fall, they created another song together—*Spring Song.* Harmony wrote the lyrics:

> Across the hill of late, come spring—
>   and stopped and looked into this wood
>   and called and called.
> Now all the dry brown things are ans'wring,
>   With here a leaf and
> there a fair blown flow'r,
> I only heard her not, and wait and wait.[10]

The music was adapted by Ives from an earlier song of 1903, which is now lost.
Spring Song dates from the late summer of 1907.[11] By then, the couple saw each
other regularly, in particular attending concerts at the Saint Nicholas Rink given
by Franz Kaltenborn, whom Ives knew from the days of *The Celestial Country.*

Despite these collaborations, it seems that Ives and Harmony were not yet
committed to marrying. Ives held back from the final step, and Harmony herself
appeared undecided. Toward the end of August she returned to Saranac, where
she was considering taking the position at Trudeau's. She wrote Ives warmly but
her letters were still signed "as ever sincerely." Ives sent her *Spring Song*, and
she responded approvingly twice.[12]

The position at Trudeau's would have required Harmony to remain at Saranac
through the winter. David wanted her to accept it but Harmony wavered. Under
other circumstances, she could have made a worthy career there in agreeable
surroundings with friends and family close by. She wrote Ives, "The tragedy of
this place strikes you all over again when you've been away as long as I have."[13]
Still, she was lonely. Ives had evidently still not declared himself.

It was Harmony who finally made the decision. She wrote him resolutely on
September 17, 1907: "I feel as if I had a lot to say to you. In the first place I'm not
coming up here for the winter."[14] Feeling much relieved, she had already informed David and Dr. Trudeau. "So I'll probably be in N.Y. sometime," she
wrote coyly, "I hope you are glad I am." From that point, events moved swiftly.

Harmony was back in Hartford by October 10, Ives visiting weekends. Scarcely two weeks later, on October 22, the decision to marry was reached on a tenderly remembered walk, Harmony commemorating it in *Our Book* as "the wood road to Farmington." It sealed that for which she had returned. He had just turned thirty-three.

In the interim between Harmony's resolution and her return, she and Ives were considering writing an opera. Harmony was already in the habit of suggesting things for Ives to read; she had been delighted at his response to Charles Lamb. The text for the proposed work, however, was considerably less auspicious. *The Red Patrol*, by the Canadian novelist Sir Gilbert Parker, was one of a collection of stories published serially, called *Pierre and His People* (1892), about the adventures of a French-Indian outlaw-mystic.[15] In a tale that today can only be read as a parody of the genre, Pierre wins a wager with a college-bred man of God, a missionary in the North Country of French Canada who then abandons his Bible and heads with Pierre to the Kimash Hills. There the wise men of the Red Patrol, led by the Scarlet Hunter, mystically pursue a greater good in the House of Judgment. Ives and Harmony had a lively exchange of letters about the plot and characters. Harmony suggested adding to the otherwise all-male cast a sweetheart for Pierre.

The appeal of the mystical and an undisguised belief in the right and the good continued to be a part of both of them. The element of rescue stems no doubt from the nurse Harmony, who suggested that at the end of *The Kimash Hills* "nothing but the combined entreaties of the girl and the good man [can] save [Pierre] from being scorned and punished, and it can all end happily."[16]

In the course of the correspondence, it was not long before the naively high ideals found their way home. Harmony, in spite of her travels, was distrustful of foreign elements. ("Perhaps I wasn't right about the contrast of emotions in opera—maybe that's only because those were *Italian*—I must learn of more")[17] More than this was a shared patriotism deeply felt. It is clear that the relationship with Harmony was already becoming a shaping force in Ives's life. The growing bond between them had antecedents in earlier relationships, particularly with their fathers, both of whom were seen as heroes by their children. The father-child bond was the source of their patriotism, although for Ives patriotism also screened a sense of shame and guilt. The mention of Lincoln and Gettysburg drew together images cherished in each case for different reasons: Lincoln, according to family lore, had praised George Ives, the young bandmaster; and Chaplain Joseph Twichell had heard Lincoln speak at Gettysburg. In both cases, love of the father translated into love of country and into an unembarrassed patriotism, which in time became part of an aesthetic.

By the beginning of 1908, as both lost interest in the project of *The Kimash*

Hills, Harmony wrote: "Charlie, of course the place for the good man in *our drama* to come from is *our country ennobled*—our own country, as our fore-fathers planned her, and as Mr. Lincoln desired her in his Gettysburg speech, and as we hope she will be in the good process of time—don't you think so."[18] By then, the opera had accomplished the task of cementing a relationship in a spirit of creative collaboration.

It may be that Ives endeavored to encourage Harmony in her writing as he pursued his own. On her part, Harmony encouraged Ives to read literature. Books were important to her, and she envisaged that they would have an impor-tant place in their married life. She wrote to him during the winter of 1908, "We must plan to have times for leisure of thought & we must try & read a lot, the best books—we can live with the noblest people that have lived that way—& we will have your music."[19] Burkholder wisely points out how the "companionship of reading" helped Ives separate from his bachelor friends. He also suggests ways in which Harmony continued in the steps of Ives's English professor, William Lyons Phelps, in both fostering Ives's desire to read and guiding his choice of reading matter.[20] By the time of their wedding, Ives had envisioned a series of overtures called *Men of Literature,* which was never fully realized. From about 1907 or 1908 he worked on several of these, including the *Robert Browning Overture*[21] and the *Matthew Arnold Overture;*[22] Browning and Arnold were favorite authors of Harmony's.

Ives, for his part, introduced Harmony to many aspects of music that were unfamiliar to her. With her he seemed capable, at least at that point, of being the patient teacher his father was. He introduced her to opera—real opera, *foreign* opera—and they went to concerts together during the summer of 1907 in New York. In their correspondence, he stimulated a lively interest in both music and musicians. Harmony was characteristically responsive and expressive.

Harmony was poised for a particular kind of partnership in marriage through her relationship with her father. The young girl who had served as a companion on the minister's speaking engagements had grown up to pursue in fantasy what amounted to a holy collaboration. She took from her father a sense of optimism expressed in the ideal of progress stemming from his mentor, Horace Bushnell, a "belief in the presence of the divine in all human beings and in nature."[23] It informed her capacity for everyday friendship and a fierce loyalty to those to whom she was close. Above all it contained the idea of service that had led her to become a nurse. But despite the attraction of a life of worthy celibacy at Dr. Trudeau's sanatorium, she was of too passionate a nature to deny herself mar-riage.

Such a passion, imbued with a need for caring and service, eventually led to the wish to have children. But this most fundamental of creative partnerships could be expressed in many derivative ways as well. The couple had already tested these possibilities in the simple but heartfelt songs they had written together and in the dismal *Kimash Hills*. The romantic streak in Harmony's character did not confine her to a single set of fantasies or strivings, and she now added the wish to be an artist's wife, his inspirational companion. Perceptibly, Harmony began to shift her goals in this direction.

Ives showed Harmony his sketches for *The Unanswered Question* and *Central Park in the Dark*. What could she have thought of these pieces? They were worlds distant from the homey sentimentality of *The World's Highway* and the banal, hackneyed ideas of *Kimash Hills*. Harmony later generously said, "He fixed it so I could understand it somehow."[24] These works may even have appealed to a trend toward mysticism that the two of them shared. Meanwhile, her dream of becoming the composer's wife, like the role of composition in Ives's life, would be private. The man she would marry was publicly a struggling but promising young businessman of good education and background. Privately, he composed, and in that sphere she would seek to help him as devotedly as she attempted everything else. During the remaining days of their courtship, she gave a great deal of thought to music and to Ives's music, developing elements of a personal aesthetic which, however untutored, had considerable influence on Ives. She already had a way of knowing what was good for him.

The Reverend Twichell solemnly noted in his diary, on November 17, 1907, the event that everyone in the family had long anticipated:

> Going up to my study in the afternoon, I found Young Harmony and Charles Ives there. In answer to my look of inquiry for the reason of it, they explained that they wanted my "Blessing." It was not much of a surprise, for we had been aware of their growing intimacy, and had been pretty sure of the issue to which it was tending. I found later in the day that Charles had already made his confession to H. We have known him a good while: he is a classmate of Dave's who has loved him fondly. We were prepared to sanction the engagement, which seemed to us suitable and auspicious in its promises to us all.[25]

This happened just short of a month after they had made their decision to marry. Harmony and Ives let as few people know about the betrothal as possible and wished the wedding to be as private as feasible. They soon completed the ordeal by telling Aunt Amelia.

That week Ives wrote two letters, one each to his future wife and his future father-in-law:

> Dear Mr. Twichell
> I want to write you, not because I feel it a matter of duty—I know you *understand all*—and only write because I feel, this afternoon, like talking things over with you, though there is nothing that I could say that could tell

what I feel. It is impossible and futile for me to try to *write down* or *say* what Harmony means to me. You must know, because you know *her*. She is not only my idol but the reason for all highest and best things that a man could live for.

I have always felt unworthy of her but don't think it best for her to let myself think much about that. I can only keep pounding away at myself until I do know that I deserve all that she has given and done for me, and though it may be years, I feel that, with her help, that day *will* come.

I don't feel, and Harmony doesn't either, as though I'm taking her away from her mother and from you. I like to think, rather, that I happened to be the one appointed to guard and care for her when the time comes that you all cannot; and one of the thoughts that I'm most grateful for is that I seem to have been steered through all these years, pretty straight down to Harmony— without having any big things to look back over, that I'm ashamed of—though lots of little things—and the whole reason seems to me, more and more closely, to have been "only through the Grace of God."

But what I wanted to ask and wanted to write you especially for—(for all the rest you must have known and understood or you couldn't have given us your blessing and been so kind and gracious as you were last Sunday; you don't know how happy you made Harmony and you've no idea what a "do or die" feeling and determination you gave me)—but I want to ask if you will let me come to you, as Dave does when he wants to talk things over and get your advice and encouragement.

Father died just at the time I needed him most. It's been years since I've had an older man that I felt like going to when things seem to go wrong or a something comes up when it's hard to figure out which is the best or right thing to do. I don't mean by that a shifting of responsibility, but I know talking it over with you would clear things up and make it easier to decide.

I hope you'll let me—*Please do.* Whenever you come to New York, if you can conveniently, I hope you'll let me see you if only for lunch or something like that. We should all enjoy having you stop with us at the flat at any time—I think we could make you comfortable. . . .

One of the pleasantest things that Harmony and I have to talk over is that we're going to have a home that her mother and father will always be glad to come to, and a home that will remind everyone who comes into it of the love, faith, and peace that is in our hearts.

Sincerely Chas. E. Ives[26]

Ives's longing for the love of an older man had come to rest on Joseph Twichell. Through marriage, he sought to gain a father as well as a wife. Earlier objects had been Griggs and the disappointing Parker. Ives had turned to the helpful Myrick, even younger than himself, when he was ill. David Twichell was a contemporary, whose relationship with *his* father Ives had doubtless envied since freshman year at Yale. He had now, in effect, elevated himself to the position of son, on a par with his friend (now become sibling); and through marriage to Joseph's beloved Harmony he might even become the favorite son once again. In the letter to Twichell, Ives confesses his deeply felt vulnerability and low esteem. At the same time, he presents himself not as a rival, although in declaring that he shall care for Harmony "when the time comes that you all cannot" he tactfully looks forward to Twichell's death. Until that day, he seems to beg, "love us both." He is as much the suitor to Twichell as to Harmony. And in marrying Harmony, Ives became as much a Twichell as she became an Ives. In gaining a wife, father, brother, and distinguished circle of friends Ives was regaining the ideal family of his dreams, of his earliest life, and he was understandably ecstatic. In addition, the distinguished circle of friends that came with the family served to raise esteem, perhaps even to promise further business contacts.

For the first time, Ives now addressed Harmony affectionately in a letter, "Dear little old Harmony T." They had talked about starting a book of memories: "Did you get our book so that we may put down all the perfect days? Please start on Oct. 22 and bring it to New York and we'll keep it together." He notes, "This is Nov. 22—a month after Oct. 22 and the greatest event in the history of the country although the populace doesn't know it—poor souls!" Ives was elated; he was even optimistic about his still-struggling business venture with Myrick: "Our business, I really think is on a sound basis, and is not suffering any more, and not so much as most firms are."[27] It was a relief to have come to a decision even if it had required Harmony's determination to help him do so.

But no solution is perfect, and in the scenario Ives devised two abandoned objects would have to be dealt with. The first was the ever-present father of mental life, the George Ives of memory, displaced in fantasy by a fickle, betraying son. The second was the all-too-real presence of the keeper of the Ives tradition, the matriarch Aunt Amelia.

Both Harmony and Charlie had a generational problem to deal with before marriage. If Joseph Twichell merely walked around with a long face, Amelia Ives was articulate enough for them both.[28] She made her claim on Ives promptly—in fact, only days after the couple privately decided to marry. Not yet knowing of the marriage plans but aware of Ives's growing attachment to Harmony and the Twichells, Amelia wrote, "I *try* to be thankful for your friends you are glad to go to when you need a rest or change—and this old house has not sufficient attraction."[29] "This old house" doubtless refers to Amelia herself. In the same letter, she described a recent trip to the Berkshires and reminisced about her first visit to an inn, the Maple Shade in Salisbury, fifty years earlier, on her honeymoon with Lyman. "I feel as your Uncle Lyman used to—the year is not complete unless I see the Housatonic Valley & the mountains beyond." She pressed Ives to relive these times with her: "I wish you would take some of these trips with me for I should enjoy it so much & I think you would—I fear by the time you learn to take vacations of this kind I shall not be here to go."[30] Ives responded guiltily, agreeing to a trip with his aunt during the very exciting month he and Harmony were letting others of the family know of their engagement. Amelia planned the trip meticulously as a re-creation of her honeymoon with Lyman: "There is a quiet country hotel with a good table & with good hills to climb, & walks and drives to take in every direction. What more can you ask but a good bed to sleep in—which we both won't need—with that good air as tonic & sedative. . . . If only I could *trust* you to surely come . . ."[31]

If Ives's courtship had spurred Amelia's rather passionate claim on him as a substitute husband, her anger, spilling over from her disappointments by Lyman, was no less evident. A few days later she wrote, "Your vacations are of the same nature as Uncle Lyman's invitations were, to go with him to Hartford where he was a member of the legislature—to go "any week but the present one."[32] And having mentioned Hartford, she suggested that they meet there, leaving Harmony with her father while they went off to Salisbury. Sometime in the next weeks the trip actually took place; Harmony duly noted that it had been sweet of Ives to go away with Amelia.

Harmony, in turn, spent much time with Joe Twichell. A confinement at home was occasioned by the "touch of peritonitis" she developed immediately after the engagement was announced.[33] It kept her home as a semi-invalid—for nine months. Later in the spring, it provided the occasion to spend time with Amelia recuperating in Lakewood, New Jersey, and in Atlantic City. By then, the tension of waiting was great for all concerned. Harmony was eager for the wedding. Even Amelia appeared to wish they were finally married—but not without a final gesture. In a letter to Ives on April 8, Amelia sounds like she is expecting a funeral instead of a wedding: "If you knew how lonely I get at times (which I hope you may never know) you could begin to realize what your being here would mean to me. I do not mean to *over*-persuade you but I do want you to know my wishes in this matter. Besides I am getting where it would be for my comfort to drop some of the care on the shoulders of those younger & more capable."[34] Although Amelia was seventy, there is no evidence that she was ill, and she would live to eighty-one. She wrote, however, as if the end were at hand and the future urgently needed to be planned. "I hope I shall not live to be a burden to anyone. If I need care you and Harmony and Aunt Nell will give it." Nell, Mollie's unmarried sister who now lived with Amelia, would need a home after Amelia was gone. Amelia also mentions the mysterious Mollie Ives, who had "left her house" some time the previous year and "was five months out of the 12 with us."[35]

Harmony's passage to adulthood took place in the nine months she remained in her father's home before her marriage. If some girlish fantasy of having father's baby was being enacted during the confinement, her conscious fantasies all related to Ives and their life to come. Her letters, increasingly tender, reveal the wish—at times urgent—to care for him as if he were her child. In part this was a response to his neediness. She appeared to become increasingly attuned to his changeable moods. Love, service, and adoration merged in the mind of the minister's daughter at Christmas, when she addressed him as if he were the Christ child:

Dear Lamb—

I want to *do* things for you & to see that you are taken care of & have what you need. It's harder when I know you're going to get to N.Y. on a dreary day like this too. . . . I can *see* you—I wish I were with you my *blessed blessed* child.[36]

In Harmony's letters, passionate and at the same time deeply religious in tone, the ideas of service and caring are repeatedly expressed. "May I live to guard & grow more worthy of the love you give me—of the dependence you will let me feel you have on me for some things—and always, darling, we will give God thanks & praise for revealing Himself as much as he has in each of us to the other."[37]

Harmony's need to ease and heal through love was intense and her capacity great. They were destined to become the dominant sustaining forces in the marriage. She had already done much for Ives. It was doubtless her decision that had led them to marriage, and it was she who, taking Aunt Amelia's measure, could help him free himself from her. There never seemed to be any question in Harmony's mind that they would live in New York. She remained always respectful to Amelia Brewster but made Ives her own. Amelia knew as their marriage approached who the winner was. Bitterly, she gave herself up to old age and unrequited love, all against the background of family and the role of loving aunt.

Harmony accomplished in nine months what Ives could not in a lifetime—a psychological leaving of her father. This did not mean that she did not continue to be devoted to Joseph Twichell. On the contrary, she was now free to do so. Twichell's relations with the couple were cordial, and he became a frequent visitor. Later, when he was ill and in a sanatorium in Vermont, Harmony was with him for nearly a month, the longest she ever would be away from Ives. From then on, Twichell ebbed away slowly. When he died in December 1918, Harmony was as capable of mourning him as she had been of loving him and, having chosen another, of leaving him. By contrast, Ives, at thirty-four, had not yet come to terms with his father, living and dead. In achieving a fine marriage and adopting a new family, Ives had vanquished George more than he had Amelia.

Amelia was aware that the Iveses might not measure up to the world of the

Twichells. When wedding invitations went out in May and one relative failed to respond appropriately, she wisely wrote to Ives, "Please don't think the naive ways of your Aunt Sarah are peculiar to your family. There's no family without such persons, I think."[38] But in Ives's family, it was not only a question of the Sarahs and Ikes. It was Ives's mother who was socially out of sight, for obscure reasons. That the maternal position required bolstering by the distinguished Mrs. Lyman D. Brewster only made the fact more apparent.

If Harmony's private view of George Ives was anything other than respectful and reverent, this was never in evidence. Even before her engagement, she had come to know George through Ives. Early in their courtship, visiting Danbury at Christmas, she got the received version of family history from Amelia. Later, in January, when she was recuperating in Atlantic City and Ives sent a bunch of family photographs, Harmony responded, "I think your father is wonderful looking. I wish I might have known him—I love him." Ives, with his sense of place and its nostalgic elaboration, would have told her of a Danbury already scarcely evident. When she wrote him of wanting "so much to see & grow familiar with the places you grew up in and love,"[39] she might have expected a nineteenth-century country town. By February, she was well familiar with the present-day Danbury, having by now stayed in the Ives homestead and met the rest of the Iveses—uncles Joe and Ike and their families. On her return, Harmony wrote, "It had been very sweet to me to be in your home & to be so happy here. They all love you . . . your Uncle Joe said how proud your father would be of you two boys if he were here now—well, I feel sure that your father knows your lives & sees what his love & thought has meant to you."[40] This intuitive and tactful remembrance reflected the knowledge Harmony had already gained of the rent in Ives's inner life that required constant mending. It may also have become clearer to her after visiting Danbury that the composing life of her businessman fiancé had something to do with restitution and repair. Although she may have played with the romantic notion of being the composer's creative companion, she knew well enough not to come between father and son. Amelia was her rival, but never George.

Out of *Kimash Hills* there had emerged for Ives and Harmony a homegrown aesthetic as well as a habit of creative sharing. Harmony responded sensitively out of long experience with her father. Before long, she had scrapped the abstractly absurd settings of *Kimash* for something they both knew better—"our own country . . . our forefathers." Soon she was elaborating a deeply personal version of conventional romantic ideas about inspiration in music.

It seems to me too, dearest that inspiration ought to come fullest at one's happiest moments—I think it would be so satisfying to crystallize one of those moments *at the time* in some beautiful expression—but I don't believe it's often done—I think inspiration—in art—seems to be almost a consolation in hours of sadness or loneliness & that most happy moments are put into expression after they have been memories & made doubly precious because they are *gone*—I think that is what usually happens tho' I don't see *why it should.* I think as you say, that living our lives for each other & for those with whom we come in contact generously & with sympathy & compassion & love, is the best & most beautiful way of expressing our love—and the Bravest way too, dear love, but to put it too into a concrete form of music or words would be a wonderful happiness wouldn't it? I think *you will* & that will be doing it for both of us, my darling, my blessed lamb.[41]

Ideas such as these, lived out within a growing relationship and not merely intellectualized, profoundly influenced Ives. Much of his work already incorporated that personal, deeply psychological element expressed against the background of his relationship with his father. Harmony, grasping its essence, reflected it back. At the same time, her respectful interest in George rendered Ives's private ruminations about him more acceptable. Similarly, revealing his Danbury of memory to her rekindled his interest in representing it musically. Persons, places, objects, and events of memory became more meaningful as the latent and even manifest content of music as he shared them with his bride. Ives made his music a celebration of commonplace experience. He now constructed a more specific framework than he had had before for expressing elements of inner life musically.

From within this framework developed such works as the feelingful Civil War pieces, *St. Gaudens in Boston Common* and *Decoration Day.* The sense of place as the organizer of rich association came to fruition in *Three Places in New England* and such brief works as *The Things Our Fathers Loved.* Ideas relating to the passage of time—its anchoring in the events of recorded memory as well as its fluidity in mental life—were revealed in the four seasons of the *Holiday Symphony.* These works (considered in later chapters) best display Ives's ongoing relationship with George and his preoccupation with the past. This is the thread that runs through Ives's total output, the thread that leads eventually to the *Concord Sonata* and the organization of the autobiographical *114 Songs.* But it is the same thread that eventually frayed as the substance of mental life itself failed. When that began to happen, Harmony moved to hold mind and music together.

The wedding took place on Tuesday, June 9, 1908, the Reverend Joseph Twichell officiating. "Uncle Mark" (Twain) had already inspected the groom, turning him round and declaring him fit "fore and aft." "Uncle Cornelius" (Dunham) had Harmony to dinner, presenting her afterward with a gift of gold pieces. "I thought he'd never stop," Harmony wrote Ives; "he gave us $250."[42]

The couple spent their honeymoon in the Berkshires, and in their little leather book Harmony recorded leisurely June days. She duly noted that the "C. E. Ives family continued to N.Y. via N. Haven," and marked June 30 as the start of a new life—"a Vita Nuova": "First meal at our own table—breakfast."[43] It should be no surprise that a new life soon include a new *life*. Both were poised for it, Harmony eagerly and fervently, Ives quietly, deeply. Her poems written for Ives to set to music all contain scarcely disguised metaphors of impregnation and generation. In the last collaboration before the wedding, *The South Wind* (her transcription of Heine's *Lotos Blume*), Harmony had written, "Beneath the snow she waits him and keeps her leaves' brave dress, her fair blossom opens at his first caress . . ."[44] Now Harmony was free to bear a child. She became pregnant within the first few months of marriage.

In Ives's mental life, virtually everything pointed in the direction of fatherhood. Through it, normal, everyday life would provide an opportunity for his long-standing wish to be reunited in fantasy with his lost father of childhood. At the same time, a reconciliation would be effected—a reunion not only in love but in a truce negating hostile and competitive strivings. Here, in marriage with Harmony, was one of those rare, timely, miraculous, yet completely ordinary opportunities to set things right. In the compromise, Ives could glimpse a further reward: to relive childhood experiences with a son.

It seems certain that Ives desired a boy child, and his later attitude toward children—for example, urging his nephews to father sons when all their offspring had been daughters—supports this view. Harmony may already have been pregnant when they celebrated their first New Year's Day "in our married life & our home. A very happy one."[45] Not only the so-called biological clock but also the psychological calendar exerts an influence on when a couple conceives a child. The memorializing, reconciling unconscious will, along with the body's dictates, determines when the hour is right. November was the month of George's death, and it had remained a time when Ives was especially vulnerable to depression. It may thus have been a time each year when another piece of the unending work of mourning could be accomplished. Such a set of circumstances is psychologically propitious for the conception of a child, here at least with regard to its father. For mourning fosters restitution.

In April 1909, Harmony's pregnancy was terminated by an emergency hysterectomy (the medical reason is unclear). Whatever the couple's grief, which must have been intense, their expression of it remained private. Even in their diary, the only trace of the event is a terse entry:

Apr. 20 H went to hospital
May 15 Home again
June 8 to Hartford[46]

Harmony recovered medically from an event from which full psychological recovery is scarcely possible. But her resources were many, and there was a new resource in her life now—Ives himself. Harmony's younger sister, Sally, who was visiting at the time, stayed on to help keep house for Ives while Harmony was in the hospital. Their mother wrote to Harmony:

> My heart is full of joy and gratitude over you, over Sally, and I must say over dear Charley with his great loving heart. I thought myself so happy in my trust in him, but now, after the revelations of tenderness in him through the great trial that has come to you, I feel that I did not appreciate half of what was in him. With him to protect you, life cannot bring you anything you cannot bear— and still have in your heart abiding happiness.[47]

Eventually, Ives became central in Harmony's life not only for what he might give but for what he might need. The termination of the pregnancy was only the beginning of much that Harmony would have to bear. A year later, her mother died.

The fullest, happiest, and (except for the operation) healthiest time of her marriage to Ives was destined to last less than a decade of their forty-five years together. Throughout these years, the sharing not only of a personal tragedy but also of a creative life fostered a bond that served each well in the next phase of life, after Ives suffered a physical and mental breakdown in 1918. That was when, in his words, "Mrs. Ives decided to take charge, and I am almost well again—how could be other wise?"[48] From the vantage point of Harmony's loss of the child, she would at length find her child in Ives. Their loss early in marriage resulted in a turning toward each other which made this kind of caring the more possible when the necessity arose.

There is only one document that may suggest the couple's closely guarded feelings about Harmony's operation. It is possible that some version of the song *Like a Sick Eagle* was written before 1906, but Ives ties it to the events of April 1909 with a notation on the manuscript: "H.T.I. in hospital—Sally singing 70 W. 11, April 29, '09."[49] The text of the song is a fragment from Keats, perhaps recalled from Phelps's classes at Yale: "The spirit is too weak; mortality weighs heavily on me like unwilling sleep, and each imagined pinnacle and steep of God-like hardship tells me I must die, like a sick eagle looking toward the sky."[50] The vocal line, largely through the use of quarter tones, evokes a crushing weariness and animal despair. Only in the upward movement of the last five diatonic tones is there a faint optimism—an inflection of feeble aspiration. Only in the last minia-ture musical image is some redeeming relief offered from the grinding heaviness and sense of inexorable fate of the earlier portion; only here is some answer faintly suggested for the overwhelming question of mortality.[51] There is as little left biographically of Ives's reaction to the loss of the pregnancy as there is to the death of his father. Significantly, the earlier song that most resembles *Like A Sick Eagle* in its employment of quarter tones is *At Parting*, in the section written after George's death.

Almost a year to the day after her operation, Harmony had new cause to mourn: first the death of family friend Samuel Clemens; then, three days later, the death of her mother (on April 24, 1910). Ives and Harmony once again collaborated on a song—the first since their marriage:

> Low lie the mists; they hide each hill and dell;
> The great skies weep with us who bid farewell.
> But happier days through memory weaves [*sic*] a spell,
> And brings new hope to hearts who bid farewell.[52]

Despite recent bereavements, in these lyrics Harmony somehow summoned a note of optimism. At the same time, in the music, Ives created a by now characteristic musical gesture of the question and answer, the optimism of "but." Despair is answered by hope, oblivion by memory.

In both 1909 and 1910, after the trials of April, the Iveses took summer vacation at Pell Jones', on Elk Lake in the Adirondacks. The manuscript of *Mists* notes, "last mist at Pell's Sep 20 1910." Ives created a small jewel in the setting of the modest poem.[53] The song is unusually symmetrical for him, beautifully balanced with an aspiringly rising line at the climax, "happier days." Characteristically, in a domestic, even sentimental context he was stimulated to invent music at once expressive and innovative while remaining deeply personal in content and style.

Other Twichells joined them at Pell Jones', including Sue, Sally, another brother, Burt, and Joseph Twichell. It may be expected that Deac was not far off. Until 1912, when the Iveses bought some fourteen acres at West Redding, the Adirondacks were their favorite summer vacation spot and, for Ives, a place for more concentrated work. There he started his *Fourth Symphony*, and there in 1911 he noted the "idea of a Concord Sonata."[54] What is important is the association of place rather than precise dating. Ives associated the great culminating works of his creative life with a person, a time, and a place—Harmony, the very first years of marriage, and the mountains. The experience of "the last mist at Pells'" condensed much that was to develop creatively.

The first decade of marriage coincided with a creative ferment in the composer's mind. The major and even the final works were germinating all at once, and he regularly worked at them even while composing other works. Meanwhile, he continued to write songs, which serve almost as diary entries recording the events of his inner and outer life. Ives composed in the evenings and on weekends and no doubt mentally during a good part of the working day at Ives and Co., later called Ives and Myrick. Nothing else could account for the vast creative output of so short a period.

The first decade of marriage was also the period of greatest business growth at Ives and Myrick, and Ives engaged in it vigorously. Letters to Harmony during her rare visits alone to her family brim with enthusiasm. In September 1910 he wrote, "Business has been booming."[55]

In spite of Harmony's dream of a life spent in quiet reading with her husband, their life together was not reclusive, at least during this period. Relations with family were rich on both sides. Tensions between them and Amelia eased soon after their marriage. Having come to terms with the loss of Ives to Harmony, and with the two of them as a couple, Amelia now often turned to them for counsel on family matters. She remained the matriarch and conduit of family news and problems but could identify with the couple, seeing in Harmony and Ives something of Lyman and herself at an earlier time. Such a shift in perception eased the burden of competitiveness and permitted her to settle her grievances enough to care for them both. Even Moss noted how pleasant things were when Harmony was in Danbury: "Aunt Amelia feels easier."

Beyond family and closely associated friends, life was too busy for a New York social life of a more conventional nature. There was, for example, little entertaining related to business. On January 1, 1910, Julian Myrick married Marion Washburn, with Ives as best man. Marion was the daughter of a tennis enthusiast wealthy enough to afford a private court at the family summer house. After marriage, Julian's interest in tennis and his considerable organizational skill led him to an active social life. The Iveses were certainly social equals but had little interest. Even with Julian, despite the respectful closeness the two men enjoyed in business, after-hours relations were more or less formal. Years later, Harmony still addressed Mike as Mr. Myrick. Ives for his part did not appear to have missed his companions of Poverty Flat. Life rapidly became concentrated in business, in music, and in Harmony. The last two were linked as she sought to make a place for an endeavor that must have appeared eccentric, to say the least, within a conventional life. He missed her greatly during her occasional visits with her father in Hartford. In October 1910, two days before his thirty-sixth birthday, he wrote her at 125 Woodland Avenue, Hartford: ". . . I have finished the score of the 1st movement and I feel fairly satistfied with it. Its free from extraneous substances & closely woven & the product of our summer at 'Pells'" outside of that its value I believe doubtful . . . how much I love to work when you're by me & how hard it is without you . . ."[56] The creative partnership was in some ways as unusual as the music. Ives was here referring to his *Fourth Symphony*, a visionary work of massive proportions full of the innovations that were characteristic of his evolving style. He did not choose to share these creative experiences with peers who might understand his work technically; he never sought out such musicians during his greatest period of productivity. Harmony could not have understood in any depth what he was attempting to do musically, although certain related religious and transcendental ideas would have been meaningful to her. Perhaps this was one reason Ives cultivated those ideas in music. Ives was not the first innovator who chose to work out his ideas—here musical ideas—in isolation with an encouraging partner who, in important respects, was more a mirror than a participant.

Ives's need for space and for an atmosphere of relative isolation spurred a move from New York City to the suburban town of Hartsdale, New York, in the spring of 1910. He and Harmony returned to the city in November only to move back the following spring. From Hartsdale, Ives could readily commute while living in a more rural setting. Hartsdale occupied a curious position psychologically, being in some sense a midpoint between Danbury and New York. Meanwhile, they looked for property further in the country. By the summer of 1913, they were in their house in Redding, Connecticut.

There was a further and ominous motivation for these moves. In the first years of marriage, Ives was already beginning to show signs of troubling personality alterations. Depression had shown through periodically, as in the "composer's slump" of 1905 and the ruminations of 1906. His adult life was characterized by extreme moodiness. Earlier, at college, he could be withdrawn and shy yet at times energetically enthusiastic.[57] Later, the tendencies exacerbated, rendering him reclusive and at times explosive. It is more the intensification of such character traits than any radical change that would have become noticeable to Harmony in the early years of their marriage. Isolation, physical and social, was a possible solution, one that favored both creative activity and a private, intimate style of marriage. Although Ives eventually became a cantankerous old man, now only intimations of the eventual deterioration flickered.

By the time Ives turned forty in 1914, the picture was more distinct. He had become irritable and was given to outbursts of anger and depression. By then, Harmony had developed a well-established attitude toward his behavior. From Hartford, she shook a finger at him as if she were dealing with a bad boy, a beloved truant: "I am *very glad* you are really going to put a check on your profanity—I don't mind an occasional appropriate expression—but frequent consecutive cursing such as you've indulged in lately is what I don't like to hear—poor old lamb—you get so mad, don't you."[58] Rationalizing, she acknowledged the recent stresses in their lives—the impending move to Redding, and perhaps the increasing infirmity of her father, which occasioned their only separations.

"We must try to take life as easy as we can—lately we have been sort of complicated. It is silly to let things one has get in the way of pure enjoyment—of course we are in a transition now & must be upset."[59]

Sensitive to Ives's increasing disequilibrium and no doubt troubled by it, she also attempted to deny it. She became by turns scolding and soothing. Ives's outbursts were hardly the antics of a delinquent and gradually revealed a growing emotional instability. If Harmony could not yet permit herself to see that something was wrong, it was because of her love for Ives. She wrote, "If you can't go to heaven with me on account of your badness I'll go somewhere else with you."[60] Her hope was that a peaceful family life at Redding would settle his nerves.

Many have noted that Ives was upset about the start of World War I and deeply troubled by America's entry in 1917, even attributing his decline in health and creativity to the war. But Ives's decline was gradual: his emotional instability antedated the war by several years, and his agitation about the war was more a result than a cause of his emotional state. In spite of this, during the war years he managed to do some of his best work both as a businessman and as a composer.

In the years prior to the war, the Iveses were establishing a pattern of life, wintering in an apartment in New York and spending much time in Redding from spring through fall. As the house was being readied in 1913, Harmony noted, "Charlie and Deac planted 3/4 acres of potatoes." In the spring and fall of 1913, "lilacs, roses, syringia about the house—all from old roots of Aunt Amelia."[61] In the summer of 1915, Harmony and Ives arranged through a favorite charity, the Fresh Air Fund, to have needy families use a small cottage on the property to get out of the city for a few weeks in the summer. That was how they came to know the Osborne family, whose frail fifteen-month-old child, Edith, they fell in love with. The Osbornes, along with their four older children, left in mid-August, but Edith "stayed on with us and continues to."[62] That year, they either remained in Redding until early December or at some point took a portion of their vacation at Keene Valley in the Adirondacks. In either event, Edith was with them, and the delight that both took in the child is evident from their exchanges when Harmony stopped at her parents' in Hartford on the way home. Already, Harmony reports, "she called 'Ma-ma' & 'Charlie' several times."[63]

Ives's memory may have failed him when in his *Scrapbook* he recalled being at Keene Valley that autumn. But the significance of the memory is twofold. First, he seemed to have accepted Edith as his daughter long before any formal arrangement had been made with the Osborne family. Second, he associated this event with the germination of the idea of his *Universe Symphony*: "When we were in Keene Valley, on the plateau, staying in the fall of 1915 with Sue and Grossie—and with Edie (and Edie's second mother)—I started something that

I'd had in mind for some time."[64] Grossie was, of course, Joe Twichell—already treated as Edith's grandfather.

Their attachment to the child was so rapid and so complete that it was frightening to Harmony. There can be no doubt that Ives was particularly taken by her given name, Edith. "Edie" was as close as he would get to "Eddy," the nickname that both father and son had shared. Edie was said to have been sickly and, it was implied, a burden to her mother, who worked in a New York City sweatshop. Harmony, according to this version, had appealed to Mrs. Osborne, citing Edith's favorable response to a wholesome diet and fresh air.[65] But by December Harmony was writing, "I feel as if I *couldn't* let her go from us. . . . She is a love—I'm afraid we made a mistake from *our* point of view ever to keep her."[66]

At some point, the Iveses opened negotiations with the Osborne family, and money was exchanged. What had started as charity had engaged needs too intense to deny. The means that made it possible to help the Osbornes and families like them also made it possible to have the child as their own, thus completing a family that each longed for as well as restoring the losses earlier in their marriage. Whatever arrangements were made were not without uncertainty and anguish. Ives's secretary at the time, who managed the Iveses personal accounts, spoke of their generosity to the Osbornes: "they were a very poor family, and they didn't have any money. After the Iveses took Edith, her family bothered him to death for more money, and he kept giving to them."[67]

The conclusion that the Iveses bought Edith is inescapable, although it would be a long time before they felt secure about their purchase. Well into Edith's school years, Ives remained anxious that she would be taken from them. He warned his secretary that if anybody tried to reach him regarding the child, she was not to reveal anything.[68] Denying the effects of Edith's separation from her family, they felt the attachment between themselves and her to have been mutual long before an agreement was reached with the Osbornes. In February, again from Hartford, Harmony wrote, "The baby was very sober after you left her— *us*—for sometime & asked 'Where's Slolie?'—ever so many times."[69] Deac instantly became the favorite uncle and looked forward to spending more time with them all at Redding. The baby was inexorably fusing the couple into a family even before she was theirs. "We are very incomplete without you—I mean the baby & me—mostly *me!*"[70] Yet constantly Harmony feared, "I am getting too fond of her."[71] Harmony's entry in their diary on October 18, 1916, four days short of Ives's forty-second birthday, was simply, "Edith now our own."[72]

Over the years, the joy the couple took in Edith corresponded rather imperfectly with the child's reactions. What had repaired a rent in their lives had created a tear in her own. She had been separated from living parents, presumably for more loving parents, at a year and a half. The Iveses could give her much; their life soon centered around her. But they may not have been able to give what she most wanted. According to Brewster Ives, Charles's nephew, "She seldom left home as she was not physically well and in fact was handicapped with illness all her life."[73] Others, too, convey the impression of a melancholy child.[74] A childhood acquaintance recalled a game they played: "she was a sleeping princess who would be awakened one of these days."[75]

Harmony was born to marry a great man. At the time of their engagement, Ives had had a good education but few accomplishments. He had given up any semblance of a respectable job in music and was only starting in business. Much of the music he had written to date would have been unintelligible to most people. If it was not Ives's own conviction that he might do something great in music, then it may have been Harmony's. If her husband were not quite—or not yet—a great man, she would do all in her power to help him become one. And she was prepared to shore him up where he was vulnerable and minister to his needs.

With the loss of the possibility of bearing children, these strivings of Harmony's were redirected toward her husband. The adoption of Edith effected a compromise between the needs of a child and those of a husband who before long would require much additional attention. Early in marriage, Harmony sought to encourage Ives and to create a domestic environment conducive to an unconventional life lived in a most conventional framework. Later, after an illness which, as we shall see, was in fact vaguer in character than the received diagnoses indicate, she faithfully served as nurse. Still later, when illness had exacted mental deterioration and there was less left of the greatness she had sought to instill, she served as amanuensis, often reinventing the man she wished to continue to admire and love.

Harmony balanced and stabilized Ives's life. In the fourteen years between George's death and his marriage to Harmony, Ives had never quite righted himself. He floundered at first in both music and business, not quite able to find his place. Harmony helped him focus his considerable impulse to compose and influenced the content of his music through what they shared together.

Marriage restored a living love object in Ives's life. At the same time, it fostered a reconciliation. On one level, Ives had a need to introduce Harmony to his deceased father, the person who had been most influential in his life, and thereby to reexperience George through her. Memories and feelings were revived that ultimately found representation in music. More deeply, she *was* for him the lost object. She became the creative collaborator Ives had lost in George. He also construed in her ideal features of character that he could attribute to both his father and himself—ideals of loyalty, comradeship, and patriotism. And in marriage, the earliest loss of all found restitution in a reunion with a caring mother who sought her life in his.

FOURTEEN

"CONTENTED RIVER":
MOLLIE REVENANT

E lizabeth Parmelee Ives—Mollie—
remains the unanswered question of her son's biography. She is scarcely mentioned in any of the family materials. What little correspondence remains from
Charlie's adolescence reveals her to be concerned, connected, and competent.
Early in Charlie's life, the Iveses seemed to have shared parental responsibility
with the Brewsters. By the time of Ives's marriage, however, Mollie had apparently abdicated all but nominal motherhood, and the executive role had passed to
Amelia. The single—possibly pivotal—datum that stands out as inconsistent
with what little is known about Mollie is the reference to her in George's last,
depressed letter: "Mother has another new nurse."[1]

Amelia was the doyenne of Charles and Harmony's wedding, and if Mollie was
present, none of the photographs in the Yale collection identifies her specifically.
During the courtship, Mollie had remained mysteriously in the background as
Aunt Amelia made her claim on Ives, at the same time reminding him perhaps of
some debt: "If I don't have you, I have your mother (at present), your Aunt
[Lucy Parmelee] & Cousin Ethel as my family—so perhaps it is all I can ask."[2]

During the honeymoon tour of New England, the couple had visited with
several members of the family, but here too Mollie is omitted. She is acknowledged in a single entry in the Ives's black leather diary, *Our Book*, the occasion a
week's visit to New York during the first year of marriage.[3] In Ives's auto-

biographical writings (the *Memos*) there is not a single reference to Mollie in her son's hand.

As the manifest content of biography, Ives's silence with regard to Mollie may be potentially as significant as his loquacity with regard to George. Of course, the wealth of information about the father's life from sources other than his son at least provides a vantage point from which to sort out potential fact from defensive distortion. In the absence of such material, one is on far more speculative ground. However, the symbolic representations of primary objects in art and their transformations and vicissitudes exist no less for one parent than for the other. It is inconceivable that one parent could be represented in mental life to the exclusion of the other, although the form each representation takes may be quite different. Where, then, is Mollie to be sought in the music?

The Housatonic at Stockbridge, the closing movement of *Three Places in New England*, commemorates Ives's marriage to Harmony and symbolizes Harmony as a person. In his *Scrapbook*, Ives provides a program note: "*The Housatonic at Stockbridge* was suggested by a Sunday morning walk that Mrs. Ives and I took near Stockbridge, the summer after we were married. We walked in the meadows along the river, and heard the distant singing from the church across the river. The mist had not entirely left the river bed, and the colors, the running water, the banks and elm trees were something that one would always remember."[4] He commented that "Robert Underwood Johnson, in his poem, *The Housatonic at Stockbridge*, paints this scene beautifully." The summer of 1908, after returning from the honeymoon in the Berkshires, Ives sketched a beginning for strings, flute, and organ. He worked on the piece at various times in the following years, was scoring it in the spring of 1911, and completed the orchestral version in 1914. (A version for voice and piano was later included in the *114 Songs*.)[5]

On the sketch, written in their new home at 70 West Eleventh Street, Ives reminisced: "This is to picture the colors one sees, sounds one hears, feelings one has, of a summer day near a wide river the leaves waters mists etc. all interweaving in the picture & a hymn singing in church away across the river." Later, he prefaced the orchestral score of the movement with an excerpt from the Robert Johnson poem that had seemed so congruent with his own impressions (or perhaps influenced them to begin with).

> Contented river! in thy dreamy realm—
> The cloudy willow and the plumy elm . . .
> Thou hast grown human laboring with men
> At wheel and spindle; sorrow thou dost ken; . . .
> Thou beautiful! From every dreamy hill
> What eye but wanders with thee at thy will,

Imagining thy silver course unseen
Convoyed by two attendant streams of green . . .
Contented river! and yet over-shy
To mask thy beauty from the eager eye;
Hast thou a thought to hide from field and town?
In some deep current of the sunlit brown
Art thou disquieted—still uncontent
With praise from thy Homeric bard, who lent
The world the placidness thou gavest him?
Thee Bryant loved when life was at its brim; . . .
Ah! there's a restive ripple, and the swift
Red leaves—September's firstlings—faster drift;
Wouldst thou away! . . .
I also of much resting have a fear;
Let me thy companion be
By fall and shallow to the adventurous sea![6]

Centered in an extraordinary experience shared with Harmony, this piece, like virtually all Ives's work, has both a pre- and a posthistory. At some earlier time, he made note of a musical idea accompanied by a hastily written memorandum on the sensory impressions—visual, auditory, and even tactile—that inspired it: "River mists, leaves in slight breeze river bed—all notes & phrases in upper accompaniment . . . should interweave in uneven way, riversides, colors, leaves & sounds—*not* come down on main beat."[7] The experience with Harmony in June 1908 served to organize the idea within the composer's mind. Multisensory impressions were revived and fused mentally with poetic images, resulting in expressive musical forms. In his own way, Ives too "paints the scene beautifully" in one of his most openly avowed biographical programs. Musically, his notes to himself on earlier and later sketches are realized as the "interweaving" of various elements, the sense of distance, and even "*not* coming down on the beat" is accomplished through orchestral layering, polytonality, and polyrhythms. Among other musical devices in *The Housatonic at Stockbridge* is one that Ives practiced repeatedly, a variant of question-and-answer: a deceptively simple two-part element within a more complex form. The device of the burgeoning answer is characteristic of a scattered group of the songs as well, invariably accompanied by texts relating to fervent optimism, the denial of death, and fantasies of immortality. As for the symbolism of the river, it is also encountered in the song *At The River*, derived from the *Fourth Violin Sonata*, and in the sense of sound across water in *The Pond*.

A melodic line is distinguishable through the dense, impressionistic texture, like some object discernible through the competing stimuli of nature. It is first carried by the solo horn, later by lower strings and woodwinds in a rich, late-romantic fashion reminiscent of Dvořák and late nineteenth-century usage. The melody contains a quotation from a long-familiar hymn tune that Ives utilized in several major works, the *Missionary Chant* by H. C. Zeuner ("Ye Christian Heralds, go proclaim / Salvation through Emmanuel's name."). In the thrice-repeated third note of the scale followed by a descent by an interval of a major third—the opening motif of *Beethoven's Fifth Symphony*—Ives found a common ground for musical idea and philosophical concept. He explored it further in the *Alcott* movement of the *Concord Sonata*. In his *Essays*, he calls the motif "that human-faith melody—transcendent and sentimental enough for the enthusiast or the cynic, respectively—reflecting an innate hope, a common interest in common things and common men."[8] In *The Housatonic at Stockbridge*, the setting is at once more sentimental and religious, associated with nature and with experiences shared with Harmony.

Harmony brought contentment into Ives's life, that sense of concord intrinsic to Johnson's poetry and to the music Ives strove for in *The Housatonic*. Ives's own text and music parallel the poem: an atmosphere of union and a near loss of boundaries in the multisensory soothings of nature. The sounds, sights, and tactile sensations of the outer world were all part of the experience. The complex affect that predominates in both song and story is that of a satiated contentment within a dreamy, intoxicated state. The restlessness of nature and of soul gather in the end toward a fervent assertion of optimism and hope. At once movement is "away" yet "adventurous," towards companionate reunion.

Perhaps only in such musical statements as these can we expect to find a representation of mother, albeit an earlier Mollie, in the composer's mental and creative life. There is verbal silence because the experiences of which the music speaks were preverbal. The state of mind is no simple depiction of gratified orality. It is a state poised sensitively between the polarities of soothing and stimulation, unreality and hyperreality, fusion and separation. Intensely sensual, it harks back to earliest individual prehistory and to that first human "marriage"—the union with mother—to which one forever yearns to return.

The Johnson poem as program note draws us more deeply toward early experience and primary object. The river is an undisguised metaphor for woman: it has "grown human laboring with men." And it is the body that is central as if nature itself constitutes the landscape of mother's body writ large: "Thou beautiful! From every dreamy hill / What eye but wanders with thee at thy will." Embedded in the poem is a tribute which may well be appropriate from the older man to the woman who no longer exists: "praise from thy Homeric bard, who lent / The world the placidness thou gavest him."

Praise as well as sympathy for the mother occurred in the texts of two songs of the Yale period, *The Old Mother* and *Songs My Mother Taught Me*. Both were exercises in the emulation of European song and each would later find its way into the *114 Songs*.[9] But unlike the later *Housatonic*, text and music alike have the mechanically banal sentiment of the parlor song. Each had a further history as well. Ives wrote no less than three versions of *The Old Mother*, the last in 1900. *Songs My Mother Taught Me* had a curious fate. Early in the century, perhaps 1902 or 1903, around the time he completed the *Second Symphony*, Ives arranged the piece for clarinet (or English horn), harp, and string quartet. The music itself remained unaltered except for instrumentation and the omission of text. The title, however, was changed to *An Old Song Deranged*.[10] Here is Sam, the Yale punster, at work. But could this have been a private, if bitter, joke?

What little is known about Mollie suggests a considerable degree of invalidism. If not medically an invalid, strictly speaking, she appears to have been treated as one socially, by and large respectfully ignored by the family as others assumed her rightful role. Something happened to Mollie, or perhaps emerged in her, during Charlie's adolescent years, something that the family—including Ives himself—wished to keep private. Mollie was forty-five when the nurse was mentioned in George's last letter to Charlie. She may have been beginning to undergo some form of mental deterioration at that time in the nature of a mood disorder or even presenile dementia. She was almost sixty when Ives married. We have already observed the instability that appeared to be well entrenched in Ives's character as he entered marriage at age thirty-four. He was in his forties when creativity began to fail, and by the time he was sixty the only thing he was writing was what came to be known as the *Memos*.

Rich representations of the mother in music, such as in *The Housatonic*, are fewer than those of the father. As might be expected in a revival of childhood experience, representations of the two parents are often fused. Even *The Pond*, Ives's quintessential memorialization of his father which later became the song *Remembrance*, suggests memories of mother as well. They are found in the very scene of nature, reminiscent of *The Housatonic*, and in the unsung words of the love song *Kathleen Mavourneen*, whose slowed-down notes comprise the substance of *The Pond*'s melody and which ends:

> Oh, hast thou forgotten this day we must sever?
> Oh, hast thou forgotten this day we must part?
> It may be for years, and it may be for ever;
> Oh, why art thou silent, thou voice of my heart?

As a final example, the nocturnal, muted, polyrhythmic clash of bands depicted in *Putnam's Camp, Redding, Connecticut*, the second of the *Three Places in New England*, may also represent a universal childhood experience. This is the child's invariably distorted sense of his parents' lovemaking. Ives wrote a preface to *Putnam's Camp*, significantly the only one of his several prose passages in which a woman appears.[11]

The "place," the site of General Israel Putnam's Revolutionary army winter quarters of 1778–79, is near Mollie's birthplace. The prose piece—part remembrance, part historical pageant—begins like a fairy tale: "Once upon a '4th of July' . . ." It incorporates a dream as the boy wanders off from the other children hoping to "catch a glimpse of some of the old soldiers." As "the tunes of the band . . . grow fainter and fainter" he falls asleep. In the dream (as in historical fact) "a few hot-heads" were attempting to break camp and retreat in frustration. Suddenly, "'mirabile dictu'—over the trees on the crest of the hill he sees a tall woman standing. She reminds him of a picture he has of the Goddess of Liberty. But the face is sorrowful—she is pleading with the soldiers." Idealized in an image of purity, the goddess has failed to deter the impulsive men. She abruptly disappears from the dream in the din and the sudden appearance of a triumphant Putnam, "coming over the hill from the center."

Thus unconscious elements, here a fantasied primal scene, come into play in an image of art. Music is a natural medium for representing an unseen phenomenon so strongly infused with affect. In the music of *Putnam's Camp*, two ghostly bands clash in a slow march, one softly but close by, the other (noted in the score) "as a distant drum beat." In the prose dream, as doubtless in the life of Ives the child, music both puts to sleep and awakens.

The American goddess of the dream, pleading, is overcome in battle and triumph. But she plays the role of reconciler and soother, the caring woman who Mollie very likely was in Ives's early life. Harmony assumed that role now.

FIFTEEN

A BOY'S CIVIL WAR

Or Charles Ives, the Civil War was the most important event in history. Other wars, in particular the Revolutionary War, were significant historically to Danbury and to the family. Ives himself had lived through the Spanish-American War and would in time live through two world wars. But the Civil War was for him that event in national and personal history to which all other historical events related because of his father's legendary involvement. Its effects were everywhere—in Danbury, in the world beyond, and most particularly at home. The despair of the war as well as the unbridled joy of its ending were well remembered and deeply ingrained in the lives of the local people. Monuments and artifacts were ubiquitous, and in Ives's home, as in so many, the living memory of the war in human form—in the father, brother, or son who had served—made it vivid.

In the arcane mental representation of time that each individual keeps, periods of life are variously distorted. Entire epochs may be enlarged, squeezed to near extinction, or even deleted completely from memory. Others may be elaborated out of scant experience. And still others, from before a person's birth, may be experienced as if lived. Such was Ives's sense of the Civil War years through the enduring memory of his father and his experience of the music. All of America's other wars carried associations for Ives to the Civil War. Even the music associated with the Revolutionary War, like *Putnam's Camp* and *The Fourth of July* (from the *Holidays Symphony*), contain quotations of Civil War music: *Marching Through Georgia* appears as a thematic element in both, and the second recalls *The Battle Hymn of the Republic* and *The Girl I Left Behind Me*, the traditional sprightly recessional following executions and other punishments.

At the distance of a generation, the gravity of the issues over which the war was fought and the toll it exacted might have been blurred in the child's mind by fantasies of adventure and images of bloody pageant and glory. Two elements fostered the inclination in this direction. First, the Civil War was in certain ways a boy's war. The youth of the fighting "men" was captured in the slang terms "Johnny Reb" and "Billy Yank." Second, for Americans, it was the most musical of wars. In addition to the universal gestures of martial music and their elaboration in the American band tradition,[1] music tracked the sentiment of the war in the most intimate of ways. By the summer of 1864, the belligerent patriotism of *Marching Through Georgia* and *Rally Round the Flag* had given way to the weary yearning for peace inherent in *Tenting on the Old Camp Grounds*. Sheet music sold in the millions. That the war had woven itself into the emotional fabric of family life was clear in *Bear This Gently to My Mother, Brother, Will You Come Back?* and *Tell Me, Is My Father Coming Back?*

George Ives was among those who came back from the war, and the tales he told became a part of his son's history. The stories of George's being the youngest bandmaster in the Union Army and of what Lincoln said about the regimental band were sources of pride for Ives, and he loved to recount them. What he knew about George's actual war record is unclear. George's record had been an estimable one before his court-martial and he received an honorable discharge. And many men never saw combat but served their stint waiting to be called to battle, as George did at Fort Richardson. But these were not the heroes, and Ives needed his father to be a hero.

The boy's need for a hero is governed by rules beyond reason and conscious control. The boy himself, emulating an image of the father, aspires to a heroic manhood. However, the possibility of the boy's achievement may become enmeshed in a fantasied rivalry that shakes the foundations of the father-son bond. As a result, feelings of guilt mingle with sadness and nostalgia, a painful constellation of affects that must be warded off. Where there is an element of shame from either real or fantasied sources, the normal developmental tasks of growing up are made more complex and the boy's distress is intensified. For it is as difficult to identify with an object tainted by shame as it is painful to vanquish so devalued an object. One solution that is close at hand is to preserve the image of hero and thus avoid a confrontation with reality that might entail painful affects. This was Ives's course, and it led to an idealization of George. The solution is necessarily fragile, however, requiring more or less constant mental energy for its maintenance. Ives's idealization of his father is apparent in many aspects of his life, but especially in his music related to the Civil War.

When Ives introduced Harmony to the memory of his father, he inducted her into a private and sacred sphere of his inner life. Her own experiences in life, in particular her relationship with her own father, made her receptive. Harmony came to know a sainted George Ives through his son Charles and his older sister, Amelia. She had no reason to doubt the authenticity of this picture. When she told Ives of her sense that his father knew and saw their lives, she meant it sincerely, literally. She shared this conviction with Ives along with the firm belief in life after death. Harmony later told a friend, "Yes, he'd always say he would see and talk with his father."[2]

Thus Harmony encouraged the memorialization of George. In so far as she was a psychic replacement for George, Ives had found in her a companion and collaborator. In telling his wife-to-be about his relationship with his father, he could reexperience what had been lost with appropriate grief; he might still mourn, however belatedly. In this way, the marriage was healing and liberating for Ives, at least for a time.

Among Ives's major works following their marriage were two relating to the Civil War, *Decoration Day*,[3] which became the second movement of the *Holidays Symphony*, and *The "St. Gaudens" in Boston Common*,[4] the first of the *Three Places in New England*. It was his practice to work on many pieces at once, all in different stages of composition. Thus he completed *The "St. Gaudens"* at Saranac in the autumn of 1912, working on *Decoration Day* around the same time. The *Fourth Symphony* was also in the making, and "the idea of *Concord*" was still being worked out. It seems possible that concentrating on Civil War themes and their associated affects led to a cathartic discharge of emotion. If so, the *Second Piano Sonata* (the *Concord*), among his finest works, may represent an act of sublimation in the psychological as well as the aesthetic sense, prepared for in the expression of the more personal, worldly, erotic, and aggressive elements inherent in the Civil War themes. And in writing the Civil War pieces Ives accomplished a further act of mourning.[5]

The small library of Ives's grandparents, George White and Sarah Wilcox Ives, testifies to the family's interest in social justice.[6] It included a well-worn copy of *Uncle Tom's Cabin* as well as *The Works of John Woolman*, a Quaker abolitionist. In the latter book, the chapter on the slave trade, "On Loving Our Neighbors," is particularly worn. Nor was the issue of slavery merely a subject for armchair reading. Sarah was said to have led a group of women to New Fairfield to rescue a captured slave threatened with return to the South.[7]

George Ives had continued the tradition in a manner even more personal than his mother's when he "adopted" a ten-year-old slave, Henry Anderson Brooks, in Virginia. The family endorsed his generosity warmly and participated in it, keeping in touch with Brooks for more than twenty years after the war.[8] Ives was proud of this episode in George's military life, citing it in his *Scrapbook*, where it is woven into a description of Negroes singing gospel hymns and the effects of syncopation and "off-accents."[9] The evangelical spirit of the revival had addressed social issues and spawned reform, most specifically abolitionism. Sin was renounced and redemption sought. And "the most heinous social sin" as James M. McPherson put it, "was slavery."[10] This was the tradition of the Iveses. Ives had experienced it not only through family stories and in books but also through the music of the camp meetings, in which he perceived his father as a central figure. Young Charlie, who had seen him on the stage of the meetings, construed him in fantasy as champion of the revival's religious and moral ideals as well as of its music.

In one of the earliest of his Civil War projects, Ives conceived of a Civil War set, the middle movement of which was inspired by Wendell Phillips, a gifted orator who delivered an eloquent protest in Faneuil Hall in 1837 upon the assassination of Elijah Lovejoy, an abolitionist editor.[11] No trace of the music exists, if indeed it was ever notated. It was broadly conceived in a slow-fast-slow form. Ives conceptualized the two outer movements similarly in terms of places in Boston with Civil War associations. The first would be "The Common (Largo) Emerson & Park Church" and the third "The St. Gaudens in Boston Common."[12] Only *The "St. Gaudens"* was completed, and it eventually became one of the *Three Places in New England*. Central to the music, to the Saint-Gaudens monument, and to Ives's image of the Civil War is the idea of equality. He attempts to express that idea at its loftiest and most abstract, as well as its most mundane, human, and corporeal, in the auditory image of men moving together.

On July 18, 1863, Colonel Robert Gould Shaw of Boston led a charge of the Fifty-fourth Regiment of Massachusetts on the intransigent Fort Wagner, a Confederate bastion in South Carolina defending Charleston's principal channel to the sea.[13] An earlier attempt to take the fort had failed. Shaw accepted the assignment despite the risk and the weakened condition of his men, who responded enthusiastically. The Fifty-fourth consisted of black volunteers, many of them former slaves and among the first to serve following the Emancipation Proclamation of January 1863. Frederick Douglass, himself an escaped slave, had two sons in the regiment. Others, recruited from Boston, included two brothers of William and Henry James who were officers. When the contingent left Boston at the end of May, 1862, Shaw and his men had passed the very spot where their monument would later stand.

Their first engagement was as inauspicious as their next and final one was disastrous. They were ordered to raid an undefended Confederate town. Soon thereafter, they redeemed themselves in actions related to the capture of strategic areas protecting Fort Wagner. Weary after a forty-eight-hour march and short of rations, they assumed the duty of assaulting the fort itself. Shaw led the charge on foot and was among the first to be killed. The few who reached the fort were wounded in hand-to-hand combat; only a handful were captured. An exception to the respect usually accorded a fallen Union officer by the Confederates was made in Shaw's case. His body was stripped and covered with the corpses of the black soldiers under his command before burial in a mass grave. Although it was later denied, the Confederate commander of the fort was said to have commented, "I knew Colonel Shaw before the war, and then esteemed him. Had he been in command of white troops, I should have given him an honorable burial; as it is, I shall bury him in the common trench with the negroes that fell with him."[14]

In the Northern press, this translated as "He is buried with his niggers," an inflammatory rendering of the already outrageous, which led to a tenfold increase in black enlistments. Shaw and his men had become martyrs.

Robert Gould Shaw was born into a Boston abolitionist family. Even as a colonel, he was one of the boys of war, having enlisted in 1861 at the age of twenty-four. War department records list his occupation as "student." So high did anti-slavery feeling run that many parents had no desire to shelter their children from war. Shaw's mother was bitterly disappointed when her only son at first declined leadership of the Fifty-fourth. When Shaw changed his mind, she wrote to him, "Now I feel ready to die, for I see you are willing to give your support to the cause of truth that is lying crushed and bleeding."[15]

Engaged by the Shaw Memorial Committee to create a statue, Augustus Saint-Gaudens conceived an equestrian monument—on more suited, as he admitted later, to his own youthful aspirations than to its subject. The family felt that his plan was pretentious. Besides, in his brief career Shaw had not attempted to transfer to the more dashing cavalry as many of his fellow officers had. "Accordingly," wrote Saint-Gaudens, "in casting for some manner of reconciling my desire [to have a horse] with their ideas, I fell upon a plan of associating him directly with his troops in bas relief, and thereby reducing his importance."[16] In the compromise, Saint-Gaudens condensed something of the human experience of the war. It was captured in the poem Charles Ives wrote as preface to his own work, The "St. Gaudens" in Boston Common (Col. Shaw and His Colored Regiment):

> Moving,—Marching—Faces of Souls!
> Marked with generations of pain,
> Part-freers of a Destiny,
> Slowly, restlessly—swaying us on with you

Towards other Freedom!
The man on horseback, carved from
A native quarry of the world Liberty
And from what your country was made.
You images of a Divine Law
Carved in the shadow of a saddened heart—
Never light abandoned—
Of an age and of a nation.
Above and beyond that compelling mass
Rises the drum-beat of the common-heart
In the silence of a strange and
Sounding afterglow
Moving—Marching—Faces of Souls![17]

Ives's sketches suggest that he worked on the manuscript during the summer of 1911 in Hartsdale, and in September 1912 at Lake Kiwasa and Saranac Lake.[18] It was scored completely for large orchestra in 1914. Ives dubbed the piece his "Black March."

Like many of Ives's works, The "St. Gaudens" had a clearly indicated companion-piece, in this case An Elegy for Stephen Foster. Of the elegy, Ives wrote, "This was worked on about the same time as the Black March from the first set and is something like it."[19] Later, when the Second Orchestral Set, of which the Elegy is the first of three movements, was drawn together, he renamed it An Elegy to Our Forefathers.

The musical material quoted in this companion piece supplements the historical background of the Civil War and its ethical background in abolitionism with more personal associations. To this must be added what Stephen Foster meant to Ives: he was the father of American music and, in fantasy, Ives's own father's friend. The two Foster tunes quoted in The "St. Gaudens" and An Elegy for Stephen Foster—Old Black Joe and Massa's in the Cold, Cold Ground—are related to slavery. Ives had already used the latter tune in the Second Symphony (1897–1902) and one of the Studies (no. 21), Some South-Paw Pitching (1908).[20] During the period when he was composing The "St. Gaudens," Ives quoted these songs in at least three major works: the Second String Quartet,[21] the Fourth Symphony,[22] and, most prominently, the Thoreau movement of the Concord Sonata.[23] In the Elegy, as well as the other works, it is generally the downward-oriented melody of the chorus "Down in the cornfields" that is quoted.

But to suggest that mere quotation was an end in itself, as in a medley, is to miss the train of musical thought as it developed in the mind of the composer. Tunes were like found objects; they had their own private verbal and affective associations but were woven into new forms in the process of musical thought. In these forms, idea and affect were forged into highly condensed nonverbal acoustic structures, music endowed with meaning quite different from that of the original tune. The musical quotation in Ives's work provides a bridge from verbal to nonverbal representation and a key to interpretation. But the music has its own unique logic. The ambiguity involved in nonliteral quotation of popular tunes—that is, in musical allusion—allows more subtle and complex ideas and affects to be encoded in the newly formed musical ideas. This was Ives's achievement in his music after 1908 and marriage to Harmony. It can be seen in full flower in the two orchestral sets, *Three Places*, and the four "Holidays."

In *The "St. Gaudens"* (the *Black March*), two Civil War songs are intrinsic to the thematic elements of the work, *The Battle Cry of Freedom*, by George Root, and Henry Clay Work's *Marching Through Georgia*. Foster's *Old Black Joe* provides a central organizing element in thematic development in the minor third of its verse, "I'm comin'." At the same time, it becomes a germinal idea for the construction of musical sonorities.[24]

The *Black March* is a highly stylized and individual slow march—a dirge. It proceeds at a weary, halting pace for about its first third.[25] It is as if the beholder of the Saint-Gaudens sculpture did not fasten on the drummer leading the procession until he had fully absorbed the exhausted followers in the procession, enervated to a dream-like state. Where the timpani and drums pick up the military drumbeat, Ives made a notation in the score: "From here on, though with animation, still slowly and rather evenly. Any holding back and variation should be of a cursory kind. Often when a mass of men march up hill, there is an unconscious slowing up. The drum seems to follow the feet, rather than the feet the drum."[26] The drumbeat ostinato is subtly in the background, more apparent to the eye in the score than to the ear. Ives's notation demonstrates his keen empathy with the people and events depicted. The men move together hypnotically, like automatons. And a close look at the sculpture reveals the illusion created by the artist of their walking uphill. In most of the figures, especially those immediately in front of and behind the figure of Shaw on horseback, the men appear to lean, shifting their center of gravity forward, their heads in front of the left, forward foot. In his manipulation of rhythm, Ives manages to create a parallel auditory image.

The snatches of Civil War tunes evoke events in history. George F. Root wrote *The Battle Cry of Freedom* in the summer of 1862, when Union morale was at a low ebb following the military failure at Richmond and the full retreat of the Army of the Potomac. On July 2, Lincoln had issued a call for three hundred thousand volunteers. It is impossible to convey in these days of rapid communication the effect a song could have in inspiring patriotic sentiment and galvanizing support.[27] It was probably in response to Lincoln's call that the seventeen-year-old George Ives joined the Union army.

Marching Through Georgia, by Henry C. Work, on the other hand, commemorated General William Tecumsah Sherman's triumphant Atlanta campaign and his uncontested "march to the sea" in the spring and summer of 1864—the summer of George's court-martial. The band from George's regiment had served as siege artillery brigade band, although it is unlikely that George led it on that occasion. Ives was particularly fond of Work's tune and used it in at least fifteen pieces. (Perhaps its appeal to him had something to do with the word association of George and Georgia.)[28] The use of the tune *Old Black Joe* introduces a sense of nostalgia for days gone by and for reunion with "the gentle voices calling." In the ghostly fabric of the music, one has the illusion of hearing other songs of the period; at times *Oh Susanna*, among others, seems to peek out.

The *"St. Gaudens" in Boston Common* traces an auditory image parallel to the visual image of Saint-Gauden's black foot soldiers, which conveys a sense of the weary desperation of the war by the time of their martyrdom. A climax of sonority three-quarters through the piece marks an attempt to portray Colonel Shaw.[29] The penultimate ascending musical figure outlines a phrase of *Marching Through Georgia* that is set to the words, "Sing it as we used to sing it fifty-thousand strong" and "So we sang the chorus from Atlanta to the sea." At the same time, the disposition of the melodic lines of the brass choir lends the impression of a hymn both as seen on the printed page and as heard through the massed orchestral forces. The horn leads in what might be a quotation, although it is not readily identifiable, and the quick glimpse of a grand chorale is hushed immediately in the return of the former musical mood.

It would be difficult to construe this climactic moment as either triumphant or joyful. Of the chief songs quoted, neither the hortatory *Battle Cry* nor the jubilant *Marching* is given full measure. Rather, it is a grim and tragic musical image, somewhat threatening in its sudden intensity, in stark contrast to the visual image of the equestrian statue. For in the Saint-Gaudens sculpture, the hero sits erect upon the powerful horse in the midst of his weary men. His horse, taking the brunt of the hill, inclines him upright against gravity, in contrast to the men who strain forward. He appears courageous, his left hand grasping the saddle, but his eyes are ghostly and sad, different from those of the heavy-lidded, exhausted men. He looks far older than his twenty-six years, hardly a boy of war any longer.

Ives captured much of his sense of the war in both its public and private aspects in his musical imagery of Shaw, whom he must have strongly identified with his own personal hero, George Ives. From Ives's writings, there can be no question but that he saw George thus, a view reinforced by Amelia and the rest of the family. It was this father he shared with Harmony, and she encouraged him to express his vision in music through the well-worn romantic aesthetic she espoused when she wrote to him about "inspiration . . . in art" and "memories."[30] While this might be the rationale behind much program music, it was nonetheless deeply felt, and Harmony came upon it freshly and sincerely, from personal experience with Ives. In marrying a composer, the long-standing reader in her wondered about the autobiographical side of art. "I never thought about it before either—that is that a composer shows *him-self* less in music than in any other line. . . I'm afraid I'd find it easier to guess the meaning of the music thro' knowledge of the man than vice versa."[31] Harmony nurtured this autobiographical tendency in her husband, and Ives, responding, produced works of far greater depth than these naive aesthetic notions might suggest.

The images, visual and sonic, conjured in *The "St. Gaudens"* are those of the tragic hero, the victor, and the vanquished, the boy become a weary man. In Ives's mind, beside the memory of the bandmaster-leader, the mythologized hero of fantasy, lay the failed soldier and defeated youth he must somehow have known from the sad entry in his father's notebook: "A space of three years servitude as Leader . . . and one year sick."[32] But his favorite, if distorted, manner of remembering George was closer to that of John Greenleaf Whittier, the Quaker abolitionist poet,[33] who wrote, "The only regiment I ever looked upon during the war was the 54th Massachusetts on its departure for the South. I can never forget the scenes as Colonel Shaw rode at the head of his men. The very flower of grace and chivalry, he seemed to me beautiful and awful, as an angel of God come down to lead the host of freedom to victory."[34] It remained for Ives to write his own poem as well as the music: "Moving—Marching—Faces of Souls!"

Ives's greatest memorialization of George is to be found in the *Decoration Day* movement of his *Holidays Symphony*.[35] In the *Scrapbook* he noted that the "set of pieces for Orchestra called *Holidays* had its career from 1897 to 1913."[36] It thus spanned the greater part of his creative lifetime, a period encompassing the four symphonies, the two string quartets, a violin sonata, a piano sonata, much church and chamber music, and many songs. In addition, he was completing the *First Orchestral Set*, of which the *Black March* was a part, and had already begun work on the *Concord Sonata*. *Holidays* was chiefly written from 1904 to 1913, with the final spurt of activity in 1912–13, when Ives brought together the many diverse elements of the work and scored the second and third movements, *Decoration Day* and *Fourth of July*.

Similarly, in the *Scrapbook* Ives recorded some of the history of *Decoration Day:* "It was started at about the same time the *Washington Birthday* was [1913]. The middle section . . . was taken from an organ piece written some years before. In my opinion this is the poorest part of the movement. The melody of the march before the end is from Reeves's 'Second Regiment Quickstep'—as good a march as Sousa or Schubert ever wrote, if not better."[37] Ives conceived of

Holidays as a kind of New England *Four Seasons*, "pictures of a boy's holidays in a country town."[38]

Whereas Ives had written a poem to supplement and underline the musical content of *The "St. Gaudens,"* in the case of *Decoration Day* he wrote an elegiac, quasi-fictional memoir appended as a postface to the printed score:

> In the early morning the gardens and woods about the village are the meeting places of those who, with tender memories and devoted hands, gather the flowers for the Day's Memorial. During the forenoon as the people join each other on the Green there is felt, at times, a fervency and intensity—a shadow, perhaps, of the fanatical harshness—reflecting old Abolitionist days. It is a day as Thoreau suggests, when there is a pervading consciousness of "Nature's kinship with the lower order—man."
>
> After the Town Hall is filled with the Spring's harvest of lilacs, daisies and peonies, the parade is slowly formed on Main Street. First come the three Marshals on plough horses (going side-ways); then the Warden and Burgesses *in carriages*, the Village Cornet Band, the G.A.R. [Grand Army of the Republic], two by two, the Militia (Company G.), while the volunteer Fire Brigade, drawing the decorated hose-cart, with its jangling bells, brings up the rear—the inevitable swarm of small boys following. The march to Wooster Cemetery is a thing a boy never forgets. The role of muffled drums and "Adeste Fidelis" answer for the dirge. A little girl on the fencepost waves to her father and wonders if he looked like that at Gettysburg.
>
> After the last grave is decorated "Taps" sound out through the pines and hickories, while a last hymn is sung. Then the ranks are formed again and "we all march back to Town" to a Yankee stimulant—Reeves' inspiring "Second Regiment, Quick-Step,"—though to many a soldier, the sombre thoughts of the day, underlie the tunes of the band. The march stops—and in the silence, the shadow of the early morning flower-song rises over the Town and the sunset behind West Mountain breathes its benediction upon the Day.[39]

Decoration Day is, above all, a construction of memory on several levels. First is the ubiquitous human phenomenon of recalling the past as memory emerges spontaneously or is consciously summoned. The artistic reconstruction of a memory is of a different nature. Even if an artist has explicitly stated his or her intent to remember (that is, to construct or re-create a memory) in a work of art, this conscious intent can never gain complete control over a mass of unconscious content related to that memory or over the process by which it would emerge. Thus, even if a composer were to state this intent—for example, in a program—it would bear the same relationship to the music as does manifest content to the latent content of dream or fantasy.

In the postface, Ives has provided us at once with a program and a piece of autobiographical writing. Like all such writing, it is an amalgam of memory traces of events as they may actually have occurred, either once or repeatedly, and both conscious and unconscious distortions variously motivated. In relating it to the piece, he states, in effect: This is what this work is about; this is what I remember. Yet nowhere in the Postface does he use "I" to identify the rememberer. The rememberer is constituted by different aspects of Ives, disguised as "those who, with tender memories and devoted hands, gather the flowers," "the inevitable swarm of small boys," and even "a little girl on the fencepost" waving to her father, wondering what he looked like at Gettysburg.

This last is the only passage in Ives's prose writings where he reveals the fantasy of being a girl. I have noted earlier bisexual elements in Ives's mental life—not only those typical in human development but those that were intensified in a close, ambivalent attachment to his father. The wish to be a girl and to possess one's father passively is a development of this theme, a common solution to conflicts relating to love and aggression. For Ives, conscious glimmers of such strivings were so abhorrent as to elicit vociferous responses which escalated in proportion to the resulting anxiety. Only in *Decoration Day* is the little girl in the man permitted a place on the fence along the route of the parade march, looking with admiration at her father and lost in a reverie about him. Ives's retrospective masculinization of his musical experiences with his father asserts their intimacy while denying any hint of effeminacy.

"The march to Wooster Cemetery is a thing a boy never forgets," wrote Ives. Two marches are heard in the music. The first is the slow march in *Adeste Fidelis*, quoted by Ives from a youthful organ prelude, an early collaboration with George;[40] the second is D. W. Reeves's *Second Regiment Connecticut National Guard March*. Wooster Cemetery is where George is buried and where Ives, approaching forty as he completed *Decoration Day*, had every reason to believe he would be interred. The first march—more accurately, the dirge—would indeed have been memorable to the twenty-year-old Ives, hurriedly returning to Danbury from his first weeks at Yale for his father's funeral. And it would have been heavy with irony, for the journey up Main Street to the Wooster Cemetery had often been made by the village cornet band, led by the uniformed George, with Charlie himself occasionally among the snare drummers. In actuality, the celebrations and parades had come first, and the last march had been the dirge; in *Decoration Day*, the order is reversed, with Reeves's "Second Regiment, Quick-Step," the "Yankee stimulant"—as Ives put it—bursting into the music with near-hallucinatory vividness. For a moment, reminiscence comes close to resurrection. But reality holds sway, and mourning must be accomplished. The march stops, and in a special kind of silence created by the composer in both the prose and the music, a sense of peaceful benediction prevails.

Perhaps if Ives had attempted to be even more concretely and consciously autobiographical, the result would have been a more contrived, less subtle re-creation of memory. It was surely his intent to "remember" in all the sections of the *Holidays Symphony*. Behind the manifest purpose, however, lie subtle representations of memory, certainly with elements not conscious to the composer. *Decoration Day* is one of the most important constructions of memories of George.

The hero whom Ives memorializes in this musical reconstruction cum program is his father. Numerous discrete elements of memory and fantasy are consciously elicited and organized by the composer in a musical invention. Other elements emerge, their content latent but potentially analyzable. The final, composite portrait shows George at his finest, and the construction of this memory serves multiple functions—not memorialization alone. The most important is idealization of the hero, restoring esteem to both father and admiring son and in the process denying some painful realities. The construction of the memory thus serves to rescue the idealized image of the composer's father. The means, through music, involves the auditory sphere, the chief channel of intercourse between father and son in life and in death.[41]

A memory is not image and idea alone but also embodies associated affects. One of the functions of reminiscence is to encourage the reexperiencing of such feelings. Accordingly, it is an essential adjunct to mourning and the working through of painful affects related to loss and ambivalence. Ives's lifelong collaboration with George was part of this mourning process, and *Decoration Day* is an unusually specific instance of it. Ives's reconstruction of the idealized memory of George in music results in a representation intended for the composer himself to experience and for the responsive listener to share. This process could not have been under the composer's conscious control.

The peaceful first section of the work serves as a counterweight to the raucous diverse elements that follow, creating a sober "once-upon-a-time" atmosphere at the inception. The second section is full of musical quotations that plunge us squarely into the Civil War period, including *Marching Through Georgia* and Stephen Foster's distinctively Southern *Oh Susanna* and *Nelly Bly*. After a brief reference to *Adeste Fidelis*, Ives quotes another Civil War song, *Tenting Tonight*. Following its defeat at Fredericksburg, the Union Army spent the winter of 1862–63 camped in the Virginia mud. The demoralizing experience and resultant longing for home inspired *Tenting Tonight*, written the following summer by a draftee, Walter Kittredge. It was subsequently sung "in the South as well as the North" and "for fifty years afterward brought tears and fond memories to veterans as they gathered at reunions and encampments."[42]

The section closes with a quotation of *Taps*, the requiem of the military. The sense of distance in time and place in the music further emphasizes its memorial quality, and its amalgamation with a tolling bell in the final portion is a curious condensation of the ideas of arousal and sleep or death.

The climax of the movement is the startling rendition of the Reeves march, the favorite march of both father and son, which contains the germ of many shared experiences. It provides another example of a posthumous collaboration since Ives used George's own copy of the Reeves march in working on *Decoration Day*, which already had some markings in George's hand.[43] At the same time, the march goes back to what was probably their first such collaboration, when Ives was thirteen (dated "X-mas '87"). This was the *Holiday Quickstep*—Ives's first use of the word *holiday* in a title—for which a set of parts exists mostly in George's hand.[44] (Ives quoted the Reeves march on one previous occasion, the *Yale-Princeton Football Game* of 1899.)

The intense silence that reigns in the final section of *Decoration Day* is quite poignant. It places the Reeves march in a new light, as if it had been framed all along in some underlying context that is now revealed. That context is a musical representation of the composer's mental state, one of reminiscence and mourning.

In the score of *Decoration Day* Ives calls for an "extra" violin. Throughout this piece, this part has a dissonant relationship to the body of the strings, usually that of the major seventh. In a footnote to the score, Ives called this a "shadow": "It should be always kept at a much lower intensity than the other parts. It stands in the background as a kind of shadow to the other strings."[45] This may be a concrete representation of George, who played violin (among several other instruments) and seemed to have been practicing it during the first years of Ives's life.

The use of the Reeves march in *Decoration Day* constitutes a compound aural memory of George at his finest. It is at once a constructed memory, in the artistic psychological sense, a reminiscence, and a memorialization. It is George himself—in his son's fantasy the greatest hero of the Civil War—who is paraded. It is the George of George's own youth, the Union's youngest bandmaster, leading the First Connecticut Heavy Artillery Regiment Band in Reeves's *Second Regiment Connecticut National Guard March*. And it is the George of Charlie's youth, the hero of the village, still in uniform (perhaps the uniform donned for special occasions), leading the Danbury Brass Band down Main Street. A photograph of George dated around 1890 shows him in uniform and holding his cornet, an object Ives kept with him all his life. In a photograph of Charles Ives's studio in West Redding, the same cornet appears on a shelf near the window in view of the piano.

Thus in *Decoration Day* George is vividly actualized, idealized. But nowhere is the sad Civil War boy to be found, the boy who passed "one year sick." Neither here nor in other works or writings is he depicted as the village eccentric and jester, the musical hired hand. Nor do we find the debased clerk confined to a menial task in his family's business, supervised by a young nephew. These painful perceptions were expunged from Ives's memory.

Certainly any image of the nineteen-year-old George who destroyed the instrument so proudly featured by the village cornet band has been erased completely. What other aspects of George may be hidden, deleted, or distorted in the creation of the hero we cannot know. Frequently, the screening function serves to blot from memory events and experiences related to trauma. In addition to memory, painful or otherwise unacceptable affects may be similarly screened. The adult Ives, now married into a family with a more distinguished father, was pursuing a career that already promised success far beyond that to which his father had aspired. Feelings of shame and guilt as well as the memories that produced them had to be shielded from consciousness. In the process, a highly original work of art was created and a family myth upheld.

Ives's presentation and representation of his father to Harmony ushered in a new stage of remembrance and mourning. Much was revived for Ives during the initial sharing of intimacy in courtship and early marriage. The immediate feelings elicited by George's death had been too intense for Ives to come to terms with when he was twenty, and as we have seen, not more than a word or two about the event remains in any of his writings. In Ives's thirties, with Harmony's help, a new George emerges. The distortions inherent in this representation followed a predictable path, that of the family romance.

At the core of the family romance, which Freud first described, is the imaginative activity of the child (here refined in the imaginative processes of the artist),[46] which gives rise to the universal fantasy that one's parents are not one's real parents and that one is the offspring of a man and woman of higher and nobler station. These elements of alienation and ennoblement can be spun into endless variations. The alienation may be repressed or denied, and the ennoblement may become extreme, giving rise to an image of exalted parentage. In Freud's view, the motives for the child's elaboration of a distinctive family romance are, first, the inevitable disappointment in parents idealized from earliest childhood and, second, the similarly inevitable provocations of real or perceived slights experienced in the process of growing up. The child's earliest image of parents, according to Freud, hark back to "the happy, vanished days when his father seemed to him the noblest and strongest of men and his mother the dearest and loveliest of women."[47]

With marriage Ives sought, as all men do, to restore a relationship with that dearest of women. And in rather successfully doing so, he gained in the Twichells a new family as well, a distinguished one more along the lines of his own family romance. Indeed, even earlier he had found an alternative family in the Brewsters. And as time went on, an enactment of the classical alienation of the actual parent could be seen in Ives's respectfully distant attitude toward his own mother. But increasingly, the George Ives of fantasy and imaginative re-creation was endowed with the status of hero. In Ives's Civil War pieces we find the most striking of these representations.

Ives's family romance in music had been apparent from his days with Horatio Parker. Aligning himself with Parker's European tradition, Ives had hoped for a brief time to inherit Parker's musical patrimony. *The Celestial Country* was the result, shortly before Ives abandoned this striving in order to enter a private world of music. Increasingly, the family romance assumes an important position in this private world, which Harmony now shared to the degree she was able. And it extends still further in such later works as the *Concord Sonata* and, at an extreme, the *Universe Symphony*.

In his musical reconstruction of an ideal heroic father, Ives has preserved and memorialized his own father, at the same time creating a minor but appealing American legend. For the unique relationship between father and son became well known; scarcely a program or record jacket fails to mention it. Thus did Charles Ives himself bridge the gap from private fantasy to public legend. In doing so, he may have accomplished a memorialization of George beyond those of *The "St. Gaudens" in Boston Common* and *Decoration Day*, and beyond his fondest dreams.

SIXTEEN

PLACES IN THE SOUL

Ⅰt is no coincidence that the titles of many of Ives's major works denote particular places, persons, periods, events (both private and historical), concepts, ideals, and objects. These are the stuff of memory and of life, building blocks in the formation of autobiography.

Owing to the influence of Lyman Brewster, Ives's musical evocation of the Revolutionary War antedated any deliberate representation of the Civil War. The *Overture and March: "1776"*, begun around Christmas, 1903, (to make restitution for the delay in composing the music for Lyman's play, *Major John Andre*), was "dovetailed" by Ives in 1911 with the *Country Band March* to become the second of the *Three Places*, retitled *Putnam's Camp, Redding, Connecticut*.[1] In his *Scrapbook*, Ives referred to this amalgamated version as *The Children's Holiday at Putnam's Camp*.[2] He probably started it soon after his marriage.[3]

A memorial park still stands outside Danbury on the site where General Israel Putnam of the Continental army (and a hero of Bunker Hill) encamped in the winter of 1778–79. It commemorates events of the Revolutionary War contemporaneous with General David Wooster's service in Danbury. Isaac Ives had not yet come to Danbury, but Charles's great-great-grandfather, the Reverend Ebenezer White, had; and, in the general destruction wrought by the British attack on Danbury, the liberal minister's new church was burnt down in 1777.

Putnam's Camp is, among other things, a battle piece, like Beethoven's battle symphony, *Wellingtons Sieg,* and Tchaikovsky's *1812 Overture.* Ives's version is distinctly American and replete with associations to local, regional, and personal history. It is also cast in the form of a small boy's experience. Ives added the following preface to the printed score:

> Near Redding Center, Conn., is a small park preserved as a Revolutionary Memorial; for here General Israel Putnam's soldiers had their winter quarters in 1778–1779. Long rows of stone camp fire-places still remain to stir a child's imagination. The hardships which the soldiers endured and the agitation of a few hot-heads to break camp and march to the Hartford Assembly for relief, is a part of Redding history.
>
> Once upon a "4th of July," some time ago, so the story goes, a child went there on a picnic, held under the auspices of the First Church and the Village Cornet Band. Wandering away from the rest of the children past the camp ground into the woods, he hopes to catch a glimpse of some of the old soldiers. As he rests on the hillside of laurel and hickories, the tunes of the band and the songs of the children grow fainter and fainter;—when—"mirabile dictu"— over the trees on the crest of the hill he sees a tall woman standing. She reminds him of a picture he has of the Goddess of Liberty,—but the face is sorrowful— she is pleading with the soldiers not to forget their "cause" and the great sacrifices they have made for it. But they march out of camp with fife and drum to a popular tune of the day. Suddenly a new national note is heard. Putnam is coming over the hills from the center,—the soldiers turn back and cheer. The little boy awakes, he hears the children's songs and runs down past the monument to "listen to the band" and join in the games and dances.
>
> The repertoire of national airs at the time was meagre. Most of them were of English origin. It is a curious fact that a tune very popular with the American soldiers was "The British Grenadiers." A captain in one of Putnam's regiments put it to words, which were sung for the first time in 1779 at a patriotic meeting in the Congregational Church in Redding Center; the text is both ardent and interesting.[4]

The preface is a construction of fact, memory, and fantasy. Ives has merged a story of mutineers marching out of the camp, only to return inspired by the triumphant Putnam, with boyhood memories of George's musical experiments, in which two bands approached each other from opposite directions, playing all the time.[5] In such events, since the bands would never be at precisely the same distance from the listener, the sounds from them would never seem in synchrony and always appeared distorted. *Putnam's Camp* creates the illusion of two distinct marching bands playing simultaneously, in the same rhythm but at slightly different speeds. Ives noted that the repertoire of national airs at that time was meager. Accordingly, he takes the liberty of supplementing *The British Grenadiers* with *Hail Columbia, Marching Through Georgia,* and even Sousa's *Semper Fidelis,* as if all wars were interchangeable.

The prose piece is one of those elegiac fictions that crop up not only in the prefaces to the *Places* but in the texts to some of the songs as well. *Tom Sails Away*,[6] *The Things Our Fathers Loved*,[7] and *Old Home Day*[8] are examples, dealing consistently with the mental and material artifacts of childhood. Usually the music seeks to evoke a dream-like atmosphere. In *Putnam's Camp*, the child, a boy this time, presumably has fallen asleep, for he awakens to the music. The change in state is dramatized by a gradual decrescendo and ritard.[9] This is followed by an orchestral arpeggio on a dissonant chord, which heralds the dream. The full chord as played by the piano shows that the dissonance is related to one of the "piano-drum" chords Ives was fond of using, which reminded him of his own boyhood musical experimentation and his father's guidance.[10] Immediately thereafter in the musical dream, the two ghostly bands clash in a slow march—one softly but close by, the other "as a distant drum beat."[11] The fictitious child awakens as a more moderate march time resumes following this musical episode.

The music that results is, of course, far more than these constituent elements derived from childhood. It produces complex polyrhythms, arresting and innovative in its time and even now requiring considerable conducting skill to bring off successfully. Similarly, in *Putnam's Camp* the incorporation of borrowed material has reached a highly sophisticated level, resulting in an amalgam of dense musical quotation. Accordingly, from the building blocks traceable to the past and to the mental life of the composer, Ives created something greater here and in other works of his mature period: musical formations that hardly require a program in order to be artistically cogent. At the same time, listening to such musical passages in Ives's works suggests a chink in the surface of "pure music," a knothole in the fence through which one may observe what is happening within. Some may call such music flawed, and it may well be. But it nonetheless remains a point of entry into the mental life of the artist that permits us to relate his private life to the notes on the page in a manner that few, if any, other composers have allowed.

The door to one's childhood is never completely sealed, yet some gifted individuals retain a more constant access, not only to memory, but also to a kind of mental function more characteristic of earlier life. Phases of development may never achieve full closure, and what may in some people seem a defect may for the artist be a source of creativity.[12] What we find in *Putnam's Camp*, the other two *Places*, and indeed all of Ives's mature works is the composer's continued capacity to daydream as a child might, intensely if briefly, and the ability to incorporate diverse elements of meaningful experience into a whole that is endowed with the illusion of reality. In the music, a complex texture is achieved, one that is both sophisticated and naive-sounding.

The prefatory sketch about the child—sentimental, nostalgic, guileless, and, in its final paragraph, pseudo-scholarly—says much about Ives. Above all, it reveals access to childhood memory and to the fluctuations of mental state characteristic of childhood. This capacity to access and to revive continued well into maturity and was one of the wellsprings of his creativity. Very often for Ives, one such state, the daydream, facilitated reminiscence in addition to fostering more fanciful elements of imagination which were outside of everyday experience. The Fourth of July sketch contains elements of both. The child's falling asleep on a July Fourth picnic seems unlikely. Rather, the author is inadvertently describing his own lifelong capacity to utilize mental states to distance himself (even from so compelling an event as a child's Fourth of July festivities) and to retreat into the even more compelling and concentrated imaginative world in which the adult artist manipulates alternative forms of reality.

As for the imaginative element, the child in Ives—and *pari passu* the artist—neither plays soldier nor plays with soldiers. He manipulates soldierly symbols and images, here in their auditory representations. The authentic field of action is hardly the literal site in Redding, Connecticut, but plainly that within the artist's mind, where he may freely furnish the symbolic objects of his choice, invent their interaction, and dictate their entrances and exits. In doing so, he must introduce elements of personal experience and memory. In this context, the memory of passing bands is reproduced. Nor can one assume all is under the conscious control of the composer, even if his intent was to reproduce a childhood auditory memory. Latent, unconscious meaning regularly sneaks aboard and, like a stowaway, remains hidden.

In *Putnam's Camp* the music, putting the boy to sleep and waking him up as well, replicates a general condition of the composer's childhood as well as the specific one of arousal by his father as disturber. The local bands of the composer's childhood sometimes practiced in the yard; at other times he could hear them at a distance while asleep or falling asleep. On a few occasions, following celebrations with massed bands, the child put in bed might hear the various bands on their way home, dispersed. At such times, blendings and crashings could be heard in the night. But beyond this are hidden two constellations of memory and affect screened by the benign "Once upon a '4th of July'" atmosphere. Discussed earlier, the first was that of the primal scene clash; the second, the earliest auditory trauma of childhood. Never quite mastered, they appear in later musical incarnations.

Threads of experience bind *Putnam's Camp* to two other works associated with places, times, and events of memory. These are two movements of the *Holidays Symphony:* the *Fourth of July*[13] and *Washington's Birthday*.[14] Lyman Brewster and George Ives stand in the background as parallel and perhaps, in the mind of the composer, contending influences. He called these works "attempts to make pictures in music of common events in the lives of common people (that is, of fine people), mostly of the rural communities." Ives acknowledged that they could be played as "abstract music," but this would mean "a covering up, or ignorance of (or but a vague feeling of) the human something at its source."[15]

The "human something" of *Washington's Birthday* relates to both George and Lyman. "The first part of this piece," Ives wrote, "is but to give the picture of the dismal, bleak, cold weather of a February night near New Fairfield."[16] It was familiar country weather, and in his prose postface, he associates it to "the sternness of the Puritan's fibre," quoting Thoreau: "Cold and Solitude are friends of mine."[17] Ives goes on to remark on the middle and brief final section of the piece:

> But to the younger generation, a winter holiday means action!—and down through "Swamp hollow" and over the hill road they go, afoot or in sleighs, through the drifting snow, to the barn dance at the Centre. The village band of fiddles, fife and horn keep up an unending "break-down" medley, and the young folks "salute their partners and balance corners" till midnight;—as the party breaks up, the sentimental songs of those days are sung half in fun, half seriously, and with the inevitable "adieu to the ladies" the "social" gives way to the grey bleakness of the February night.[18]

There is a profusion of musical quotation—as Hitchcock put it, "bald tune-quotations, not so much developed as coming to mind, some half recalled or even mis-remembered."[19] Kirkpatrick cites at least nine, ending with *Home Sweet Home* and *Goodnight, Ladies*. In fact, Ives's description suggests the barn dance of his father's time more than his own, and he notes the connection in a comment on the multiplicity of rhythms.

> As I remember some of these dances as a boy, and also from father's description of some of the old dancing and fiddle playing, there was more variety of tempo than in present day dances. In some parts of the hall a group would be dancing the polka, while in another a waltz, with perhaps a quadrille or lancers going on in the middle. . . . Sometimes the change in tempo and mixed rhythms would be caused by a fiddler who, after playing three or four hours steadily, was getting a little sleepy—or by another player who had been seated too near the hard cider barrel.[20]

Ives attempted to create an imaginative aural image of the event, to preserve "the old breakdown tunes and backwoods fun and comedy and conviviality that are gradually being forgotten." This description best fits the days of George's youth, when Danbury was more rural than it was in Ives's day. Moreover, elements of memory have been condensed in the passage from one generation to another both temporally and, in the picture of the barn dance, spatially. The entire scene is viewed as if through a distant convex mirror.

The "dismal, bleak" winter of the first part bore a relationship to February 1778 and George Washington's encampment at Valley Forge, depicted in Lyman Brewster's *Major John Andre*. In this scene, Benedict Arnold comes to see Washington to request a commission. The scene is anticipated by a pious panegyric to Washington, sentimentally rendered by an old soldier.[21]

Probably the finest of the three associated works is the *Fourth of July*, which has a rather typical patchwork history. Completed in 1912–13, it was started in Hartsdale in 1911 "from chords in 'Cage' 1905."[22] In *Putnam's Camp*, Ives had devised a scheme to achieve "a composite sounding noise" from the orchestra, and he returned to it in composing the *Fourth of July*. Here once again bands clash, and the piece is marked by two "explosions" of sound, one of which carries this description in the sketch: "Town Hall fireworks blow up, skyrockets, firecrackers." He also elaborated on the "band jokes" of *Decoration Day* and, wishing to make sure that the copyist did not make "corrections," wrote on the score, "Mr. Price: Band stuff—they didn't always play right & together and it was good either way." For a title, he wrote sassily, "III Fourth of July (a boy's '4th of July' in these here you Knighted States)."[23]

Despite its polyglot origins, the *Fourth of July* coheres. The quotations themselves are organizing elements, among them the Civil War *Battle Cry of Freedom*, *Battle Hymn*, and *Marching Through Georgia*.[24] Ives said that his *Fourth of July* was pure program music but was also pure abstract music, as the music stands on its own. Its composition, however, linked him to his boyhood as much as *Washington's Birthday*, *Putnam's Camp*, and *Decoration Day* did. He wrote:

> I remember distinctly, when I was scoring this, that there was a feeling of freedom as a boy has, on the Fourth of July, who wants to do anything he wants to do, and that's his one day to do it. And I wrote this feeling free to remember local things etc., and to put [in] as many feelings and rhythms as I wanted to put together. And I did what I wanted to, quite sure that the thing would never be played, and perhaps *could* never be played—although the uneven measures that look so complicated in the score are mostly caused by missing a beat, which was often done in parades.[25]

Thus he described the access to memory that characterizes this group of pieces. The "band stuff" variations on a theme, differing somewhat in each of these works, reevoked experience from the beginnings of conscious life to the death of George. In a real sense, it went back even further, to George's musical stories from the Civil War and the years of Reconstruction before Ives's birth. Even technical devices Ives used in these works were frequently associated with George—for example, Ives said of his *Fourth of July*, "Technically, a good deal of this movement was suggested by the old habit of piano-drum-playing."[26]

Through such devices George's experiments, and George's permission for Ives to experiment, lived on. The music—on the page, in the "air," perceived in the inner ear or hallucinated in the mind's ear—had the function of maintaining the connection through time.

The places, things, days (both holidays and ordinary days) and ideas that occupied Ives's mind provide an index to the raw materials of imagery and, at the same time, outline his individual human profile. For example, when Ives spruced up several songs for publication in *114 Songs* in the early 1920s, he gave each a date, presumably the original date of composition. Although the accuracy of the dating has been challenged, it is nevertheless interesting to consider possible psychological motivations behind Ives's ascription of certain songs to certain dates.

Two songs are frankly called *Memories*, listed as "A,—Very pleasant" and "B,—Rather Sad." Ives dated them 1897, but since there is no manuscript, he may have written the pieces either after or even before that year. The date may be appropriate in an idiosyncratic way: to Ives, 1897 meant the past, the Yale years, the first years of bereavement, and the end of boyhood. The first song is a miniature memoir of a boy in the "opera house"—probably Taylor's, built in 1870 and popular in Ives's boyhood. Minstrel and other musical shows were presented there, some by the best professional traveling companies. The opera house had been the scene of many of George's quasi-professional performances. As he usually did in such "memories," Ives wrote the text in the present tense, the time frame of remembering:

> We're sitting in the opera house, the opera house, the opera house;
> We're waiting for the curtain to arise
> with wonders for our eyes;
> We're feeling pretty gay,
> and well we may,
> "O, Jimmy, look!" I say,
> "The band is tuning up and soon will start to play."
> We whistle and we hum, best time with the drum.
> [*Whistle———*]
> We're sitting in the opera house, the opera house, the opera house,
> awaiting for the curtain to rise
> with wonders for our eyes,
> a feeling of expectancy,
> a certain kind of ecstasy,
> expectancy and ecstasy,
> expectancy and ecstasy—Sh'—s'—s'—s.
> [*Curtain!*][27]

The music is marked *presto* and, on the oom-pah piano part, "As fast as it will go." It conveys a sense of breathlessness, which is heightened by the literal whistling, the letting off of steam, and the sibilant shushes before the curtain. It vividly re-creates childhood excitement quite aside from the terms "expectancy" and "ecstasy," the retrospective footnote of the sophisticated adult.

The "rather sad" memory is more nostalgic than truly unhappy. In fact, in their retrospective ways, words and music seem to represent a variety of affects in which the "rather sad" events are rather pleasantly recalled, albeit with a pang of muted pain:

> From the street a strain on my ear doth fall,
> A tune as threadbare as that "old red shawl,"
> It is tattered, it is torn, it shows signs of being worn,
> It's the tune my Uncle hummed from early morn,
> 'Twas a common little thing and kind 'a sweet,
> But 'twas sad and seemed to slow up both his feet;
> I can see him shuffling down to the bar or to the town,
> a-humming.[28]

The most important thing about this apparently insignificant sentimental song is that the "tattered" object is a hummed tune. The gently syncopated melody is hummed at the end and includes a soft echo of itself. Though not a literal quotation, in its diatonic simplicity it might recall dozens of well-worn popular or folk tunes with similar phrasing, and earlier phrases of the brief piece contain simple variants of it. The tune is, in this sense, as "threadbare" as a physical object might be, but not less beloved.

In the metaphorical comparison to a literal object, "that 'old red shawl'," the composer suggests the earliest beloved object of childhood, what has been called the transitional object.[29] To the child, the object is precious because it partakes of the earliest experiences with caring persons—usually, but not exclusively, the mother. In its subtle texture and smell, it relates ultimately (but again, not exclusively) to the breast. Equally important, the experience harks back to an early period of childhood when reality is unfolding and thus, so to speak, the curtain is about to rise. During that period, the self has not yet become fully distinguished from, let alone independent of, the other. If a physical object such as a child's blanket can be endowed with magical properties, why not a tune,[30] especially in an acoustically sensitive child? In Charlie's earliest experiences, memories of self blended with mother and the father-mother of George Ives; tunes came to represent such objects and combinations. In this earliest layering of experience, music was closer to the image of the body than it ever would be subsequently. Accordingly, tunes were appreciated pleasurably in the most tactile, kinesthetic, even olfactory manner or, alternatively, were experienced as frightening, disgusting.

This "memory" depicts no literal uncle that Ives ever had—certainly not the sophisticated Lyman, the entrepreneurial Ike, or the successful Joe. Mollie's only brother died young, and besides, it is a fruitless exercise to seek the literal in so primitively imaginative a context. The uncle here is a bisexual image, masculine in gender but associated with the "old red shawl" of the transitional object. The "shuffling" body is specified in words and alluded to in sound in the monotonously lumbering accompaniment of the piano. Pastness is evoked by distant humming and the archaic "doth fall" of the poem. Even taste and smell are summoned in the delectable hum, "a common little thing and kind 'a sweet," and the reference to the barn. These are the ways in which the "rather sad" memory relates to the "contented river" of *The Housatonic at Stockbridge* and Mollie Ives.

As transitional object, the tattered "old red shawl" is precious and worthless, good and bad. This set of circumstances also creates the potential for a deep ambivalence toward "tunes" and the music that might be constructed from them, a condition that might permit the composer to love or hate them in a fiercely primitive way. Quoting a tune may represent a tender citation of memory or, on the other hand, a wish to master, distort, or obliterate memory entirely. Music itself, one's own or that of others, might similarly be loved or hated.

Sentimental tunes, in particular, were vulnerable to attack from Ives because they might reveal the vulnerability of the person affected by them; so, too, were gospel tunes. For Ives, to be moved by an old song—say, *The Sweet Bye and Bye* (quoted at least seven times) or *Bringing in the Sheaves* (quoted ten times)—was to experience a loss of control that could not have been completely pleasurable. Further, potential pleasure may run counter to the aesthetic judgments that education and taste impose. It may also involve the taint of the effeminate. A desire to distort, obliterate, or destroy—alongside the original unabashed love of the tune—may then show through in the choice of musical device.

Of the nostalgic songs Ives wrote, two works stand out for their manifest sentimentality and biographical reference to the past. The first is entitled, appropriately enough, *Old Home Day*.[31] The second, which I will take up later, is *The Things Our Fathers Loved*.[32] Ives wrote the words to both. So dense are the symbolic references in word and music to the things, events, places, and, above all, feelings of childhood in *Old Home Day* (originally called *Old Home Town*) that the six-bar introduction seems to have been an afterthought. There, in a biographical reference of another sort, the composer quotes Virgil: "Go my songs! Draw Daphnis from the city."[33] Yet in these initial measures, Ives evokes a characteristic dream-like atmosphere, used as a device in several places and invariably associated with childhood in the text or accompanying notes.[34] There follows a limping, syncopated melody which promises to break out into a march, quoting the tune of *Battle Hymn of the Republic*, when it spends itself in a brief measure's ghostly repetition. At that juncture, the piano accompaniment sounds a full band "roll-off," and the remainder of the song is a march complete with repeat and finale ad lib for "fife violin or flute."[35]

The song is as densely packed with aural images of ancient sounds and old tunes as it is with visual images. Among the many tunes quoted is *Saint Patrick's Day*, a memoir of the popular Irish tunes of George's time. The text of Ives's song contains a curious reference to "another sound we all know well, it takes us back forty years, that little red schoolhouse bell." If Ives added it in revising the song in 1920, it would refer to his own boyhood forty years earlier, when he was about six years old. If, on the other hand, one takes the composer's word that the song was originally written "before 1914," it could again be an instance in which his childhood and George's were merged among the symbols of boyhood. Perhaps that has something to do with the belabored repetition of the word *old* in the text, including the "dear old trees," the "old church bell," and the "old home town"; there is even a musical episode called "an old breakdown." Certainly, Ives himself never attended a "little red schoolhouse." In the music, the wistful *Annie Lisle* (Cornell's *Alma Mater*) underscores "the note of sadness."

The affect perhaps most characteristically associated with the music of Ives is nostalgia. At the same time as the artist achieved representation of this affect in his work, it served important psychological functions in his inner life. That it is a universal human experience accounts for its responsive audience.[36] Nostalgia as feeling should be distinguished from the associated fantasies that generate it. For it may be valued as an experience in its own right. Further, in yearning for the past, one does not necessarily desire to return to it. The vehicle for the nostalgic experience is frequently reminiscence, a state of mind in which the past may be reexperienced.[37]

Charles Ives's most concentrated work of nostalgia is *The Things Our Fathers Loved*,[38] composed in 1917 when he was forty-three years of age. A brief song (only twenty-two measures) written for voice with piano accompaniment, it had been adapted from a *Piece for Small Orchestra and Organ*, which was probably composed in 1905 and is now lost.[39] The text was written by Ives himself:

> I think there must be a place in the soul
> all made of tunes, of tunes of long ago:
> I hear the organ on the Main Street corner,
> Aunt Sarah humming Gospels; Summer evenings,
> the village cornet band, playing in the square.
> The town's Red, White and Blue, all Red, White and Blue.
> Now! Hear the songs! I know not what are the words.
> But they sing in my soul of the things our Fathers loved.

The music is literally "made of tunes . . . of long ago." Not only are many actual musical quotations incorporated into the musical structure, but there are also musical fragments that sound as if they *ought* to be portions of old tunes. Further, the song contains more subtle allusions to bygone tunes, such as certain characteristic accompaniment figures. Personal allusions abound that can be traced in the mental life of the composer. Above all, this is not a medley or a random pastiche but a tightly fashioned work of art, a miniature masterpiece whose affective features are highly condensed in representation and intense in quality.

The words alert us at the start that the locus is in inner life, "a place in the soul." The music, through various devices, likewise discloses the inward quality characteristic of private mental experience. For example, no tune achieves anything approaching full performance; only snatches, fragments, vague allusions are perceived as they might exist in memory. The progress of the text in time resembles free association, and this is reflected in the music, although in no simple way. Brief sequences reveal themselves to be past experiences through their association musically with the "tunes of long ago." They are presented in a style of spontaneous reminiscence in which they appear to be recollected, episode following episode without benefit of conjunction or preposition: "I hear the organ . . . Aunt Sarah humming . . . Summer evenings . . . The village cornet band . . . The town." The music portrays its pastness even more subtly through affective attitudes objectified in musical form. Fragments of tunes, in addition to conjuring up places (for example, "home" in the condensation of the tunes of *The Banks of the Wabash* and *My Old Kentucky Home*), cast an image of emotion— the longing association with places in these sentimental songs. There is no question in the listener's mind that these episodes exist only in the now of memory. Perhaps the most striking feature of the text is that it is almost entirely in the present tense. Only in the last line is it made explicit that vivid experiences evoked with so strong a sense of presence belong to the past.

Despite the literalness of musical thematic quotation and even the "quotation" of other stylistic devices (such as the parlor song accompaniment figures), it is clear that the artist has constructed an image of the past, not an imitation or a parody. An intrinsic element in this image is the emotion associated with the past, as if it were a commentary on it, realized in the materials of music. This emotion often harbors a profound ambiguity that opens vistas of allusion with regard to the historical past. Here, in word and music, is that peculiar tension between past and present that is characteristic of nostalgia. Thus an experience which is universal may be translated by a range of listeners to fit the particular circumstances of their mental life. Although his music was experienced as forbidding even by many sophisticated listeners, Ives believed that his music was written for the common man, and the heart of his patriotism was reflected in a conviction that the common man was the competent listener.

Among the main elements in the song—time, place, and person—time is apparently the most ambiguous. Yet the places are entirely unambiguous and specific in the text: Main Street corner and the village square. The people, somewhat less distinct, are Aunt Sarah and the village cornet band. (In fact, there are several potential Aunt Sarahs in Ives's biographical dramatis personae.) These references, apparently so private, paradoxically become universal symbols that can accommodate literal referents as well as those of greater symbolic complexity.

The flag as an object, the songs that celebrate it, and even the concepts with which it is associated extend the range of content from time, place, and person to things and even concepts. Ives's feelings for the past were often objectified in such things. One of the tangible objects most precious to him was his father's cornet, which Ives kept throughout his life on a shelf in his studio. The present song makes a disguised allusion to this in "the village cornet band." The concept of "Liberty" is literally referred to as the "greatest" of "the things our Fathers loved" in the subtitle of the song.

In *The Things Our Fathers Loved,* Ives achieves an organized musical structure that both represents and communicates nostalgia. He does so through an intrinsic morphology that mirrors the mental organization underlying the affect—the mental phenomena of pleasure/unpleasure and idea, and of mood structure.[40] The affect in mental life and its externalized representation in music are in some sense parallel and coextensive.

The product—even so brief and apparently simple a song—is a highly condensed form of knowledge. It is rich in history, both personal and social, and in examples of private and public memory. The connotations of the music as well as the words are far-reaching, all within a musical framework of brief duration. The rich ideational content of nostalgia is an inherent part of the affect that is, in turn, represented and communicated in musical form. It constitutes yet another kind of knowledge: the artist's intuitive, unconscious knowledge of himself, hence of other human beings and of the nature of human feelings. A regressive state is not necessary to gain access to this knowledge. If anything, its pursuit is associated with a heightened state of awareness and realization in a work of art accomplished only through the fullest technical mastery over the symbolic and formal potential of the artist's medium. Fundamentally, the artist's knowledge, as in Charles Ives's nostalgia, is that of human sentient life.

The intensity of Ives's nostalgia for the Danbury of his boyhood gave substance to this knowledge. During his most creative years, it fostered a characteristic style and a number of his finest works. In the course of time, the feeling of nostalgia was destined to become too intense for mastery through the creation of musical form. Ives would experience it as increasingly painful as Danbury inexorably changed, the people who linked it to the past died, and his own capacity to symbolize in art began to fail. In the end, Ives could not even bear to return to Danbury, preferring the sustenance of memory to a reality that seemed to obliterate the past.

SEVENTEEN

CONCORD

The first decade following Ives's marriage was probably the best time of his life since childhood, and certainly his most creative period. During this time he wrote the most complex, most original, and most characteristic of his works. His business life was becoming increasingly challenging. No sooner had Ives and Harmony married than Washington Life, the parent company of Ives and Company, sold out to a firm that did no business in New York, leaving the partners stranded after less than two years in business. But before the year was out, Mutual, their old benefactor, came to the rescue, and a new agency was created, Ives and Myrick.

It was a time when new kinds of policies were being devised to meet new needs of individuals and families. The two partners were agile not only in creating them but in promoting them as well. In addition, they proved to be gifted administrators and made the training of agents a vital part of their organization.[1] Although both Ives and Myrick could be aggressive, each in his own way, the foundation of their successful partnership lay in their mutual noncompetitiveness. Each seemed content to let the other have his own sphere of influence.

Various observers have commented on the span of Ives's most creative period. The Cowells dated it between 1910 and 1918.[2] Ives himself said that the body of his work was completed "in the twenty years or so between 1896 and 1916."[3] Burkholder, among others, concludes that he stopped composing "sometime in

1916 or 1917," associating this date with the beginning of the *Essays before a Sonata.*[4]

It was during this same creative period that Ives was most vigorous in business, most fertile in formulating ideas for advertising copy and bureau memoranda, and most active in training agents. As a consequence, his income more than tripled. In 1913, the first year of the individual graduated income tax, Ives reported a personal income of $10,342; by 1918, it had become nearly $30,000. (His income peaked in 1922, when he earned more than $56,000.)[5] The partners again found themselves in the right place at the right time. That they made the most of it was in good measure due to Julian's adroit management and Ives's ideas, the latter as much a result of the stimulating collaboration with Julian and his accepting nature as Ives's music at this time was a result of the nurturing partnership with Harmony. At home, Harmony saw to the stability that favored composition. At work, Julian was tolerant of an unusual division of labor in which Ives worked somewhat in isolation, from an inner office. It was a felicitous and productive time of life—truly a period of concord.

The honeymoon trip of 1908 had taken the couple to Concord, Massachusetts, and in 1916 they visited there again. Sometime in the interim, "shortly after 1911, at Pells' [in the Adirondacks]," Ives wrote, "I got the idea of a Concord Sonata."[6] The first trip to Concord would have included a visit to the Alcotts' Orchard House. Ives had completed an *Orchard House Overture* in 1904, of which fragments remain;[7] the *Missionary Chant* and perhaps the opening motif from Beethoven's *Fifth Symphony* were explicit. Years later, he recalled—perhaps erroneously—having worked on an *Alcott Overture* even earlier, in 1902–04 on Pine Mountain; the interest in Concord may have been of long standing. Then, of course, Walden Pond was in Concord—another stimulus to Ives's imagination. It may have struck Ives that it was in the year 1845, the year of George Ives's birth, that four great men of literature—Emerson, Hawthorne, Alcott, and Thoreau— were all living in Concord. They remain there in death: Ives and Harmony doubtless visited Sleepy Hollow cemetery, where the four are buried close by one another. The only other place where they are drawn into such proximity is Ives's *Concord Sonata.* Ives transformed the sense of their presence there into the related parts of the *Second Piano Sonata: "Concord, Mass., 1840–1860."*

The "idea" of Concord had a deeper significance to Ives. Its meaning may be enriched by an understanding of the discordant elements in his mental life. Emotional instability was already in evidence during the early years of marriage. A tendency to moodiness in which nostalgia trenched upon depression had emerged clearly in early adulthood. Moods characterized by excitement and even elation occasionally vied with more subdued moods for ascendancy. Yet Ives was able to mobilize enough energy to compose effectively and to make a living. The entire system had broken down briefly in 1906, when in either state he became overwhelmed—by the burdensome preoccupation and psychic slowing typical of depression or by the overstimulation that threatened him with psychic disorganization. Features of the artist's mind inevitably become characteristics of his artistic style: the music was frequently expressive of these extremes of mood and ideas relating to them. His sensitivity to potentially overwhelming stimuli often gave rise to musical ideas. *The Housatonic at Stockbridge*, written on the eve of his marriage to Harmony, is an example. Against this background, the need for intense involvement in two simultaneous and contrasting careers, each with its own demands, taxed Ives's considerable integrative capacities. This need in itself was a reflection of inner conflict, perhaps even the result of an attempt at resolving it. The shadow of George Ives fell irregularly and fragmentarily upon the two careers of his son. Similarly, conflict lay behind depression in the guilt of the successful survivor and in chronic, unresolved mourning.

No doubt Ives also had a biological endowment that made him receptive to the sensory data that serve as raw material for the creative works. Such an endowment, common in artists, may in itself be a hazard to balanced living. As noted earlier, Ives was subject to shifts of mood which could be subtle or extreme. A variety of cyclothymia, this was more a tendency of character than a pathological condition. But late in life Ives clearly did succumb to such a condition: a gradually emerging senile dementia, in part an accident of longevity itself. By that time, however, he had long ceased to function as a composer and had retired from the business world as well. Earlier, yet another variety of emotional instability was occasionally in evidence, the tendency toward extreme affective excitement that would challenge and often overwhelm his self-control. Most frequently, the affect was an anger that, once elicited, could hardly be contained. It seemed to feed on itself, gradually peak, and then discharge only with difficulty. A number of situations or issues might spark the expression of inner rage. As time went on, the stimuli for such outbursts became both more specific, focusing on designated bêtes noires, and the resulting reaction became more diffuse, threatening not only affective equilibrium but even reason itself. At such times, Ives's thought skimmed the edge of reality, and psychosis threatened. To complicate matters, the musical ideas he generated in this state of mind tested the boundaries of art and madness.

Aunt Amelia and Harmony were sensitive to this aspect of Ives's mental life, and each in her own way sought to soothe. It is clear from correspondence that Harmony was sensitive to Ives's moods early in their relationship and intuitively made soothing an important aspect of her role in the marriage. Ives was also much loved and admired by the extended family. Endowed with a good sense of humor and a knack for punning when he was in a high mood (which could also serve the function of aggressive verbal attack), he was accepted as a lovable eccentric—the more so for his odd combination of careers. Later, this respectful protectiveness within the family found a parallel among those who came to admire him artistically. It became difficult to separate out the crazy from the creative, the bizarre from the innovative—and for good reason. The innovator regularly straddles the border of the rational and the irrational, the possible and the impossible. Thus the very quality of mind that privately plagued Ives and those around him had creative issue. Certainly entire passages of the *Essays before a Sonata* as well as other published writings do not make a great deal of sense. What parallel there may be in the vast output of music creates an ambiguity that is part of its fascination.

Behind the writings, the music, the everyday behavior, and the moods was a mind in tension. The etiology would lie somewhere in the borderland between organic illness and functional disturbance of the mind.

In the autumn of 1911, at Pell Jones' camp in the Adirondacks, Ives was already struggling with unruly, even chaotic elements in mental life. At their root was an aggression that at times defied modulation. It might either be experienced as depression or externally directed as anger. Nonetheless, Ives's capacity for integration remained prodigious, and it was expressed in many aspects of life, not least composition. He was able to modify such impulses, divorce them from expression in affect or behavior, and sublimate them in music. There were lapses, of course, but these were relatively few and private at this time. It was in this mental environment that Ives worked on his *Second Piano Sonata* between 1911 and 1915. The choice of its subtitle, *Concord*, has many determinants, among them his search, ultimately fruitless, for freedom from conflict and for inner peace.

The idea of the *Concord* had its precursors during the period of courtship. At first, Ives had the general notion of writing overtures representing literary men. He considered Whitman, Browning, Arnold, Emerson, Whittier, and Henry Ward Beecher. Ives later recalled having made some sketches toward a work about Whittier or Whitman—he could no longer remember which. Several of these ideas found their way into songs and, ultimately, into the collection *114 Songs*, where Arnold, Browning, and Whitman are featured.[8] Ives spoke of having had the "overture habit" in those days, but the idea was never expanded. At least one piece, however, *Browning*, "got somewhat out of the overture shape" and was duly called a tone poem.[9]

Despite the earlier *Orchard House Overture*, with its association to Alcott, it was not until his relationship with Harmony took a serious turn that his interest was kindled in self-consciously literary themes. Harmony helped make reading a part of the background stability and orderliness of Ives's life. Programs of reading, with lists of recommended works, became a part of the structured life she made for him. Words, literary ideas, and philosophical concepts played an increasingly important role in composition. They spilled over into other writings and in the ensuing years found expression in his political writings as well as in his advertising copy and sales manuals for the insurance business. Toward the end of the 1910s, as his musical creativity was failing, he gradually came to write more prose than music. One result was the *Essays before a Sonata*, which was finished in 1919, only after the completion of the *Concord Sonata*. Harmony's influence was thus exerted not only in the formation of the *Concord* but, in a sense, in the prolongation of Ives's creative function.

The *Concord*, as Ives wrote in the preface to his *Essays*, "is a group of four pieces, called a sonata for want of a more exact name, as the form, perhaps substance, does not justify it. . . . The whole is an attempt to present (one person's) impression of the spirit of transcendentalism that is associated in the minds of many with Concord, Mass., of over a half century ago. This is undertaken in impressionistic pictures of Emerson and Thoreau, a sketch of the Alcotts, and a *scherzo* supposed to reflect a lighter quality which is often found in the fantastic side of Hawthorne." The music, like a massive auditory mobile, is poised in the balance of the outer movements representing Emerson and Thoreau. The inspiriting figure, however, was Emerson, with whom Ives had become fascinated.

If Harmony was the catalyst for Ives's interest in the American transcendentalists, Ralph Waldo Emerson was the chief reagent. To be sure, Ives had read Emerson in college, in Phelps's course, and had even written a paper on him. A thread of proud family history weaves back to the 1850s, when Ives's grandmother, Sarah Wilcox Ives, heard Emerson lecture on the New England reformers. It was said that Emerson had been a guest at the homestead on Main Street during his visit to Danbury and that Uncle Joe had met him in Boston. But the notion that Ives was a long-standing philosophical Transcendentalist as a result of family tradition (hence its latter-day musical exponent) is erroneous.[10] Ives used Emerson and his ideas as a vehicle for integrating and organizing ideas of his own. Further, his romance with Emerson served some intrapsychic function related to Concord as place and state of mind. At the same time, private fantasies were at work in the choice of Emerson as the musical subject for the first movement of the *Concord Sonata* and the philosophical subject of its accompanying *Essay*. At this point in Ives's life, Emerson was truly his Representative Man.

In 1907, during the period of the "overture habit," Ives had worked on an *Emerson Overture* for piano and orchestra—in effect a concerto. It was either never completed (only sketches remain) or lost in that form; in any case, the material was ultimately transformed into the first movement of the *Concord Sonata*, completed in the summer of 1912. Ives went on to complete the second, or Hawthorne, movement that fall. The Alcott and Thoreau movements were done by 1915, around the time Ives turned forty-one, but Emerson continued to fascinate him. Some time after 1915 and the completion of the *Concord*, he returned to the overture that had been the original Emerson inspiration and transcribed it for piano. Meanwhile, the last of the major works were completed, the *Fourth Violin Sonata* in 1916 and the *Fourth Symphony* in 1916 or early 1917. Three more Emerson transcriptions for piano were made over the next few years of dwindling creativity. He did some work on these even after 1919, the year all the *Essays* were written. Still, Emerson continued to captivate Ives, and the last of the transcriptions were said to have been written a year or two after the *Concord* was published in 1922. By that time, Ives was doing virtually no other composing. Emerson, then, the subject of one of his finest achievements, attended his decline.

A clue to Ives's fascination with Emerson rests in Ives's decision to write essays, the form central to Emerson's work, and to write them in somewhat imitative style. Emerson's style has been aptly described as "brilliant, epigrammatic, gem-like; clear in sentences, obscure in paragraphs. . . . The coherence of his writing lies in his personality. His work is fused with a steady glow of optimism."[11] In the *Essays*, Ives appears to strive for a scholarly, reasoned, and inspirational texture peppered with quotes and epigrams—almost a caricature of Emerson's style. Moreover, in Ives's fevered brain, Emerson's "glow of optimism" periodically ignites in cosmic conflagration and grandiose gesture.

Ives's Emerson is prophet, guide, and explorer. He is "an invader of the unknown—America's deepest explorer of the spiritual immensities."[12] As prophet, he is in the business of revelation; as guide, he is closer to Prometheus than to Virgil. In a recurrent image, "we see him—standing on a summit at the door of the infinite where many men do not care to climb, peering into the mysteries of life, contemplating the eternities, hurling back whatever he discovers there—now thunderbolts for us to grasp, if we can."[13] A quotation from Emerson's essay *Circles*, "every ultimate fact is only the first of a new series," captured Ives's imagination. Supplanting Emerson's contemplative reasoned tone and poetic imagery is Ives's frenzied picture of the leader at the edge of the cosmos.

Not only does Ives identify with Emerson; he also identifies Emerson with himself as composer: "Jadassohn [German author of a music theory textbook], if Emerson were literally a composer, could no more analyze his harmony than a Guide-to-Boston could. A microscope might show that he uses chords of the ninth, eleventh, or the ninety-ninth, but a lens far different tells us they are used with different aims from those of Debussy."[14] Ives equates Emerson's philosophical ideas with musical ideas as if they were mutually translatable. "On the other hand, if one thinks that his harmony contains no dramatic chords, because no theatrical sound is heard, let him listen to the finale of "Success" or of "Spiritual Laws" or to some of the poems."[15] This notion is neither poetic image nor logical error. Rather, it is an expression in musical terms of the transcendentalist ideas elaborated in the last section of the essay on Emerson, where they are presented in terms of Emerson's character, the "courageous universalism that gives conviction to his prophecy." Everything reflects the universal, and Emerson's "symphonies of revelation begin and end with nothing but the strength and beauty of innate goodness in man, in Nature and in God—the greatest and most inspiring theme of Concord Transcendental Philosophy."[16] In the Emerson essay, Ives sums up his personal concept of transcendentalism: "Nothing but the strength and beauty of the innate goodness in man."

Ives ends each of the essays with a brief coda, in which he relates some musical idea to an extramusical, philosophical concept. In "Emerson," that idea is the opening motif of Beethoven's *Fifth Symphony*, which is musically quoted in the *Sonata*. He translates Beethoven's image of fate knocking at the door into Emersonian terms, as "the soul of humanity knocking at the door of the divine mysteries, radiant in the faith that it *will* be opened—and the human become the divine." This is what he understands to represent "the 'common heart' of Concord."[17]

Ives's essays are often rambling, pseudo-scholarly, and at times illogical to the point of irrationality. The essay on Emerson is peppered with tirades and softened by tender personal reminiscence. But the essay cannot be reduced to these elements, and much can be understood through them. Despite the grand phrases and dense writing, Ives's conception of transcendentalism is not complex, and it resolves to such basic religious convictions as a belief in man's innate goodness.[18] Ives's elaboration of his rendering of transcendentalism incorporates trends already well established in his own musical and nonmusical thought. Characteristic is the fervent utopian optimism Ives generates at the end of his Emerson essay. Above all, a rationale is established for the idea of music as something more than music. Just as there is music in Emerson's essays and in his character, so there may be character and philosophical thought encoded in music. Ives understands both music and nonmusic to be aspects of a more fundamental transcendental ideal. Thus, the music of the *Concord Sonata* is as much a guide to the *Essays* as the *Essays* are a guide to the music. Ives wrote that he had intended to print the music and essays together, but the volume would then have been too cumbersome. As it turned out, he included a page of music as frontispiece to each essay, in token acknowledgment of his original idea.

The musical frontispiece to "Emerson" is a dense five staves, starting with an efflorescent musical figure that rapidly rises to a double-forte. Further climaxes are apparent even to the casual reader of music: "agitando . . . faster and faster . . . FFF . . ." It requires a master musician, however, to do the piece justice in performance. By contrast, the hymn-like musical frontispiece to "The Alcotts" can be grasped by anyone with enough training to play a hymn tune. The combination of verbal and musical concept was to serve Ives as vehicle for a more fundamental communication. Neither music—at least not traditional music—nor words alone could accomplish this. In the epilogue to the essays, Ives wrote, "Maybe music was not intended to satisfy the curious definiteness of man." But he hoped that "music may always be a transcendental language in the most extravagant sense."[19] In Ives's somewhat murky aesthetic, music can express the sublime and the commonplace of human experience—individual moments, human characteristics, and ethical values. In this function, the ordinary materials of music—individual organized phrases, notes, sound itself—were beside the point. In a prose climax, he exclaims, "My God! What has sound got to do with music!"[20]

It must be remembered that the *Essays* were written in 1919 after most (if not all) of the music had been completed. The idea of paired forms, however, appears to have been germinating earlier, centering around Ives's *Concord* group and, in particular, the figure of Emerson. Although the *Concord Sonata* of course stands on its own without the *Essays*, the prose highlights an aspect of Ives that could perhaps never be explicit in the music. It reveals a similar but intensified Ives.

The *Essays before a Sonata* contain a curious mixture of sense and nonsense. Ostensibly complementary, a parallel work in another genre intended ultimately to form a whole along with the music—literally to be concordant with it—the *Essays* are many other things as well. The essay on Emerson, for example, is an appreciation of heroes and a densely formulated aesthetic statement. It is also a self-serving vehicle for the ventilation of rage and personal rivalries. A kind of philosophical theory appears to organize itself out of the rambling texture, heavily indebted to diluted transcendental ideas. At other times, what purports to be aesthetic theory veers into what might generously be called poetry, and the poetic soon tends to the prophetic, all apparently driven by some grandiose impulse. So the prose seems to perch on the ledge between concord and chaos. In this sense, it mirrors the mind at work, the obstacles that were beginning to confront it, and the attempts at solutions.

John Kirkpatrick likened Ives's persistent idealization of George Ives to "ancestor worship."[21] If there had been room for another hero, it would have been Ralph Waldo Emerson. Years after publication of the *Concord*, and even after he had ceased working on the four *Emerson Transcriptions*, Ives spoke of his feeling about Emerson. He had by then lived with his Emerson music for some twenty-five years: "It is a peculiar experience and, I must admit, a stimulating and agreeable one that I've had with this Emerson music. It may have something to do with the feeling I have about Emerson, for every time I read him I seem to get a new angle of thought and feeling and experience from him."[22] Ives in effect transformed the transcendental ideas he had extrapolated from Emerson into musical terms for his own contemplation. Thus, as he played the transcriptions for himself, he found himself refreshed and stimulated by new "angles" and directions. Even after he had the manuscript photographed, thus apparently freezing the document in time, Ives made frequent amendments and usually did not play the music as written or the same way each time. Nor did he "feel like" doing so: he lived and relived in music the idea of "Circles," perhaps his favorite Emerson essay. Emerson had written: "Our life is an apprenticeship to the truth, that around every circle another can be drawn; that there is no end in nature, but every end is a beginning; that there is always another dawn risen on mid-noon, and under every deep a lower deep opens."[23]

Ives could not write a sentence like that, try as he might. Nor was it within the range of his musical style to compose with such elegance and balance. But the expression of ideas in music was another matter. Emerson wrote in *Circles*, "The eye is the first circle; the horizon which it forms is the second; and throughout nature this primary figure is repeated without end."[24] We cannot know whether the notion of individual human centrality with which Emerson's essay opens struck Ives in its auditory literalness—the circle of the human eye homologous with the human "I"—but it is entirely consistent with Ives's musical outlook. To bring the idea into full alignment with Ives's body image, we could change the quotation to read, "The ear is the first circle." If, as Porte argues, the opening passage of "Circles" is "an epitome of Emerson's thought,"[25] then in auditory terms there is something in it of the essence of Ives's music.

Emerson, then, was Ives's most important teacher during his later years. The pantheon of Ives's *Concord* was dominated by Emerson just as Emerson was central to Concord, Massachusetts, in the 1840s. When Emerson died in 1882, Bronson Alcott said of him, "The change was very little, he was living in the spirit here."[26] This was a notion Ives grasped imaginatively. One did not have to know Emerson to know him; his influence was entirely spiritual and mental, permeating and enduring. In this regard, he differed from such earlier heroes as Griggs, Parker, Joseph Twichell, and Lyman Brewster. In a sense, however, the spiritual teacher and mentor Emerson represented was closest to the George Ives of Ives's mental life, a transformation of the hero of childhood, the idealized father.

The image of the father as hero stemming from the family romance of childhood may persist in consciousness or remain latent, to be revived under compelling circumstances. The transformations of this image make it possible, and at times necessary, for a father who was ordinary to become extraordinary, for the modest to become awesome, the disgraced exalted. The child in Ives could recall the awesome creator of massive sound of earliest childhood and identify him as the "noblest and strongest of men."[27] From such memories as of his father's attempts to pick out the overtones in the village bells, Ives construed a seeker into the unknown. From memories of a tinkerer running violin strings on the clothesline to produce quarter tones comes the myth of a pioneer in the discovery of a new art. And the ridiculous Herr Schwergeblassen, as played by George Ives, laughed at by the townsmen and his son alike, is transformed into the inventor of the subtlest and most humanistic of musical instruments, the Humanophone. The master of all these attributes has the rare gift of inculcating his hard-earned knowledge and thereby inspiring his students. This is the image of George Ives that informs his son's hero-worship of Emerson. In the repeated metaphor of Ives's *Essays*, Emerson is the advance guard of mankind.

Ives's personal "canonization of Emerson"[28] contains within it the private hagiography of his father. At mid-life another stroke was added to this portrait in Ives's sense of his own failing creativity. The years of the *Concord* ironically span both his finest musical achievements, the sonata and the *Fourth Symphony*, and his demise as a composer of music. By the time the *Concord* was published, Ives could be a composer only of words. Yet only Ives himself could perceive a drying up of sources, a premonition of creativity coming to an end and with it, life itself. One source of grandiosity lies in portents of its opposite, that is, in intimations of insignificance. At the peak of mastery, a sense of helplessness threatens, resulting in a pressure toward the assertion of magnificence. Embedded in Ives's exalted admiration of Emerson is the transformed image of the father and Ives's fused identification with both men. In these, he arrives in fantasy at the further reaches of the family romance.

The idea of Emerson as spiritual father had its source in the revived grandiose father of childhood and was fueled by Ives's need to exalt father and family in the service of denial of reality. In later life, the threatening perception of limitation, failure, and helplessness gave impetus to creativity. Fact and tradition in the actual family connections with Emerson provided the merest scaffolding on which the elaborated family romance was built.

Certain hidden parallels in the lives of Emerson and Ives, of which Ives could not have been totally unaware, suggest a further source of identification. Emerson's economic independence in his maturity made the rest of his life fundamentally different from that of his scholarly, philosophical, or artistic contemporaries.[29] Hawthorne, a devoted Democrat, constantly worried about money as his fortunes shifted with those of the party. Thoreau, the only bachelor in the group, had modest needs, which were for the most part met by proceeds from the family pencil-making business.[30]Alcott's school at Boston's Masonic Temple was a financial failure—parents were unwilling to have their children educated together with a black student—and the sheriff seized its assets to pay Alcott's considerable debts.[31]

Emerson once wrote that "in its effects and laws" money was "as beautiful as roses."[32] Ives could scarcely permit himself so frank a view about money, although the economic solutions he had found for himself put him in at least a financially comfortable position. In his preferred view, however, money was not central; it was merely incidental, the means toward some other, higher goal. Aware of the value Emerson placed on money, Ives rationalized money transcendentally, as "essential parts of the greater values." "Material progress," he wrote loftily, "is but a means of expression."[33] Interestingly, in this very section of the Emerson essay Ives careens into dense, ill-reasoned political philosophy. The passage is manifestly poorly controlled and subsequently unedited. When he quotes Emerson's "Calm yourself, Poet," he may be referring to his own excitement, born not only of the sense of injustice about which he purports to write but perhaps also of the elemental, libidinal excitement of money and the conflict it engendered.

Ives writes in this passage of "the 'hog-mind' of the minority against the universal mind, the majority."[34] Ives's majority is idealized—in fact, sanctified: "God is on the side of the majority (the people) . . . he is not enthusiastic about the minority (the non-people) . . . he has made man greater than man . . . he has made the universal mind and the over-soul greater and a part of the individual mind and soul . . . he has made the Divine a part of all."[35] Citing Emerson again in his optimistic mode, he writes, "If a picture of economics is before him, Emerson plunges down to the things that *are* because they are *better* than they are."[36] In his pseudo-transcendental view of money, Ives distanced it as far as possible from the everyday economic facts of life, idealizing and purifying it in the process. If this can be called sublimation, it is sublimation gone wild—a contradiction in terms. Ives's prose enters a murky tunnel, densely inhabited by the likes of Montaigne, John Stuart Mill, and the economist David Ricardo, all of whom Ives cites. By the time it emerges, he has touched upon theories of labor without reaching any conclusion, radical or conventional.[37] The economic issues he seemed to need to raise troubled him and soon led him to write his longest essay, "The Majority."

In Emerson, then, Ives found more than a spiritual ancestor; he found a realization of his family romance and a kindred spirit who had evolved a formula for living not unlike the one Ives had stumbled onto—with one glaring exception. Emerson's economic living was not divorced from his creative work. Ives, however, vociferously turned that separation into a virtue; he believed it made him purer. The view of Emerson as a mystic with a good head for money was prevalent in Emerson's lifetime despite the secular canonization. In identifying with Emerson, Ives envisioned a similar public image for himself. In the psychological bargain, he found a universally admired spiritual father who could create art and make money too.

The other Concordians of the *Sonata* fall under Emerson's shadow there as they had in actual life. The Hawthorne movement is Ives's scherzo. Its substance is much like the image of Hawthorne conveyed by that writer's *Mosses from an Old Manse* and *Tanglewood Tales*. It is, as Ives said of Hawthorne, "dripping wet with the supernatural, the phantasmal, the mystical; surcharged with adventures, from the deeper picturesque to the illusive fantastic."[38] Here Hawthorne is the American brothers Grimm, the creator of American fable, just as Ives created an essentially American scherzo by incorporating elements of jazz. Surprisingly, an intrusion of the *Country Band March* pierces the gossamer texture of the music, pulling the listener away from Hawthorne's fantasy land to the parade path of Main Street, Danbury, and the parade ground of Putnam's Camp in nearby Bethel. It is like an abrupt but pleasant awakening or a dream within a dream.

The Alcotts was written during the summer of 1913, the first summer the Iveses spent in their new home in Redding. As concrete a statement as *Emerson* is abstract, it re-creates an idealized home life in the Alcott household. Ives wrote of the "commonplace beauty about 'Orchard House.'"[39] Basically, it is a scene from childhood not quite literal yet scarcely disguised. And, characteristically, its terms of presentation are auditory. Ives invokes the voice of Bronson Alcott, not so much his words as the music of his voice: "an internal grandiloquence made him melodious."[40] Ives fantasizes about what might have resulted if "the dictograph had been perfected in his time." Alcott was "Concord's greatest talker," and had his words been recorded "he might now be a great writer."[41] Like George, in Ives's distorted view, the Bronson Alcott he invokes left no writings behind (which is not true in Alcott's case) except those enshrined in the hearts of those he influenced. Ives notes that Alcott had a "strong didactic streak," shared by his daughter Louisa May, author of *Little Women*. Thus are father and daughter Alcott related to father and son Ives—not the first time the persona of the artist is female with reference to father. Bronson was like George: "his idealism had some substantial virtues, even if he couldn't make a living."[42] And Ives resembled Louisa May: "The daughter does not accept her father as prototype—she seems to have but few of her father's qualities 'in female.'"[43] In his own special blend of masculinity and artistic endowment, Ives and Louisa were cut from the same alien cloth. Louisa, he writes, "leaves memory-word pictures of healthy New England childhood days—pictures which are turned to with affection by middle aged children—pictures that bear a sentiment, a leaven, that middle aged America needs nowadays more than we care to admit."[44]

It is just such a picture that Ives strives to evoke in *The Alcotts*, though here it is a memory-sound picture. He creates a mise-en-scène consisting of characters, objects, and, above all, sounds drawn from his own childhood or Louisa May's as he imagines it; at times, they overlap. Moving from "the broad-arched street," one comes to the "home under the elms." In the parlor "sits the old spinet piano" just as it did in Ives's childhood. From this point, auditory images predominate: "a kind of common triad of the New England homestead, whose overtones tell us that there must have been something aesthetic fibered in the Puritan severity" and thus in "the human-faith melody" of Beethoven's *Fifth Symphony*.[45] Not mentioned in the prose but heard in the music is the musical cognate of that melody in the descending third of the Zeuner's *Missionary Chant*. That the quotation is unbarred in the score (as much of the sonata is) allows a tentativeness of performance characteristic of a child or amateur at the spinet. The words are silent: "Ye Christian Heralds, go proclaim Salvation through Emanuel's name." (Missionary Sunday was November 18, two weeks after George Ives died.) Shortly, an unidentified, sweetly melodious, gospel-like tune is heard, harmonized in thirds in parlor-song style. Its sentimentality and slowed-down jaunty rhythm fairly beg that words be sung.

The thread that was hidden in each of the three preceding movements of the *Concord* becomes increasingly apparent in the final section, *Thoreau*. Its elegiac mood, its apotheosis of Thoreau as a great musician, and finally its manifest reference to George Ives's death on some fantasied Indian summer day at Walden Pond reveal it to be at once a memorial and an artifact of mourning. Essay and music purport to evoke in word and tone a mood that is remarkably specific: the traditional blend of commemoration and eulogy, and the particular touching sadness that characterizes the elegy. The mood is past lamentation and redolent of comfort.[46]

On completing *Thoreau*, Ives wrote in a memo, "finished May 30, 1915 from some ideas"—"Walden Sounds—Ch Bells, flute, Harp (Aeolian) to go with Harmony's Mist . . . Elk Lake 1910."[47] The shorthand "Harmony's Mist" harks back to the autumn of 1910 and their experience of "the last mist at Pell's," which had led to the first collaboration of their marriage—*Mists*, also an elegy. The emotional background of *Mists* lay in Harmony's loss of her mother and Uncle Mark (Twain) the previous spring, virtually on the anniversary of her miscarriage and hysterectomy a year earlier. Perennially working through these events, she used a fragment from Thoreau as setting for another poem (now lost), "Smoke": "Light-winged Smoke, Icarian bird . . ."[48] This became the inspiration for the opening measures of the musical piece *Thoreau*. The memo was Ives's way of encapsulating the complex experience that inspired the work. Mist (as well as smoke) is visual and tactile, but all other elements mentioned in the memo are auditory, like the "Walden Sounds" at Elk Lake.

The *Essay* begins, "Thoreau was a great musician not because he played the flute but because he did not have to go to Boston to hear the Symphony."[49] Ives's Thoreau is the acoustic Thoreau. In Thoreau's well-known image, which Ives quotes near the end, of "An evening when the whole body is one sense,"[50] the sense that is most central to the *Essay* and to Ives's Thoreau is hearing. Ives observes, probably correctly, that "Thoreau's susceptibility to natural sounds was probably greater than that of many practical musicians."[51] Indeed, the "Walden Sounds" section of his memo is quoted (or slightly misquoted, suggesting that it had been memorized) from the chapter "Sounds" in *Walden*. Comparing Thoreau to Beethoven, Ives suggests that it is only because Thoreau could not readily expose his feelings that he did not actually express himself in music. The emotion thus avoided is love, presumably love of humanity. "When the object of love is mankind, the sensitiveness is changed only in degree." Here Ives writes, "a composer may not shrink from having the public hear his 'love letter in tones,' while a poet may feel sensitive about having everyone read his 'letter in words.'"[52]

The great natural musician, who, Ives rationalized, was too sensitive to cast his passionate emotions in Beethovenian form, is the persistent idealized image of the father of childhood. This accounts for the curious form of Ives's essay on Thoreau as well as certain elements of disorganization. For the tone of much of the writing is not only that of eulogy but also that of polemic and apology. Ives deals with some of Thoreau's least attractive traits—his withdrawal, isolation, cynicism, feistiness, and downright "contrary cussedness"[53]—taking on such formidable critics as Henry James, James Russell Lowell, and Mark Van Doren. When it comes to defending Thoreau's "mysticism," Ives asserts that it is "with no mystic rod that he strikes at institutional life." Thus starts an angry tirade which at length rather illogically arrives at the issue of "property" and at some of his ideas about "the majority" and a "People's World Union." He finds it "conceivable that Thoreau, to the consternation of the richest members of the Bolsheviki and Bourgeois, would propose a policy of liberation, a policy of a limited personal property right."[54] Here Ives, one of the "haves," in a fantasied and unlikely alliance with Thoreau, becomes champion of the "have-nots" of the world, motivated by the guilt of having and surviving.

Again, one notes the span of time between the writing of the music and the essays; in the instance of *Thoreau*, it was about four years, from 1915 to 1919. Does the essay here reveal some process in the intervening years that led to a rambling, belligerent, disorganized, and illogical trend? Or did this tendency already exist when the music was written?

In the last section of the Thoreau essay Ives re-creates in words the elegiac mood that informs the music, and it is here that he quotes Thoreau extensively in his role as "great musician." Thoreau's "Aeolian harp" is cited as well as excerpts from the long musical passage of his "Sounds" that starts with the hearing of the Concord bells on Sundays: "At a distance over the woods the sound acquires a certain vibratory hum, as if the pine needles in the horizon were the strings of a harp which it swept . . . a vibration of the universal lyre."[55] This is truly a love letter to Thoreau and to the father-hero he represents—"my Thoreau—that reassuring and true friend, who stood by me one 'low' day when the sun had gone down, long, long before sunset." Thus he refers to the death of George on November 4, 1894. Addressing Thoreau's critics and detractors, he exclaims, "You may know something of the affection that heart yearned for but knew it a duty not to grasp—you may know something of the great human passions which stirred that soul—too deep for animate expression—you may know all of this—all there is to know about Thoreau . . . but you know him not—unless you love him."[56]

A mood of resignation and comfort pervades the conclusion of the essay: "And if there shall be a program for our music, let it follow this thought on an autumn day of Indian summer at Walden—a shadow of a thought at first, colored by the mist and haze over the pond."[57] Harmony Ives's *Mists* ("Low lie the mists . . .") seems fused with a poem of Thoreau's from *A Week on the Concord and Merrimack:* "Low anchored cloud, / Fountainhead and / Source of rivers . . ."[58] Significantly, the day in Thoreau's *Week* under which the poem appears is Tuesday, which was one of Ives's "low" days, the day of George's funeral.

The fused image of Thoreau and George Ives is represented in the *Concord's* final movement in the musical quotation of Foster's familiar *Massa's in the Cold, Cold Ground.* Fragments from the song's chorus are heard: "Down in de cornfield . . ." When Ives adapted themes from the sonata as a song (*Thoreau*) for the *114 Songs,* he introduced the verbal quotation from "Sounds" as if it were a spoken meditation. The words he chose to set to music were, "He grew in those seasons like corn in the night, rapt in revery, on the Walden shore, amidst the sumach, pines and hickories, in undisturbed solitude."[59]

The image of Thoreau's cornfield by Walden Pond invokes the peaceful setting of the pond in Wooster Cemetery, in view of the knoll where George Ives was laid to rest. In the earlier piece, *The Pond*, the very sound of Ives's father was re-created in the muted trumpet: "A sound of a distant horn, / O'er shadowed lake is borne, / my father's song." At the close of the *Concord Sonata*, George's instrument is heard once again. This time it is his first instrument, the flute of family legend, which George had wanted so much as a child that he resolved to stay back from the Fourth of July picnic in order to earn money. That sacrifice was said to have persuaded his father, George White Ives, to let him take music lessons and so begin his career as musician.

In the final measures of *Thoreau* Ives inserted an optional part for flute, the occasion rationalized by the fact that Thoreau played the flute and had one with him at Walden. In the last pages of the *Concord,* Thoreau is virtually brought to life as the "great musician." Here, too, the essay serves as program to the music. In penning the flute part, Ives performed a creative act that has meaning on other levels as well. It would seem strange to expect the flutist to sit on stage through a lengthy, massive composition only to join in the last few seconds; but it would be stranger still, even eerie, to have the unanticipated flute music waft in from offstage. In either event, the actual rendering is of little consequence since it is clearly the *idea* of the flute song that Ives intended and with it some actualization of the spirit of his father. It was perhaps a part of the original "idea of a Concord Sonata" that struck him at Pell Jones' that autumn of 1911, its germ in the musical idea of the flute echoing across the misty pond. "It is darker," he wrote at the end of *Thoreau,* "—the poet's flute is heard over the pond and Walden hears the swan song of that 'Day'—and faintly echoes . . . is it a transcendental tune of Concord?"[60]

Charles Ives's *Second Piano Sonata,* the *Concord,* along with its companion *Essays before a Sonata,* constitutes one of his greatest achievements. He started it along with his *Fourth Symphony* sometime around 1911, when he was thirty-six. The music was more or less finished in rough form when he was about forty-one and the essays when he was forty-five. The *Fourth Symphony* occupied him simultaneously until about 1916. Together, symphony, sonata, and essays constituted three-quarters of his culminating work. With the composition of the *Concord Sonata,* something was spent in Ives as well as accomplished. He would never again write works of so complex a nature and massive a scale as the *Second Piano Sonata* or the *Fourth Symphony.*

Ives could hardly have been aware that beyond the creative peak of these years loomed a creative desert. As he entered his forties, the creative impulse began to falter, although little more than half his life had elapsed. Not until he was just past fifty could he acknowledge that it was extinguished completely. Emerson wrote, in a passage buried in his *Journal,* of the Indian summer days in the year following the death of his son, Waldo: "These are the reconciling days which come to graduate the autumn into winter, & to comfort us after the first attacks of the cold. Soothsayers, prediction as well as memory, they look over December & January into the crepuscular lights of March and Spring."[61] For Ives, the *Concord Sonata* was an act of reconciliation in which he accomplished an apotheosis of his father. Concord was for him a place in the mind, the ultimate "place in the soul," somewhere between Olympus and Danbury.

Harmony Twichell Ives (1876–1969), in nurse's uniform, ca.1898–99.

David Cushman Twichell (1874–1924), brother of Harmony.

Charles and Harmony in front of cabin at Pell Jones' Camp, Elk Lake, in the Adirondacks.

Harmony Ives with Edith Osborne Ives (1914–56), ca. 1916.

Julian Southall Myrick (1880–1969).

Charles Ives (right) and Julian Myrick, ca. 1947. Photo: W. Eugene Smith.

Passport photo of Ives and Edith, 1924.

Passport photo of Ives and Harmony, ca. 1932.

Harmony and Ives at West Redding, ca. 1948.

Ives's studio at West Redding. Among the memorabilia are photographs of George Ives and Abraham Lincoln, a thirty-year-old Danbury felt hat and a baseball cap from Yale, and George Ives's cornet.

Charles Ives in the barn at West Redding, ca. 1947. Photo: Frank Gerratana.

EIGHTEEN

JOURNEY'S END

The mist at Pell Jones' was germinal. Those late summer days of 1910 and 1911 were a time of intense private meaning for both Ives and Harmony. They were days of sadness and reflection as the two found comfort in each other and in the beauty of the natural surroundings at Elk Lake. Later, Ives would erroneously date that first Indian summer to 1909, associating it with Harmony's hospitalization. But it was at Pell's in 1910 that the nuclear musical ideas that spawned the *Concord Sonata* and the *Fourth Symphony* were formulated.

Not only is the *Fourth Symphony*, in Kirkpatrick's words, "in every way one of [Ives's] most definitive works";[1] it is also as much a culminating work as the *Concord*. Indeed, in some respects it should be considered *the* final work, although Ives was only forty-two when he completed it in 1916 or early 1917, after working on it sporadically for a half dozen years. When Ives gave an interview to Henry Bellaman a decade later, he made the work sound far more organized and planned out than it had in fact been. In this regard, the act of recollection only continued the process that had given rise to the work, one of assemblage, organization, and reorganization from diverse elements, a procedure long since characteristic of his music.

As in the *Concord*, each of the movements of the *Fourth* had its own history and had been individually conceived. Indeed, each was written for virtually a different orchestra. The overall orchestral forces are vast, Ives's largest ensem-

ble short of the musical legions he envisioned for his *Universe Symphony*. Henry
Bellaman wrote, "This symphony . . . consists of four movements—a prelude, a
majestic fugue, a third movement in comedy vein, and a finale of transcendental
spiritual content. The aesthetic program of the work is . . . the searching
questions of What? and Why? which the spirit of man asks of life. This is
particularly the sense of the prelude. The three succeeding movements are the
diverse answers in which existence replies."[2] Thus the perennial question again
makes its appearance in Ives's work. Later, he elevated diversity to a transcendental ideal: "Eclecticism is a part of [a man's] duty."[3] The symphony constitutes
the grandest, loudest, and most searching representation of the question and
answer in Ives's music, a far cry from the simple "Shall we gather at the river?"
of an earlier time. The first movement is essentially a setting for chorus of the
hymn tune *Watchman, Tell Us of the Night* with two accompanying ensembles,
the main orchestra and an ethereal-sounding group of solo strings and harp. The
question and the answer are intoned:

> Watchman, tell us of the night,
> What the signs of promise are:
> Traveler, o'er yon mountains' height,
> See that glory beaming star!
> Watchman, aught of joy or hope?
> Traveler, yes; it brings the day,
> Promised day of Israel.
> Dost thou see its beauteous ray?[4]

Ives felt that this work was an essentially religious one, but quite different
from earlier works with religious themes or those written for religious services.
Moreover, he found himself working on it with a "more natural freedom"—
perhaps, he speculated, because he knew that "the music was not going to be
inflicted on anyone forced to listen."[5] He reasoned that because he had given up
being a professional musician he could "feel justified in writing quite as I wanted
to, when the subject matter was religious." He contrasted the *Fourth Symphony*
to the *Third*, whose composition he dated to 1901,[6] although in fact he completed
it at Elk Lake in the summers of 1910 and 1911, when he began the *Fourth*. Thus
he associated one work to the time before 1902 when he "gave up music," and the
other to the time after this decision.

Further, the *Third* and *Fourth* symphonies vastly differ in the "religion"
inherent in their programs. The *Third Symphony*, subtitled *The Camp Meeting*,
is full of the daily religious life of Danbury in its verbal program and auditory
imagery. The movements, entitled "Old Folks Gathering," "Children's Day,"
and "Communion," are scenes from childhood, as far from the theological apparatus of religion as Danbury is from Rome. The *Third* is a work of relative youth,

its nostalgia rooted in the wrenching changes inherent in growing up and continuing with resignation through the revisions undertaken in mid-life. The *Fourth*, on the other hand, is a work of middle age, its religion tinged with premonitions of death and fervently desired intimations of immortality.

During the six or seven years when Ives was creatively engaged in writing the *Fourth* (1910–16), his life was outwardly conventional. A sign of this was his more or less regular churchgoing. During most of this period, Harmony and Ives lived in Hartsdale, New York, where they attended the local Methodist church. The churchgoing tradition was strong on both sides. The liberal Protestantism of the extended Ives family made it the more possible for Ives to be influenced through the Twichells by the teachings of their spiritual mentor, Horace Bushnell. For Ives, this represented upward mobility, religiously speaking. His most intense religious experiences derived from the revival meetings he associated with his father in contrast to the intellectually heady and spiritually inspiring experiences Harmony associated with *her* father. Despite the influence of the liberal Christian tradition—Ives dutifully sat through sermons and even commented on them—for him the "'let out' souls" were the ultimate bearers of religion.

From such diverse elements emerged the nucleus of a kind of private religion developed by the couple. Burkholder calls it a "private spiritual mysticism,"[7] and Kirkpatrick perceives it as "a mystical vision of reality" intrinsically related to the couple's "devotion to each other."[8] The peculiar religious pastiche the pair evolved did seem to be related to a spiritual withdrawal in the midst of an apparently active business and family life. This withdrawal accommodated Ives's increasing irritability as well as his need for the opportunity to compose. Indeed, in some ways the two were related as composition served the function of personal integration. In their intensive spiritual readings the couple unearthed elements that were drawn into a system of beliefs. The ideas of the Transcendentalists, particularly of Emerson, were thus incorporated, and any fundamental differences between conventional Christianity and the farther reaches of transcendental idealism were accordingly blurred.

The couple worshiped conventionally, but their ideas about religion were idiosyncratic, as if they were a sect of two. They accepted Christian morality, but the figure of Christ was scarcely present except in the iconography of hymn tunes. Their saints were Emerson, Hawthorne, and Thoreau. It was Harmony who held this patchwork religion together. As Ives strove to organize the chaotic elements of his mental life within his music, Harmony provided him with a stable background. Their "private spiritual mysticism" was intimately shared with an intensity that was probably displaced from the sexual intimacy whose issue had been such a disappointment.

In religious ideas the irrational in Ives's mental life could be readily masked. Similarly, Ives's political ideas of the time often had a visionary, even prophetic cast. Even now, some scholars see only these positive elements in his political convictions, failing to perceive the disorder and irrationality Ives was capable of, particularly when he became angry. Indeed, his increasing inability to contain and modulate anger was itself a sign of mental deterioration.

The start of World War I came during the period when Ives was working on the *Fourth Symphony*. Ives's attitude toward the war was complex. It both stimulated his anger and served as a focus for his growing rage. His efforts to contain his feelings are apparent in both the music related to this time and the political writings that were more and more replacing the writing of music. By the time the United States entered the fray, Ives was bellowing in his diary that "this [was] started by rich . . . degenerates, fought for rich degenerates, but fought by the people against the people." On the back of an envelope he railed against "gov[ernment] by property," asserting that "compulsory service means fighting for the rich."[9] His solutions to war were economically reductionistic and fundamentally simplistic, among them to impose a limit on the amount of property a person could own. Rossiter concludes that "by this time his thinking had moved beyond mere political democracy to social democracy."[10] Perhaps so, but the style in which such ideas were cast had become uncontrolled and grandiose.

The events in Europe of August 1914, although two and a half years before America's entry into the war, stimulated in Ives a wave of anger and patriotism. On Columbus Day, 1914, he sketched the first of several songs associated with the war, *Sneak Thief*.[11] At the top of the sketch he wrote, "People of the World rise and get the Sneak Thieving Kaiser." Later he thought, "*Sneak Thief* is a Better Titel [sic]." *Columbia, the Gem of the Ocean*, still a favorite, was quoted in an introductory trumpet fanfare. A short pencil sketch indicates that the unfinished piece was apparently intended as a "Chorus for a P.W.U." (Peoples' World Union)."[12] Echoes of the Civil War persisted with the fiftieth anniversary of its end close at hand: *Sneak Thief* also quotes *Reveille, Marching Through Georgia*, and *The Star Spangled Banner*.

For all his ideals and his outward belligerence, Ives was no activist, or at least not an effective one. His interest was in ideas more than actualities, and those ideas were often idiosyncratic and invariably had a sentimental basis in the past. In this lay many contradictions, including the call for limiting property ownership by a man at the peak of his income-earning years who showed no inclination to rid himself of property in the future. As Ives moved into his fourth decade, inner agitation manifested itself as political agitation. Its intensity increased even as any basis for effective political action diminished. This process paralleled the gradual decrease in the writing of music, which was supplanted by the writing of words. The prose he produced ranged from pseudo-scholarly essays to crank pamphlets. His efforts soon became quixotic as he tilted at social institutions. The start of the war in Europe only served to exacerbate this tendency.

From Ives's comments on the conceptual work of those summers of the mist at Pell's, it seems likely that the common element in the *Concord* and the *Fourth Symphony* was to be found in the writings of Hawthorne. Ives worked first on what would become the Hawthorne movement; the "idea of Concord" did not come until the next summer. The Hawthorne idea that was central to the *Fourth Symphony* was that of a journey, as in Hawthorne's story of "The Celestial Rail-Road." It was elaborated in Ives's mind as a personal celestial journey.

The *Fourth Symphony* reflects Ives's fascination with Hawthorne's short story "The Celestial Rail-Road." The story, a potboiler, nonetheless is filled with brilliant passages characteristic of the best of Hawthorne. Intended as a parody of John Bunyon's *Pilgrim's Progress*, it depicts a railroad journey from the "city of Destruction" to the "Celestial City." The traveler's companion, Mr. Smooth-it-Away, who guides him past the "Valley of the Shadow of Death" for an enticing sojourn in "Vanity Fair" before reaching the Celestial City, proves to be the devil's accomplice, perhaps Satan himself. In the end, the city is suggested to be an illusion. The story is in the form of a dream, and at the conclusion, when the dream has turned into a nightmare, the narrator awakens and thanks heaven. But before this horrifying turn of events, the dreamer in the story awakens *within* the dream and finds himself in "the pleasant land of Beulah." The pastures of heaven lie before him in a naive vision of the Garden of Eden as the gospel tune *Beulah Land* is among the several tunes quoted in the often dense texture of the music. [13]

Ives found in this minor Hawthorne piece a vision kindred to his own and felt drawn to it and inspired by it. Hawthorne depicts the Celestial City before its fall in auditory terms: "We heard an exulting strain, as if a thousand instruments of music, with height, and depth, and sweetness in their tones, at once tender and triumphant, were struck in unison, to greet the approach of some illustrious hero, who had fought the good fight, and won a glorious victory, and was come to lay down his battered arms forever." [14] This spirit informs the whole of the *Fourth Symphony*.

The pilgrim's journey not only appears in literary allusion and musical quotation but underlies the fantasy of the personal journey through life and transforms the music into autobiography. This is conveyed in John Kirkpatrick's elaborate preface to the score of the *Fourth*. [15] For in order to clarify the "formal and poetic contributions" of earlier works to this "definitive one," Kirkpatrick found that he had to trace Ives's musical biography back to the Yale days and even earlier.

The musical thread weaves from a fugue Ives wrote for Parker based on Lowell Mason's *Missionary Hymn* through its persistence in the *First String Quartet* and a revival service at Center Church in New Haven. The thread is picked up in a *Memorial Slow March* based on Mason's *Bethany* from Ives's days as organist at New York's Central Presbyterian Church in 1901, a tune that recalled the camp meetings of Ives's youth. Thus Kirkpatrick wound his way through the Ives biography as he sought to identify musical and other ideational elements within the formal and poetic aspects of the *Fourth Symphony*. The biographical journey continues with acknowledgment of the *Country Band March*, whose source lay in Ives's relationship with Lyman Brewster—and so on, through the *Orchard House Overture*, which quotes Charles Zeusner's *Missionary Chant* and in turn found its final place in the *Concord Sonata*, which was largely composed during the same period as the *Fourth*. Many other works are cited by Kirkpatrick for their ultimate contribution to the symphony, but most striking is the spontaneous biography that emerges as though inadvertently in the course of an exegesis of the music. Kirkpatrick, a musicologist, found himself writing biography because for Ives the line between art and life was blurred.

Intrinsic to the fantasy of the journey is the idea of the journey's end, presaged at the very opening of the work: "Watchman, tell us of the night." If the journey behind the music states, "this is where I was and this is what I have done," then intimations of its ending are implicit in the first step. Even the most meticulous or controlling autobiographer cannot write the final chapter. The philosopher may speculate, however, and the poet invent alternatives. Ives discovered the most appealing of those alternatives in the journey of Hawthorne's "Celestial Rail-Road": the Land of Beulah, the gathering at the river. It was consistent with a personal eschatology already revealed in his own earlier *Celestial Country*. Now, barely fifteen years later, Ives was capable of a far grander and infinitely more complex auditory image, one closer to that rendered in literary terms in Hawthorne's "exulting strain." In the preferred version of the fable, one awakens to "the thousand instruments of music." But behind the fantasied awakening lay another, explicit in Hawthorne's story, feared and fervently denied by the composer: the awakening *to* a nightmare and to intimations not of eternity but of eternal punishment. These are the fears that drove Ives, as he approached mid-life, to transform the naively untroubled world of the *Third Symphony* into the haunting religious vision of the *Fourth*.[16]

Following the ironic "comedy" of the second movement, Ives introduces a fragment of personal past by way of the fugue that constitutes the third movement. He took it from his *First String Quartet*, where it stood as the first movement, called *Chorale*.[17] To say he adapted it would not be quite accurate, since he literally "transferred" it (as Kirkpatrick put it) from the earlier work to the symphony. In his mind, the movement no longer existed as a part of the earlier work; a memo on the score suggests that the mental transfer took place "at Pell's" in 1909. As the *Fourth* finally came together in his mind—about 1916, as Ives recalled—he positioned the fugue as the third movement. As for the sleight of hand that removed music from one time and place and advanced it some twenty years, Kirkpatrick suggests that it represents "an extreme of New England privacy. . . . Its past was nobody's business but his own."[18] One wonders, however, whether there is more to this concretization of the music such that it could be transferred as if it were a person or object. For Ives, music always retained a primitive potential to subsume the most concrete and abstract elements. Perhaps the clearest example of this attitude is in what amounts to a bill of rights for music in the postface to the *114 Songs*. Ives writes of "an excuse" for the existence of some of the songs: "A song has a *few* rights the same as other ordinary citizens."[19]

The original version of the quartet, for strings and organ, was subtitled *A Revival Service*, and portions had been performed by Ives at revival services at Center Church in 1896. At least one of them, performed in October, Ives called "mild." This may have been a performance on Choral Sunday for a revival gospel service at Center Church. One of the two gospel tunes prominent in the *Chorale* suggests a further association. The second Sunday in November was Men and Missions Day, honoring the evangelical mission of the church. The two hymns most related to this observance in the Protestant hymnal are the *Missionary Hymn* and the *Missionary Chant*. Both are used as thematic material in the *Fourth Symphony*, and the *Missionary Hymn* is one of two hymns constituting the double fugue of the "transferred" third movement. Its original composition in 1896 commemorated a personal event: George Ives died on the first Sunday in November 1894, and Missionary Sunday was the next service Ives played afterward. The original movement was itself a commemoration; now, advanced some twenty years, it revived a specific time and occasion.

The process of incomplete mourning was beginning to extend to Ives's own middle years. He had now reached the age at which he believed his father had given up music, settling for a more conventional if restricted life. In a sense, Ives felt that his father had done so for him, and his identification with George Ives demanded a parallel sacrifice. Intimations of things coming to an end are found in the musical summation of life revealed in Kirkpatrick's commentary on the *Fourth*. Equally, its valedictory quality suggests it to be a premature final work.

In the final movement, Ives created an imaginative musical construction of journey's end in a musical fantasy of hymn tunes. Vastly complex in texture and rhythm, the entire movement proceeds against a background of a closely woven ostinato in the percussion (called "battery unit"), which requires a second conductor. It ominously opens the section and continues at the end, fading into silence; it is a representation of eternity. As in the first movement, there is an independent distant choir of instruments—here a group of violins and harp—as well as a choir of human voices. The most prominent hymn tune is Mason's *Bethany* ("Nearer My God to Thee"), fragments of which appear at the beginning of the symphony. At the conclusion, the ostinato fades into a silence, which intimates the infinity of time.

Beyond this is a more remote level of autobiography, one that pertains to childhood. It is the re-creation of the earliest auditory environment as originally experienced by the child and mastered by the artist, and it manifests itself in the intricate and often tangled musical texture Ives devised in the fourth movement of the *Fourth Symphony*. This texture, apparent in a number of earlier works, is a stylistic feature in which musical cumulations are gradually built up from relatively simple elements. In the *Fourth Symphony*, one finds perhaps its fullest and frankest expression, especially in the second and fourth movements.

In a critical article on the *Fourth*, the musicologist Kurt Stone skillfully characterized the style.[20] He noted, for example, that there are essentially no original themes and that the borrowed materials seem "to have been chosen largely for their non-musical connotations, picked for the role they have played in Ives's personal life." He characterized them as "peep[ing] out of every crevice" with little reference to either the work as a whole or, for that matter, each other. He uneasily suspected that other tunes would have served equally well musically. Harmonies are largely "the coincidental result of simultaneous horizontal lines," for the most part (except for the fugue) "non-functional." Massive musical "agglomerations" result.[21] But "unfortunately, . . . most of these kaleidoscopic interactions and transmutations cannot be heard because the total texture is usually too crowded and over-composed to permit such subtle and complex lacework to become perceptible in the general pandemonium."[22]

The critic, in capturing something of the listener's experience, opens a window on the motivation of the composer. It was just such an overwhelming mass of sound, made up of everyday hymns and parlor and patriotic songs, that confronted the acoustically sensitive child, Charlie. Auditory agglomerations, through which discernible meaningful elements gradually "peeped out," describe well both the child's raw experience and the stimulus for the gradual ordering of chaos. Endowment provides the capacity for creative ordering, here in music. It fosters maturation and, where successful, lays out the developmental path of the composer. But the motive force is, above all, mastery, its task set by the potential for trauma. The mind of the child thus hovers between chaos and order, between anxiety and satisfaction. Where mastery fails, so may motivation itself. Where it is successful, deeper gratification awaits when the child abandons the rigid imposition of form in favor of the continual creation of forms; that is, when the child's focus shifts from the goal of order to the process of ordering. The aim of this process is to revive and master, not to reach an end; to do, not to die. In pursuing a more flexible and challenging solution (a process that is unconscious in any event), the artist puts himself at risk. Chaotic elements may be called forth that are beyond his capacity for mastery.

By the time Ives was writing the *Fourth Symphony*, he was already having considerable difficulty in containing and ordering emotion. Harmony attempted a social solution in setting up a rigidly structured and rather withdrawn life. To the extent that it served as a tranquilizer, it was an emotional solution as well. A true psychological solution, however, in the most extreme instance would have been a true giving up of music, which not only served to organize but also to challenge organization. But in the *Fourth Symphony*, Ives does the opposite by confronting, not avoiding. He thus unconsciously persists in his lifelong endeavor to master threatening early auditory traumata through the re-creation of the infantile auditory environment. At the same time, and in part as a result, he finds himself at the peak of mastery of his unique, idiosyncratic style, which allowed a dynamic tension between order and chaos. Fundamentally, this tension exists in the psyche of Ives the composer, but he achieves a representation of the struggle in the music. It may become audible to the listener, an experience not always comfortable to share. As Stone observed, "Whether the listener will consider [the second movement of the *Fourth Symphony*] an unforgettable glorious noise or an equally unforgettable cacophonic horror, he will not be able to escape its almost traumatic impact."[23]

The end of the journey of the *Fourth Symphony* augurs the end of another journey. Stone notes that the final movement "has a quality of portentousness rarely if ever encountered in Ives's music."[24] Adult portent replays the childhood threat of becoming overwhelmed by chaotic forces that can be neither mastered nor contained. And whether the threat experienced by the adult stems from inner mental life or outer reality, it may assume the form of a fear of death.

On April 6, 1917, America entered the war in Europe. Ives's personal concerns regarding aging and death blended with common public ones, lending force to his preoccupations about the destructiveness of the war in Europe. His ever-threatening sense of inner chaos was externalized. Ives warmed to Julian Myrick's suggestion that he set *In Flanders Field* to music, to be sung at a meeting of Mutual managers in mid-April at the Waldorf.[25] The author of the poem, Dr. John McCrae, had done medical consultations for Mutual in Montreal. Ives pulled out all the stops in quoting discernible fragments of patriotic tunes. The piece opens with a quotation from *The Red, White, and Blue* and at structurally important points sounds out *La Marseillaise* and *The Battle Cry of Freedom*. *America* and *Reveille* are also prominent, all imbedded in a dissonant, impressionistic setting with ominous overtones.

The baritone who attempted to prepare the song, a friend of Myrick's who struggled with it as a favor, said he could not make head or tail of it, finding the dissonance "unbearable."[26] One can imagine what the insurance agents who heard it as entertainment at their business luncheon must have thought. Unlike Myrick, they failed to dissimulate, and the performance got a tepid reception, which hurt Ives greatly. Yet one must question his judgment in having it performed at that time and in that place. This fiasco reflects the degree to which he was already out of touch not only with what was socially appropriate but also with the Great War as others experienced it. In a sense, he was still writing music for the Civil War, and Flanders might just as well have been Gettysburg.

Ives was fervent about the righteousness of the war in Europe and troubled by the rise of the peace movement—"agitated," according to his nephew, Bigelow Ives.[27] This stimulated him to write the next of his war songs, *He Is There*. He tried to get Bigelow, then a small boy, to sing it: "If I didn't sing it with enough spirit or gusto, he would land both fists on the piano. 'You've got to put more life into it,' he'd say. There was one little passage which called for a real shout, but I shouted very timidly and he nearly hit the roof. 'Can't you shout better than that? That's the trouble with this country—people are afraid to shout.' "[28]

Ives wrote *He Is There* on Decoration Day, May 30, 1917. The song—words as well as music—again reflects the merging of the Civil War and World War I. Unlike *Flanders Field*, it is a rousing, easy-to-follow march replete with written-in cheers and a Sousa-like "flute or fife" obligato in the final chorus.[29] If Ives had not been so earnest about the piece and about the war, one might almost hear it as a parody:

> Fifteen years ago today
> A little Yankee, little Yankee boy
> Marched beside his granddaddy
> In the decoration day parade.
> The village band would play those old war tunes,
> and the G.A.R. would shout,
> "Hip Hip Hooray" in the same old way,
> As it sounded on the old camp ground.
> That boy has sailed o'er the ocean,
> He is there, he is there, he is there.
> He's fighting for the right,
> but when it comes to might,
> He is there [etc.].

The scene is a variation on the one Ives depicted in his prose companion to *Decoration Day*. The little girl on the fence looking at her father and wondering what he looked like at Gettysburg has been transformed into the grandson who bridges the generations. The little boy who had marched in the parade with his veteran "granddaddy" is now presumably old enough to fight a war himself:

> As the allies beat up all the warlords!
> He'll be there he'll be there,
> and then the world will shout the Battle Cry of Freedom
> Tenting on a new camp ground . . .

Represented here is the minimally distorted experience in the earlier life of the composer of watching and hearing the parade in which other boys marched, with his own father very likely leading the village band playing "those old war tunes." Among the tunes boldly quoted are two in the coda, *The Battle Cry of Freedom* and *Tenting Tonight:* "Tenting tonight, tenting on a new campground / For it's rally round the Flag boys / Rally once again / Shouting the battle cry of Freedom." Ives wrote the piece when America was barely two months in the war, and he wrote it in dead earnest.

The fantasy of fighting in the war gained impetus in the ensuing months and was associated with a flood of childhood memories relating to the other war, the one in which his father served. In a fantasied solution to the twin specters of aging and failing creativity, Ives pictured himself as the youth his father had been when he entered *his* war. Like every fantasy, this one was a patchwork. It included an opportunity for restoring the family honor, although one dared not speak of the shame. At the same time, the Gettysburg of Europe loomed, beckoned perhaps—Flanders. In *He Is There* Ives wrote, "'Hip Hip Hooray!' is all he'll say, / As he marches to the Flanders front."[30]

In September, this fantasy manifested itself as the third of the *Three Songs of the War: Tom Sails Away.*[31] It is a song of parting and departing: "In freedom's cause Tom sailed away for over there, over there, over there!" The words are set in a dreamy, impressionist texture: "Scenes from my childhood are with me," wrote Ives, and a literal scene is reconstructed with the immediacy of the present tense. At this point, the world war might, by some idealistic stretch of imagination, still be construed as a "boys' war," and no doubt it was in this romantic sense, informed by the patriotic idealism of the past, that Ives experienced it. It was a time of rallies and parades, as in the enthusiastic early days of the Civil War. The first American engagement was still six months off, and the casualty lists were not yet a reality. Ives now relived his family's past with a growing inner urgency. At age forty-two, when he had finally become a father himself (he and Harmony had adopted Edith), he was seriously considering enlisting. Somehow he would find a way to get into the war.

NINETEEN

SHADOW ON THE GRASS

The year 1918 was the most critical of Ives's life. It dawned with Ives characteristically feisty and vigorous, warding off ever-threatening overstimulation while at the same time harboring the fantasy of volunteering for war service. It ended in illness, with Ives out of the insurance office during a long autumn and then, in the winter, on his way south to recuperate. Dreams of glory were dashed, and, saddest of all, he came to experience the fading of his creative impetus.

In January, he sketched out a short piece for chamber orchestra, *Premonitions*, in a style reminiscent of the earlier experimental works of 1906.[1] The piece was associated with a text by Robert Underwood Johnson, from whose works Ives had already drawn *The Housatonic at Stockbridge*, and it would later appear in the *114 Songs:*

> There's a shadow on the grass
> that was never there before;
> and the ripples as they pass
> whisper of an unseen oar;
> And the song we knew by rote
> seems to falter in the throat,
> a footfall, scarcely noted,
> lingers near the open door.
> Omens that were once but jest,
> Now are messengers of Fate;

and the blessings held the best
cometh not or comes too late.
Yet whatever life may lack,
not a blown leaf beckons back.
Forward! Forward! is the summons.
Forward! Wherever new horizons wait.[2]

Before the year was over, omen had become reality, as a disabling illness (discussed below) marked the close of Ives's most creative period.

The Iveses now spent winters in New York so that Edith could have regular schooling there. From the deep attachment that had burgeoned earlier, there had evolved a close family of three. Separations were now rare, and only for Harmony's occasional visits to Hartford. With the start of the new year, Ives fit into an already busy schedule whatever he could do for the war effort. He became avidly involved in the Red Cross and Liberty Loan drives instituted in his office. One Saturday in January he went with Reber Johnson, assistant concertmaster of the New York Symphony, to entertain soldiers at Camp Upton on Long Island. He probably did not repeat his *Flanders Field* misjudgment, and he was still a good pianist and improviser with a feeling for jazz. But the "premonition" proved true: after the beginning of 1918, he did "almost no composing."[3] He did not seem to feel like it.

By June, he had devised a plan: he would serve for six months in France with the volunteer ambulance service of the YMCA. He was unable, however, to pass the required medical examination, for reasons that remain obscure. "Everything had straightened out except the medical side," he wrote later. The experience was "humiliating to say the worst." Leaving the YMCA building, he ran into an acquaintance to whom he behaved so rudely that he later apologized, making the lame excuse that he had had a pressing appointment.[4]

Ives spent three weeks in July in Redding working on the farm of his neighbor, Frank Ryder, to get himself into better condition for a repeat physical, scheduled for October 2. Just two weeks before then, on September 20, Aunt Amelia died at the age of eighty-one. Ives attended the funeral in Danbury but returned for several days' more physical exertion in Redding before coming back to New York. The day before the scheduled exam he developed, as he put it, "the serious illness that kept me away from the office for six months."[5]

The illness of October 1918 is believed to have heralded the end of Ives's intensive composing years. It is also widely believed to have been presaged by the illness of December 1906. All the major biographies link the two events, and those that venture to classify periods of Ives's creative life place the end of active composition at or close to 1918. The Cowells date "the period of his most energetic creative production of music" to 1910–18,[6] and Burkholder identifies "the years of maturity" as 1908–17."[7] Ives himself wrote, "My . . . things [were] done mostly in the twenty years or so between 1896 and 1916. In 1917 the War came on and I did practically nothing in music. . . . In 1918, I had a serious illness that kept me away from the office for six months."[8] The illness, the Cowells wrote, "left him with permanent cardiac damage." Rossiter agrees. Only Wooldridge gives details of the 1918 illness, but no source for his information is cited.[9]

The medical records raise doubt about whether Ives suffered an actual heart attack—that is, a coronary occlusion along with certain sequelae. Some data suggest, rather, that although Ives and later Harmony used the colloquial term "heart attack," the very real symptoms he experienced were not a result of organic cardiac damage at all.

In 1931, Ives went to the Joslin Clinic in Boston for treatment of diabetes. His personal physician, J. Godfrey Wells, sent along a note summarizing Ives's past medical history: "For a period of several years he was subject to tachycardia of a severe type—of late he has had none." The examining physician at Joslin elicited the following history: "Broke nose years ago; always healthy. In 1906 had heart attack with marked tachycardia & palpitation. Has had several other attacks since. None recently."[10] His physical examination at Joslin failed to reveal any abnormality of the heart—size and sounds were judged normal. Despite a possible predisposition to hypertension—his father had died of a stroke—Ives's blood pressure, 150/85, was normal for his age. The single electrocardiograph extant from one of two later hospitalizations revealed no evidence of permanent cardiac damage.[11]

It is certainly possible that Ives suffered a coronary occlusion in 1918, as Wooldridge states and others assume. Wooldridge reports that Ives "collapsed complaining of giddiness, fever, pains in his chest. The preliminary diagnosis was Spanish influenza. A more thorough examination showed a coronary thrombosis with suspected extensive cardiac damage, and his doctor ordered him complete rest for at least six months."[12] But Wooldridge does not substantiate his account, and it is subject to question for two reasons. First, cardiac pain was unlikely to have been confused with Spanish influenza. Second, the phrase "thorough examination" is both inaccurate and anachronistic. Diagnosis at the time would have been made on the basis of medical history; technological diagnostic means—electrocardiograph and blood tests, not to mention more sophisticated techniques—were either not yet in general use or had not been developed.

It is appealing, in the search for patterns in Ives's life, to believe that the period of his creative maturity was inaugurated by a heart attack in 1906 and brought to a close by a second in 1918; but there is scant evidence to support this view. Julian Myrick, who had accompanied Ives to Old Point Comfort in 1906, recalled later that Ives "had *something like* a heart attack"[13] (italics added). It was his belief that a long-standing condition was diagnosed at that time; but if so—that is, if some congenital organic condition had been detected—it would likely have been noted on subsequent examination at the Joslin Clinic or at Roosevelt Hospital in the 1950s. The only medically reliable information tells us that Ives suffered from episodes of tachycardia and palpitation, that is, a rapid heart rate or the perception of it. Never is there any mention of pain, the cardinal symptom of a heart attack. On the other hand, a rapid heart rate may be caused by other conditions than influenza and heart attack—most commonly bouts of severe anxiety, often called "spells" or "attacks" even in Ives's time. And even if Ives did in fact sustain cardiac damage later in life, the evidence in 1906 and 1918 points more to attacks of anxiety in conjunction with the depression observed earlier.

Yet even if Ives did suffer a crippling heart attack in October 1918, this does not necessarily explain the degree of his disability or specifically the failure of his creativity. Far less gifted individuals return to some diminished activity following critical illness, and many artists resume creative work. Ives, however, gave up both his careers, composition and business. The process was gradual though not prolonged. His creativity was not extinguished with a single blow but at first assumed new guises and pursued changing goals. Accordingly, the quality of summing up observed in the *Fourth Symphony* was very shortly transformed into a summing up of earlier accomplishment in the preparation and publication of the *Concord Sonata* (with its accompanying *Essays*) and the *114 Songs*. This was part of a final creative impetus which began as early as the period of convalescence in 1918. But aside from a few songs, minor pieces, abortive attempts at larger works, and certain ongoing projects to which he sometimes turned his attention, he never again composed as he had before.

Instead of ascribing Ives's creative decline largely to the effects of a presumed physical, organic illness, we should consider the profound psychological jolts Ives sustained at the time. In 1918 he was rejected by the YMCA Ambulance Corps. By applying, Ives was attempting to deny his sense of aging and his fear of death. By providing an opportunity (albeit a "peaceful" one) to discharge aggression by participating in the war, his acceptance would have proved (in his eyes) his vitality as a man. Intimations of failing potency—physical, sexual, creative—intruded into consciousness. It was the "shadow on the grass," a predisposition of mind, that drew him to *Premonitions* and the inclination to set it to music early in the year. Masculine potency and musical creativity, long since associated conflictually, were henceforth more tightly linked in his mind. We do not know why Ives was turned down by the corps. Perhaps it was his age or his prediabetic status; or perhaps the episodes of otherwise unexplained "spells" or "attacks" alerted the screening doctors to a nervous condition. But the blow to

Ives's self-esteem was enormous; too much hinged on the enactment of a compensatory fantasy in an unrealistic, quixotic endeavor. It would be difficult to imagine Ives near the trenches of the Marne, where the battle raged that summer, when Harmony was continuing to shield him and to balance his life between Gramercy Park and Redding. One wonders what she thought of the venture; perhaps she hoped—and assumed—the impulse would pass.

The underlying mental events of the greatest significance relate to the meaning to Ives of the progression of his life toward his late forties, as he approached the age of his father's death. George Ives, in his forties, had given up the thankless career of village musician and entered the business world in order to earn the steadier income his commitment to his children now required. He was forty-four when he accepted a part-time job as clerk in his nephew's business, and forty-seven when he began a regular job with the bank founded by his father, a position he held when he died two years later at age forty-nine.

Ives averted George's fate. In fact, he carried forth the Ives business tradition more visibly and successfully than any of his generation, but in doing so he bound his life inextricably with that of his father. He was well prepared owing to the education pressed on him by his father and the Brewsters. In business, his identification with George White Ives, his father's father, proved fruitful. Uncles Joe and Ike, father's siblings and rivals, were also drawn upon in the patchwork quilt of identifications. In his entrepreneurial insurance writing, Ives was more like Ike than he would have wished to acknowledge.

With George's death, Ives's idealization of his father had become rigid; intensified later, it became a fixture of mourning. Music, in turn, became a praxis of mourning, an unconscious sharing in fantasy of what had once been shared in actuality. The eminently successful career in business, however, was something his father could not have shared in life.

Thus Ives's creative decline tracks the decline in George's life in an uncanny way, for it is an unconsciously lived-out revival of the sensitive boy observing the decline in his father's esteem that lay behind the manifest changes in his life. It is a memory in action, a perception calling for some modification of one's own life. Identification with George spawned creative activity but, by the same token, determined its duration. Ives remained the composer during the same span of his life that he experienced George to have been a musician in his. Ives's adolescence had coincided with his father's early forties, and in those years of unrest the idealized image of George (which might have been shaken intrapsychically in any event) was shattered by his loss of status and esteem. The collaboration is thus a rewriting of musical history closer to the heart's desire, a realization of the father's neglected potential and a posthumous repair of esteem. For Ives, denial and idealization characterized the mourning process, which intricately involved music.

As for the precise timing of the decline in this endeavor, who can say when one has mourned enough? Mourning is always incomplete, an index of ambivalence and attachment. Perhaps as Ives entered the decade that had been his father's last, some shift occurred in his point of view: he no longer saw himself as the boy bereaved but as a father himself, possibly soon to die as his father had before turning fifty. Mourning cannot be fully accomplished with the continued burden of guilt. This burden, created by surpassing, prevailing, even surviving, hangs in mental life like a debt that cannot be repaid and that steadily accrues interest over a lifetime. Ultimately, the same dutiful impulse that generated the collaboration between Ives and his father had to call a halt to it. Aggression, which was harbored in mind and bound in art, at length turned against the self, dictating a limit to creativity. As a matter of conscience, collaboration was a duty, but its indecent continuation was an abomination and a transgression.

At Christmas, 1918, Harmony entered in the diary, "Quiet at 120 E. 22."[14] *Our Book* was never meant to be an intimate forum for sorting experiences and expressing feelings. Rather, the couple tended to note there the barest details, the milestones of the journey. Often, there would be no entry for a year; then one or the other, usually Harmony, would scribble a few dates—marking a visit, an event, a death. The diary in some way served the function of the family Bible of earlier generations, in which the rites of passage were duly noted, conveying a poignancy of its own in its simplicity and restraint. Ives himself had no need of any journal other than his music and the diaristic entries he often made on the manuscripts. As for Harmony, she was not given to complaining, and perhaps she associated the expression of feeling with discontent or even anger. She was, in fact, quite expressive elsewhere, but clearly better practiced at expressing pleasure than displeasure. The latter seemed to spur her to action, and she rarely felt sorry for herself. Ives was home, out of work, and recovering from the events of the autumn with as yet little that could make Harmony optimistic that he could return to either of his usual occupations. Plans had been made to spend the remainder of the winter in Asheville, North Carolina, for continued recuperation.

Christmas, 1918, was a milestone of another sort for the couple, the end of a generational era in their lives. A few days before Christmas, Joseph Twichell died, and Harmony made her saddest visit back to Hartford. For the previous four years, following a period in a Brattleboro, New Hampshire, sanatorium, Twichell had been at home, slowly fading. The only separations between Harmony and Ives during that time had been the occasions of her visits to her father. After Edith became theirs, Harmony always brought her along to see Grosspapa. Before long, the house at 125 Woodland Avenue was put up for sale. With the deaths of Joe Twichell and Aunt Amelia within three months of each other, the senior members of both families were now gone, leaving Ives and Harmony on their own. Ives's mother, as much a shade as ever, was destined to live another decade. The couple turned toward the nine-year-old Edith as if they were younger parents, not forty-four and forty-two, respectively.

Ives was greatly comforted by the presence of wife and daughter, and both he and Harmony took pleasure in Edie's growing up, keeping a notebook of the clever things she said. It appears that since October he had not written anything worthy of being recorded by either Harmony or himself. But a revival of interest in music was kindled by a little song they wrote together for Edith; or perhaps the song simply heralded the fact that Ives was ready to resume composing. In any event, shortly after they arrived in Asheville, Harmony wrote a poem that Ives set to music—old music, a song he remembered writing in 1892, when he was eighteen. They called it *To Edith* ("So like a flower, thy little four year face . . ."), and when Harmony later revised the verse, Ives liked it so much he left both versions in.[15] It was their first collaboration since *Mists*.

Recuperating in Asheville, Ives found within himself the renewed creative energy that led to the completion of the three works comprising his final trilogy. It was clear that out of the disorder of recent months a plan was taking shape. Ives would have the *Concord Sonata* engraved, privately printed, and published, then distribute it himself as he saw fit. Similarly, he would have the *Essays* printed. Over the course of the next month, he decided to do the same for his songs, the list of them grew to reach 114. Gradually, but at an accelerating pace, he completed various portions of the *Concord* as well as the accompanying *Essays*.[16] Before he left Asheville, he sent the completed movements of the sonata to New York to be engraved. It would be close to two years before the *Sonata* and *Essays* were printed and ready, in January 1921; and the *114 Songs* would not be ready until a year later.

In Asheville, the small family remained quite isolated, a condition that favored work. Reading was also a regular daily activity. But, curiously, Ives distanced himself from the world events in which he had been so vitally interested only months earlier. It was not until February 1919, as the three movements of the *Concord* neared completion, that he even picked up a newspaper— for the first time since October. (Perhaps Harmony had banned the papers, protectively enforcing rest for her husband.) So Ives had missed news of the Armistice and the founding of the League of Nations! He wrote, "things have gone on just about as one would imagine they would. Hence, uselessness of reading newspapers but once every four months."[17] Ives, emerging from illness, had been immersed in the nineteenth century, in his private pantheon of New England Transcendentalists. A final spurt of his accustomed creative energy had been mustered in the worldly withdrawal of invalidism. Once gathered, it continued until he had accomplished the tasks he had formulated in Asheville, that is, until the publication of the *114 Songs* in 1922. Meanwhile, his thinking about world affairs and politics was not extinguished completely; rather, it took an inward turn, strongly influenced by an idiosyncratic vision of transcendentalism and colored by grandiloquence. This trend of thought would soon become manifest in the *Universe Symphony*.

The family remained in Asheville until March, returning home for Easter. Ives's health had improved enough for him to return to New York now that the weather was better, though he did not return to his office. He resumed composition, however, at least that final phase of the preparation of a major work for publication, a far cry from the creative effort involved in conceptualizing a work and exercising artistic invention. The price of this renewed activity was a still more profound withdrawal from the world. Henceforth, Ives would maintain a personal aloofness, appearing out of touch with reality in his business and political thinking.

The trip to Asheville, despite its accomplishments, had not been an easy one, at least not for Harmony. At some point Ives had a "relapse," but Harmony's characteristically terse observation leaves no clue to its nature. She made note of it on their return, adding drily, "we didn't have a very cheerful time."[18] Nor was the return a cheerful prospect. For Harmony, it meant the sale of the house at 125 Woodland. The doctor said that Ives was still unable to commute to work, so the summer of 1919 was spent at Redding. He did not return to the office until September.

Thus "the song we knew by rote," which "faltered" in *Premonitions* in January 1918, wavered during the rest of the year as Ives endeavored to regain equilibrium after his illness. The ideas underlying the *Universe Symphony* were at once an attempt at self-healing and a part of that illness: order and disorder. And they may well have related to Ives's "relapse" in Asheville, when he may have been struggling against madness.

TWENTY

UNIVERSE

K eene Valley in the Adirondacks lies thirty-five miles south of Saranac at the apex of a triangle formed by Port Henry to the southeast and Elk Lake, the site of Pell Jones' camp, to the southwest. Ives and Harmony always found these mountains spiritually restorative. For the composer, they were mystically inspirational, a private world vastly distant not only from New York's Wall Street but even from Danbury and nearby Redding. The mountain retreat had been in the Twichell family, but Ives soon made the Adirondacks his own. Although he could work virtually anywhere—in the office, in homes and apartments, even in the crowded men's dormitory of Poverty Flat—composing in the mountains had a special quality, and he did so there with relative ease. More important, impressions, feelings, and mental states experienced during these mountain intervals remained with him when he returned to his other worlds. Ives and Harmony vacationed on Saranac Lake in the late fall of 1908, soon after returning from their honeymoon. Vacations at Elk Lake in 1909, 1910, and 1911 brought forth the *Concord Sonata* and the *Fourth Symphony*. At Keene Valley, in October 1915, Ives formulated an idea for what he thought would be his fifth symphony. He would call it the *Universe Symphony*.[1]

Characteristically, musical concepts had a long period of germination in Ives's mind; consequently, many were worked on at the same time. Although he made the first extant sketches for the *Universe* that fall, he later said that he had had the idea in mind for some time and had even made a few notes as early as 1911, the autumn of "the mist at Pell's" and "the idea of the *Concord*."[2] The "idea of the Universe" gained ascendancy in mind with the completion of the *Concord*. Only later would it become clear that the *Universe* was probably never meant to be completed. But the underlying extramusical ideas that were part of the concept preoccupied Ives during the next phase of his life—indeed, for the remainder of his life. They not only permeated his music—written and unwritten—but informed all of his nonmusical writing. Ultimately, they were destined to break the bonds of what either mind or art could successfully contain. They were part of a system of unconscious fantasies that gradually gained ascendancy from 1915 onward and were spurred by the inner and outward events of 1918. Thereafter, they assumed various manifest forms. But nowhere can these ideas and fantasies be observed more clearly than in Ives's sketches for the *Universe Symphony*.

In the *Memos*, Ives describes rather mechanically the transcendent experience and mental state that inspired the musical idea, proceeding immediately to related technical details of how it would be concretized in musical tones. He describes

> trying out a parallel way of listening to music, suggested by looking at a view (1) with the eyes toward the tops of the trees, taking in the earth or foreground subjectively—that is, not focussing the eye on it—(2) then looking at the earth and land and seeing the sky and the top of the foreground subjectively. In other words, giving a musical piece in two parts, but played at the same time—the lower parts (the basses, cellos, tubas, trombones, bassoons, etc.) working out something resembling the earth, and listening to that primarily—and then the upper [parts] . . . reflecting the skies and the Heavens—and that this piece be played twice, first when the listener focuses his ears on the lower or earth music, and the next time on the upper or Heaven music.[3]

He was thinking of "The Earth and the Heavens" as a possible title.

An unprecedented sense of elation permeated Ives's mental life at the time. Only two months earlier, the Olivers had departed Redding, leaving the baby, Edith, behind. Before leaving Redding that fall, Ives already had noted some "thoughts for fifth symphony" in manuscript sketches. United at Keene Valley, "on the plateau," were "Sue and Grossie . . . Edie (and Edie's second mother)."[4] Sue was Harmony's sister; Grossie, short for Grosspapa, was Joseph Twichell; Edie's "second mother," of course, was Harmony. Ives was, at least for the moment, head of the family.

The concept of the *Universe Symphony* was grandiose and awe-inspiring, encompassing nothing less than heaven and earth through time past, present, and future. Unusually well organized for one of Ives's initial ideas, it was visualized as having three sections:

I / Section A / (Past) Formation of the Waters and mountains.
II / Section B / (Present) Earth, evolution in nature and humanity.
III / Section C / (Future) Heaven, the rise of all to the spiritual.[5]

On one of the manuscript pages of section B, following what was meant to be a second prelude to the work, Ives wrote, "Birth of the Clean [or Clear] Waters." There is a detailed explanatory note in the margin: "The 'Universe in Tones' or a Universe Symphony. A striving to present—to contemplate in tones rather than in music as such, that is—not exactly within the general term or meaning as it is so understood—to paint the creation, the mysterious beginnings of all things, known through God to man, to trace with tonal imprints the vastness, the evolution of all life, in nature of humanity from the great roots of life to the spiritual eternities, from the great unknown to the great unknown."[6] Ives struggled to formulate his grand idea both musically in the sketch and verbally in his comments on it. The fantasy was magnificent: he wished to encompass nothing short of all, plummeting back in time to the beginnings, to the timeless "eternities."[7]

The task Ives undertook paralleled the work of God in Genesis. In every creative individual there is a propensity toward identification with the mythic Creator. It stems in part from the excitement of forming—from the libidinous and aggressive discharge attendant upon making something new, or making something from nothing, a latterday reprise of human anal prehistory. For the first human making of things proceeds from the body, from its products and childhood fantasies related to its processes. The sense of relief and satisfaction in the creation of form and the resultant exaltation persist in the adult creator. Concomitantly, there is a discharge of tension relating to the experience of chaos and its mastery. Latent in such experiences is the person's identification with his or her biological progenitors, both the man and the woman who made him; this too is part of the all. Beyond it is the realm of the spiritual.

The vicissitudes of an identification with God are many, ranging from the defensively humble posture (an aspect of identifying with God by identifying with his Son) to the frankly psychotic delusion of merging with the creator of the universe. Moreover, the underlying unconscious fantasy to which these identifications give rise, that of being God the Creator, may assume different forms at different times depending on psychic equilibrium—how the various parts of the mind are poised and interact. Such a fantasy may remain unconscious and still give impetus to creative activity. Or it may break through into consciousness, motivating behaviors that are alien to creative activity, inappropriate, even bizarre.

The childhood component of this fantasy informed the content of the imagery and endowed it with conviction. The imagery was not only religious in the sense of childhood religious experiences in home, church, or camp meeting. It was also prereligious, based in earlier experiences of the Olympian parent, a God-like father who created and, having done so, retained the power of life and death.

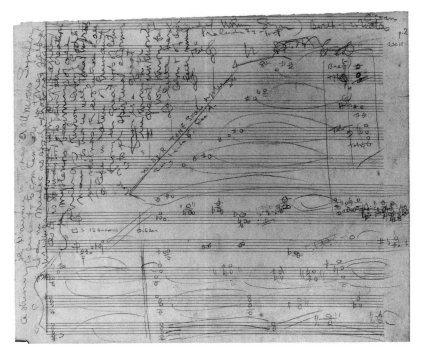

A manuscript page from the Universe Symphony, *1911–16.*

Indeed, it was this earliest image of the father that helped form and give force to all Ives's later religious experiences. In the infantile fantasy that would inform adult belief, if God made heaven and earth out of chaos, the earthly father, George Ives, did so out of tone. In later childhood, this image was reinforced by George as the temporal representative of God, moving the emotions of the multitudes at camp meetings.

The child's earliest creation myth is the legend of his own birth, at first shrouded in mystery, then related to the invariably distorted experiences of parental bodies coming together. In the compulsive artistic re-creation of the primal scene, the artist at the same time re-creates himself. The taking up and taking in of the entire world revives the childhood experience of the "love affair with the world."[8] It entails a widening and intensification of experience which in turn is related to the experience of awe, its developmental forerunner.

The mid-life component of Ives's fantasy at the time he conceived the *Universe Symphony* stemmed from his fear of aging and his approaching forty-nine, the age at which his father died. The fantasy of omnipotence was intensified defensively by Ives's recognition of his increasing mental instability and of physical illness (whether organic or psychic in origin). And his awareness of failing creativity, after more than a decade of strenuous and dedicated work, must have been devastating. He variously interpreted the loss of creative musical vitality as impotence, emasculation, and the imminence of death. So menacing a threat must be vigorously denied. Similarly, denial of a fear of death is subsumed in his personal rendering of the "future": "Life & death, and future life . . ." Ives fastened onto a fantasy of God in whose image he recast himself: Charles Ives, Creator of the "Universe." As the verbal heading of the same manuscript page on which Ives scrawled his description of his "universe in tones," he had written his own version of Genesis: "The Earth & the Heavens and lo—now it is night and lo the Earth is of the Heavens (or the Plateau, Keene Valley Oct. 1915)"[9]

The search for musical expression surpassed the verbal efforts to represent so vast a concept. Ives went about his representation of the universe near-literally, mixing prose and musical idea intrinsically.[10] For example, in a technical note he writes of five to fourteen separate orchestras representing "continents," the members of which will have memorized parts based on one "wide chord of intervals" ranging from octaves to quarter tones. *Everything* must be represented. The heavens would have their own chord system; a percussion orchestra would supply "the pulse of the universe's life beat."[11]

Ives appears to have struck a curious compromise between a concept so cosmically imaginative as to defy realization in an actual musical world and rather concrete and mechanistic artistic means. Yet both elements represented a degree of dysfunction—the unrealistic concept and the increasingly constricted means available to represent it. Equally important was Ives's failure to distinguish the artistically possible from the impossible. There was a diminished capacity for the very tasks now being completed in the composition of *Concord* and the *Fourth Symphony*. To deny this, a grandiose scheme was required, perhaps greater than any composer had attempted before, but the ebbing creative impulse fell back on formulae. Mechanical drawing superseded invention as words crowded out music in Ives's sketches for the proposed *Universe Symphony*.

From its inception, there were many intimations that the *Universe Symphony* could not be performed (at least as envisioned) and would never be performed. In his more realistic moments, Ives may not have intended it to be completed. This was music that was meant to be imagined, not performed. Ives was testing the boundaries between artistic conception and musical realization.

The idea of multiple orchestras whose musicians could come together in "conclave" suggests the vision of a mass outdoor assembly in some natural setting. The childhood origins of the image are discernible in the spatial "experiments" of George Ives, as perceived by the child, and even in the gathering of the Danbury Band in the house or backyard on Main Street. Here they are enlarged to Olympian dimensions; their purpose is utopian and their significance universal.

Ives conceptualized a thirty-two piece percussion ensemble ("Earth's motion and pulse") consisting of a dozen instruments. Among these were blocks of wood and pipes. Thus he reveals the common in the cosmic and the past in the present, as he associates these to one of George's performances: "I remember my father using (in a brass-band comedy-piece taking off *A Trip to Coney Island*), instead of some percussion instruments he didn't have . . . some large water pipes, perhaps sewer pipes."[12]

This incompletely and inadequately conceived *Universe* was Ives's "Unfinished Symphony." He never quite got over the idea that he would complete it some day, and as time went on he thought it might be possible to do so with a collaborator. Writing his *Memos* later (as he approached the age of sixty and had long since given up serious composing), he stated with regard to the *Universe*, "I want to work this out completely this summer."[13] In the event that he did not, he felt that "the themes and general plan are quite clearly indicated in the sketch" so that it might be filled in by a successor. The wish for a collaborator persisted to the last.

The ideas that gave rise to the *Universe* permeated Ives's life from his forties onward. They are manifest in his musical and nonmusical endeavors, in business and politics, and in the way in which he conducted his life. The failure of the creative impulse was painfully clear to him by 1926, at age fifty-two, and by the time he dictated his *Memos* in 1931, the capacity to compose was extinguished. The gradual deterioration of a function whose value to him was so overdetermined was a blow to self-esteem that stimulated a need for compensation. Its source was beside the point: the observing, experiencing ego perceives loss, interprets impotence, and seeks restitution where it can find it. The result was the mental trend that infused the spirit of the *Universe*. There it took the form of grandiloquence; elsewhere in life it showed itself as grandiosity. Further, it stimulated the wish for another creative partner, the ancient one, the eternal collaborator. Accordingly, Ives unconsciously sought greater and more cosmic representations. Turning to the forces of nature and to God, he pursued the most distant reaches of the family romance of childhood.[14]

During his convalescence in Asheville in 1918, Ives had become involved in yet another long-range project, which may bear some relationship to his "relapse" there, which Harmony noted. Since virtually the start of the war, Ives had been drawn to political thinking on a grand scale. Characteristically, the boundaries of musical and verbal expression were blurred, ideas germinating and blossoming in either or both forms. Thus the earliest conceptualization of the ideas related to a later prose essay, *The Majority*,[15] was in a song for unison chorus and orchestra of December 1914. Indeed, this initial effort may well have been Ives's finest statement of the humanistic ideas that underlie both music and prose. The poetry that served as text for the song contained Ives's personal rendering of transcendentalism, at once naive and romantic. Later, his thinking deteriorated, and poetry and practical politics became bizarre companions.

The Majority remains within the bounds of inspirational music. It is a fine example of Ives's mature style—"purely Ivesian," as Phillip Newman put it— with "dissonant harmonies, tonal ambiguity, complex rhythms, and a declamatory voice line." Ives wrote a text of nine stanzas (although in the final version he deleted stanzas 5, 6, and 7):

> The Masses have toiled;
>   Behold the works of the World!
> The Masses are thinking;
>   Whence comes the thought of the World!
> The Masses are singing;
>   Whence comes the Art of the World!
> The Masses are yearning;
>   Whence comes the hope of the World!
> The Masses are dreaming;
>   Whence comes the vision of God!
> God's in His Heaven;
>   All will be well with the World!

The circumstances of the musical deletions are revealing. Ives had been experimenting with schemata bordering on a twelve-tone system. (Perhaps some pictorial impulse inspired by the biblical twelve tribes who would become the "Nations of the World" led him in this direction.)[16] But unlike his sketches for the *Universe* a year later, the musical possibilities in this direction were rejected as being too calculated and diagrammatic: "It's too easy, any high-school student (unmusical) with a pad, pencil, compass and log table and a mild knowledge of sounds, and instruments (blown or hit) could do it."[17] His later sketches for the *Universe*, however, suggest something very much along these mechanical lines, though greatly inflated.

In *The Majority* of 1914 (which he alternatively called *The Masses*), Ives had perhaps said all he could musically about the ideas that lay behind the poem. The masses of which he writes were not the masses of Karl Marx, and Ives was never identified with socialism or any other movement not of his own making. More likely, these masses harked back to the half-remembered masses of the camp meetings, remnants of the distortions of childhood memory. The poem is a curious amalgam of the Bible, home-grown transcendentalism, and a utopian vision. By August 1916, following America's entry into the war in April, Ives couched some of these same ideas in terms of ordinary citizenship in an open letter entitled *Stand by the President and the People.* By then a staunch Wilsonian Democrat, he wrote, "This is a war for democracy. It must be fought by democracy. It can only be won by democracy. President Wilson has done more than any other president to voice the sentiments of the people rather than that of politicians."[18]

But the exhortation proved only to be an occasion for Ives to vent his spleen against a group of American millionaires who "have a great deal too much to say regarding the people's government." Among these were William Randolph Hearst, "who wanted war with Mexico, and owns $1,000,000 in Mexican mines," and Franklin Delano Roosevelt, then assistant secretary of the navy, who "inherited an easy living. Never made a cent for himself in any legitimate business outside of politics." Ives deplored the privilege of the "sons of the rich," who could escape the danger of combat. "The time has almost come," he wrote, "when no man who has personal property to the amount of, say, $100,000 should have any active part in a government by the people." Later, he would generalize this favorite idea, the limitation of personal property.[19]

In Asheville in 1918 Ives returned to these ideas, no longer in music or in a brief open letter, but in an eighty-four-page tract. The central verbal document of this period in Ives's life, *The Majority,* first took the form of a dialogue which he called *"George's Adventure* or A Study in Money, Coherence, Words, and Other Things (a good model for a poor story)." Kirkpatrick says that Ives began it in "a form borrowed from Plato," only to abandon dialogue in favor of a long essay. To compare this effort to Plato any further is to imply a mastery and control too obviously absent.[20] The groping, rambling, and often irrelevant text, which is meant to be humorous, is painfully unfunny. The rough question-and-answer form, however, may reflect some attempt to call upon a classical education to organize disarrayed thinking. Ives was cognizant of his tendency toward incoherence at this point in his life. On the first manuscript page, where various titles and subtitles are crossed out, he scribbled, "This is just to show how a man should write who considers himself a nice author and who everybody else considers crazy."[21] He now copied out the music he had written, and he wrote prose. He tried to organize his thoughts and hoped the act would organize him. In the process, he attempted to bind in words grandiose ideas, the impulse that gave rise to them, and considerable aggression—all now threatening to dominate mental life.

In an earlier document, *Stand by the President,* Ives had estimated the wealth of certain too-powerful men; now, in *George's Adventures,* he disingenuously revealed his own, which he rather illogically associated with transcendentalism.

He appears to struggle with his own wealth in the pseudo-rational manner in which much of the *Adventure* is written. When George's nurse-wife comments, "Many people will say that your ideas are too transcendental, too visionary," he answers, "The fundamental doctrine . . . of transcendentalism (the innate goodness of man) may be visionary, but if it was not true, there would never have been not only a world but a universe. The most practical thing I've ever done was to go into business and in twelve years make $1,800,000. But the idea that made it possible was called not only visionary but that it would ruin us within a year."[22]

In the twelve years since the start of Ives and Company in January 1907, Myrick had become a gifted businessman, and Ives had shown a knack for advertising and training and a capacity to develop original ideas. But to call their endeavor "visionary" was to grossly distort its mission and method. Ives cast himself as a prophet, in all of his writings henceforth, and the message of *The Majority* infiltrated virtually everything he wrote in words. Phrases from *The Majority* not only found their way into the essay *Emerson*, also written in Asheville, but very shortly insinuated themselves in his business writing—for example, in a revised edition of a teaching manual for insurance agents, *The Amount to Carry*.

These twilight musings of "George" contained another distortion. In the year of his illness, 1918, Ives's income tax records show him to have earned $29,535.[23] While this was a sizable sum for the time, it was no fortune. Ives and Myrick were not owners of the agency but managers. When Ives retired, he no longer owned any part of the business and retained only a pension. The $1.8 million probably represented the cumulative sum of his earnings over a number of years, not his current net worth—a further example of his disordered thinking.

In any event, Ives's call for a limitation on wealth in his writings from 1914 through 1920 seemed to proceed from a mental compartment entirely different from that of the businessman who earned the money. In 1914 he had earned a little more than $15,000; by 1920 he had raised his earnings to over $41,000. That year the Chicago manager of Mutual, Darby Day, wrote a letter congratulating Ives and Myrick for having written $3.5 million of insurance in January. He hoped it would be a "forerunner of twelve 3½ million dollar months."[24] In fact, they surpassed that goal. If Ives's makeup was such that neurotic guilt followed financial success, he was on a roller coaster that he could not—and in a way did not want to—control.

From 1918 to 1922 Ives's income continued to increase. It seems unlikely that his efficiency at work improved after his return in September 1919, but the firm, now well established, owing in good measure to Ives's earlier training program, wrote more and more insurance—over $22 million in 1919, $28 million in 1920. In 1921, the year the engraved *Concord* was sent out, Ives's personal earnings peaked at above $54,000.

If, as his writings suggest, the "relapse" in Asheville was a mental one, then *George's Adventures* tracks its murky mental disorganization and reconstitution. Out of a regressed twilight confusion, two figures emerge carrying on an imagined dialogue. Its content, however strange (or original), gradually becomes cogent and fixed. In the final analysis, one may view this effort as product or as process—either serendipitous writing that became a study for the essay *The Majority* or an imperfect healing process ending in fixed ideas short of delusion but removed from reality. *The Majority* is not easy to read. Its generalities, repetitiveness, and continual tangents invite skimming. However, it is such an extraordinary document for a composer to have created that some have been lulled into accepting the author as the kind of visionary he tries to pass for. The writer of *The Majority* is not the writer of the Civil War pieces and perhaps no longer even composer of the four completed symphonies or the *Concord*. But he is most assuredly the man who conceived the *Universe Symphony*. He still had ideas in abundance, although he no longer had the capacity to cast them in musical form. And there were plenty of words—too many.

Back in New York, Ives devoted himself to *The Majority* for the rest of 1919 and well into the following year. During this time, his thinking took another turn, which was reflected in the form of the essay. Previously a dialogue, it became an oration. It now opened with the inflammatory ring of the speechmaker: "Who are going to run things in this country—in this world, for that matter? A few millionaires, a few anarchists, a few capitalists, a few party-leaders, a few labor-leaders, a few political leaders, a few 'hystericals,' a few this, a few that, or YOU—the Majority—the People?"[25] Ives had moved from dialogue to demagoguery. The agitated had become the agitator. In this way, he could express aggression yet ward it off, contain it and externalize it at the same time. Others were greedy for wealth and power, others were aggressive, but not so the orator. Nor was he impotent—rather, he was powerful in the benevolence with which the simple transcendental ideal endowed him and in the world plan he sought to advance. Neither he nor anyone else was bad: the world plan would facilitate the emergence of the transcendental doctrine of "the innate goodness of man."

The Majority is a ranting, vituperative diatribe. In it Ives wields information in a tendentious manner, and its hold on reality is often tenuous. Its rhetoric displays the powers of persuasion that probably made Ives such a good trainer of insurance agents. He demurs on the issue of personal power: "The movement is the leader,"[26] he wrote. Yet power is one of the central issues and, if nothing else, is reflected in the style of the author. Ives's quasi-paranoid grandiosity is barely contained. At the same time, he tries to pass himself off as a man of vast, in fact universal, learning. He cites religious, literary, and historical figures by the dozen. Scientists and philosophers are mentioned as if to support his views, and people of every political belief receive their due.

The Majority is divided into five long sections, like the movements of a symphony. In the first, the "hog-mind of the Minority" is contrasted with the "Universal Mind" of the Majority, a term adapted from the Transcendentalists. The demagogue's insidious sense of knowing intuitively becomes the idealization of ignorance in the guise of wisdom, a celebration of the nonrational: "The Universal Mind Knows."[27] The Minority is of course constituted by the capitalist powermongers. Nowhere, despite Ives's liberal background and former respect for emancipation, is there any interest in or concern for the true minorities of the time. The ideal world in which the Majority would prevail would consist largely of middle-class white males if this vision were to be taken literally.

Incorporating yet another compartment of life as deftly as he formerly incorporated the vernacular in music, Ives includes in this political tract a questionnaire such as those he employed in the insurance business. The gentle question and answer of the songs and the troubled philosophical *Unanswered Question* are now assimilated into a survey ("answer 'yes' or 'no'") and adapted to the cause of self-government. In the utopian universe, questions would be settled as if in one vast New England town meeting or universal family of the Majority: "A thirty-minute daily discussion of our vital problems around the dinner tables of our thirty million families might save or help to save the world."[28] For *The Majority* was about nothing less than the salvation of humanity.

The Majority never quite comes to a conclusion. Ives simply ends it with a "summary," which he himself correctly calls an "excuse for a peroration." The point at which he decides to close is one in which fear of the Minority's power breaks out and with it an undisguised counteraggressive fantasy of murder or execution: the Minority man defeated has few alternatives. He can "abide by the winner's terms," "go to some other country," or "begin to shriek, to get nasty, hysterical, and begin to throw things around—and then the Majority will strangle him—and treat him like a farmer treats a skunk who loses his self respect."[29] The "peroration" then brings the work to a close with a cosmic image of world rightness under a deified Majority.[30]

Characteristically, music intrudes and the essay ends with the words of a song. Ives writes, "Man knows not the horizon of the soul—but Faith has yet its Olivet, and Love its Galilee!"[31] The last phrase is a quotation from the hymn *Immortal Love, Forever Full*, by John Greenleaf Whittier. It is well suited for its position in the essay, a last-minute attempt to transform oration into sermon.

The final form Ives's visionary ideas of this period assumed was a proposal for a twentieth amendment to the Constitution, a proposal for direct government by referendum.[32] In May 1920 he sent it along with a letter to eight New York newspapers and a handful of political leaders, including Massachusetts governor Calvin Coolidge and President Woodrow Wilson. He received polite acknowledgments from the secretaries of public figures and rejections from the newspapers.

Wounded, Ives "answered" such responses in penciled notes on the letters.[33] He also wrote to William Howard Taft, then a professor of law at Yale. Taft seems to have taken him seriously, expressing direct opposition to Ives's proposal, and Ives wrote him back at length, grateful for any response at all.

Undaunted, he decided to turn to a broader audience. The 1920 Republican National Convention was scheduled for Chicago. Ives had his "Suggestion for a 20th Amendment" printed up as a circular. He contacted Darby Day, the Mutual manager in Chicago, to arrange to have it distributed at the convention but did not manage to get it there in time. The Republicans nominated Warren G. Harding. Wilson made the presidential campaign into a referendum on the League of Nations, which the Senate had twice rejected and which Harding also opposed. Stimulated by Wilson's seeming criticism of representative democracy, Ives wrote another long letter to the press. Somewhat more closely reasoned than his earlier writings, it still was full of bitter sarcasm, such as a reference to "those fine old ladies in the Senate."[34]

Ives was angry and disappointed when Harding was elected. He revealed his feelings in text, music, and manuscript notations in the song *Nov. 2, 1920.*[35] The full title is *An Election or Nov. 2, 1920 or It Strikes Me That . . . or Down with Politicians & Up with the People.*[36] This soliloquy for male unison chorus is "half spoken." In fact, its entire text is within quotation marks from the reflective beginning, "It strikes me that . . . ," to the belligerent "Kick him out! . . ." to a passionate ending, "Captain, Captain, oh my Captain."[37]

Ives had worked obsessively on the project that started with *The Majority* and ended with the twentieth-amendment proposal for nearly two years. He noted in his letter to Taft that he did not have energy to spare. Not since Harmony's hospitalization, the loss of the child, and *Like A Sick Eagle* had Ives written performance directions such as those for *Nov. 2, 1920:* "Slowly . . . faster, but in an uneven and dragging way . . . slower and slower . . . In a weak and tiresome way . . . heavily." Ives looked to the past in an impassioned evocation of Lincoln, quoting musically from his own *Lincoln, the Great Commoner.* The music employs his most varied harmonic techniques while conventional, hence "safe," tonal messages satirize some of the words of its extended text: "Now you're safe, that's the easy way."[38] This is among Ives's last songs. Shortly, he would revise it for his collection *114 Songs,* where he added a subscript to the title: "Soliloquy of an old man whose son lies in 'Flanders Fields.' It is the day after election; he is sitting by the roadside, looking down the valley towards the station." In a footnote to the printed score, written sometime before 1922, he was still agitating for his twentieth amendment. He offered to send a copy of the amendment along with "an article discussing the plan in some detail and from various aspects . . . to anyone who is interested enough to write for it."[39]

Nov. 2, 1920 reveals not only the persistence but also the passion Ives brought to his ideas, however naively conceived. If his political ideas veered out of control as he vainly sought to realize them, the attempts were nonetheless heartfelt. If he could not convince the world to limit wealth, he could at least limit his own. It was said that he could have retired a much wealthier man as a senior member of Ives and Myrick. He decided not to do so; he did not "feel right, reserving to himself more than . . . his reasonable share of the country's wealth."[40]

When Ives returned to the office in September 1918, the spirit of *The Majority* infused with "universal" fantasies soon influenced his business. His role in the office evolved into a special one. He became writer, teacher, and philosopher in an organization that, after all, existed in order to make money. In some ways, he was its conscience as well, and his efforts to raise the self-esteem of the agents by striving to make the new field a profession rather than a business were keenly appreciated. The advertising copy he wrote betrayed more grandiose aspirations. Selling insurance was not merely a job; it was a mission to make people better. Agents were trained to promote programs of estate planning, not just to sell policies. They were to consider themselves as professionals providing a service, not merely as salesmen on commission.

In creating this atmosphere, Ives made good use of his Yale education. The programs he formulated had an academic ring. The Agency Instruction Courses were offered in semesters, classes held on Mondays and Fridays.[41] The program and its tone also made it possible to attract college men to the field. Indeed, it was Ives's idea to call the new agents "counselors."[42] He himself never taught any of the sessions, but the curriculum was based on his insurance writings. It included, for example, sessions on the analysis of actual cases, which was one of Ives's specialties. The question-and-answer form so frequent in his music also provided a natural dialogue between "prospect" and agent.

Ives had a knack for colorful copywriting. The voice that sounded eccentric and cranky in his political writings came across as beguiling and original in his advertising copy. The Ives and Myrick Agency put out a monthly bulletin which Ives entitled *The Estate-O-Graph*. The gadgets of George Ives and the gimmicks of Uncle Ike found their legitimate and lucrative resting place in Ives's advertising copy.

Ives's increasing isolation seemed to trouble no one at work. Julian Myrick had matured into an accomplished businessman with extraordinary social skills. In 1915, he had become president of the Life Underwriters' Association and had been elected president of the West Side Tennis Club. As Julian was "the outside man," Ives was most assuredly the one inside. His office, at the end of the hall, had two doors. One, of solid wood, was a private entrance; the other, facing the hall and open working spaces, had smoked glass so that no one could see inside.[43] By this time he had already become something of a legend in the office and seemed to be much respected, even revered. He was rarely involved in the unpleasantness of everyday management, and encounters with him were soon translated into praiseworthy anecdotes. Coworkers remembered him as kindly and never angry, a humanitarian with a high regard for others, a dedicated teacher and an egalitarian. His obvious eccentricities appear to have been all but ignored. His secretary thought he looked like Abraham Lincoln.[44] It was well known that he wrote music, which also served as an opportunity for euphemism. "Charlie was essentially an artist," summed up one of the agency men;[45] Myrick called him "a scholar."[46]

When Ives came back to the office, he made some changes. A couch was brought in so that he could lie down when he got one of his "heart attacks."[47] Perhaps by then he was experiencing angina. He was sometimes observed putting a pill under his tongue, although later medical histories fail to mention any episodes of pain. His working hours became irregular in the 1920s; he began to come into the office at ten or eleven and frequently left by two. Sometimes he would stay out for a week at a time. To his secretary, who worked for him between 1921 and 1929, he insisted not only on privacy but also on a confidentiality bordering on secrecy. Everything he dictated was "personal" and nothing was to be discussed with anybody. It was her belief that he continued to worry that someone would try to contact him about Edith, now five years old. No one unconnected with insurance was permitted to enter unannounced.[48]

When Darby Day sent a letter of congratulations to Ives and Myrick for the $3.5 million month of January 1920, Ives expressed his appreciation by return mail, breezily and disingenuously acknowledging both his withdrawal and his absences: "As it so happens . . . Mike [Julian Myrick] has had more opportunity for seeing you than I have."[49] The only substantive point that can be extracted from the letter is that the clerks' low morale, owing to inadequate salaries, resulted in poor service to clients. But tirade and harangue seem to lick at the edges as the idea of "the Progress of the Company from a bigger standpoint" took hold. Ives sarcastically expressed his dissatisfaction with the entire organization, "from the noblest Director (whatever that means) to the lowest mortality killer," all of whom have been satisfied with "the results of loose jointed, unrelated processes." One can only wonder what Day's reaction must have been to this salvo in response to a simple congratulatory note that had warmly begun, "My Dear Boys."

The dialogue of *George's Adventures* had its business counterpart in a feature entitled "Adventures of Two Different Types of Agents"—Ives liked to call it "Broadway"[50]—which appeared serially in the agency bulletin from July through September 1922. There, in story form, Ives presented dialogues between the "prospect" and two different kinds of agents. In this feature, Ives wrote something that was strictly business and very skillfully rendered. He shrewdly depicts the foot-in-the-door persistence of the successful agent. This agent is the "systematic opportunist" as opposed to the "casual" one, outlining a "system" that takes into account not only the prospect's needs and fiscal position but his psychology as well. It is engaging and scientific-sounding with occasional use of jargon, such as the agent's "Prospect Index" and the "psychological moment." One would never know from the document that Ives never had *his* foot in the door. Nonetheless, he certainly could teach. From this point on, such wildly irrational notes as his letter to Darby Day, characterized by grandiose fantasy and angry or inflated mood, were interspersed with quite straightforward letters that showed greater mental stability.

In the years to come, the system of fantasy kindled in the *Universe Symphony* of 1915 would flicker beneath the surface of everyday life. At times it would flare up, igniting some musical or philosophical or political idea. It could be consuming, spreading to other spheres of life where its presence was inappropriate at best, destructive to rational discourse at worst. At Keene Valley, in his "parallel way of listening to music," Ives took in all that was perceptible and imperceptible—in short, the universe—by a practiced inadvertence of perception in which nothing was permitted a focused clarity. Ives fell into this unfocused state of mind episodically, later perhaps chronically. At such times, and in a splendid isolation fostered by those close to him at work as well as at home, Ives—protected, respected, and even revered—could mix and match worlds to his heart's content.

BOOK FOUR

THE ENDURING FATHER

TWENTY-ONE

AUTOBIOGRAPHIES I, 1920–22

In the final years of his creative life, Ives wrote two autobiographies. One is well known; written in 1931–34, later compiled and edited by John Kirkpatrick,[1] it was published as the *Memos*. The other, arcane and accidental as autobiography, is the *114 Songs*, a product of the years 1919–22, the same period that gave rise to the *Concord*. Together, the *Concord Sonata*, the *Essays on a Sonata*, and the *114 Songs* comprise a final trilogy—Ives's last major completed work, notes on the impulse that gave rise to it, and a summation in music of the life of the composer.

The two "autobiographical acts,"[2] separated by little more than a decade, could not be more different from one another. Both are about music and a life in music; but the first is an orderly serial presentation of music, the second a ragged verbal narrative. Both are compilations, and in both cases the compiling was motivated by a long-standing biographical impulse. But the Charles Ives who was completing his fifth decade of life was not the Ives at the end of his fourth, any more than the latter was identical with an earlier Ives. The deterioration of Ives's mind and personality was gradual, insidious, progressive; hence it is more apparent and accessible in the later, verbal autobiography. In this sense, the earlier effort is in certain important ways more successful. Yet the content of each is the "I" of the artist as revealed in his life and work, artistically ambiguous in the first, discursively explicit in the second.

The *114 Songs*, as a great work of art, highlights the degree of control the artist was still capable of exercising in music between 1919 and 1921. The emotional lability and loss of control revealed in the prose *Memos* of 1931 makes the work subject to distortion. Here the revisionist temptations inherent in self-conscious autobiography are powerful, the more so where reason fails and grandiose fantasy presses for expression. The *114 Songs* is far less self-conscious although it is every bit a biography of the self. Its intricate and subtle revelations are in marked contrast to the distortions and excesses of the later work. Whereas the veracity of the *Memos* may be questioned, the *114 Songs* constitutes Charles Ives's truest "life."[3]

After the *Concord* and *Essays* were printed, Ives started assembling completed songs and those in "potential"[4]—songs for which there were earlier versions, sketches, fragments of musical ideas, and poems he thought he would one day use. Fully a third were new, newly cast from notes, or newly revised versions of earlier songs. Collecting this material in his late forties, and thus contemplating pieces he had written the day before side by side with songs written as early as his fourteenth year, Ives had before him the elements of his entire life. The task occupied him through much of 1920 and 1921, from the time he returned to the office after his illness. The songs were as surely the natural material of biography as the written notes from which he dictated the *Memos* a decade later.

The *114 Songs* does not consist only of music, however. It includes marginal notes and remarks and a closely printed two-page postface.[5] The postface, though not completely free from cranky tirades, is relatively moderate in its fist shaking and, as for world shaking, reasonably silent except for a single ecstatic transcendent moment. It is the *inner* universe that concerns Ives most in the *114 Songs* and its postface. Nor is the prose free of rambling circumstantial and quasi-philosophical musings. Coming, for example, to the concept of "progressive evolution,"[6] he focuses on the moderate if still utopian goal of each man's finding his proper work and appropriate expression of self. The products should bear the character of their maker, rooted in the commonplace and quotidian: "The instinctive and progressive interest of every man in art . . . will go on and on, ever fulfilling hopes, ever building new ones, ever opening new horizons, until the day will come when every man while digging his potatoes will breathe his own Epics, his own Symphonies. . . . He will watch his children in *their* fun of building *their* themes, for *their* sonatas of *their* life."[7] In the transcendental soup everything is blended digestibly, fit for assimilation and consequent epiphany—"he will hear the transcendental strains of the day's symphony, resounding in their many choirs, and in all their perfection, through the west wind and the tree tops." Thus the greater and lesser details of life are amalgamated with art and biography.

More specifically, Ives asks those questions that commonly spur the autobiographical impulse, but in his own way: "Wedged in between the sewing machine and the future he examines himself, as every man in his position should do;—What has brought me to this?—Where am I? Why do I do this?"[8] It is in this position—more metaphysical than physical—that he poses existential questions. Continuing the domestic metaphor, he offers an answer: "Some have written a book for money; I have not. Some for fame; I have not. Some for love; I have not. Some for kindlings; I have not. I have not written a book for any of these reasons or for all of them together. In fact, gentle borrower, I have not written a book at all—I have merely cleaned house. All that is left is out on the clothes line,—but it's good for a man's vanity to have the neighbors see him—on the clothes line."[9]

There can be little question, then, that Ives intended the *114 Songs* as a work of autobiography.[10] Indeed, he often used a song, the context of its invention, and the manuscript itself for purposes of recording diaristic events. One may observe here the influence of the nineteenth-century habit of the journal, the tradition of Emerson and Thoreau. But the whole as assembled in the *114 Songs* is more than the sum of its parts. A distinctive artifact has been created.

In the postface, Ives writes of songs that cannot be sung, and in the margins he notes others that are unworthy of being sung.[11] Although virtually all the songs have been performed at one time or another, the *114 Songs* still awaits a complete performance. Ives probably did not intend such a musical marathon; like the *Universe*, this autobiography was meant to be conceptual, never to be fully realized.

The short individual pieces that comprise the *114 Songs* range in duration from several seconds to a few minutes. While Ives did not consciously intend to create an overarching form as in the symphonies, he clearly paid attention to order and balance. The pieces were shuffled but not at random. Individually, the songs are like brief diaristic entries; in the aggregate, like a portion of a calendar or a volume of a journal. While there is no apt analogy either in music or in literature with regard to style, one is reminded of the verve of Samuel Pepys's diaries and the interiority of Thoreau's journals.

The *114 Songs* is laid out according to various time schemes, ranging from the progression of days and months to the seasons of nature and the seasons of man. Some songs refer to specific public holidays and occasions, like the "red letter days" of old calendars, others to days with singular biographical significance. There are songs about the passage of time and the affects associated with it, such as anxiety, nostalgia, regret, and grief. Finally, there is the transcendental and religious time after human time: eternity.

As in a book of hours, Ives re-creates every phase of the day somewhere in the songs, from the optimistic dawn of *Mists* to the melancholy dusk of *Children's Hour* to *Evening* and *Night Thoughts*. Among the months, there are songs titled

August, September, and *December,* and October is mentioned in *Maple Leaves.* Similarly, the seasons are named in *Autumn, Spring Song,* and *In Summerfields,* and winter is evoked in *December* and *A Christmas Carol.*

The phases of human life progress from infancy (*Cradle Song* and *Berceuse*) to grave; the *Slow March* with which the work closes is after all the scene of a funeral, albeit of "the Children's Faithful Friend" (the family cat). Childhood is referred to literally in the *Children's Hour* as well as in *Two Little Flowers,* but many scenes from childhood and youth fill other songs. Youth is celebrated in *Disclosure* and Wordsworth's *The Rainbow;* adulthood finds literal representation in such songs as *Luck and Work* and the Emersonian *Duty.* Experiences of boyhood, both "very pleasant" and "rather sad," are cited in *Memories. The Sideshow* and *The Circus Band* represent boyhood pleasures, and even cowboys and Indians have their day in *Charlie Rutledge* and the wistful *Indians.* The Yale years receive their due in such songs as *In the Alley* "after the session at 'Poli's'" and the rambling two-step *Son of a Gambolier.* The many songs of a frankly biographical nature and those relating to ethics, love, and the admiration of heroes enlarge on Ives's mature years. The *Last Reader* and *Evening* are valedictory, and among the songs of death are *At Sea* and *Immortality.* The last serves as a transition to the songs that describe afterlife in the heaven of *Charlie Rutledge,* the utopia of the *Celestial City,* the deliverance of *The Waiting Soul,* and the reunion in *At the River.* But the truest terminus and goal of life are to be found in the transcendental and universal experiences explicit in such songs as *Disclosure, The Rainbow, The Housatonic at Stockbridge,* and *Evidence.*

Of the songs with an explicit biographical context, *The Housatonic at Stockbridge* commemorates marriage and honeymoon; *Like a Sick Eagle,* Harmony's hospitalization; and *Slow March,* the earliest recorded loss, which latently represents still earlier losses and all subsequent ones. The title of one song indicates an extreme of temporal specificity in an actual date: *"Nov. 2, 1920."* Aside from being the date of the presidential election that year, November 2 may be a fantasied date of inception, the temporal "now" of the collection. November, too, was an anniversary month: the month of George Ives's death more than a quarter century earlier.

In fact, *"Nov. 2, 1920"* may well have been the first of the new songs Ives wrote for the collection. Among the other new songs were the four "month" songs noted above and the three melancholy evening songs: *Afterglow, Disclosure,* and *Evening.*

Ives had in mind a time sequence that would roughly reverse the now all-too-rapid flow of time: the last would come first and the first last (although this scheme was not slavishly pursued). Thus the *114 Songs* was originally planned to open with one of the last completed songs, *Evening,* and end with the earliest,

Slow March, written when the composer was thirteen or fourteen—thus spanning the thirty-four years of his truest creative lifetime. It is likely that Ives thought of *Evening* as a farewell song, for it closes with a recondite quotation of Beethoven's "les adieux" theme from the opus 81a piano sonata. Despite the reversal of time, then, the *114 Songs* begin and end with valedictory themes. Even the words of the first and last songs bear a strong poetic resemblance. The dignified elegance of *Evening*, drawn from Milton's *Paradise Lost*, contrasts curiously with the homespun sentimentality of the boy Charlie Ives:

Now came still evening on, and Twilight gray
Had in her sober livery all things clad;
Silence accompanied; for the beast and bird,
They to their grassy couch, these to their nests were slunk. (*Evening*)[12]

One evening just at sunset
we laid him in the grave,
although a humble animal
his heart was true and brave.
All the family joined us,
in solemn march and slow,
from the garden place beneath the trees
and where the sunflowers grow. (*Slow March*)[13]

The theme that binds the two is indeed that of paradise lost.

Intimations of a later Charles Ives—the author of the second autobiography, the *Memos*—intruded on his initial intention to begin the collection with *Evening*. In a fury against the "old ladies" of music who were even then beginning to elicit from him outbursts and diatribes, Ives aggressively altered the planned sequence at the last minute. Every paranoid conjures his own enemy and brings into focus the central issue. In Ives's case, the enemy would be the putatively effeminate members of the old guard and the issue masculinity in music. Ives later wrote that "the way some of the 'old ladies' purred out about playing the piano with a stick—and how just terribly inartistic to have octaves of all white or black chords of music . . . made me feel just mean enough to want to give all the 'old girls' another ride—and then, after they saw the first page of *The Masses* as No. 1 in the book, it would keep them from turning any more pages and finding something 'just too awful for words, Lily.'"[14] Thus he came to substitute *The Majority* (whose opening words are "The Masses!") at the beginning of "the book," flaunting the massive, boxed tone clusters with which the volume opens, imparting a shocking and aggressive appearance to the page itself. Later, Ives regretted this, feeling that "stupid or unfair" criticisms and remarks had provoked him "to do something that his better judgment knows it's not quite best perhaps to do."[15]

This episode reveals the Charles Ives of 1920–21, the autobiographer of the *114 Songs* in conflict with the autobiographer of *Memos* of 1931–32. Earlier, while his inner forces were sporadically out of control, he was still capable of mobilizing his creative energy and exercising artistic judgment. When inner pressures shortly gained the upper hand and paranoia flourished, informed by fantasies of grandiosity long held in abeyance, effective composing failed completely. This state of affairs characterized the period of the second autobiography. The scarcely controlled rage that led to the substitution of the belligerent and grandiloquent *Majority* for the gently accepting *Evening* served another purpose—that of fierce denial of death.

Within this framework, the temporal elements of biography emerge in verbal, visual, and auditory imagery in a present which is anchored in November 1920 but opens onto the past. The *114 Songs* was the "disclosure" (as Ives put it in one of his texts) of the "range of soul," accomplished in a unique language formed of music and word. Since it lacks a conventional narrative surface, the inherent autobiography is all the more transparent. By the same token, experience is rendered with immediacy, unobscured. There is no consistent "I" in it and scarcely a "he." In the *114 Songs*, Ives has created something of a palimpsest, on which layers are superimposed on other layers which are never completely erased. Thus the past enriches and informs the present.

The person in the autobiographical portrait is defined by experience, not by name, but other persons and their roles and functions in life are more definitive. The mother so conspicuously absent from the *Memos* as well as from the extant letters and other biographical materials is acknowledged in the *114 Songs*. She appears in the student composition *Songs My Mother Taught Me* and in one of the German songs, *The Old Mother*. Ives dated the latter to the turn of the century although an earlier version exists, possibly written as early as 1894. Its verbal message is simple and sentimental—a song of praise for having reared the poet-singer to manhood.

Father virtually materializes in the sound of the horn heard across the lake in *Remembrance*. But he is present throughout the work, especially in the nostalgic songs related to the remembered (and misremembered) boyhood paradise of Danbury. Both *Old Home Day* and *Down East* open with that impressionistic, spell-weaving musical texture that whispers, "Now we are going back." They richly catalog the human and nonhuman objects of which George is at the center. The nostalgia is intensified powerfully in *The Things Our Fathers Loved*. George is also invoked in the four "Hymntune Theme" songs, the last of which is *The Camp Meeting*.

Among the new songs of 1921 was a setting of a poem from the New York *Evening Sun* of June 7 by Anne Collins, called "The Greatest Man." A piece of unabashed hero-worship cast in a homey boyhood vernacular, it is the musical equivalent of a Norman Rockwell illustration: "My teacher said us boys should write / about some great man, so I thought last night / 'n thought about heroes and men / that had done great things, 'n then / I got to thinkin' about my pa." The cliché-ridden verse makes the expression of affect acceptable.. This is the "Pa" of feeling, who, despite his masculine feats, "won't kill a lark or a thrush," wept "when my mother died," and "once when I was sick . . . rubbed the pain right out." At the end, he is compared to "George Washington 'n Lee" (the latter doubtless for the rhyme).[16] In this song, the hero-father is grafted onto the domestic father. Elsewhere in the *114 Songs*, the ego-ideal in the form of the heroes of boyhood and the later idols appears in the abstract images of man taken from Browning's "Paracelsus" and Whitman's *Leaves of Grass* and in *Lincoln, The Great Commoner*, by Edwin Markham.

Brotherhood receives scant attention except as the idealized Brotherhood of Man. In fact, the only human brother who peers through the maze of memories is the fictitious Tom of *Tom Sails Away*. The text convincingly reflects the human experience of early memory in the vividness of detail. Such memories, of course, are much distorted: "I'm in the lot behind our house upon the hill, a spring day's sun is setting, mother with Tom in her arms is coming towards the garden; the lettuce rows are showing green." In the end, "Tom sailed away for over there, over there, over there!"[17] The repetitions (marked *slower* and *diminuendo)* are wistful, not sprightly. The listener is left in little doubt as to Tom's fate; the sibling's death wish is tenderly and artistically realized, art serving the purpose of defending against it.

The notes read, "Where no author is indicated the words are by Harmony Twichell Ives or her husband."[18] Thus, Harmony is recognized by the inclusion of several songs whose texts she provided: *The World's Highway, Mists, Autumn,* and *Spring Song.* Her birthdays were the occasions for *The Last Reader* (thirty-fifth) and the Wordsworth *Rainbow* (thirty-eighth).

Ives's attachment to his adopted daughter, Edith, was strong, and one episode involving her had so powerful an impact on Ives that he recorded it in the *114 Songs* in the form of two songs. In February or March 1922 the seven-year-old Edith suffered a severe infection whose consequences could well have been disabling or even fatal. Harmony later said that the occasion "prompted" the writing of *Immortality*, with words by Ives: the challenge, "Who dares to say our child is dead!" is answered, "If God had meant she were to die, she would not have been."[19] The entire song is based on the hymn tune *St. Peter*, which appears undisguised following a dissonant climax in the last line accompanied by rich, organ-like chords. The score is marked "quietly and firmly."

St. Peter is quoted again in *Two Little Flowers,* the text of which was written by Ives and Harmony together and set by him after Edith's recovery later that spring. While not itself in question-and-answer form, it seems to serve as an expanded answer to the questions of *Immortality*. The musical quotation in both *Immortality* and *Two Little Flowers* is benignly lyrical. In the allusion to Saint Peter as keeper of the gates of heaven Ives is signaling his trust in an idyllic afterlife.

Two Little Flowers, with harp-like accompaniment, musically depicts a moment of heaven on earth in a backyard Garden of Eden: Edith playing with her little friend Susanna in the sunny urban yard is one of several images of heaven in the *114 Songs*. In *At the River*, "the throne of God" is evoked. In *Charlie Rutledge* (a song about an unfortunate cowboy who was killed when his horse fell on him), although his "relations in Texas his face never more will see," the singer hopes that "he'll meet his loved ones beyond in eternity, in eternity, I hope he'll meet his parents, will meet them face to face, And that they'll grasp him by the right hand at the shining throne, the shining throne of grace."[20]

The future is not commonly the concern of autobiography, although the aspirations and fears it engenders are constantly latent. If, in intrapsychic life, the object is immortal, a portion of its mental representation must include its potential for survival *after* life. In the *114 Songs* Ives ponders the fate of this aspect of the internalized relationship with his father. Reunion is prominent among the various fantasies this mental mechanism may engender. At length, the homely reunions of the backyard and the river are transformed into the utopias implicit in *The Majority*, the *Celestial Country*, and the transcendental visions of *Disclosures* and Harmony's *Mists*.

Celestial Country was inspired by Parker's cantata *Hora Novissima*. In fact, the musical ancestry of both George Ives and Horatio Parker pervades the entire work. Overall, the idiosyncrasies of the *114 Songs* reveal it to be a kind of musical "contraption" second to none of those created by George. Curiously, a more distant musical ancestor, Elam Ives, is exhumed in *Cradle Song*. A poem by his daughter, Miss A. L. Ives, published in his *Musical Spelling Book* of 1846, was used as text for the song. There is no evidence in the rich Ives genealogy of any actual relationship.

Music itself is the subject of *The Last Reader, Disclosure*, and *On the Counter*, which are songs about other songs. Elsewhere, Ives evaluates or criticizes some of the pieces in prose. A footnote to *In the Alley*, for example, asks, "which is worse? the music or the words?" In the postface, he suggests that some of the later songs cannot even be sung, "—and if they could they perhaps might prefer, if they had a say, to remain as they are,—that is, 'in the leaf.' "[21]

Two other groups of songs bear particular mention, those depicting the ethical and affective aspects of life. Fully a dozen of the *114 Songs* deal with ethical subjects. Not only are such issues as slavery and equality dealt with in *Lincoln, The Majority,* and *Tolerance;* the wrongness of war and the fading ideals for which the world war had been fought are treated in *"November 2, 1920"* and *In Flanders Field.* Minorities other than black slaves are the concern of *The Indians* and *West London,* the latter about grinding poverty; and the more general issue of the wrongs men do to men is treated in *Night Thoughts.* Ecology is the subject of *The New River,* which has to do with the waste and noise pollution brought about by technology. The work ethic is celebrated in *Duty* and *Luck and Work,* and plain human decency in *The Greatest Man.*

The range of affects expressed either explicitly in the text or implicitly in the music is nothing short of that encompassed in life itself. The songs portray everything from simple pleasure to joy, hope, inspiration, and exaltation. On the darker side, wistfulness gives way to nostalgia, sadness, mourning, and grief. Anxiety is expressed as well as reverence and tenderness. Finally, love finds its place, romantic and patriotic, gratified and unrequited—love for parent, wife, child, friend, nation, and humanity.

Thus the *114 Songs* is the record of the life and times, the inner and outer experiences, of one man. It is a portrait of the self without the "I." Although Ives would later call it a "book" and published it as such, in the postface he took pains to inform the reader, "I have not written a book at all—I have merely cleaned house. All that is left is out on the clothes lines."[22] The statement is perfectly apt—a line of clothes, a few new but mostly old, spruced up for the occasion. Passersby may infer what they will about the person who wears them from a string of images which are auditory as well as visual.

The interval between 1922, when the *114 Songs* was published, and the summer of 1931, when Ives began his *Memos,* was Ives's musical Indian summer. By the mid-1920s, it had become clear that his ability to compose had effectively failed forever. The few songs he wrote were but brief reminders of a creative life that was already behind him. Like the Emersonian "reconciling days," Indian summer was not only a reprise of the past but also an intimation of the future. When it became all too clear that Ives would have to retire, his long-standing ability to find creative solutions did not fail him; he was able to exercise it one last time.

The Cowells coined the phrase "the career of Ives's music" in their biography and aptly wrote, "Composers are born, but a career is always made."[23] As the born composer in him was dying, Ives made a new career of his products, as if the manufacturer had turned marketer. It was, after all, Ives himself who decided to print and distribute the *Concord, Essays,* and *114 Songs.* The act was an odd combination of modesty, pride, and grandiosity, reflecting the contrasts in his character—the exhibitionism in the recluse. The clothes may have been "out on the line," but Ives hardly waited for them to be discovered in the backyard. He had the laundry delivered! On the one hand, he did not think his works worth anyone's paying for; on the other, he believed they were priceless. The compromise was a gift: he published all three of the works without copyright and sent them out to dozens of musicians, music journals, and newspapers.

The response was not overwhelming, but a brief article did appear in the *Musical Courier* acknowledging receipt of the *114 Songs;* the article was entitled, "Who Is Ives?" Ives bridled at the writer's observation that "to print such a book costs a lot of money and it is out of reach of most of us."[24] He replied immediately: "I'm *not* eager for publicity—and I ask that you give me no more no matter how favorable (or I might say charitable) you make it."[25] Why, then, had he sent the material to the *Musical Courier,* or, for that matter, to local newspapers such as the New York *Sun?*

Ives clearly was conflicted not so much about publication of his work as about the means that made it possible. The *Courier* had touched a sore spot, eliciting in him a sense of guilt for being the beneficiary of life's unfairness. Unlike most artists, he was in a position to serve as composer, editor, and publisher all in one. There was, of course, no guarantee that anyone would look at let alone perform the music, but it was at least out there, like a message in a bottle.

Meanwhile, Ives was open to considering performances and even began to pursue them actively. He had sent conductors scores as early as 1911, when he wrote to Walter Damrosch.[26] Despite the lack of a response from Damrosch, Ives again sent him material in 1915.[27] In 1920, he wrote Josef Stransky, conductor of the Philharmonic Society of New York,[28] and in 1921, Leopold Stokowski, then conductor of the Philadelphia Orchestra.[29]

For the most part, the publication of the "trilogy" was either ignored or received critically. Ives was deeply wounded by such responses. He had a long memory for the pain they inflicted and for the individuals who shrugged off his efforts, criticized them, or simply did not like or understand the music. Harmony stood by him as ever, convinced of the value of his work. She continued to keep in touch with the old Hartford families, and when the *Concord* was printed she sent a copy to the daughter of her uncle, Albert Sprague. Elizabeth Sprague Coolidge was by then, along with her husband, a musical philanthropist. It must have been Harmony's hope that her friend would pass the sonata on to knowledgeable and influential acquaintances. Mrs. Coolidge sent a copy to "a friend in Boston, who is very interested in new work and modern ideas." She confessed, however, "I did not in the least understand your husband's work myself. . . . I found nothing in it that I liked." The Boston friend's response was "not encouraging to Charlie's work. I do not want to quote him because I think it would hurt you."[30] Ives drafted an answer himself, which was never sent:

Thank you for your letter to Harmony. If it isn't asking too much I would like to hear all your Boston friend has to say about my music (I *still* call it that). He can't hurt my feelings—I've been called all the names in the criminal code. Favorable comment, to a great extent, is negative—that is, in effect, it sends one up too many 'blind alleys'. . . . But whatever he says won't be discouraging—that can only come from one source—you forget that. . . . The whole thing, of course, is but an experiment—and it was not written primarily to please. I thought that would be generally understood. However I was surprised to find so many men were interested in a thing so repellent in form.[31]

The letter is a study in denial: he is *not* hurt—indeed, *cannot* be hurt—by negative criticism. Favorable comment is even worse. In any event, he is *not* affected by the opinions of others—only his own opinion counts. Besides, he was only trying things out—this is *not* the finished, completed, statement.

One person who did receive the message in the bottle was Henry Bellaman, a writer and lecturer on music. Bellaman had received the *Concord* in 1921 and immediately sent off a warm letter of congratulations to Ives. He wrote a review of it in the *Double Dealer* later that year and persuaded a young pianist, Lenore Purcell, to play parts of the piece as illustrations for his lectures. Bellaman was the first of several critics who "discovered" Ives as a result of Ives's own efforts.

In the fall of 1923, a lucky accident led to the further dissemination of Ives's music when French pianist E. Robert Schmitz came to Ives to talk about buying insurance. Schmitz was the founder of the Franco-American Musical Society, later called Pro Musica, a group committed to the performance of new and unfamiliar music.[32] The relationship between the two men led to a performance by Schmitz of Ives's quarter-tone music in 1925. In 1927, Schmitz was instrumental in arranging the premiere of the first movements of the *Fourth Symphony*. Eugene Goosens conducted, with Schmitz performing the piano part. Henry Bellaman provided the program notes.[33] The critical response to this performance was unprecedented for Ives. Two prominent New York critics, Lawrence Gilman and Olin Downes, recognized the uniqueness and importance of the work in their reviews.[34] That same year Bellaman published an article on *The Music of Charles Ives* for the *Pro Musica Quarterly*.[35]

As for further composition, it was Harmony who acknowledged that creative life was over in her poignant description of her husband just after they moved into a new house at 164 East Seventy-fourth Street in New York in 1926. The house would remain their permanent New York home. A room on the top floor had been designated the "music room." "He came downstairs one day with tears in his eyes, and said he couldn't seem to compose any more—nothing went well, nothing sounded right."[36] But by then, this could hardly have been a revelation to either of them.

The year 1927 was one of promise and a watershed for the new career. By now,

Ives rarely went to the office. Diabetes, with its medical sequelae, was beginning to plague him. Cataracts were obscuring his vision, and the resulting frustration increased his now habitual irritability. Harmony continued to play nurse. A stabilizing element in their lives was the East Seventy-fourth Street house. And it was in 1927 that Ives was first contacted by Henry Cowell.

Cowell, at some point in the early 1920s, conceived the idea of a society to promote contemporary music. He started with concerts on the West Coast. Other enterprises followed, including the publication of the *New Music Quarterly*.[37] During the course of 1927 and 1928, Cowell solicited subscriptions for the new journal, in which he proposed to print complete scores of new and unknown music. He sent out some eight thousand circulars and personal notes. Cowell may have heard some of Ives's music by then. Although he had not been sent the *Concord Sonata* or the *114 Songs*, he certainly knew of their existence since Charles Seeger, then head of the music department of the University of California at Berkeley, had them, and they had talked about Ives. Sidney Cowell reported that Seeger (along with the composer Carl Ruggles), "felt strongly that one shouldn't waste time on this music: it was the work of an amateur, a dilettante and a clown."[38] Earlier, Henry Cowell may have been convinced by his conversations with Ruggles, but now he invited Ives to submit some of his music to the proposed *New Music Quarterly*.[39] He also invited Ives to serve on the advisory board.[40]

Ives responded immediately and with enthusiasm, taking out two subscriptions at two dollars each for the new publication to which he would be a regular contributor for years; in fact, he became its largest single supporter.[41] This was also the start of a friendship and a fruitful collaboration with Cowell, twenty-three years his junior, that would continue, with a single unfortunate hiatus, until Ives's death.

The correspondence between the two men reveals Ives to be as much a backer of Cowell's efforts as Cowell was to become the promoter of Ives's. Through Cowell, Ives became the major underwriter for the newly organized Pan American Association of Composers.[42] His check for the renewal of his subscriptions to the *New Music Quarterly* the following year, far in excess of the amount billed, was called a "lifesaver" by Cowell. Meanwhile, plans were being made for the publication of one of his own works; little more than a year after their first exchange of letters, Ives was preparing the second movement of his *Fourth Symphony* for publication in volume two of the *New Music Quarterly*.[43]

Ives's relationship with Cowell led to important performances that resulted in wider, if controversial, recognition of his music. It also created the circumstances surrounding the writing of his second autobiography, the *Memos*. In late July 1929, Ives wrote Nicholas Slonimsky, founder and conductor of the Chamber

Orchestra of Boston, reminding him of a request he had made to Cowell for an Ives score.[44] Ives sent him the *Three Places in New England*, which Slonimsky conducted several times two years later. With these performances and the publication of the *Fourth Symphony*, Ives's new career was launched. It was none too soon, for 1929 was the final year of his business life.

In a sense, the end was only ceremonial, since his participation in the business had become minimal. Ives was not involved in the stock market at the time of the crash in the autumn of that year. *His* descent was purely personal. The year began with the death of Mollie Ives at the age of seventy-nine. Nothing is known of her son's immediate response. Ives had long since tried to put Danbury behind him, as he and Harmony invested their lives in New York and, more important, in Redding. Now only Moss and his family remained in Danbury, which by the 1920s hardly bore any resemblance to the town of Ives's youth. Of the older generation, only Mollie's sister Lucy, Aunt Nell, survived.

As for Harmony's family, David and his wife, Eva, had remained close to her, visiting frequently. In 1921, they spent the summer at Redding. When David died in 1924, Harmony lost the third most important member of her family and the sibling to whom she had been closest. Now she became nominal head of the family. Ives had lost a friend and brother in David, and his death at forty-nine must have had haunting overtones of this father's death at the same age. This loss isolated him further from the past as it drew him into it.

In many respects, it was the past Ives still favored, and he attempted to preserve it, as physical health and mental capacities were failing, by remaining invested in the promotion of his music. The Iveses now virtually never went to Danbury, only minutes away. From Redding they had a view of Pine Mountain with its associations of the family camp and an earlier time. It continued to represent Ives's preferred view of Danbury.

Ives's letter to Myrick in July (the same month he wrote to Slonimsky) announcing his decision to retire on January 1, 1930, could hardly have come as a surprise. It was, however, a sad occasion for the friends of twenty-five years, as Myrick publicly acknowledged in a full-page open letter in the *Eastern Underwriter* that, by its combination of eulogy and assessment, reads like an obituary.[45] Julian described Ives as a "remarkable student, seated in his Connecticut home with pen in hand." Ives's creative contribution had been to "evolve literature . . . in the cause of life insurance progress."[46] By the time this tribute was published, Nicholas Slonimsky was already preparing the *Three Places in New England* for performances in Boston, New York, Havana, and Paris.

After Ives sent his letter of resignation to Julian, he worked at Redding on what was probably his final effort at a song, not an original one but a simple harmonization of the Negro spiritual *In the Mornin'*[47]: "In the mornin' when I rise, give me Jesus! / . . . 'Twixt the cradle and the grave, give me Jesus! / You can have all the world, but give me Jesus!" The piece underlined an irony in Ives's life. With the demise of one part of his life came the rise of the new, the fantasy of rebirth enacted. Although the visionary ideas of the *Universe* bordered on the impossible and skirted madness, the composer had managed to bring about some portion of its prophecy in his actual life. Like his last original song of 1926, *Sunrise*,[48] *In the Mornin'* marked both an end and a beginning, a Thoreauvian new day. The context, words, and music of the spare song looked back to a time forever past. Its people were gone. With the passing of Mollie earlier in the year, the last of Ives's four parents had died. Nineteenth-century Danbury was no more. But—the *but* that introduces the answer in Ives's optimistic songs—as in *Sunrise*, "a light as a thought forgotten comes again, and with it ever the hope of a new day." This, too, was the hope of *Premonitions:* "Forward is the summons. Forward! Wherever new horizons wait."[49]

Sunrise alludes to the close of *Walden*, "The sun is but a morning's star." Thoreau was never far from Ives's mind. In the discursive 1929 "footnote" to the *Fourth Symphony*, Ives paraphrased him in the "symphonies of the Concord Church bell when its sounds were rarified through the distant air." Ives ends the passage by quoting "an unknown philosopher of a half-century ago": "How can there be any bad music? All music is from heaven. If there is anything bad in it, I put it there—by my implications and limitations. Nature builds the mountains and meadows and man puts in the fences and labels."[50] Not even now was the George Ives of boyhood forgotten. In 1924 the Ives's, including Edith, went abroad for the first time, traveling in England. The trip, too, signaled an end and a beginning; it remained to be seen whether body and mind could rouse themselves to meet the new morning. Ives was fifty, his musical work essentially complete as the "trilogy" was published and his business work diminished as he did less in the office. The trip was no doubt devised by Harmony as tranquillizer, to get away from that which could not be escaped: Ives's mental state. Later, in the 1930s, they would be abroad for as much as a year. But the trip also brought new places to their lives just as the growing career of the music was bringing new names. Earlier, life centered around New York and Redding as both Hartford and Danbury faded more and more into memory. In the summer of 1924, foreign places—London, Oxford—were added for the first time. Shortly, the *Three Places in New England*, Ives's scenes from deepest childhood, would be performed in Paris.

TWENTY-TWO

AUTOBIOGRAPHIES II, 1931–34

At about the midpoint between the two autobiographies, the ten-year-old Edith, emulating her parents, kept a diary.[1] She started it on her birthday in May 1924, continuing until July, when the family left for their first trip abroad. Edith reveals a rich imaginative life centered about a fantasied "Lady Beautiful." In her drawings she depicts herself as a queen with a wardrobe of dresses, jewels, purses, and lockets for both "evenings" and "church." There is even a picture of "her thrown [sic]." The names of Edith's invented family royalty were Prince Rollo and Princess Lily: her adoptive father must have been speaking at home about the "Rollos," "Lilies," and "Lily Pads," invectives he hurled at musical enemies, real and fabricated, in his remarkable second autobiography.

Throughout the late 1920s Ives's health continued to deteriorate. Successive physical illnesses left him enraged and exhausted. Additionally, his mental condition was becoming more complicated. A growing affective instability gave rise to periods of depression and episodes of excitement. His ideation was at times grandiose, and he harbored paranoid suspicions. The parsimony one seeks in medical diagnosis is often impossible when one is confronted with a human life. What is more, character itself, which ordinarily comprises the more stable and enduring features of personality, may become "progressive" as certain traits are exaggerated with age, others subdued, and still others newly developed with the challenges later life brings. Finally, an element of mental disorganization may supervene whether its source be organic—the result of natural or premature aging—or functional—the fragmentation of reason by inner rage. *All* were operative here.

Still, the picture of the human being is complicated by the person's most engaging characteristics. Ives had long been famous for his sense of humor, with which he once entertained college classmates and now endlessly amused his nephews. His music itself is deeply imbued with humor. But at some point humor veered into sarcasm, at times vitriolic and uncontrolled, bordering on madness. He became especially fond of punning and neologism. His habits of speech soon encroached on his writing style, which could scarcely hide the underlying anger; the result was a crazy quilt of word and clang associations. Later, in the last and senile stages of life, Ives would be perceived as harmlessly idiosyncratic— "tetched," as one person put it, or frightening, as his grandson would experience him.[2]

The "attacks" continued, although the distinction between frank bouts of anginal chest pain and those of anxiety was blurred. Later, the sequelae of actual heart disease supervened as Ives had difficulty breathing. The diabetes had neurological consequences as well, which produced problems with vision. By the end of the 1920s, Ives had begun to develop a tremor that interfered with his handwriting. Probably the greatest source of disability as the 1930s approached, the emotional sphere, shows through most strongly in Ives's writings, especially the "second autobiography," which came to be called the *Memos*. In these years Ives seemed to become increasingly irritable and phobic, and was given to outbursts. Harmony made every effort to keep domestic life tranquil. They saw few people other than family and even then only in their own homes in New York or Redding. His suspiciousness, which bordered on paranoia, was associated with anxiety and fostered withdrawal. Critics of his music became "enemies" of his music, enemies of progress in music, and hence enemies of music itself. Because his own music was so radical-sounding, Ives could rationalize his outrage. For the same reason, there was more than a grain of truth in his suspicions and judgments.

Like Ives's major musical works, the prose *Memos* were "assembled" rather than written all of a piece. It is fairly certain that they were begun in 1931, another pivotal year for Ives in his new career. He worked on the autobiography until 1932, when he left on a fourteen-month trip abroad with Harmony and Edith. He brought the typescript with him, correcting and adding a few words to a few pages. After he came home, he returned to it from time to time and even added a few notes on a subsequent trip to England in 1934. Returning just short of his sixtieth birthday, he lost interest or energy or perhaps the capacity to resume. Alternatively, he may have considered the work complete, or, as in the case of the *Universe Symphony*, perhaps he never intended to complete it. By then, it had served its immediate purpose. Later, when he wanted to give the typescript to his first biographers, the Cowells, he could retrieve only about three-fifths of it. It remained for John Kirkpatrick to assemble the autobiography after its author's death by uniting its two natural halves, the *Scrapbook* and the *Memories*, prefacing them with introductory material initially written by Ives as the idea was gaining impetus. As editor, Kirkpatrick, invoking an Ivesian pun, called this first portion *Pretext*. It provides an opportunity to understand at least the manifest occasion for the writing of the *Memos*.

In January 1931, Ives was present when Nicholas Slonimsky performed the *Three Places in New England* at New York's Town Hall. This may well have been one of the last concerts of his own music he attended. Among the other pieces played was Carl Ruggles's *Men and Mountains*. Ives had not yet met Ruggles and had very likely been shielded from Ruggles's low estimation of his work. But he knew *Men and Mountains*, which had been the first publication of the *New Music Quarterly*.[3] Ives had not responded, at least outwardly, when his own music was booed and jeered. But when the Ruggles work brought hisses, he jumped up shouting, "You God damn sissy . . . when you hear strong masculine music like this, get up and use your ears like a man." He was proud enough of his stand to report it years later when he was interviewed for a never-published *New Yorker* profile.[4] But he seldom went to concerts thereafter.

Slonimsky repeated the controversial program in Boston, at the New School in New York, and in Havana. In June, he gave a series of two Pan American Association concerts in Paris. By then, Ives was principal backer of the association, and his piece was included in one of the concerts. The critical response to Ives's work in Stravinsky territory seemed to go to the heart of the matter: issues of innovation and priority. Appreciative reviewers found the piece original, imaginative, and strong; acknowledging that it was written twenty years earlier, they recognized Ives as an innovator, a "precursor." Critical reviewers, on the other hand, found the music derivative of Stravinsky and Schoenberg.[5]

Early the following month, with the European reviews in, Philip Hale of the Boston *Herald* wrote an article about the event. Whereas many of the Europeans had praised Slonimsky, one calling him a Christopher Columbus, Hale asserted that he had essentially misrepresented American music to Europe since the composers whose works he performed were "not those who are regarded by their fellow countrymen as leaders in the art." He suggested that a fairer idea would have been given by works of Charles Loeffler, Deems Taylor, or Arthur Foote, who, "working along traditional lines, have nevertheless shown taste, technical skill and a suggestion of individuality." He feared that the Europeans would form the impression that American composers are simply "restless experimenters," lacking melodic gift, displaying their ingenuity in "rhythmic inventions and orchestral tricks." Although he was clearly no admirer of Stravinsky, Prokofiev, or Hindemith, Hale called the Americans "followers, but with unequal footsteps." None of the Americans was singled out for specific comment.

Slonimsky's manager, A. H. Handley, had sent Ives the Hale article. A sketch of his angry response to Handley survives, its style characteristic of that which would shortly pepper the *Memos:* "Thank you for note and the enclosed pretty lines from a nice old lady . . . (Mr. Hale has quite the philosophy of Aunt Maria— When you don't understand some'n, scold some'n)." Ives's letter must have been in the mail when the Sunday New York *Times* of July 12 appeared with a review of the previous season by the Paris correspondent, Henry Prunières. The Slonimsky concerts, Prunières reported, had not been a great success. "If it be true that Charles Ives composed his *Three New England Scenes* before acquaintance with Stravinsky's *Le Sacre du Printemps* he ought to be recognized as an originator. There is no doubt that he knows his Schoenberg, yet gives the impression that he has not always assimilated the lessons of the Viennese master as he might have."[6]

Prunières's review rankled Ives as Hale's had not, no doubt because it singled him out. In a letter to the sympathetic pianist, Schmitz, a few weeks later, Ives sarcastically vented his anger: "[The review] wasn't so unfavorable as unfair or weak-eared. He says I know my Schoenberg—interesting information to me, as I have never heard nor seen a note of Schoenberg's music." As for not having applied his lessons—this elicited one of Ives's homey analogies, sparked by anger: "It's funny how many men, when they see another man put the 'breechin' under the horse's tail, right or wrong, think that he must be influenced by someone in Siberia of Neurasthenia. No one man invented the barber itch."[7] In fact, Ives liked the thought so well that rather inappropriately he tried to put it to Schmitz in rhyme but soon abandoned the effort. Something more needed to be said, although he had constrained himself with Schmitz while slyly implying that Prunières was a horse's ass. He confined his further thoughts to an open letter of the same date, addressed to no one in particular and to the world:

Dear Sirs and Nice Ladies:—
(This is not for publication, but anybody who can read can read it.) The following statement is made, not because it's important to anything or anybody, but because there are "lilies" taking money from newspapers and other things, whose ears and brains are somewhat emasculated from dis-use. They have ears, because you can see them—they may have brains, but you can't see them (in anything they write). Every so often, an article or a clipping or a "verbal massage" is sent to a man (see name on dotted line), which shows that Rollo has a job, writing his opinion about things the facts of which he doesn't know and doesn't try to know—or about music he doesn't hear or try to know. If he can't

hear and doesn't know it, he's a mental-musico-defective (from his neck up)—if he doesn't try to hear and knows he doesn't know, then he is getting money under false pretenses! In other words, these commercial pansies are either stupid or they are liars (mean word, but put there after careful consideration). . .[8]

The letter remained a marker for a rage Ives could neither discharge nor contain. All the themes that subsequently appear in the *Memos*, interspersed among the musical and biographical material, are already present: Rollo and the "lilies," the emasculated ears and brains, and the notion of the musical prostitute who is castrated and defective but paid for his services. Prunières, although unnamed, is one of the "commercial pansies." Philip Nathan Hale (who is named) "is either musically unintelligent or deliberately unfair. To say it quickly, he is either fool or crook."[9]

Even the open letter failed to quell Ives's outrage. He continued in a long tract that centered on Hale, called "Aunt Hale," "a nice and dear old lady from Boston (with pants on often) who sells his nice opinions."[10] He dissects Hale's brief article point by point. Again, this extension of the "Dear Sirs and Nice Ladies" open letter turned on priority and justification.

Ives was still licking his wounds from the reviews on Thanksgiving, when Kirkpatrick believes it "occurred to him to make something bigger out of the letter Dear Sirs and Nice Ladies"—that is, to write an informal autobiography.[11] He started to do just that in March of the following year, when he began in earnest to dictate the material that became the *Scrapbook* and *Memories*. In May, he wrote another introduction that purports to answer the questions he had already asked himself when he wrote the *114 Songs:* "What has brought me to this—Where am I? Why do I do this?"[12] Casually (and inaccurately), he attributed the inception of the *Memos* to a request for biographical material he had just received from the composer Wallingford Reigger, who had heard some of Ives's songs at Yaddo.[13] Ives's prefatory remarks are accurate but hardly cover all the ground. "When you get started putting things down (a good deal was dictated offhand and not looked over), one thing would come up from another thing—incidents that I or Mrs. Ives or someone of the family, or old friends, might remember or refer to—various family scrapbooks, old letters, programs, clippings, margins in old books, music and manuscripts, even a quotation over the wood house door. Some of the remarks may be rough, but they're the way I feel about things, right or wrong, and I don't apologize for them as such."[14]

This was, of course, written after the agitated twin letters and the "Aunt Hale" tract. In a different mood here, Ives pictures the planned autobiography as if it were like the bulletin board he had at Redding. Indeed, some of the items mentioned had found a place by this time on the board or in his studio. In a sense, this more reflective "introduction" better describes the earlier *114 Songs* as autobiography than it does the *Memos*. By now, something within Ives had been stimulated that needed to be discharged. Prunières and Hale had triggered issues that went beyond the technical details of the music and even the narcissistic issue of priority. Rather, issues of priority, innovation, fairness, and self-justification became urgently meaningful in the broader context of two questions Ives seemed pressed to address in the *Memos:* "Who is Ives?" and "What is music?" Once aroused, they informed the autobiographical impulse that led to the writing of the *Memos*.

By this point, however, the man attempting to grapple with these questions was much changed, even from the man who had compiled the *114 Songs* a decade earlier. First, his musically creative days were past, although their products remained "on the line." The autobiographical impulse now expressed itself entirely in words. Second, the personality changes already noted were much in evidence.

Ives's impulse toward autobiography gathered force in the context of the Prunières and Hale letters. The stimulus could not be contained by brooding or tirades or discharged in communication with Harmony. Nor could the excitement induced be assuaged by an evening's tranquil reading. Ives felt obsessively driven to answer for himself and for his music, and the answers inherent in the musical autobiography of a decade earlier no longer sufficed. In any event, because of the inner narcissistic magnification of the issues, a louder voice and wider stage were required. Moreover, the musical capacity that had made it possible had now passed. Hence Ives embarked on a proper *apologia pro vita sua*. By the time Reigger wrote expressing "curiosity about the facts of your life," Ives was well into the process of creating the "life." Indeed, he had already dictated much of it. The image of Ives that emerged derived from the dominant theme in his mental life—the complexly fused image of father and son. This was intuitively clear to those who knew Ives well at this point in his life. Chester Ives, his youngest nephew, recalled, "Uncle Charlie idolized his father. In fact, he used to speak of his father as if he felt his presence all the time."[15] Kirkpatrick, who met Ives only after he had dictated the *Memos*, speaks of his being almost "in a state of Chinese ancestor worship."[16]

Accordingly, the *Memos* are as much about George as about Ives, and in this final opportunity to immortalize him, a unique picture develops full of fact and fiction, memory and distortion, revelation and concealment. Ives portrays a George closer to the heart's desire, one more befitting the requirements of the son whose creative life was now over. In the heroization of George in the Civil War pieces, *Decoration Day* and *The "St. Gaudens" in Boston Common*, a monument had been created that was fixed for future appreciation and repeatable in performance. Now, the prose effort of the *Memos* was the final opportunity to assert joint identity, to fix its structure for all time.

The vicissitudes of Ives's family romance had long been accompaniment to this process, enriching past and present with fantasy, endowing the ordinary with the extraordinary, and creating the stuff of myth and legend. It made life past and present worth living by assigning an exaggerated value to the parental figures of the past and their representation in the present. It also rendered life tolerable, for the fantasies had a protective function, subserving the denial of reality and the avoidance through repression of such painful affects as anxiety and shame. Late in one's life, particularly after the loss of creativity, the fear of personal extinction is added to the threatening array of affects. This ultimate narcissistic blow may intensify the family romance fantasy and produce a change in its content. If nothingness threatens, then in denial everythingness must be asserted. Needs and wishes were projected back upon parental origins: he could not have had a modest background. Urgently, origins had to be aggrandized.

In the *Memos*, the exalted life of the father is fused with that of its author. Only on the surface has fantasy assumed a more human dimension. What is important in considering Ives's return to his origins and to Danbury is that the grandiosity of *Concord* and the straining of reality to the breaking point found in the *Universe* and *Majority* are not absent from the *Memos*. They merely assume another form and are employed in the service of new functions. The occasion for writing only manifestly concerns issues raised by some early performances of Ives's work and the Prunières and Hale correspondence. Reigger hardly had to press the button for the machinery to start up. The *Memos* show a father and son motivated by the pressure to revise what had been, and to repeat and reexperience this most gratifying version of reality. The life story informed by the family romance is a favorite story told to one's self. Many of the "facts" are there, but Ives alters and reshuffles them according to a more compelling pattern.

Beyond this, the disinhibition characteristic of certain portions of the *Memos* permits a glimpse of fantasies that were normally unconscious, hence in large measure defended against and under control. In the *Memos*, Ives's references to his father, the exclusivity of the pair in Ives's mental life, the affects of love, reverence, and nostalgia, and the apparent absence of the mother as an important object suggest the fantasy of a family of two, father and son. In such a "family," men beget men. How this would be accomplished would be shrouded by the veil of unconscious fantasy, but the conscious mind could go so far as to be aware of an incomparable love and intimacy that could be shared by men, the creative power that could be generated by this communion, and the creative products that might result. In such an unconscious fantasy, conception would be immaculate and women unnecessary.

The fantasied notion of man's making man is an extreme variant of the self-made man, a strong element in the Ives family myth. One example is George's own father, George White Ives, who started the Danbury Bank in the parlor of the family home. George himself is repeatedly endowed with no less creative capacity in the *Memos*, where his modest musical accomplishments are grandly inflated. At one point, Ives attributes a series of visionary statements to George with regard to the technical possibilities of music.[17] If these had been realized in music before the turn of the century, they would have encompassed atonality, dissonant harmony, polytonality, and polyrhythmic as well as quarter-tone techniques, among others.

In the family picture that emerges, Ives is the only partner, the only sibling, the only heir. Moss is scarcely mentioned, and such other influential figures of early life as Amelia and Lyman Brewster are noted only fleetingly. Similarly, George appears to be virtually the only significant teacher; Parker receives short shrift. In George is focused the best of family tradition and the best of musical tradition. The latter lies both in George's classical training and in his role as the Union's youngest bandmaster. Further, Ives was the only rightful inheritor of this tradition just as George was its sole source. From this lofty viewpoint, other contemporary composers either did not exist or, for various reasons, were depreciated.[18]

Ives disavowed music he had previously not only admired but emulated. Even Dvořák appears as little more than a foreign musical carpetbagger.[19] By contrast, while aggrandizing George's contributions to music, Ives claims the credit for them. When Moss admonishes him for conceit in implying that his music was "greater, less emasculated, and more to the point than any of the so-called great masters," Ives replies, "I don't imply any such thing—I don't have to—I state [that] it is better."[20]

As for charges that his style derives from Stravinsky, in the *Memos* Ives supports his claim as originator: "I've never heard or seen the score of the *Sacre du Printemps*. The places in this movement [*Putnam's Camp*] which some say come from Stravinsky were written before Stravinsky wrote the *Sacre* (or at least before it was first played), and came direct from the habit of piano-drum playing."[21] Thus disavowing influence, let alone flagrant musical plagiarism, and asserting priority, he at the same time shares the credit with George, with whom the piano drumming was long associated. George is the only avowed influence. Stravinsky is relegated to the same Gallic limbo as Ravel: "morbid and monotonous."[22]

This passage, which is elaborated with musical examples, occurs toward the end of the *Memos*, but it is central to the impulse that gave rise to the autobiography. Ives felt that he had been attacked, and the pressure to justify and rectify stimulated yet another revision of the family romance fantasy. The latent image of George which had been expressed in action and in music now became explicit in words. As it became organized, it became the more exaggerated. A revised past was created. If a "fact" came loose from its matrix, this was because it served the more pressing need of survival. The aggrandizement of the father would empower the self and deny the recent failure of creativity which portended death. It was thus that Ives sought to answer the question, "Who is Ives?" in this second autobiography.

A further system of unconscious fantasy is central to the question "What is music?" There are two factors that make the autobiographical *Memos* the essential document for understanding this fantasy. First, the *Memos* have the quality of a discharge phenomenon: Ives, angry and agitated, had to get something off his chest. Having done so, some of the *Memos* appear calmer and certainly better organized, with reminiscences about the past and detailed notes on his compositions. Second, this discharge betokens a degree of disinhibition—a failure of the normal, mature function of restraint or censorship of the expression of emotionally laden thoughts and impulses in the service of appropriate social relations.

While this disinhibition bears a superficial resemblance to the free association of psychoanalysis, in disinhibition control of the regulatory barrier of censorship itself is lost. In some ways, it is closer to a condition of perpetual parapraxis—slips of the tongue and of behavior. The point of similarity is that both give access to content long under control and characteristically of long duration in mental life, albeit in differing ways. Thus, in either instance the essence of the boy's fantasy life may be found in the mind of the aging man just as the relics and artifacts of past times may be found buried in the ground beneath us. Under circumstances of discharge, attempts at verbal expression may become uncontrolled, colorful, or bizarre, and metaphor and its elaborations will reveal the outlines of unconscious fantasy. With the stimulation of strong affect and the loosening of the bonds of logical discourse, the flow of disinhibited thoughts and feelings will inevitably include elements from the past. This process may be perceived in Ives's *Memos* and accordingly provides access to important elements of his fantasy life.

So it is with Ives's fantasy of a shared musical "ear." Molded and remolded in every stage of development, this fantasy nonetheless retained its primitive, somatic origins in memories of the earliest experiences of hearing and the pleasurable and unpleasurable affects with which they are fused. The human objects associated with aural experience become an intrinsic part of the mental image of the ear, and in the course of time one may come to stand for the other. To the infant Charlie, George was music; later, music became George. Music served as the medium of memory, through which Ives established a lifelong attachment to his father. After George's death, it became the medium of mourning.

The question of whether it was father or son who first harbored the fantasy, or it was the result of a father-son collaboration, is answered ambiguously in the *Memos*. There Ives quotes from a letter of George's in which one literally cannot distinguish where George leaves off and Ives begins. The letter was purportedly written by George to Orrin Barnum, a student of his and a former classmate of Ives's in Danbury, when Barnum was studying at the New England Conservatory of Music. Kirkpatrick makes an editorial guess that effectively bisects the letter, separating George's part from Ives's commentary.

> *George:* The older I get (he was about 42 [at] this [time]), the more I play music and think about it, the more certain I am that many teachers (mostly Germans) are gradually circumscribing a great art by these rules, rules, rules, with which they wrap up the student's ears and minds as a lady does her hair—habit and custom all underneath. They (the Professors) take these rules for granted, because some Prof[essors] taught them to them, and [before that some other] Prof[essors] taught them to them, etc., ad lib. And when you begin to really consider it, you ask, "Why? Why do you say this should never be used—this is [the] right way—this [is] wrong?" They['d be] surprised, sometimes dazed, and babble something that some old Prof. has told them fifty years ago. What they teach is partly true, but is it all true? See what Helmholtz says about natural laws—the danger of restricting music to habits and customs and [giving] these natural laws as an excuse.

> *Charles:* I am fully convinced [that], if music be not allowed to grow, if it's denied the privilege of evolution that all other arts and life have, if [in the] natural processes of ear and mind it is not allowed [to] grow bigger by finding possibilities that nature has for music, more and wider scales, new combinations of tone, new keys and more keys and beats, and phrases together—if it just sticks (as it does today) to one key, one single and easy rhythm, and the rules made to boss them—then music, before many years, cannot be composed—everything will be used up—endless repetitions of static melodies, harmonies, resolutions, and metres—and music as a creative art will die—for to compose will be but to manufacture conventionalized MUSH—and that's about what student composers are being taught to do.[23]

The actual letter could not be found after Ives's death. Ives asserts its existence when he comments that, in transcribing it, he had been unable to make out some of the words and so had made some editorial guesses of his own (in parenthesis; Kirkpatrick's emendations are in brackets). It is possible, of course, that George never wrote any such letter. Solomon believes "there is no compelling reason to accept that it ever existed."[24] It is also possible that the letter did exist—but only in Ives's fantasy. On the *Memos* manuscript, presumably when copying a portion of his father's letter, he wrote, "can't make out."[25] Perhaps what he couldn't make out were the elements of distorted memory employed in the service of reconstructing a letter in his mind that may or may not have been written. As it stands in the *Memos*, however, if the letter is indeed part Ives (as seems likely), it is an example of collaboration between father and son in prose, and an instance of the son's developing what he liked to think of as his father's words and ideals. Screening and revision went hand in hand. There can be no doubt that Ives was also inventing at the same time. This process led to the kind of writing, in prose as well as music, that might appear to have been done by two different people.

Ives dwells on George's colorful metaphor—the image of a lady with her hair drawn back to cover the ears. But the image is far from an attractive one. She is constricted, her ears as rigidly bound as the feet of Chinese women of that time. The comparison is apt since the rationale is that of "rules" derived from "habit and custom." The result is a deformity: fundamentally, these ladies are deaf. The organs of hearing have been crushed, as implied by the association of *music* and *mush* in Ives's continuation of the letter.

Kirkpatrick's judgment as to where the "George" portion of the letter ends and the "Charles" part begins is astute since the vocabulary, syntax, and metaphor of a more educated man are apparent in the latter half. (In fact, his portion may well have begun with the reference to Helmholtz.) If, indeed, the letter was either a reconstruction of his father's words or a frank fabrication, then we are given a glimpse of two aspects of Ives's personality, separate and unintegrated for the moment. One is the boy Charlie fused with his father, speaking with his voice; the other, the aging adult. Both are unstable, the earlier suffused with the anger and anxiety arising from the taint of the feminine in music, the latter with intimations of grandiosity. At the same time, the persona of both parts is that of a musician who cares intensely about music and its future. Perhaps one is of the nineteenth century, the other of the twentieth. Only the language is different. The colorful metaphor of the first gives way in the second to the technician's detail and the visionary's dream. Only at the end does metaphor reappear in the literal crushing contraction of "music" to "mush." But the substance of his remarks about the future of his art are not unreasonable and are admired and shared by many, if not so colorfully stated.

The imagery is powerful and graphic as in much of Ives's writing in this "genre"—that is, tirade against the effeminate in music, a subject which (as Rossiter put it) he "could not leave alone."[26] Elsewhere, as the image of the ear becomes further elaborated as a fantasy of some unique human organ, the boundaries of creator and created blur; the ear comes to have the qualities and potential of a living offspring. Later in the *Memos*, after giving examples of "piano drumming," Ives goes on to say, "I just mention the above . . . to show

how the human ear (not one but all) will learn to digest and handle sounds, the more they are heard and then understood . . . going back to the usual consonant triads, chords, etc., something strong seemed more or less missing."[27]

First and foremost in all of Ives's writings, the ear was strong and brave. Yet at the same time it was receptive. It thus paralleled the function of other body orifices, the mouth in particular. Never completely passive, the organ itself was capable of mastery, by touch and manipulation. In this way, it could achieve strength. Incorporating the phallus, it became the phallus. The danger of losing it was fraught not only with anxiety but also with the sadness incurred by the loss of an object of value. If the ear was prehensile, it was vaginal as well; able to grasp it, to give it, and to take it. Yet one was in constant danger of losing it.

Dissonance as well as other disjunctions in the fabric of music were experienced as welcome and challenging intrusions, strong and tough. Beethoven ("a great man"), masculine as he was, only made one long for something even stronger: "Oh for just one big strong chord not tied to any key. . . . The more the ears have learned to hear, use and love sounds that Beethoven didn't have, the more the lack of them is sensed naturally."[28] Beethoven was admired yet criticized; but withal he was exempt from the vitriolic scorn Ives reserved for other composers. It is Beethoven who is honored by being quoted in Ives's *Concord Sonata*, where the famous four opening notes of the *Fifth Symphony* serve as an important musical motif. Ensconced in Ives's pantheon along with Emerson, Hawthorne, Alcott, and Thoreau, Beethoven appears as the natural ancestor of George and Charles Ives and, unlike the "mediaeval" Richard Strauss, seems "always modern."[29] Although his symphonies are "perfect truths," he would not have objected to the reorchestrations of Gustav Mahler, which made them "more perfect": "Beethoven is big enough today to rather like it."[30] The image of a male musical progenitor is latent, his presence imminent. At issue is not only psychological identification but a family romance fantasy of ancestry, even reincarnation. Ives was aware of envisioning the *Universe* as his own *Fifth Symphony*.

In the *Memos*, a description of George's experiments follows the comments on what Beethoven lacked. The family romance implications are clear: ancestry proceeds from Beethoven through George Ives to Charles Ives. The "one big strong chord not tied to any key" was to be Ives's creation, and he makes it clear that it all came from George. Ives cites the "wide jumps in the counterpoint and lines" of some of his own music, providing a musical example in which a simple chromatic scale is extended through intervallic leaps through five octaves: "The ears got gradually used to these, as they, like the piano drumming, started in fun."[31] George is credited with having encouraged these experiments: "If you must play a chromatic scale, play it like a man." A man's space is wide, upward, and outward, a projection of his own organ of masculinity. In music, it may assume this form on the printed page, a graphic representation of auditory form. It looks male, and it sounds male.

One of the songs Ives cites as an example of the wide interval in his own work is *The Majority*. As a matter of fact, there is not one exposed "wide interval" of a ninth in either the vocal line or the piano score in the version in the *114 Songs*. Rather, another aspect of strength, of masculinity, and of space is represented. The score looks dense; its visual appearance can only be described as menacing. In performance, the instrumentalist must take an aggressive approach, to say the least, as complex chords comprising up to fourteen notes in one hand are best played with fist, forearm, or stick. The text is about the masses, and the music itself represents mass—indeed, *has* mass. It is massive in space and in sound, as are many passages in Ives; in fact, such passages are what makes much of his music awe-inspiring.

George's explorations of musical space included not only its widest extreme but also its narrowest. Just as ears and the sounds that entered them were stretched, so too sounds could be atomized, reduced to their smallest particles, which could in effect burrow into the accommodating ear. Thus an opposite, feminine component is introduced into the fantasy. Ives presents himself as sharing such percepts and the musical and acoustical explorations of his father with intense interest and utmost seriousness. He continued them in his own way long after his father's death. They became at once the medium of fantasy and the field in which fantasy was elaborated.

The underlying, unconscious fantasy was of a collaborative ear. It was both hard and soft, encompassing outer space and inner space, capable of being awesome and shameful and of engendering creativity, even life itself. Fundamentally phallic and male, it had a female component that was both enriching and frightening. If it was absent, annihilation threatened. It was, in fantasy, a truly bisexual organ, and therein lay its power and its threat. This fundamental fantasy was represented in all aspects of the music—its sound, its look, its creation and its re-creation in performance. Ives desperately warded off its feminine implications: intrusion, castration, annihilation, and death.

Ives took an aggressive pride in his celebration of the masculine in music. He boasted of a kind of musical heroism in achieving the ability "to keep five, and even, six, rhythms going in my mind at once, so that I can hear each one naturally by leaning toward it, changing the ear in each measure."[32] Ives's "heightening" of the dissonance in late transcriptions of his music, observed by Elliot Carter, is a further example of this compensatory masculinization.[33]

In idealizing the masculine, Ives indulged in a somewhat paradoxical overkill of anything he associated with the feminine, including sentimentality. He himself was openly emotional about things he loved in the human and nonhuman world, especially father, Harmony, and Danbury. The past continued to fill him with a sense of nostalgia and often found representation in quotations of "the tunes of long ago." It seems likely from their recurrence and their context that he actually loved and revered these old sentimental melodies and what they represented for him. He often quotes them tenderly, but, as he writes in the *Essays*, the "thoughts and memories of childhood are too tender, and some of them too sacred, to be worn lightly on the sleeve."[34] Such feelings were associated with the feminine, and the feminine within him had to be strenuously denied. Hence Ives ended up virtually phobic of anything feminine, including the powerful emotions he himself experienced.

Accordingly, disparagement of the feminine came to play a large role in the *Memos*. The actual or fantasied critics of his music are repeatedly dubbed "ladies" or reproached for their contaminating association with ladies. For example: "Too much of the American ear has become Soft-Static Co. (Limited), and the Gabrilowitsches et al. have the money and coll[ect] the ladies smiles."[35] By the time the emotional discharge is spent, Ives has concluded that "many or most of the celebrities of world fame are the greatest enemies of music—unless the art is going to lie forever as an emasculated art, degenerating down to one function and purpose only—that is, to massage the mind and ear, bring bodily ease to the soft, and please the ladies and get their money."[36] In the *Memos*, men are exalted, women (with the exception of Harmony) deplored, and boys wistfully revered. Ives is nostalgic when he writes, "The boys got going," uneasy when recalling how "The boys laughed out loud."[37] Music itself "is a nice little art just born, and they ask 'Is it a boy or a girl?'—and one voice in the back row says 'It's going to be a boy—some time!'"[38]

Ives recruited a fictitious boy for purposes of further derision. Rollo, the hero of a series of books popular during George Ives's boyhood, was the quintessential good boy to whom everything had to be explained. Ives no doubt knew of the character from his father. Rollo must have served as the object for vitriolic discharge as early as 1924, when Edith in her diary adopted that name for a member of her own imaginary family. Ives's Rollo first makes his appearance in the *Memos* with regard to Hale: "Rollo has a job, writing his opinions about things of which he doesn't know and doesn't try to know."[39] The music critic William Henderson is called "Rollo Henderson" and similarly criticized for "taking money for telling the public about something he knows not enough about."[40] Ives's imaginary dialogues in the *Memos* reveal Rollo as unmistakably effeminate and exaggeratedly phobic—the quintessential sissy. The putative Rollo is quoted as responding "just hoorid" or "not nice" to unconventional sounds. Ives parodies the bloodless responses of the Rollos to music: "You see, Rollos, I rather seem to tend to compare my music to a lion, and the music you like to a chicken."[41] He pictures "Rollos resting all their nice lives on, and now hiding behind, their silk skirts—too soft eared and minded to find anything out for themselves."[42] They are emasculated and, by contamination, can emasculate.

What is more, they do it for money. For Ives, even worse than the specter of effeminacy was that of prostitution. In a section of the *Memos* entitled "Emasculating America for Money," Ives's tirade reaches fever pitch as he questions, "Is the Angle-Saxon going 'Pussy'?"[43] Here he extends his criticism of things "going soft" to the commercialism of broadcasting companies, tabloids, and crooners, "the most popular defectives—the ladybirds—the femaled-male crooners." "Is America 'losing her manhood'?" he asks.

In "Emasculating America," Ives, looking back thirty-five or forty years, addresses himself as Rollo in speaking of his own earlier musical taste. "I feel like saying, 'Rollo, how did you fall for that sop, those 'ta tas' and greasy ringlets?'" In this relatively late portion of the *Memos*, Ives reaches the apogee of his diatribe, abandoning reason and eschewing the traditions that nurtured his earlier development as a composer. For he lumps together not only Wagner's *Preisleid* (from *Die Meistersinger*) and Ethelbert Nevin's *The Rosary* but also "a certain amount of Mozart, Mendelssohn, a small amount of early Beethoven, with the easy made Haydn, a large amount of Massenet, Sibelius, Tchaikovsky, etc. (to say nothing of Gounod), most Italian operas, . . . some of Chopin." Only Carl Ruggles—whom he had recently met for the first time and whose *Of Men and Mountains* had been on the same Slonimsky programs that spurred the *Memos*—was stronger and greater. As for himself, Ives asserts that his own music is "greater, less emasculated than any of the so-called great masters!"[44]

That the Charles Ives who completed the *Memos* was no longer the Charles Ives of the earlier autobiography, the *114 Songs*, or the contemporaneous *Essays* is painfully revealed in two letters to William Lyons Phelps, one from each of the two periods. Ives maintained a lifelong admiration and respect for his Yale professor and sent him a copy of the *Essays* in 1920, which Phelps, by then Lampson Professor of English Literature, reviewed favorably in the *Yale Alumni Weekly*.[45] Phelps sent Ives a thank-you note: "I'm so proud of you! And this is the work of 'Ives '98' my pupil and friend."[46] Ives in turn tried to help Phelps by attempting to get Bellaman and others to publish some of Phelps's poems.[47]

In 1937, after a long hiatus, Ives wrote to Phelps again. The occasion was his and Harmony's outrage at certain inaccuracies regarding Joseph Twichell in a recently published book on Mark Twain.[48] A typescript of the letter—the draft that was no doubt sent—contains a warm, affectionate, and grateful reminiscence, the nostalgic reflections of an alumnus, written in a cogent and measured style.[49] A draft in Ives's own hand, however, dated two days earlier, bursts out in a gratuitous tirade: "Emasculating America for money seems to be a business today, and one not wholly a monopoly, tabloids, movies, & radio with their headline 'picture pap' of defectives, mush scenes, jelly music, of money getting prima donnas, crooners etc."[50]

This, then, was the Charles Ives of the second autobiography. He is different from the Ives of the first autobiography, but the change reveals an underlying fantasy that had long been in operation but earlier had been under control. Nevertheless, the two autobiographies complement and supplement one another. The *Memos* are explicit where the *114 Songs* are ambiguous. One speaks in music about ideas, the other in ideas about music. Each serves to accomplish the aims of autobiography, to define the man and the particulars of his work—in Ives's case, his music.

TWENTY-THREE

FINAL COLLABORATIONS

Charles Ives was at core a collaborator. When he wrote in the *Memos* that if he had "done anything good in music, it was, first, because of my father, and second, because of my wife," he acknowledged the two essential collaborators of a long life.[1] Together, the lifetimes of father and wife encompassed all but a dozen years of Ives's life, those between the death of George and the first musical collaborations with Harmony. And it was during those years that Ives met Julian Myrick, who became his partner in Ives and Myrick.

In his sixties and later, his physical and mental infirmities required more than the devoted attention of his nurse-wife. Ives was ill-prepared to manage the new career he had launched. More than a secretary was needed for the flow of correspondence that he generated, and more than a music librarian to locate and help organize the sketches and manuscripts that Ives could now see only with difficulty. He needed an amanuensis and perhaps even something like an alternate self. For Harmony not only took from dictation the letters he could no longer write because of a hand tremor; she also came to write the letters herself, creating in them a more stabilized version of the personality of the supposed author. In this correspondence, and over the course of years, she organized him, tidied him up, and, where necessary, invented him. When she was exhausted or ill, Edith wrote the letters, conveying to the recipient what her father said or, later, the sense of what her father wanted to say. At times, when one or the other of the Ives nephews was staying at 164 East Seventy-fourth Street, it would be

Bigelow or Chester who would pen the letter. The "career of the music" became something of a family business and cottage industry.

The music needed help too. In fact, it invited collaboration. Much of it was unrevised and in sketch form, and a good deal of it was complex to begin with. Composers who found the music interesting soon found themselves involved in the very process of composing it. That is, they would be drawn through their own interest into operations normally performed by the composer—revision, arranging, even adding passages where gaps existed. Usually this was done according to Ives's instructions, and he retained a prodigious memory for what he had put down in score or sketch from years earlier. At the same time, he welcomed the active, creative participation of those composers who worked with him—Cowell, John Becker, Lou Harrison, even the performers of his music. For these men, the music seemed to carry the fascination of an unsolved puzzle, and they were drawn into the enterprise of creating musical gestalts in collaboration with the composer.

Against this psychological and historical background, and considering as well Ives's failing physical and mental capacities, it would be hard to overestimate the significance of the new people who were coming into his life around this time. The association with Henry Cowell had set off the series of events leading up to the writing of the *Memos*. A many-faceted collaboration between the two men developed rapidly, involving not only Cowell's promotion of Ives's music and Ives's financial support of Cowell's endeavors but also a joint effort to advance the music of other composers.

Perhaps most important to Ives was finding someone, and later a group of people, who were responsive to his music and validated it for him as well. There is a note of despair in the *Memos* where he writes of the isolation he had experienced: "I felt . . . that perhaps there must be something wrong with me. Said I to myself, 'I'm the only one, with the exception of Mrs. Ives (and one or two others perhaps, Mr. Ryder, Dr. Griggs), who likes any of my music. . . . Why do I like to work in this way and get all set up by it, while (others only get upset by it) and it just makes everybody else mad, especially well known musicians and critics. . . . (Are my ears on wrong? No one else seems to hear it the same way . . .).'"[2] The pathos of the entry is underscored by the fact that Frank Ryder, a neighboring farmer in Redding (and later his son, Will), was caretaker for the Ives's property.

The new group who sought him out, however, was made up of musicians and critics who could "hear" his music. A few were drawn into creative, hands-on musical collaborations with him. In 1936, for example, Cowell produced a performable version of *Calcium Light Night* from Ives's autograph sketch.[3] The sketch contained hardly the germ of the idea, the substance of which Ives was somehow able to convey to Cowell. Since there is no intermediate version, there can be little doubt that Cowell exercised considerable freedom in his realization of the music. It was, in effect, a true collaboration. Cowell was modest with regard to his contribution, writing to Ives, "I enclose the Calcium Light score which I have made—it is probably just what you already have there, but with some few minor adaptations in order to fit the scheme together and with added markings for the parts, etc. Although seemingly so simple, it took a long time to think on it and live with it until I felt that it was right."[4]

Two other composers who corroborated for Ives that his ears were not "on wrong" were John Becker and Carl Ruggles. It was Ruggles, only a year and a half younger than Ives and plainly a Yankee, whose music Ives considered bigger and stronger than that of the Three B's. Their earliest correspondence stems from Ives's congratulatory telegram of February 1932 on the occasion of the performance of Ruggles's *The Sun Treader* by Slonimsky in Paris: "We are all elated that Paris is up with you treading the sun." Kirkpatrick notes, "They soon became each other's favorite living composer."[5] Ruggles possessed a great, burly personal warmth and frequently addressed Ives in his letters as "Charles Dear." Their wives became friendly, and the couples saw each other from time to time.

But it was with the Beckers that the closer relationship developed; they became "family." Indeed, there was more than a casual family resemblance between John Becker and Ives in terms of values, regional background, musical training, and, above all, style. Additionally, Becker was an archetypical family man in ways that were bound to impress Ives. He struggled to support his wife and three young boys as an academic in a small Midwestern college while remaining uncompromising with regard to his music.

John J. Becker was twelve years younger than Ives. He grew up in a middle-class environment in a small town in Indiana, and although there does not seem to have been a significant family figure in his early musical experiences, his formal training was largely conservative and academic in the European tradition. After earning a doctorate from the Wisconsin Conservatory of Music, he had a series of associations with Catholic colleges (including Notre Dame) which led him in 1929 to the chairmanship of a new department of fine arts at Saint Thomas College in Saint Paul, with a student body of five hundred. This became a base of operations for the composition of his own radical music: the period between 1929 and 1933 becoming one of "intense creativity and restless experimentation for Becker, and a crusade for new music and the 'ultra-modern' in American arts." He was energetic and feisty and wrote prolifically in an "unsentimental" prose style that could be belligerent, even "scathing."[6]

Becker, too, had responded to Cowell's 1927 flier for the *New Music Quarterly*, and this had led to a rich correspondence between them and a productive relationship in the service of publishing and performing new works. Cowell saw in Becker the potential leader of a progressive midwestern center for the development of new music,[7] and Becker in turn provided what support he could muster for the fledgling journal.

Ives's relationship with Becker dates from 1931, when Cowell sent him a copy of a 1930 article—polemic might be more accurate—of Becker's entitled "Fine Arts and the Soul of America." There Becker aggressively advanced his fiercely individualistic views on "the loss of spiritualism and the rise of materialism among the masses." He invoked the "American Babbitt," who smugly speaks of "America's progress" while "America . . . from an esthetic viewpoint . . . is floundering blindly, nearly lost, served only by its starving artists."[8] The Ives of "Emasculating America" might well have wished he could have put it thus. In any event, he responded to Becker's broadside immediately, expressing his admiration and requesting a dozen copies. Recognizing in Becker a kindred spirit, he sent him at the same time a copy of the *114 Songs*, portions of the *Concord Sonata*, and photostats of several other pieces.

From these beginnings there ensued a relationship that lasted until Ives's death and involved both families in such personal matters as finances, family illness, and even insurance. The correspondence between the two families numbers well over three hundred items. Ives saw a spiritual brother in Becker, addressing him in a letter of the fall of 1933 as "Dear Fratre in ipsis viabus"— Ives's garbled Latin for "Dear Brother along the same road."[9] As Don Gillespie suggests, Becker's penurious life as an academic and professional composer was not the road taken by Ives himself. Gillespie further wonders whether "a tinge of guilt may be detected in Ives's attitude toward Becker."[10]

By 1934, Ives was drafting a letter of support for Becker's application for a Guggenheim fellowship, in a shaky hand and now familiar style (the actual letter that was sent would have been revised by Harmony): "Mr. Jackie Becker is a —— of a nice (some boy) baby & he has 3 nice kids—Bully for him. He [is] one of our crowd. Mr. B is a musician & composer of considerable ability. His work has a solid foundation of years of experience, thoughtful study, a wide knowledge of theory & practice in all of music."[11] In the course of time and as the families became closer, generosity of other kinds became much in evidence. In the Becker family, "Mr. Ives" was legendary, the source of the New York postmark on the packages that bore Christmas gifts to the three young boys. When one of the boys was sick in 1935, Ives sent a check. In 1937, when Becker was trying to reach a decision on his life insurance, Ives wrote him a long, detailed letter of advice: He counseled Becker to not give up his insurance and to let Ives know if he was unable to pay for it.[12] Later the following year, although Ives had been in one of his "down slants" (as he now called them) or "those usual, chronic low swings," he roused himself to bolster Becker after a particularly wounding criticism: "That g— d— sap! who said you were a defeatist—composer—is a half-wit or a liar—you are a great composer—to Hell with the lily-ears."[13]

Like Cowell, Becker became a true collaborator. In fact, writes Gillespie, "Becker and Ives can be approached solely in terms of their musical collaboration." The first of these was in 1934, when Becker prepared a performing version of two of Ives's three *Harvest Home* chorales,[14] which date to 1902. The pencil sketch by Becker contains a few notations by Ives.[15] Around the same time, Becker orchestrated and arranged the song *General William Booth Enters Heaven*. Ives's collaboration is preserved in a page of humorous "memos" regarding this.[16] In 1943, Becker also attempted a "realization" of the final movement of the *Fourth Symphony* from Ives's sketches.[17]

A set of unfortunate and bizarre circumstances led to a break in the relationship between Ives and Henry Cowell in 1936. The previous year had been rich in the fruits of Cowell's collaboration with Ives. In July 1935, following a somewhat pressured correspondence, Ives had managed to get to Cowell the material for the *Eighteen Songs* slated for publication in the October issue of *New Music Quarterly*, now in its ninth year. In fact, in the course of the give-and-take, no one bothered to count, and nineteen songs were printed.[18] Continuing medical problems had delayed Ives, who delivered the last songs with an apology for not doing more for the quarterly and hoping that "the next 5 mos. will be better ones." A check was enclosed. In fact, Ives covered the cost of the engraving of the issue and expressed concern that whatever funds existed be reserved "for the others' music."[19]

In May 1936, Cowell was arraigned on a morals charge in his native California. Despite his artistic sophistication and considerable organizational ability, he could be something of a naïf in personal matters. Although the full story remains to be told, it appears that his defense in court was inadequate. He was convicted and served time in San Quentin, from which he was released in June 1940.[20] Cowell was able to carry on a few of his musical activities during that period, remaining enthusiastic about Ives's music.[21] He was, however, forced to give up his *New Music* enterprises, turning over the entire operation to a colleague in October 1937. As sole "owner," he sold the quarterly for the nominal sum of one dollar.[22]

It hardly seems possible that Harmony would not have somehow heard of Cowell's misfortune before the summer of 1936. The New York *Herald Tribune* of May 23 reported the arrest and stated that the charges involved a seventeen-year-old boy.[23] While Ives no longer had any interest in the newspapers and did not subscribe to one, others in the family who would have known of Ives's connection with Cowell were avid readers. It was John Becker who told Harmony about Cowell's arrest, having learned of it that June in Chicago. Harmony, in turn, wrote to Charlotte Ruggles: "Have you heard this hideous thing about Henry Cowell—that he has been guilty of Oscar Wilde practices—a crime in California. Mr. Becker wrote me—fearing to write Charlie whom I shall not tell until I have confirmation. . . . If true I think it is the saddest thing in our experience—had had no inkling of this defect, had you? . . . Of course it is a disease—a quirk of nature, as Mr. Becker said."[24]

The following week Harmony received a letter from Cowell, who also enclosed one for Ives, to be given him if she saw fit. She wrote again to Charlotte (her only confidante in this matter), finding it "strange" that there was "no *suggestion* of contrition" and even "a spirit of bravado," although he freely admitted "the commission of the offence." "Anyway I told Charlie. . . . A thing more abhorrent to Charlie's nature couldn't be found. He will never willingly see Henry again— he *can't*. . . . He said characteristically, 'I thought he was a man & he's really a g— d— sap.'"[25]

Ives could not have put his attitude more precisely. It would indeed have been impossible to conceive of an act calculated to disturb him more than Cowell's, for it shook the foundations of love and work. The reciprocal love of a man and a boy and its vicissitudes in the mourning of one for the other had by now cast its shadow on a lifetime. Its ambivalent side had been a cause of conflict as its sexual side had been an ever-potential source of anxiety. Rarely if ever had its deepest sources broken through into Ives's consciousness, and never had such a homo-erotic fantasy been enacted. Indeed, his entire career had been spurred and sustained by the sublimation of fantasy and desire in creative life. Only in disguised, derivative, and desexualized form had such fantasies entered con-scious mental life, such as the fantasy of the collaborative "ear." Ives, through a combination of luck and art, even in his sixties found ever-renewing potential for a sublimated realization of these fantasies in those he encountered. There is a point in the *Essays* where the underlying homoerotic wish is revealed in a single moment of unguarded longing. It occurs in "Thoreau" and is associated with the "one 'low' day" of George Ives's death: "You may know something of the affec-tion that heart yearned for but knew it a duty not to grasp." Cowell had enacted the forbidden wish, and it was bound to be experienced by Ives as, in Harmony's word, "abhorrent."

As a result, the Iveses immediately broke off their relationship with Cowell. During his imprisonment, Cowell did what he could for Ives's music, apparently unembittered by their abandonment of him. As for the *New Music Quarterly*, now in other hands, Ives continued to support it. After Cowell was paroled in June 1940, he attempted to contact the Iveses again with regard to music and business matters. Harmony's response was impatient and scolding: "I think you do not realize Mr. Ives' condition. He has not been at all well for over a year and is in a very low state. He has to keep quiet. The doctor says this is very important to lessen the heart attacks. He feels he has been so out of touch with things that he would not be of much help in planning for New Music but he will be glad to continue the present monthly contribution. . . . He hopes you are well & that things will go well for you."[26]

In what business correspondence continued, Cowell was solicitous: "I hear from John Becker that Mr. Ives has been worse, and was extremely sorry to hear it. One feels so helpless; I wish so much that there was something that I could do to be helpful."[27] Their personal relationship, however, did not resume until Cowell announced his intention to marry in the fall of 1941. He presented his bride, Sidney Robertson, to the Iveses in terms calculated to gain their approval: "She is a musician, plays the piano well, and has collected folk-songs through the country. She is very successful in being on friendly terms with country people and wins them over completely. She is thirty-seven years old, of old American stock."[28] The response, in Harmony's style, was not only prompt but also signed by Ives in the shaky hand he now called "snaketracks": "It was great to hear your good news—Our kindest wishes to you both. May the marriage bring a happiness which will last thro' 'to the end of eternity and then on.'"[29] A check was enclosed ("we can't enclose a book-case or sofa") and a promise to see the Cowells when the Iveses returned from Redding. Henry was redeemed.

The relationship between the two couples picked up the next spring when Harmony called on Sidney, who was ill with phlebitis following a miscarriage, at the Cowells' Greenwich Village apartment.[30] This formal visit—Harmony wore white gloves—revived some semblance of the earlier relationship. In visiting, Harmony expressed an empathy with Sidney stemming from her own experiences in the first year of marriage. The friendship between the couples proved to be a productive one, resulting in the first biography of Ives not in his own hand. Yet things were never quite the same between Ives and Cowell. In the last letter Cowell wrote to Ives before the scandal broke, regarding his work on *Calcium Light Night*, he addressed him, as had been usual, "Dear Charlie." He never called him Charlie again.

The eclipse of Cowell was the more regrettable because of the continuing losses in Ives's life during the 1930s as he entered his sixties. His physical and mental health continued to decline. His failing eyesight, a progressive symptom of diabetes, worsened over the course of the decade. A fine tremor of the hand was making writing impossible. Eventually, the sensory-receptive apparatus of the brain also deteriorated (whether owing to the same process as the tremor or a different one is uncertain), causing a wavery distortion of sound that seemed to increase when he listened to music. And before the decade was out, frank signs of senility made their appearance.

Meanwhile, the remaining fragments of old Danbury were passing from existence. In 1939 Moss died, like George, of a sudden stroke. Later that year, Ives's aunt Lucy Cornelia Parmelee died, the last of her generation and the last inhabitant of the old house, which by now had been moved from Main Street to Chapel Place. Between the two events, Ives made his final visit to Danbury, although he continued to spend much of his time in Redding, only a few miles away. Bigelow

Ives described his uncle's pain in revisiting Danbury that last time while staying at the house where he was born:

> Uncle Charlie spent the night there and wandered through the old house and spoke very feelingly about the north parlor, and recalled how changed it all was. I went out walking with him late that evening, and we went up as far as the Civil War monument in the City Hall Square. . . . He actually moaned aloud when he got up there and saw how it had all changed from his recollection of it. . . . He leaned up against a sandbox which was on the corner by the curb, and he buried his head in his hand and moaned. "I'm going back," he said. "You can't recall the past."[31]

Ives had been devoted to Moss's children, and after his brother's death he and Harmony played a role in their lives like the one the Brewsters had played in his own life. Ives and Harmony were careful to pay special attention to whichever of the children was most in need at any given time. The boys, in turn, viewed Ives and Harmony as "almost an ideal couple."[32] Earlier, in 1920, when Ives was assembling the *114 Songs*, fifteen-year-old Moss, Jr., was living with them. The boy was mentally and emotionally handicapped, which only drew them to him even more. They hired a tutor for him who said later that they treated him like a son.[33] Moss was considered to have an ear for music, and Ives gave him music lessons.[34] Moss eventually had to be institutionalized, Ives having made provision for him.

Later, Chester Ives lived with the couple on East Seventy-Fourth Street when he was starting out in business, and Moss's other children visited frequently. Ives helped all of them financially with their educations. He took them to concerts at the time he still attended them and when he was still writing, played his music for them, asking their opinions. The genuine affection he felt is revealed in a note to Chester, who in 1940 tried to repay a business loan: "Send this interest to your mother during her lifetime; then to the one of the children who, by popular vote, is said to be nicest."[35]

The cycle of family life completed and renewed itself as Edith married in 1939. Two new people came into Ives's later life: a son-in-law, George Grayson Tyler, who became his attorney and executor, and a grandson, Charles Ives Tyler, born in 1946.

During the early 1930s, the five composers "most conspicuously concerned with innovation" were Ives, Ruggles, Cowell, Becker, and Wallingford Riegger. Gillespie has called them "the American Five."[36] It was Ives who seemed to have an inspirational effect on younger, aspiring composers, a number of whom managed to contact him at one point or another. One was Lou Harrison, who first wrote him in 1936, and Ives responded by sending copies of his music. In 1944, he engaged Harrison to proofread and correct the parts for the *Second String Quartet*, which was being prepared for performance. Harrison, in a postscript to the letter accompanying his bill, notes, "I took the liberty of reconstructing several measures in the 4tet where there was an obvious omission & the sketches were likewise vague." He admired Ives enormously, writing to him, "I am, of course, nearly a generation removed from you & in any sensible society I should be able to hear your major works preferably under the most sympathetic conditions."[37]

In hoping that orchestras might someday be led by composers instead of "Chicago gangsters" and deploring the "rampant prostitution of a great creative art to purely commercial ends," Harrison sounded like Ives himself.[38] "Mr. Ives was," Harmony wrote, "quite affected by your letter. . . . You know how to write music, Mr. Ives says, but you don't know how to write bills."[39] Harrison had billed six dollars for work that Ives considered to be worth "several times more"; a check was sent for twenty-four dollars.

Two years later, Harrison worked with him on what Ives termed an "old almost illegible score of [the] 3rd Symphony." Complicating the task was Ives's eyesight, by then extremely impaired. He could, however, recall the parts with clarity—a good copy had been made some thirty years earlier—and could communicate details to his amanuensis. Ives told him that he need not return the parts for review: "What you do will be all right & he can't see them anyway," wrote Harmony.[40]

Harrison conducted the premiere of the *Third Symphony* with the New York Little Chamber Orchestra on April 5, 1946. He was the perfect collaborator, and his comments following the performance demonstrated his responsiveness to Ives's hearing impairment as well: he described acoustic details that Ives would not have been able to discriminate even had he attended the performance.[41] That Ives's *imaginative* ear still functioned was revealed when the following month he suggested changes in the orchestration based on Harrison's report. "Distant church bells" had been called for at the end of the last movement, and Ives proposed instead "a piano off stage perhaps—but better small chimes, celesta or glockenspiel."[42] Although he was unable to read the completed score, he liked Harrison and trusted him. Harmony wrote, "He knows you have done it all wonderfully well."[43] On the yellow sheets that Ives used to write what he could of the drafts that she turned into letters, those to Harrison were marked, "Lou Harry sun" or "to Son harrylou" or "Lou Harry Son."

Ives offered to pay for the publication of one of Harrison's works, an offer that Harrison declined. Later, after Ives's *Third Symphony* was awarded the Pulitzer Prize in 1947, Ives had the opportunity not only to reward Harrison but also to show him a generosity that he had been incapable of showing Henry Cowell. Ives learned from John Cage that Harrison had been hospitalized at Stony Lodge Sanatorium for what Cage called "a curable case of schizophrenia." Cage was writing Harrison's friends to raise money to pay the bills.[44] Ives was compassionate in an immediate response to Cage, enclosing "not a present but a recognition of help": he had already written the check when he received Cage's letter. Ives's response, in Harmony's hand, included a note to Harrison as well: "Mr. Ives says, 'As you are very much to blame for getting me into that Pulitzer Prize Street and for bringing a bushel of letters to answer and for bringing a check of $500 thrown at me by the trustees of Columbia you have got to help me by taking 1/2 of this.'"[45] That summer, he sent another portion of his prize money to John Becker.[46]

It was this kind of generosity, along with his sense of humor, that the extended Ives family would remember him for. There was no question of Ives's loyalty and support for "family," which included all relatives and close friends. Increasingly, they were polarized from enemies of his music, actual and fabricated. Between these lay an increasing number of friends of the music as Ives entered his seventh decade.

As for Ives's humor, it disintegrated with encroaching senility, losing its sharpness while preserving its vitriol. Ives's human instrument was tensely poised—mind and body alike—and agitation constantly threatened. The Cowells wrote of an "excitable flow of paradox and incomprehensible punning."[47] His was not a gentle decline, nor was it easy for those who cared for him to bear. Harmony had set the example by her protectiveness, and others followed suit, eventually including biographers and other scholars.

The final collaboration was with the Cowells, and it resulted in the biography that is the main source of the received view of Ives—an idealized portrait of the businessman composer from Danbury with his bandmaster father. Although ground-breaking and informative, the Cowells' biography maintained a tone that was respectfully silent on some matters as if in order not to disturb someone who is ill. Henry Cowell proposed the project in February 1947, hardly daring to hope that Ives would be well enough to consider it.[48] Harmony hesitated at first: "You know, I have never really liked seeing our name in print."[49] Although the Cowells consulted many in gathering data and were given access to family material, as they say, "Ives speaks for himself." They referred, of course, to quotations from published works by Ives—the *Essays* and other printed material in prefaces and postfaces to the music—as well as to the autobiographical manuscript that would become the *Memos*. Thus it was that an earlier Ives came to participate in the creation of his first published "life."

By 1947, already well into his seventies, Ives in many ways lived in the past and in a future defined by the fate of his accomplished work, on the one hand, and the infinity of the uncompletable *Universe Symphony*, on the other. The years of the Second World War had revived in him the ever-latent spirit of earlier wars, especially the Civil War. On a commission from the League of Composers, Ives attempted a revision of his World War I song *He Is There*. Calling it *They Are*

There, he also referred to it as his "War Song." It was orchestrated and completed by Lou Harrison "with a certain amount of internal recomposition."[50] On a sketch for the title page, Ives wrote: "music by Chas. E. Ives [crossed out] an American with reflections from the Old War Songs of Kittredge, Root and Work."[51] These were the composers, respectively, of *Tenting on the Old Camp Grounds*, *The Battle Cry of Freedom*, and *Marching Through Georgia*. Nevertheless, there was a sense of urgency in Ives's feeling about the music, as if a song might still galvanize a nation as it could nearly a century earlier. Ives wanted it "banged and shouted out down the corner and up Main Street."[52] In support of the song, he had Harmony write Cowell that "he has heard from many who feel that it would help in these days if it could be sung often—we have been told that soldiers who have seen or heard it felt the same way. One said that it made him feel like fighting harder as did his friends. So Mr. Ives says it is more than just a matter of music good or bad."[53]

Never did Ives quite give up the idea of the *Universe Symphony*. At one point, his conversations with Henry Cowell during the Cowells' visits to the East Seventy-fourth Street house were mainly about the symphony, on which Ives hoped Cowell would collaborate. Sidney Cowell described "energetic discussions about the advisability of adding this note or that, and about the consequences each note might have as the music developed."[54] There seemed to be an understanding between them that "the concept of the *Universe Symphony* . . . would express aspects of the Ideal so various and so lofty that no single man could ever complete it." Nor, of course, could these two men.

When all else left him, the aspiration for the *Universe* seemed to remain. On February 22, 1951, Leonard Bernstein conducted the New York Philharmonic in the premiere of Ives's *Second Symphony*, a milestone for the career of the music. The seventy-six-year-old Ives did not attend. When the performance was rebroadcast on the radio, he listened to it at the home of his Redding neighbors, the Ryders. His reaction was inscrutable. Mrs. Ryder said: "He stood up, walked over to the fireplace and spat! And then he walked out into the kitchen. Not a word. And he never said anything about it." But even in his final years, he still spoke occasionally of the *Universe*. The Ives's typist, who worked for them at Redding until three years before Ives's death in 1954, spoke of his "real and continuing interest" in it. "Once after he stood looking out the picture window toward the mountains, he restlessly paced about, not conversing but as if he were thinking aloud with gestures, and humming and singing bits of music. He said, 'If only I could have done it. It's all there—the mountains and the fields.' When I asked him what he wanted to do, he answered, 'the Universe Symphony. If only I could have done it.'"[55]

But above all, the tunes were what persisted in mind. They had been a part of the first experiences of his life and, nearly eighty years later, were the last to remain. Throughout his life, Ives had been known by many in the family to improvise endlessly at the piano, carrying on a running commentary as if music and word blended in reminiscence and free association. The tunes would remind him of people and places and of the events and experiences of the past; and as he recalled them, the memories stimulated recall of still more tunes, which then emerged in the musical improvisation. The words and the music were always about the past.[56] Now, in his final days, tunes continued to come to mind, and at the end perhaps they were all that was left. Sometimes he would emit a "loud hoarse chant derived more or less from 'Columbia the gem of the ocean,' a tune that seemed to float into his mind whenever it was otherwise unoccupied."[57] It was thus that after Ives had long outlived the composer in him, and after the grandiosity had burned itself out, and even after mind itself had atrophied, the tunes lingered, "tunes of long ago," his father's songs.

Charles Edward Ives died on May 19, 1954, at the age of seventy-nine. He was buried in Wooster Cemetery in Danbury, close by the grave of George Edward Ives, overlooking the pond. Harmony Twichell Ives joined him there in the spring of 1969. She had chosen the epitaph, from Psalm 108:

"Awake psaltery and harp: I myself will awake right early."

The Ives gravesite, Wooster Cemetery, Danbury.

APPENDIX A

ON THE VERACITY OF IVES'S DATING OF HIS MUSIC

In a 1987 article entitled "Charles Ives: Some Questions of Veracity," Maynard Solomon undertakes to investigate Ives's datings of his music.[1] In this appendix I consider the merits of Solomon's findings and assertions.

Solomon notes that the nine separate lists of Ives's works "painstakingly setting forth his claims as to when they were composed" were prepared between 1929 and 1950, long after the works were said to have been written. He observes further that Ives's "autographs are liberally sprinkled with Ives's notations about putative dates of composition, including hundreds of datable addresses and phone numbers, other external references to datable biographical or historical events, and many specific dates for the commencement, sketching, copying, completion, and performance of the works." But, Solomon asserts, "Ives added many of his notations retrospectively and often these entries are self-serving, in conflict with other datings, or patently false." The examples he offers include sections of the *Three Places in New England*, which, he suggests, "may well have originated as a polemical attempt to deny the influence of other composers" and "a brief to establish Ives's priority as a modernist." Specifically, Solomon judges *Putnam's Camp*, dated 1908 on a patch of manuscript, to be "clearly in Ives's later hand." He goes on to observe that Ives "subsequently gave up this attempt to pre-date *Putnam's Camp* to 1908, placing the words "Whitman's house, Hartsdale N.Y., Oct. 1912," on the score sketch in dark pencil, thus oblit-

351

erating another date." Solomon concludes, "There is no independent evidence that this work was composed prior to the premiere of *Le Sacre du Printemps* on 29 May 1913, or indeed, completed much before its own first public performance on 10 January 1931."

Solomon's evidence fall into two categories. First, there is a group of retrospective datings which he finds to be mutually contradictory; and second, there is a group of works on which the date of a revision is suppressed and an earlier date substituted. He also comments on problematic datings of earlier works such as those done at Yale. The lists themselves contain contradictions. Further, he observes a "striking oddity": "identifying publisher's marks" in some instances have been cut out of the music paper. These data lead Solomon to the "working hypothesis" that "the evidence thus far suggests a systematic pattern of falsification."

Solomon finds yet another pattern—a psychological one. At the beginning of his essay, he notes that "Ives was by nature a reviser" and that this "had fairly predictable psychological consequences but quite unexpected musicological implications." Commenting on Ives's "innate competitiveness" with his father, he adumbrates the oedipal pattern: "Unable to surpass his father in his most fundamental roles and perhaps hoping to avoid reprisals for imagined transgressions, we may surmise that Ives was impelled to make his father his permanent collaborator, idealizing their relationship, purifying his own motives, and professing a filial piety of immaculate quality." He perceives Ives's "retrospective monumentalization of his father" as taking the form of crediting him with "having anticipated if not invented more than a handful of the procedures and techniques of twentieth century musical modernism." No confirmation exists of George Ives's musical experiments, Solomon asserts; his son made it a point to note that George did little composing and did not write textbooks. The capstone of Solomon's argument is George's single extant letter (see chapter 22), which even Kirkpatrick observes sounds like Ives. Solomon concludes, "In the absence of the original, there is no compelling reason to accept it ever existed." This, in sum, constitute those "fairly predictable psychological consequences but quite unexpected musicological implications" that proceed from a consideration of the rivalrous and revisionist Charles Ives in the context of his relationship with his father.

Indeed, Ives may well have been psychologically poised for retrospective falsification in the dating of his manuscripts. He certainly harbored the wish for priority, as revealed in his grandiosity. Further, we have observed the failure of emotional control that could well have facilitated enactment of this wish. In fact, a far richer and more complex motivational case can be made for Ives's having altered the scores than the one Solomon advances. This does not, however, mean that Ives actually did so. But moreover, other emergent psychological elements, whose underlying sources were organic, make it unlikely that Ives was capable of the "systematic pattern of falsification" Solomon alleges.

In addition, the criterion of dating scores to which Solomon holds the composer, although certainly not unknown to Ives, was inimical to his style of composition and foreign to his pseudo-philosophical and idiosyncratic concept of what music was—in effect, his fantasies about music. The practice of orderly dating one's manuscripts at the time of composition—Schubert is Solomon's example, "who so conveniently noted on his manuscripts the dates of the commencement and/or completion of works"—was alien to Ives.

Solomon's psychological formulation is not so much wrong as incomplete. It misses the complexity of motivation, hence the richness of the mental life that underlies all human efforts, including both creating and lying. Although Solomon's observations seem to assume the existence of unconscious motivation, he appears to ignore its role in actual behavior. Clearly, he is writing of mendacious behavior, but it is not at all clear that Ives was a conscious liar and fraud. In any event, the well-traveled psychological interpretations Solomon offers would not fully account for these behaviors.

In a brief but similarly incomplete review of conventional and psychoanalytic Ives studies,[2] Solomon deplores the "utterly idealized relationship between father and son" portrayed by some biographers. He finds this "at best a partial view." But he has substituted an equally partial view in his oedipalization of the Ives legend. In this respect (as in Ives's putative dating), one thing has been erased and another substituted. In Solomon's formulation, anger is written over love crossed out, and rivalry and competition revise attachment and identification. Motivation itself is viewed here through the narrow lens of defense while, at the same time, processes that are normally unconscious (including the defenses of the ego) are treated as if consciously determined.

If Solomon finds the above conflict-free aspect of Ives's relationship with his father (and *pari passu* the conflict-free sphere of mental life) "consoling . . . for both subject and biographer," I suggest that his own purely oedipal view may be equally consoling. For what Solomon has lost sight of is a vast panoply of pre-oedipal elements, the revival of which in mental life bring us to the crossroads of creativity and psychosis. Additionally, the dyadic, pre-ambivalent relationship of father and son lends a richness to the relationship which relates to the strong affects associated with it as well as the enduring bond.[3] There can be no question that with Ives, as with all human beings, the oedipal constellation is a solid stone in the arch of mental life—perhaps its keystone. But Oedipus in a straitjacket can provide too neat and comforting a view of mental life, tending to obscure other elements. For example, oedipal guilt may disguise shame, and depression may appear to be exclusively a displacement of aggression where early loss is important. Above all, a narrow rendition of the oedipal struggle stressing affects and strivings in the aggressive range, while characteristic of the phase, may obscure psychological events occurring before and after its ascendancy which are of the utmost human significance.

The pre-oedipal, indeed pre-conflictual, relationship with a father provides the foundation for the love of father. This affective flow, once initiated, not only spills over into other relationships but energizes other human endeavors, including, in the life of Ives, business, music, and politics. Similarly, an exclusive focus on the aggressive and rivalrous component may overshadow the successes and contributions of the post-oedipal period. Ives's adolescence was, as we have seen, a critical time in his life whose outcome was not completely unsuccessful. The positive force of identification with the father and the compromises forged with the evocation of family romance fantasies ultimately gave it a unique direction. This direction included, incidentally, a very satisfying and constructive marriage. Although one can hardly point to an ideally "healthy" resolution of the oedipal phase, many of the solutions Ives found for himself were creatively idiosyncratic and ultimately successful.

A psychoanalytic view of the progress of life must pay attention to the later fate of each of the earliest phases. But the manifestations of, say, the oedipal phase, while consistent, are not identical in adolescence, mid-life, and later life. There are many new influences, not least among them the organic, and each phase modifies the next. Progression is not only developmentally genetic in the psychoanalytic causative sense but epigenetic in the Eriksonian sense. Life evolves, and within the framework of the "fairly expectable," the fairly *unex*-pectable often occurs. We may not have been able to predict such events, but the human context that made them surprising may help us understand them. If so, however, it would not be through a rigid application of theory. If Ives, for example, did lie (in the conscious, literal sense) in the *Memos* and deceive in the manuscripts, it should be borne in mind that these were acts of a man approaching sixty, many of whose worlds were falling away. Acts in extremis, stemming from reality or fantasy, are not the same as those performed under ordinary circumstances.[4] It is not a matter of excusing them from a moral point of view but of understanding them as thoroughly as possible from a human one.

Two things seem clear, one from a musical and another from a psychological point of view. With regard to the music, it has long been known that Ives repeatedly altered his scores. Indeed, this has been a perennial problem for those engaged in editing scores for performance. No one knew better than Kirkpatrick that "all datings in Ives are problematical." Elliott Carter had observed the revisions firsthand. Visiting the East Seventy-fourth Street residence in 1929 while

Ives was preparing the *Three Places in New England* for performance, he watched as Ives "hacked up the level of dissonance": "A new score was being derived from the older one to which he was adding and changing, turning octaves into sevenths and ninths, and adding dissonant notes."[5] As a result, Carter wondered whether "he was as early a precursor of 'modern' music as is sometimes made out," suggesting that "a study of the manuscripts would probably make this clear." Carter considered himself to be "temperamentally unsuited for the task."[6] Whether Solomon has accomplished it remains in question. Hence, the datings I have adopted adhere to those of Kirkpatrick, who spent many years unscrambling Ives's manuscripts. When the issue of lying arose earlier, Kirkpatrick responded: "It's not that you can't believe a word he says because he was a liar. He was not a liar, but he had a very sly sense of humor and a very acute New England sense of privacy, and often he'd just throw smoke in your face."[7]

Solomon's evidence is in itself circumstantial. His vigorous assertions are curiously at odds with the statement that his findings are "obviously . . . data for a working hypothesis that remains to be fully substantiated."[8] Nevertheless, the fuller musicological inquiry Solomon anticipates is likely to be eagerly pursued by scholars on both sides of the issue. Carol Baron has already advanced data refuting Solomon's hypothesis. Her painstaking analysis of Ives's handwriting supports his final dating of *Putnam's Camp* and its earlier sources. Further, her work throws light on Ives's method of composition. She states that the "combination of ink and pencil seems to have led to the erroneous conclusion that the short score emanated from two different periods: the writing in ink from 1911–1912; the writing in pencil from 1929. Their identical provenance suggests new ideas about how Ives composed this manuscript and important new evidence for dating *Putnam's Camp* and the musical innovations found in this work."[9] Refuting Solomon's "working hypothesis," Baron's evidence shows that no revisions were made. Rather, "the music written in pencil consists of additions, filling out a thin sketch."[10] Baron's data also support Ives's dating of *The Celestial Country*, the *Three-Page Sonata, Country Band March*, and *March: "1776."*

To go on to the psychological issue, Solomon points to "a systematic pattern of falsification" and its implications. It is clear from the amplified psychological point of view I have developed here that events of falsification would not be incompatible with Ives's mental state late in his life. However, whether he would have been capable of a thoroughly systematic effort is highly doubtful. Indeed, the very "pattern" described is a confused one. Ives might have been poised for it mentally, but if so, it would not be only because of the fate of the oedipal struggle. He had by now lost more than his father. He had lost his health, his creative faculty, and the capacity to practice those occupations that had brought him a sense of esteem and even power. Already his sense of reality showed signs of softening under the strain. Grandiosity supplanted real achievement and grew apace with the sense of powerlessness. It became organized in content in terms of the family romance fantasy as increasingly unrealistic and cosmic renditions were elaborated. Moreover, the pressure of fantasy both strained reality and impelled its alteration. With the failure of creativity and the threat of the extinction of life itself, not only did the past have to be manipulated but the future assured. Fantasy had invaded the territory of prophecy in the last bastions of the family romance.[11] It is in this sense that the pressure of fantasy served to push aside the details of reality. The stage had long been set mentally, and its background was not necessarily or completely pathological.

Ives's concept of the reality of music lay somewhere between the animate and the inanimate world, stemming from that period in his own early development when music served as transitional object. Music never completely lost this quality for him, much to the benefit of the imaginative content of his work. The notion was perhaps best put in the postface to the *114 Songs*, which presents in effect a Bill of Rights for music, which ends, "In short, must a song / always be a song!"

Despite the pseudo-scholarship of the *Essays* and the various lists, Ives never had a genuinely scholarly concept of music. The notion of scholarly or even orderly documentation was foreign to him during his creative period. Kirkpatrick perceived something of this when he observed Ives handling his music as if, having made it, it belonged to him and he could do what he liked with it. More primitively, it was also like a living entity. When, for example, he "transferred" a movement of the *First String Quartet* to the *Fourth Symphony*, it did not exist for him in the quartet any more; the other movements just moved up in place (see chapter 18). Ives had a similar view toward other people's music, and it found its way amply into his own through quotation or "take-offs," a method of incorporating another's music that did not necessarily imply stealing. It was precisely this talent for take-off that Ives would have employed had he in fact incorporated some of Stravinsky's innovations into the *Three Places*. Carter admired Ives's capacity for improvisation, which sometimes took the form of derisive commentary on the music of others. He recalled vividly "his 'take-off' at the piano of the Ravel chord and the repetitiousness of Stravinsky. Ives was very literate and sharp about this—he seemed to remember quite clearly bits of what he had heard and could parody them surprisingly well."[12]

In addition to the structure and function of mind, one must always take the past into account in speculating about motivation. There is nothing in Ives's past to suggest anything like the order of falsification Solomon posits. With regard to conscious behavior, Ives appears to have been scrupulous in his personal dealings with others. He entered the business world after a wave of corruption in the industry and was never identified with anything but its best elements. Further, by the 1930s, Harmony Ives was full collaborator as well as caretaker. Little was done without her surveillance, and little could be accomplished without it. Is one then to consider Harmony Ives a co-conspirator? It might be argued that her devotion would dictate tolerance of whatever might calm her agitated husband. But at no point does she show herself to be the kind of person who tolerated lies and fraud; quite the contrary.

Finally, a distinction must be made between a "systematic pattern" and isolated attempts at falsification. Even the "pattern" adumbrated by Solomon is a crazy quilt of efforts somewhat consistent with Ives's performance at work. It is doubtful that Ives had been doing much effective work at Ives and Myrick for some time before his announcement of retirement in 1929. It seems equally doubtful that he was capable of the organized mental effort necessary for a systematic revision of his life's work. Nevertheless, it would not have been inconsistent for the grandiose and sometimes agitated Ives of this period to have wished or even been impelled to make the attempt. A disorder of mind would then have given rise to the impulse, but the same disorder of mind would have rendered its accomplishment highly unlikely.

Charles Ives's idol, Emerson, once wrote, "The world is upheld by the veracity of good men: they make the earth wholesome."[13] Solomon's musicological assertions remain to be evaluated, their ethical as well as their scholarly implications fully appreciated. His psychological formulations, however, oversimplify the workings of a complex creative mind. The issue of Ives's datings is no simple matter from either point of view. And, as is frequently the case in matters both psychoanalytic and musicological, a degree of ambiguity may have to be tolerated. What is not in question from any quarter is the authenticity of Charles Ives's voice as an original and unique composer.[14]

APPENDIX B

A DISCOGRAPHY OF THE *114 Songs*

There are three discographies of the music of Charles Ives. For recordings issued before 1972, see Richard Warren, *Charles E. Ives: Discography*, Historical Sound Recordings Collection, Yale University (Westport, Conn.: Greenwood Press, 1972). For recordings issued from 1972 through 1979, see "Charles Ives," in *American Music Recordings: A Discography of Twentieth-Century U.S. Composers*, ed. Carol J. Oja (Institute for Studies in American Music, Brooklyn College of the City University of New York, 1982), pp.171-80. For commercially produced recordings through 1987, see Geoffrey Block, *Charles Ives: A Bio-Bibliography* (Westport, Conn.: Greenwood Press, 1988), pp. 57–69. The selection of recordings of the *114 Songs* listed here was made by Dr. Block and is reprinted with his permission.

S1 Corinne Curry, soprano; Louise Vosgerian, piano. Cambridge CRM-1804.

S2 Jan DeGaetani, mezzo-soprano; American Brass Quintet. Nonesuch H-71222.

S3 Radiana Pazmor, soprano; Genievieve Pitot, piano; Mordecai Bauman, baritone; Albert Hirsch, piano. Composers Recordings S-390E.

S4 Choral Guild of Atlanta. Press P-5002.

S5 Roberta Alexander, soprano; Tan Crone, piano. Etcetera ETC 1020.

S6 Jan DeGaetani, mezzo-soprano; Gilbert Kalish, piano. Nonesuch 71325.

S7 Jan DeGaetani, mezzo-soprano; Gilbert Kalish, piano. Bridge BDG 2002.

S8 William Parker, baritone; Dalton Baldwin, piano. New World 300.

S9   Ted Puffer, tenor; James Tenney, piano; Phillip Corner, piano. Folkways FM 3344, 3345.

S10   Carolyn Watkinson, mezzo-soprano; Tan Crone, piano. Etcetera ETC 1007.

114 Songs

1. *Majority.* S6, S9.
2. *Evening.* S3, S5, S9.
5. *Immortality.* S5, S9.
10. *Charlie Rutlage.* S3, S5, S9.
13. *Resolution.* S3.
14. *The Indians.* S2, S9.
15. *The Housatonic at Stockbridge.* S2, S5.
16. *Religion.* S1.
17. *Grantchester.* S9, S10.
19. *The Greatest Man.* S3, S5.
22. *"Nov. 2, 1920."* S1, S9.
23. *Maple Leaves.* S5, S9.
25. *Ann Street.* S1, S3, S2, S9.
26. *Like a Sick Eagle.* S2, S5, S9.
27. *From "The Swimmers."* S9.
28. *On The Counter.* S5.
29. *The See'r.* S5, S6.
30. *From "Paracelsus."* S2, S9.
31. *Walt Whitman.* S9.
32. *The Side Show.* S5, S6, S9, S10.
39. *Afterglow.* S6, S9.
40. *The Innate.* S2.
41. *"1, 2, 3."* S1, S5, S9.
42. *Serenity.* S2, S5, S9.
43. *The Things Our Fathers Loved.* S2.
44. *Watchman.* S8.
45. *At The River.* S2, S8.
46. *His Exaltation.* S8.
47. *The Camp-Meeting.* S8.
48. *Thoreau.* S2.
51. *Tom Sails Away.* S5, S6, S9.
55. *Down East.* S5, S6.
57. *Mists.* S9.
60. *Autumn.* S5.
64. *The Cage.* S2, S5, S9, S10.
65. *Spring Song.* S5.
67. *Walking.* S9, S10.
72. *Tarrant Moss (Slugging a Vampire).* S5.
74. *The Children's Hour.* S9.
76. *Qui'il m'irait bien.* S8.
77. *Elegie.* S8.
78. *Chanson de Florian.* S8.
79. *Rosamunde.* S8.
83. *Ich grolle nicht.* S1.
85. *Dreams.* S5.
93. *Berceuse.* S5.
96. *Romanzo di Central Park.* S5.
100. *A Christmas Carol.* S2, S9.
102. *Memories.* S2, S5.
103. *The White Gulls.* S6, S9.
104. *Two Little Flowers.* S3, S5, S6, S9.
105. *West London.* S6, S9.
108. *Songs My Mother Taught Me.* S5, S6.
111. *Canon.* S9.
114. *Slow March.* S5.

Other Songs

A Farewell to Land. S1, S2, S9.
General William Booth Enters into Heaven. S1, S3, S9.
In the Mornin'. S2.
On the Antipodes. S9.
Requiem. S9.
Song For Harvest Season. S2.
Sunrise. S8.

NOTES

The primary sources cited are from the Charles Ives Papers in the John Herrick Jackson Music Library, Yale University, collected and organized originally by John Kirkpatrick, who served as curator. Vivian Perlis compiled the descriptive catalog. The papers consist of music manuscripts, literary writings, correspondence, scrapbooks, diaries, photographs, programs, and other miscellaneous materials (Yale University Music Library Archival Collection, MSS 14, New Haven, Connecticut, January 1983). The music portion is catalogued in John Kirkpatrick's "Temporary Mimeographed Catalogue," referenced below (KCAT). All dates of musical manuscripts are given according to Kirkpatrick. (See Appendix A for discussion.)

For purposes of readability and availability, quotations from Ives's autobiographical writings are cited in this work from the edited version published by Kirkpatrick as *Memos* (IMEM). Since this publication contains considerable additional scholarly material in the editor's appendixes and notes, such citations are referenced separately to distinguish them from the transcriptions of Ives's own writings (KMEM). Similarly, the *Essays before a Sonata* and other writings, such as *The Majority*, are cited in their published versions edited by Howard Boatwright (ESS). Material from Vivian Perlis's Ives Project at Yale, an oral history consisting of fifty-eight transcribed interviews, is likewise cited from its published version (VP). Unless otherwise noted, letters are from the correspondence section of the Ives Papers (ARCH). Some letters were only available in an abbreviated typescript by John Kirkpatrick which is now part of the Ives collection at Yale. All letters are identified by initials of writer and recipient. References to the *114 Songs* are by number (*114*). Historical material related to the growth of Danbury and local events were derived from surveys of contemporaneous local newspapers, the Danbury *Times* (DT) and the Danbury *Evening News* (DEN).

The following are abbreviations used for frequently cited primary and secondary sources:

ARCH   Charles Ives Papers, compiled by Vivian Perlis, Yale University Music Library Archival Collection, MSS 14, Catalog (New Haven, 1983).

BUR   J. Peter Burkholder, *Charles Ives: The Ideas Behind the Music* (New Haven: Yale University Press, 1985).

COW   Henry Cowell and Sidney Cowell, *Charles Ives and His Music* (London: Oxford University Press, 1955).

DEN   Danbury *Evening News*.

DT   Danbury *Times*.

ESS   Charles Ives, *Essays before a Sonata and Other Writings*, ed. Howard Boatwright (New York: Norton, 1961).

IMEM   Charles Ives, *Memos*, ed. John Kirkpatrick (New York: Norton, 1972).

KCAT   *A Temporary Mimeographed Catalogue of the Music Manuscripts and Related Materials of Charles Edward Ives, 1874–1954*, compiled by John Kirkpatrick (New Haven, 1960).

KMEM   See IMEM.

ROS   Frank R. Rossiter, *Charles Ives and His America*. New York: Liveright, 1975.

VP   Vivian Perlis, *Charles Ives Remembered: An Oral History* (New Haven: Yale University Press, 1974).

114   Charles Ives, *114 Songs* (Bryn Mawr, Pa.: Merion, 1935).

PROLOGUE

1. KCAT, p. 88ff.
2. ESS.
3. *114*.
4. IMEM.
5. F. N. Crouch, "Kathleen Mavourneen," in *Ideal Home Music Library*, vol. 9 (New York: Scribner's, 1913), p. 190.
6. KCAT, p. 44.
7. VP.

1: THE IVESES OF DANBURY

1. DT, May 4, 1854.
2. James M. Bailey, *History of Danbury, 1684–1896*. (Danbury: Danbury Relief Society, 1896), p.77.
3. VP, p.3.
4. Ives Oral History Project, Vivian Perlis, director, interview of Amelia Van Wyck.
5. Ibid.
6. Bailey, *History of Danbury*, p. 281.
7. Perlis, interview of Amelia Van Wyck.
8. Bailey, *History of Danbury*, p. 183.
9. VP, p. 4.
10. Ibid.
11. Ibid.
12. Last Will and Testament, Isaac Ives, d. 1845.
13. Bailey, *History of Danbury*, pp. 226–27.
14. Ibid., p. 5.

2: A VILLAGE BOYHOOD

1. VP, p. 7.
2. DT, May 22, 1856.
3. Ibid. Despite his unfortunate experience at Yale, Joseph continued to consider himself to be a member of his class and often attended reunions in New Haven.
4. Perlis, interview of Amelia Van Wyck.
5. Bernard Wishy, *The Child and the Republic* (Philadelphia: University of Pennsylvania Press, 1968), p. 23.
6. James M. Bailey, *Life in Danbury*, (Boston: Shepart and Gill, 1873).
7. Perlis, interview of Amelia Van Wyck.
8. H. Wiley Hitchcock writes of the "dualistic musical culture in nineteenth-century America" reflected by "two bodies of American music, two attitudes toward music: cultivated and vernacular traditions." The cultivated (or genteel) tradition, based on European models was "significantly concerned with moral, artistic, or cultural idealism." Hitchcock, *Music in the United States* (Englewood Cliffs, N.J.: Prentice-Hall, 1974), p. 52.
9. James W. Nichols, Log Book, Scott-Fanton Museum, Danbury, Conn.
10. KCAT, p. 213.

3: AMONG THE CONNECTICUT "HEAVIES"

1. DT, April 1, 1860.
2. Ibid., April 12, 1860.
3. Ibid., December 20, 1860.
4. Ibid.
5. Ibid., July 11, 1861.
6. Kenneth E. Olson, *Music and Musket-Bands and Bandsmen of the Civil War* (Westport, Conn.: Greenwood, 1981), p. 62.
7. Ibid., p. 3.
8. Ibid., p. 255.
9. Ibid., p. 73.
10. Ibid., p. 70.
11. E. B. Bennett, comp., *First Connecticut Heavy Artillery: Historical Sketch* (East Berlin, Conn., n.d.).
12. W. A. Croffut and J. M. Morris, *The Military and Civil History of Connecticut during the War of 1861–65* (New York: Ledyard Bill, 1868), p. 206.
13. Ibid., p. 208.
14. DT, October 2, 1862.
15. Ibid., July 4, 1863.
16. Bruce Catton, *A Stillness At Appomattox* (Garden City, N.Y.: Doubleday, 1957), p. 1.
17. Olson, "The Field Musicians," chap. 5 of *Music and Musket-Bands*, pp. 82–126.
18. Mary Chesnut, in Olson, *Music and Musket-Bands*, p. 241.
19. Olson, *Music and Musket-Bands*, p. 180.
20. Ibid., p. 179.
21. Ibid., p. 183.
22. Croffut and Morris, *Military and Civil History*, and Bennet, *First Artillery*.
23. Croffut and Morris, *Military and Civil History*, p. 617.
24. George E. Ives, First Connecticut Heavy Artillery, File No. 2442, Service Records.
25. John D. Billings, *Hard Tack and Coffee on the Unwritten Story of Army Life* (Boston: Geo. M. Smith, 1888), p. 143.
26. Ibid., p. 149.
27. Ibid., p. 150.
28. Orders No. 13, Headquarters Siege Artillery near Broadway Landing, July 3, 1864. Transcript of Garrison Court Martial of George E. Ives, National Archives, Washington, D.C.

29. Affidavits, February 17, March 20, and April 15, 1865, Danbury, Conn., National Archives, Washington, D.C.

30. KMEM, p. 250.

31. George E. Ives, in KCAT, p. 213.

4: DANBURY DAYS, FAMILY CIRCLES

1. H. Wiley Hitchcock, *Music in the United States: A Historical Introduction* (Englewood Cliffs, N.J.: Prentice-Hall, 1974), pp. 130ff.

2. John Tasker Howard, *Stephen Foster: America's Troubadour* (New York: Crowell, 1953), p. 342.

3. Lloyd Morris, *Incredible New York* (New York: Random House, 1951), p. 44.

4. DT, advertisement, July 7, 1866.

5. Ibid., July 19, 1866.

6. Ibid., June 27, 1867.

7. Ibid., June 20, 1867.

8. Ibid., July 4, 1867.

9. Ibid.

10. Ibid., May 20, 1869.

11. DT, March 3, 1869.

12. Ibid., May 5, 1867.

13. Ibid., July 1, 1869.

14. Ibid., July 8, 1869.

15. Ibid., March 3, 1870.

16. Ibid., September 29, 1870.

17. Ibid.

18. Baldwin Family Papers, Sterling Memorial Library, Yale University, New Haven, Conn.

19. DEN, September 6, 1871.

20. Ibid., June 17, 1872.

21. Ibid., 1873, n.d.

22. The family bible, which was printed in 1829 and later owned by Charlie's maternal aunt Lucy, lists births as far back as 1802.

5: "VOX HUMANA: A COMPOSER'S CHILDHOOD

1. DEN, October 27, 1874.

2. IMEM, p. 131.

3. DEN, September 9, 1874.

4. Amelia Van Wyck, in VP, p. 6.

5. VP, p. 247.

6. Ibid., p. 247.

7. *Youth and Yale Years*, VP, pp. 3–24.

8. Bigelow Ives, personal communication, April 30, 1982.

9. Lawrence Deutch, "Overstimulation by a Father," in *Fathers and Their Families*, ed. Stanley H. Cath, Alan Gurwitt, and Linda Gunsberg (Hillsdale, N.J.: Analytic Press, 1989), pp. 327–36.

10. Phyllis Greenacre, "The Childhood of the Artist: Libidinal Phase Development and Giftedness," in *Emotional Growth*, vol. 2 (New York, International Universities Press, 1971), p. 489.

11. Ibid.

12. John Demos, "The Changing Faces of Fatherhood: A New Exploration in American Family History," chap. 27 in *Father and Child: Developmental and Clinical Perspectives*, ed. Stanley H. Cath, Alan Gurwitt, and Linda Gunsberg (Boston: Little, Brown, 1982), p. 428.

13. Amelia Van Wyck, VP, p. 7.

14. Greenacre, "Childhood of the Artist," p. 489.

15. DEN, November 29, 1876.

16. Ibid., October 10, 1877.

17. Ibid., December 12, 1877.

18. Ibid., February 13, 1878.

19. Ibid., February 27, 1879.

20. Ibid., July 23, 1879.

21. Ibid.

22. This is the concept of collective alternates described by Greenacre, *Emotional Growth*, 1:362–63, 2:490–94.

23. D. W. Winnicott, "Transitional Objects and Transitional Phenomena," *International Journal of Psychoanalysis* 34: 89–97.
24. KCAT, pp. 264–66.
25. Clayton Wilson Henderson, "Quotation as a Style Element in the Music of Charles Ives" (Ph.D. diss., Washington University, 1969).
26. Marjorie McDonald, "Transitional Tunes and Musical Development," *Psychoanalytic Study of the Child* 25 (1970): 503–20.
27. This biographical sketch of Lyman Brewster is derived from the following special collections of Sterling Memorial Library, Yale University: Alumni Records, Class of 1855; Baldwin Family Papers; Mulford Family Papers. Also, Emma C. Jones, *Brewster Genealogy, 1566–1907* (New York: Grafton Press, 1908); DT, February 14, 15, and 16, 1904, and September 21, 1918.
28. Class Book of 1865, Yale College, Yale University Library Alumni Records, Class of 1865.
29. Baldwin Family Papers, Sterling Memorial Library, Special Collecitons, Yale University.
30. DT, February 14, 15, 16, 1904 and September 21, 1918.
31. Amelia Van Wyck, VP, p. 7.

6: BOYHOOD AND ITS VENERATION

1. DEN, August 13, 1879.
2. Ibid., July 20, 1881.
3. Ibid., May 23, 1880.
4. Ibid., May 27, (Monumental Supplement), June 2, 1880.
5. Ibid.
6. Charles Edward Ives (CEI) to Amelia Ives Brewster (AIB), May 9, 1880.
7. DEN, October 20, 1880.
8. BUR, pp. 33–41, 128 nn. 17, 21.
9. DEN, July 5, 1882.
10. Ibid., December 13, 1882.
11. Ibid., January 10, 1883.
12. JK, p. 115.
13. COW, p. 24.
14. Ibid., p. 25.
15. IMEM, p. 47.
16. Laurence David Wallach, "The New England Education of Charles Ives" (Ph.D. diss., Columbia University, 1973), p. 117.
17. DEN, March 17, 1885.
18. Ibid., April 6, 1885.
19. Moss Ives Diary. ARCH, p. 162.
20. KMEM, p. 247.
21. CEI to George Edward Ives (GEI), July 18, 1886. The various misspellings are CEI's.
22. KCAT, p. 216.
23. IMEM, p. 45–46.
24. "It would have been an early suggestion to Charles of the possibilities of retuning the piano for either purposes of intervalic purity or microtonal complexity. The latter was actualized in the quarter tone pieces of 1925, while the former remained an ideal for piano music which Ives may have kept in mind when notating his conventional piano music, which abounds in strange, often cumbersome chord spellings." Wallach, "New England Education," p. 89.
25. IMEM, p. 108.
26. Ibid.
27. Ibid.
28. COW, p. 27.
29. ROS, pp. 3–53.
30. Ibid., p. 29. Rossiter's significant contributions to the biography of Ives remain at the sociological level, hence his repeated use of the term *emasculation* is metaphorical. That is, it has to do

with social roles and not personal fantasy, either conscious or unconscious. His use of the term *sociosexual* is consistent with this approach and thus he neatly avoids the implications of the term *psychosexual*, which has to do with the mental representations attendant upon sexual drives and their vicissitudes throughout the life cycle. It is to the realm of the psychosexual that dreams and fantasies belong.

31. KCAT, p. 62.
32. Ibid., p. 129.
33. JK, p. 147.

34. KCAT, p. 213.
35. IMEM, p. 97.
36. Letter to John Tasker Howard, KMEM, pp. 236–37.
37. Ibid., p. 238.
38. IMEM, p. 114.
39. Ibid., p. 45, n. 5.
40. Ibid., pp. 132–33.
41. Ibid., p. 132.
42. Ibid., p. 46.
43. Ibid., p. 132.
44. ESS, p. 83.
45. Ibid., p. 52.

7: COLLABORATIONS

1. DN, Oct 16, 1889.
2. KCAT, p. 157.
3. *114*, no. 114.
4. KCAT, p. 215.
5. *114*, no. 114.
6. William E. Devlin, *We Crown Them All: An Illustrated History of Danbury* (Woodland Hills, Calif.: Windsor, 1949), p. 19.
7. ROS, p. 29.
8. IMEM, p. 142.
9. DN, November 2, 1886.
10. IMEM, p. 45.
11. Ives attributed some of his own jagged melodies to the influence of George's "Humanophone" experiment.
12. Wallach, "New England Education," p. 135.
13. Ibid.
14. Ibid., p. 137.
15. Ibid., p. 139.
16. Ibid., p. 151.
17. Elizabeth Parmelee Ives to GEI, August 22, 1889.
18. VP, p. 16.
19. Ibid.
20. Scrapbook of George McLachlan, Scott-Fanton Museum, Danbury, Conn.
21. COW, p. 12.

22. *Variations on "America"* also begins to integrate and develop the trend of the patriotic inclusion of the vernacular, which was anticipated in *American Woods Overture* (1889), KCAT, p. 35.
23. IMEM, p. 38.
24. Ibid., p. 147.
25. KCAT, pp. 132, 214.
26. Ibid., p. 105.
27. Ibid., p. 54.
28. Wallach, "New England Education," p. 142.
29. DN, June 14, 1889.
30. Although it is not among the most frequently quoted tunes in Ives's later works, it receives a significant if brief treatment in the Second Symphony, which is both passionate and tender.
31. Wallach, "New England Education," p. 161.
32. IMEM, p. 38.
33. Ibid., p. 115.
34. Wallach, "New England Education," p. 155.
35. KCAT, p. 106.
36. Ibid., p. 136.
37. IMEM, p. 178.
38. Ibid., p. 46.

8: AT PARTING

1. ROS, p. 31.
2. Ibid., p. 248.
3. Ibid., pp. 130–31.
4. Ibid.
5. Ibid.
6. CEI to GEI, July 9, 1893.
7. Ibid.
8. CEI to GEI, July 5, 1893.
9. GEI to CEI, July 11, 1893.
10. CEI to family, August 28, 1893.
11. Lyman Denison Brewster to Amelia Ives Brewster, September 1, 1893.
12. Whatever the literary limitations of the work, one might keep in mind, as Kirkpatrick suggests, "what the events of the play meant to the Ives family and their circle of in-laws and friends. Danbury having been burned by the British in 1777, was still, well over a century later, acutely aware of the Revolution and everything it had meant including patriotism and treason." KMEM, p. 281.
13. Wooldridge has suggested that the occasion was the trip to Chicago. David Wooldridge, *From the Steeples and Mountains: A Study of Charles Ives* (New York: Knopf, 1974), p. 58.
14. DEN, October 25, 1893.
15. CEI to GEI, October 30, 1893.
16. Ibid.
17. CEI to GEI, December 3, 1893.
18. CEI to family, April 29, 1894.
19. CEI to GEI, February 20, 1894.
20. CEI to EPI, March 22, 1894.
21. CEI to family, March 29, 1894.
22. CEI to GEI, April 12, 1894.
23. CEI to GEI, May 8, 1894.
24. CEI to GEI, August 3, 1894.
25. Wooldridge, *From the Steeples and Mountains*, p. 66.
26. KCAT, pp. 157–58. *At Parting* in this earlier form was the setting of a sentimental verse by Frederic Peterson, perhaps a translation. Although Charlie's setting begins with a folk-song simplicity characteristic of sentimental songs of the 1890s, the second line introduces a skillfully managed dissonance, where a leading tone resolves upwardly in the course of a beautifully flowing line. *Rallentando* (slowing down) is not only written verbally but fluidly prolonged in musical notation. The first measure of the song apparently quotes *Flow Gently Sweet Afton* (although Kirkpatrick does not mention this); it is perhaps before the period of conscious quotation in Charlie's music. And the words themselves quote *My Wild Irish Rose* ("The sweetest flow'r that grows"). The song, otherwise uncomplicated, was sung in New Canaan in 1889 and perhaps in Danbury a year earlier at a concert in Town Hall.
27. See also discussion in Phillip Edward Newman, "The Songs of Charles Ives" (Ph.D. diss., University of Iowa, 1967), 2:27ff.
28. IMEM, p. 44–45.
29. Ibid., p. 108.

9: AT YALE: MUSIC AND MUSICIANS

1. GEI to CEI, September 28, 1894.
2. CEI to EPI, October 24, 1894.
3. CEI to GEI, October 30, 1894.
4. Ibid., September 30, 1894 (with addenda).
5. Ibid.
6. Henry Seidel Canby, *Alma Mater: The Gothic Age of the American College* (New York: Farrar & Rinehart, 1936), pp. 88ff.

7. George Wilson Pierson, *Yale College, 1871–1921* (New Haven: Yale University Press, 1952), p. 58.
8. ROS, p. 68.
9. Ibid.
10. Canby, *Alma Mater*, p. 150.
11. ESS, p. 67.
12. IMEM, p. 115.
13. Ibid.
14. Ibid., pp. 115–16.
15. Ibid., p. 116.
16. CEI to GEI, October 30, 1894.
17. CEI to JHT, November 23, 1907.
18. IMEM, p. 237.
19. Ibid., p. 49.
20. This account of Parker's life is drawn chiefly from William K. Kearns, "Horatio Parker, 1863–1919: A Study of His Life and Music" (Ph.D. diss., University of Illinois, 1965).
21. Ibid., p. 22.
22. Ibid., p. 81.
23. Ibid., pp. 85–86.
24. Ibid.
25. John Tasker Howard, *Our American Music* (New York: Crowell, 1931), p. 337.
26. IMEM, p. 49.
27. ROS, p. 37.
28. IMEM, p. 49.
29. Ibid.
30. IMEM, pp. 48–49.
31. Ibid.
32. KCAT, p. 109. Now lost, this work was later developed into the fourth movement of the *Holidays* Symphony.
33. IMEM, p. 39.
34. Ibid.
35. Ibid., p. 184.
36. Ibid.
37. BUR, p. 61.
38. Ibid., p. 74.
39. ESS, p. 66.
40. CEI to John Cornelius Griggs, in KMEM, pp. 257–58.
41. KMEM, p. 202.
42. IMEM, p. 49.
43. KCAT, pp. 12–13.
44. Ibid.
45. Dennis Marshall, "Charles Ives's Quotations: Manner or Substance," *Perspectives of New Music*, no. 2 (1968): 45–56.
46. KMEM, p. 254.
47. Wallach, "New England Education," p. 245.
48. Ibid., p. 87.
49. KCAT, p. 1.
50. KMEM, p. 51.
51. *The New Grove Dictionary of Music and Musicians*, ed. Stanley Sadie, 18: 461.
52. Ives later included several of these pieces in "a group of German Songs," borrowing the text for two of them, *Feldeinsamkeit* (from Brahms) and *Ich grolle nicht* (from Schumann).
53. *114*, nos. 80–83.
54. IMEM, p. 52.
55. In this regard, the popularity of Ives's music in France in the 1960s and 1970s is of interest.

10: 76 SOUTH MIDDLE

1. Lewis Sheldon Welch and Walter Camp, *Yale, Her Campus, Class-Rooms, and Athletics* (Boston: L. C. Page, 1899), p. 4.
2. Canby, *Alma Mater*, p. 151.
3. Welch and Camp, *Yale*, p. 58.
4. Frank R. Rossiter, "Charles Ives: Good American and Isolated Artist," in *An Ives Celebration*, ed. H. Wiley Hitchcock and Vivian Perlis (Urbana and Chicago: University of Illinois Press, 1977), p. 21.

5. KCAT, p. 113.

6. IMEM, p. 41.

7. Ibid., p. 130.

8. KCAT, p. 5.

9. ROS, p. 71.

10. Ibid., p. 64.

11. KCAT, p. 132.

12. Welch and Camp, *Yale*, p. 79. One reason for the expense, incidentally, was the inefficiency inherent in one-year control, since membership on the social committee for the event was a much-coveted position, determined annually on the basis of popularity and influence rather than competence.

13. COW, p. 97.

14. KCAT, p. 55.

15. Ibid., p. 172.

16. Ibid., p. 197.

17. Welch and Camp, *Yale*, p. 37.

18. Ibid., p. 99–100.

19. Owen Johnson, *Stover At Yale* (New York: Collier, 1968). Cited in ROS, p. 335.

20. ROS, p. 78.

21. George Santayana wrote that the Ivy League graduate of the time believed in "one's divine mission to be rich and happy." Cited in ROS, p. 86.

22. Ibid., p. 80.

23. Ibid., p. 81.

24. KMEM, p. 41.

25. KCAT, pp. 48–49.

26. Ibid.

27. He probably wrote this out in 1936, when Henry Cowell prepared a performing version of the song from Ives's 1907 sketch; in 1936 Ives was sixty-two years old and already infirm.

28. See further discussion in Stuart Feder, "Calcium Light Night and Other Early Memories of Charles Ives," in *Fathers and Their Families*, ed. Stanley H. Cath, Alan Gurwitt, and Linda Gunsberg (Hillsdale, N.J.: Analytic Press, 1989).

29. DEN, August 29, 1883.

30. There is strong evidence that the composer not only had such experiences but also could realize them in musical form. See, for example, *The Things Our Fathers Loved; 114*, no. 43. The modalities of vision and audition apparently merge at the climax in the ultimate representation of homoerotic love and excitement. Stuart Feder, "The Nostalgia of Charles Ives: An Essay in Affects and Music," in *The Annual of Psychoanalysis* (New York: International Universities Press, 1982), 10:301–36.

31. COW, p. 35.

11: POVERTY FLAT

1. The title of this chapter and much of the factual background is drawn from John Kirkpatrick's appendix 17 in KMEM.

2. KCAT, pp. 139–40.

3. Ibid., p. 121.

4. BUR, p. 79.

5. KCAT, pp. 115–20.

6. Ibid., p. 30.

7. J. Peter Burkholder, "Quotation and Paraphrase in Ives's Second Symphony," *Nineteenth Century Music* 11, no. 1 (Summer 1987), pp. 3–25.

8. COW, p. 135.

9. KCAT, p. 115.

10. Horatio W. Parker, *Hora Novissima (Op. 30)*, Kalmus Vocal Scores (Melville, N.Y.: Belwin Mills, n.d.), p. ix.

11. Charles E. Ives, *The Celestial Country* (New York: Peer International, n.d.), pp. 4–5.

12. Ibid., pp. 24–42.

13. *114*, no. 45.

14. Ibid., no. 11.

15. BUR also suggests this, citing Victor Yellin's similar conclusion.
16. IMEM, p. 34.
17. Ibid., p. 43.
18. By the time Ives, late in life, had tacked the wrong-note chord onto the original, more conservative end of his *Second Symphony*, he either no longer had to worry about approbation or wanted to be deliberately provocative—probably both.
19. *Musical Courier*, April 22, 1902. Cited in KMEM, p. 33.
20. IMEM, p. 57.
21. KCAT, pp. 40–41.
22. Ibid., p. 39.
23. BUR, pp. 83–93, calls the years 1902–08 the period of "innovation and synthesis."
24. "Fictional music" is a term coined by Peter J. Rabinowitz, in his "Fictional Music: Toward a Theory of Listening," *Bucknell Review* 26, no. 1 (1981).
25. KCAT, pp. 7–9.
26. IMEM, pp. 128–29.
27. Burkholder, "Quotation and Paraphrase," p. 18.
28. BUR, p. 84.
29. Ibid., p. 86.
30. Ibid., p. 87.
31. KCAT, p. 70.
32. KMEM, p. 269. A chapter on Julian Southall Myrick appears as appendix 18, which includes material on Myrick's early life (pp. 268–73).
33. Rossiter, who researched this period for his chapter "The Businessman" (ROS, chap. 4, pp. 110–25), from which some of this material is drawn, has failed to come up with details.
34. ROS, p. 111.
35. VP, pp. 31–38, interviews with Julian Myrick, 1968–1969.
36. Robert I. Mehr and Emerson Cammack, *Principles of Insurance* (Homewood, Ill.: Richard P. Irwin, 1976), p. 397.

37. ROS, p. 111.
38. Mehr and Cammack, *Principles of Insurance*, p. 399.
39. KCAT, p. 42.
40. KMEM, p. 281–86.
41. KCAT, p. 29.
42. It was later to be the fate of both these pieces to become a part of the *Holidays Symphony*, Lyman's music being associated with the Fourth of July and George's with Decoration Day. Similarly, in Ives's *Three Places in New England* (the *First Orchestral Set*, 1903–14), each of the "fathers" came to be associated with a place. The Revolutionary War, with its associations with Lyman Brewster, had its "place" in Putnam's Camp, a locale just outside Bethel, near Danbury. The Civil War and its leaders, associated with George, found its place on the Boston Common in the Saint-Gauden's Memorial, which commemorated the first black volunteer regiment of the war.
43. KCAT, p. 39.
44. IMEM, p. 265.
45. KCAT, p. 42.
46. Ibid.
47. *114*, no. 12.
48. KCAT, p. 42.
49. KMEM, p. 276.
50. KCAT, p. 67.
51. Ibid., pp. 82–87.
52. Ibid., pp. 74–76.
53. COW, p. 71.
54. AIB to CEI, March 11, 1908.
55. AIB to CEI, September 7, 1905.
56. KCAT, p. 42.
57. Ibid., p. 43.
58. Wooldridge, *From the Steeples and Mountains*, p. 124.
59. KCAT, p. 73.
60. Ibid., p. 96.
61. Harmony Twichell to CEI, March 24, 1908.
62. AIB to CEI, October 29, 1907.

12: QUESTIONINGS

1. IMEM, p. 61.
2. KCAT, p. 43.
3. IMEM, p. 54.
4. KCAT, p. 67.
5. Ibid., p. 65.
6. IMEM, p. 90.
7. Ibid., p. 91. "In this piece, I wanted to get, in a way, the sense and sound of a bonfire, outdoors in the night, growing bigger and brighter, and boys and children running around, dancing, throwing on wood—and the general spirit of Holloween [*sic*] night—(and at the end, the take-off of the regular coda of a proper opera, heard down the street from the bandstand). In spite of the subject matter, this was one of the most carefully worked out (technically speaking), and one of the best pieces (from the standpoint of workmanship) that I've ever done. The four strings play in four different and closely related keys, each line strictly diatonic. Then it is canonic, not only in tones, but in phrases, accents, and durations or spaces. I happened to get exactly the effect I had in mind, which is the only ([or] at least an important) function of good workmanship."
8. KCAT, p. 43.
9. Idem.
10. KMEM, p. 266.
11. KCAT, p. 43
12. Ibid., p. 46.
13. Ibid., p. 45.
14. Ibid.
15. Ibid., p. 77.
16. IMEM, pp. 58–59.
17. Ibid.
18. Letter to John J. Becker, quoted in KMEM, p. 59.
19. IMEM, p. 55.
20. *114*, no. 64.
21. IMEM, p. 56.
22. Ibid.
23. Ibid.
24. Ibid.
25. *114*, no. 12.
26. Postface to *The Unanswered Question* and *Central Park in the Dark*, KCAT, p. 45.
27. Ibid.
28. Ibid.
29. Ibid.
30. Following the entrance of the trumpet on B♭, the rising musical inflection of the motif C♯–E is "answered" in the higher octave with another wider interval, E♭–B♭, in inversion and mirror image.
31. H. Wiley Hitchcock (*Ives*, Oxford Studies of Composers, 14 [London: Oxford University Press, 1977]) designates these works as important precursors of "stereophonic and collage techniques" as well as other advances of more recent composers. In particular, he notes the handling of the time elements in music: "'time' in the usual musical sense [rhythm, meter, pulse, etc.] does not exist; the only time-sense is of the chronological continuum, and the music simply unrolls in it—like a scroll in space, at once plastic and concrete" (p. 81). The Cowells noted, "One of Ives's most spectacular achievements is the invention of a form which logically uses consonance and dissonance in a single piece" (COW, p. 340).
32. KCAT, p. 44 (*Taps* does not appear on the published score).
33. HT to CEI, August 29, 1907.
34. HT to CEI, August 16, 1906.
35. KMEM, p. 270.
36. Personal communication, David J. Johnson, The Casemate Museum, Fortress Monroe, Va. Also, advertisement for the Hotel Chamberlain, *National Geographic Magazine*, January 1915.

13: HARMONY

1. Appendix 16, on Joseph Hopkins Twichell, and appendix 19, on Harmony Twichell, in KMEM, serve as background material for this chapter.

2. Further source material on Joseph Hopkins Twichell is drawn from the only available biography, Leah A. Strong, *Joseph Hopkins Twichell: Mark Twain's Friend and Pastor* (Athens, Ga.: University of Georgia Press, 1966).

3. Robert Taylor, *Saranac—America's Magic Mountain* (Boston: Houghton Mifflin, 1986), p. 74.

4. KMEM, p. 275.

5. Ibid., p. 277.

6. HT to CEI, January 5, 1907.

7. KMEM, p. 277 (before April 1907). Text from *114*, p. 207:

My heart was brave for each
    new thing
and I loved the far away.
I watched the gay bright people
    dance,
We laughed, for the road was
    good.
But Oh! I passed where the way
    was rough
I saw it stained with blood.
I wandered on till I tired
    grew,—
Far on the world's highway
My heart was sad for what I saw
    I feared,
I feared the far away, the far
    away.
So when one day, O sweetest
    day,
I came to a garden small,
A voice my heart knew called
    me in,
I answered its blessed call;
I left my wand'ring far and
    wide
The freedom and far away

But my garden blooms with
    sweet content
That is not on the world's
    highway.

8. *114*, no. 90.
9. KCAT, p. 190.
10. *114*, no. 65.
11. KMEM, p. 277.
12. HT to CEI, August 29 and September 1, 1907.
13. HT to CEI, September 9, 1907.
14. HT to CEI, September 17, 1907.
15. KMEM, appendix 21, pp. 318–24.
16. Ibid., p. 324.
17. Ibid.
18. Ibid.
19. HT to CEI, [February 18], 1908, from transcript by Edith Ives Tyler, quoted in ROS, p. 173.
20. BUR, p. 100.
21. Ibid., p. 32.
22. KCAT, p. 34.
23. KMEM, p. 277.
24. Ibid., p. 277.
25. IMEM, p. 49.
26. CEI to JHT, November 23, 1907, from KMEM, pp. 260–61.
27. CEI to HT, November 22, 1907.
28. HT to CEI, May 13, 1908.
29. AIB to CEI, October 29, 1907.
30. Ibid.
31. AIB to CEI, November 5, 1907.
32. AIB to CEI, November 7–8, 1907.
33. HT to CEI, March 11, 1908.
34. AIB to CEI, April 8, 1908.
35. Ibid.
36. HT to CEI, December 23, 1907.
37. HT to CEI, December 30, 1907.
38. AIB to CEI, May 27, 1908.
39. HT to CEI, January 9, 1908.
40. HT to CEI, February 4, 1908.
41. HT to CEI, February ?, 1908 (dated "Tuesday").
42. HT to CEI, May 12, 1908.
43. ARCH, diaries, *Our Book*.

44. *114*, no. 97.
45. *Our Book*.
46. Ibid.
47. Harmony Cushman Twichell to HTI, quoted in p. 278.
48. Ibid., p. 279.
49. IMEM, p. 159.
50. *114*, no. 26.
51. The music, a tightly written masterpiece in miniature, merits interest from several points of view. On paper, it appears to be a study in chromatics in the form of short phrases with weary, sigh-like pauses between them. The score is marked "very slowly, in a weak and dragging way," and each phrase arches downward at the same time that a climax is aimed for at the word "God-like." From here, a single long phrase slowly drifts chromatically downward, with only the final five notes detached from it—the five that bear the faint hope, "looking towards the sky." Other than the usual marking, no indication concerning performance is given in the published version of the *114 Songs*. In a later version (*34 Songs*, in *New Music* 7, no. 1 [San Francisco, 1933]), Ives makes it clear that this was also intended to be an exercise in quarter tones and other unusual intervals: "a slide was made down or up through a 1/4 tone, in a semitone, except between the 2 or 3 tones in a whole tone interval, except between the last 5 notes." The use of quarter tones relates the song to not only the events of April 1909 but also to layers of earlier psychic life,
in particular the enduring presence of George Ives. Charles wrote in the *Memos* of "a kind of family prejudice, for my father had a weakness for quarter-tones—in fact he didn't even stop with them. He rigged up a contrivance to stretch 24 or more violin strings and tuned them up to suit the dictates of his own curiosity. He would pick out quarter-tone tunes and try to get the family to sing them" (IMEM, p. 110).
52. *114*, no. 57.
53. KCAT, p. 194.
54. KMEM, p. 202.
55. CEI to Harmony Twichell Ives, September 26, 1910.
56. CEI to HTI, October 18, 1910.
57. COW, p. 35.
58. HTI to CEI, March 4, 1914.
59. HTI to CEI, April 22, 1914.
60. HTI to CEI, March 24, 1915.
61. *Our Book*, November 1, 1913.
62. Ibid., August 16, 1916.
63. HTI to CEI, December 6, 1915.
64. IMEM, p. 106.
65. Wooldridge, *From the Steeples and Mountains*, p. 180.
66. HTI to CEI, December 8, 1915.
67. VP, pp. 48–49.
68. Ibid.
69. HTI to CEI, February 29, 1916.
70. Ibid.
71. HTI to CEI, March 2, 1916.
72. *Our Book*, October 18, 1916.
73. VP, p. 76.
74. Ibid., pp. 115–17.
75. Ibid., p. 130.

14: "CONTENTED RIVER": MOLLIE REVENANT

1. GEI to CEI, September 28, 1894.
2. Amelia Ives Brewster to CEI, October 29, 1907.
3. *Our Book*.
4. IMEM, p. 87.
5. *114*, no. 15.
6. Charles Ives, *Three Places in New England: An Orchestral Set* (Bryn Mawr, Mercury Music, 1935), p. 64.
7. KCAT, p. 17.

8. ESS, p. 47.
9. *114*, nos. 81, 108. *The Old Mother:* "Du gabst mir den starken Arm und diesen wilden Muht. / Du wischtest ab die Thräne mein, war's mir im Herzen bang" ('Twas thou my courage didst impart, my arm sturdy might? Thou'st wip'd away each childish tear, when I was sore distrest). *Songs My Mother Taught Me:* "Songs my mother taught me in the days long vanished, seldom from her eyelids were the teardrops banished."
10. KCAT, p. 64.
11. Ives, *Three Places*, p. 20.

15: A BOY'S CIVIL WAR

1. Jonathan Elkus, *Charles Ives and the American Band Tradition: A Centennial Tribute* (Exeter: American Arts Documentation Centre, University of Exeter, 1974).
2. VP, p. 112.
3. KCAT, pp. 10–11.
4. Ibid., pp. 14–15.
5. The great Civil War pieces were bracketed by a brief piano piece of 1908, *The Anti-Abolitionist Riots in the 1830s and 1840s*, and *Lincoln, The Great Commoner*, a song for unison chorus and orchestra, in 1917. Unlike *Decoration Day* and *The "St. Gaudens,"* there is nothing in the music of *The Anti-Abolitionist Riots* to suggest an autobiographical source of the kind considered here. Rather, like others of the group of *Studies* of which it is a part (no. 9), it appears to be a technical exercise, a study in ninths. This music may belong to an earlier conception, a previous phase or sequence of musical thought, while the title alone suggests another, later trend.
6. BUR, p. 34.
7. Interview with Bigelow Ives, April 30, 1982.
8. KMEM, p. 252.
9. Ibid., pp. 53 and 43. The hymn *Nettleton*, accented with a grunt on the fourth beat, is given as an example. Ives remembered hearing hymns sung this way "in some of the churches and in the camp meetings."
10. James M. McPherson, *The Battle Cry of Freedom: The Civil War Era* (New York: Oxford University Press, 1988), p. 8.
11. KCAT, p. 14. Lovejoy was murdered defending his press from an anti-abolitionist mob. When an earlier speaker likened the action to the Boston Tea Party, Phillips in his speech searingly termed the comparison a slander to the founding fathers. Burkholder suggests that Ives may have read a recent biography that recounted the event (BUR, p. 142, n. 17).
12. IMEM, p. 14.
13. The account that follows is drawn largely from Lincoln Kirstein, "The Memorial to Robert Gould Shaw and His Soldiers by Augustus Saint-Gaudens," in *Lay This Laurel* (New York: Eakins Press, 1973).
14. Ibid.
15. Ibid.
16. Ibid.
17. Ives, *Three Places*, p. 1.
18. KCAT, p. 14, 15.
19. IMEM, p. 91.
20. In its present context, there may be an Ivesian pun in "South-Paw."
21. KCAT, p. 60.
22. Ibid., p. 21.
23. Ibid., p. 90.
24. *The "St. Gaudens"* opens, for example, very quietly, over a polychord in low strings. The germ of the minor-third melody outlines a diminished chord on

B, while the divided strings (with backing from the tympani) play a foundation of an A-minor chord over which sounds another chord, in D♯ major. The piece ends with a play on the minor third in piano and viola in harmonics. Throughout, the minor third (the "I'm coming" of Stephen Foster's *Old Black Joe*) is an intrinsic motif germinating musical idea and gesture. At the start of the second section (measure 16), for example, the solo oboe flags it, as does the piano several bars later (m. 23). Shortly (m. 27) the flute develops it into the tune to the words, "The Union forever" (from *The Battle Cry of Freedom*). Only later in the work, in an irregular eight-measure phrase, is a full elaboration of the theme played by the flute.

A sense of the condensation of musical ideas generated by quotation, the uniqueness of the form invented, and its aesthetic effect can be gained from a brief four-measure passage at the start of the preceding passage (mm. 66–69). Hitchcock observes that in the phrase "I'm coming" Ives found a "common denominator" with phrases of Work's song ("Hurrah! Hurrah!), as well as Root's ("The Union forever, Hurrah boys, Hurrah"). He also points out how Ives "derives an ostinato bass from a motive shared by the two Civil War songs; and underscores the whole complex with a traditional military drumbeat (Hitchcock, *Ives*, p. 87). Elsewhere, in the middle section of the piece, the simple drumbeat is staggered at two different speeds in an interesting and typical polytempo.

The musical analysis encompasses minute temporal events which are near-simultaneous, the entire passage requiring seconds much as mental events do. It is questionable as well as highly variable how much detail can be heard by the individual listener in any conscious manner, but much is conveyed impressionistically and doubtless unconsciously. It is in this manner that much of Ives's music can be intelligible and, indeed, affecting by building up intense, often dense auditory images, simultaneous and frequently overlapping, which are more powerful in effect than their often banal constituent parts may suggest.

25. Ives, *Three Places*, "St. Gaudens," to letter D, m. 35.

26. Ibid., p. 8.

27. Kenneth A. Bernard, *Lincoln and the Music of the Civil War* (Caldwell: University of Idaho Press, 1966), p. 75.

28. KCAT, p. 265.

29. Ives, *Three Places*, "St. Gaudens," at m. 63. Continuing over the persistent but barely audible military drumbeat, a brief climax of scarcely three measures of orchestral tutti is built with the brass predominant for the only time and moving in dissonant contrary motion up to a vast triple-forte chord in C-major, the trumpet sounding E. The addition of a B in the horn renders it a major seventh over the persistent lowest A of the tympani.

30. HT to CEI, [March 10], 1908.

31. HT to CEI, March 23, 1908.

32. KMEM, p. 276.

33. Kirstein, "Memorial."

34. Ibid.

35. KCAT, pp. 10–11.

36. IMEM, p. 94.

37. Ibid., p. 102. Kirkpatrick notes that no such organ piece has survived but suggests that "it may have been an organ version of the lost Slow March for band on Adeste Fidelis (KMEM, p. 102). The latter appears in Ives's earliest listing of works, dated there to 1886 or 1887. This would extend the gestation of *Decoration Day* (and *Holidays*) over a twenty-seven year period, to the time when Ives was a boy.

38. Ibid., p. 96.
39. KCAT, p. 109.
40. Postface to *Decoration Day*, second movement from a set of four pieces for orchestra, *Holidays in a Connecticut Country Town*. Typescript, "Decoration Day," New York Public Library, Music Research Collection, Lincoln Center, New York City.
41. Stuart Feder, "Decoration Day: A Boyhood Memory of Charles Ives, *Musical Quarterly* 66, no. 2 (April 1980): 234–53; "Charles and George Ives: The Veneration of Boyhood," *Annual of Psychoanalysis* 9 (1981): 265–316.

42. Bernard, *Lincoln*, p. 75.
43. IMEM, p. 102.
44. KMEM, p. 148.
45. Stravinsky, who particularly admired *Decoration Day*, commented on the "surprise ending" and the "shadow violin as Ives called the marginal fiddle playing in major sevenths with the others." He called the ending "the loneliest and one of the most touching I know of."
46. Sigmund Freud, "Screen Memories," *Standard Edition*, 3 (London, 1955), p. 322.
47. Ibid.

16: PLACES IN THE SOUL

1. KCAT, pp. 15–16.
2. IMEM, p. 83.
3. KCAT, p. 16. A note on the manuscript records his disappointment in the presidential elections of November 1908, when, to the dismay of progressive Republicans, William Howard Taft was nominated and elected. Ives had scribbled, "Wanted in these you-be-knighted-states!—more independence . . . election day . . . 1908."
4. *Three Places in New England*, p. 20.
5. A Danbury townsman recalled George as bandleader: "They'd be going one way with the band, with another band going the other way 'round the park here, and the two would clash—that interested him [George] very much." Phillip Sunderland in VP, p. 15.
6. *114*, no. 51.
7. Ibid., no. 43.
8. Ibid., no. 52.
9. Beginning at letter F in the score.
10. IMEM, p. 43.
11. *Three Places in New England*, p. 35.
12. As Phyllis Greenacre put it, there may be "a diminished firmness of the barrier

between primary-process thinking and imagery, a condition which seems characteristic of gifted individuals." *The Quest for the Father* (New York: International Universities Press, 1963), p. 16.
13. KCAT, pp. 11–12.
14. Ibid., p. 9.
15. IMEM, pp. 97–98.
16. Ibid.
17. Ibid.
18. Ibid., p. 97.
19. Hitchcock, *Ives*, p. 84.
20. IMEM, p. 97.
21. Lyman Brewster, *Major John Andre*, in KMEM, p. 290.
22. KCAT, p. 11. In writing *The Fourth of July*, Ives assembled other diverse elements. The trio from the *1776 Overture*, left over, as it were, from *Putnam's Camp* (after he dovetailed portions with *Country Band* in 1911), was included, as well as some ideas from an unfinished work of 1904, *The General Slocum*.
23. Ibid., p. 11
24. Dennis Marshall suggests that *Colum-

bia, the Gem of the Ocean "serves as a structural framework for the entire movement in much the same way that a Lutheran chorale melody would serve as the formal model and motivic source for a cantata movement or an organ prelude of J. S. Bach." Marshall, "Charles Ives's Quotations: Manner or Substance," *Perspectives of New Music* 6 (1968): 45–46.

25. IMEM, p. 104.
26. Ibid.
27. *114*, no. 102.
28. Ibid.
29. Winnicott, "Transitional Objects."
30. McDonald, "Transitional Tunes."
31. *114*, no. 52.
32. Ibid., no. 43.
33. Ibid., no. 52. The Latin, "Ducite ab urbe domum, mea carmina Daphnin," which serves as subtitle as well, was no doubt a remnant of freshman or sophomore Latin at Yale.
34. Ibid. The words are:

Go my songs! Draw Daphnis from
the city.
A minor tune from Todd's opera
house
comes to me as I cross the square,
there,
We boys used to shout the songs
that rouse
the hearts of the brave and
fair,
of the brave and fair.
As we march along down Main
Street,
behind the village band,
The dear old trees, with their arch
of leaves
seem to grasp us by the hand.
While we step along
to the tune of an Irish song,
Glad but wistful sounds the old
church bell,

for underneath's a note of sadness,
"Old home town" farewell.

A corner lot, a white picket fence,
daisies almost everywhere, there,
We boys used to play "One old
cat,"
and base hits filled the air,
filled the summer air.
As we march along on Main
Street,
of that "Down East" Yankee town,
Comes a sign of life,
from the "3rd Corps" fife,
strains of an old breakdown;
While we step along
to the tune of an Irish song,
Comes another sound we all know
well,
It takes us away back forty
years,
that little red schoolhouse bell.

35. *114*, p. 117.
36. The small but highly interesting psychoanalytic literature on nostalgia has been reviewed in Feder, "Nostalgia of Charles Ives."
37. Peter Castelnuovo-Tedesco, "The Mind as Stage: Some Comments on Reminiscence and Internal Objects," *International Journal of Psychoanalysis* 59 (1978): 19–26. David S. Werman, "Normal and Pathological Nostalgia," *Journal of the American Psychoanalytic Association* 25 (1977): 387–95.
38. *114*, no. 43.
39. KCAT, p.43.
40. Charles Brenner, "On the Nature and Development of Affects: A Unified Theory," *Psychoanalytic Quarterly* 44 (1974): 532–56. Edward M. Weinshel, "Some Psychoanalytic Considerations on Mood," *International Journal of Psychoanalysis*, 51 (1970): 313–20.

17: CONCORD

1. COW, p. 52.
2. Ibid., p. 98.
3. IMEM, p. 112.
4. BUR, p. 112.
5. ARCH, Correspondence, Miscellaneous, Tax Records, box 38.
6. IMEM, p. 202.
7. KCAT, p. 42.
8. *114*, nos. 30 (Browning), 31 (Whitman), 105 (Arnold).
9. IMEM, p. 76.
10. BUR, p. 109.
11. Henry Van Dyke, "Emerson," *Encyclopeadia Brittanica*, 11th ed., 9: 335.
12. ESS, p. 11.
13. Ibid., p. 12.
14. Ibid., pp. 24–25.
15. Ibid., p. 25.
16. Ibid., p. 35.
17. Ibid., p. 36.
18. BUR, p. 26.
19. ESS, p. 71.
20. Ibid., p. 84.
21. John Kirkpatrick, personal communication, January 13, 1978.
22. IMEM, p. 79.
23. Ralph Waldo Emerson, "Circles," in *Essays and Lectures* (New York: Library of America, 1983), p. 403.
24. Ibid.
25. Joel Porte, *Representative Man: Ralph Waldo Emerson in His Time* (New York: Oxford University Press, 1979).
26. Josephine Latham Swayne, *The Story of Concord, Told by Concord Writers* (Boston: Geo. H. Ellis, 1923), p. 87.
27. Sigmund Freud, "Family Romance," *S.E.*, vol. 9, p. 241.
28. Porte, *Representative Man*, p. 3.
29. See ibid., pp. 247–84.
30. Robert D. Richardson, Jr., *Henry Thoreau: A Life of the Mind* (Berkeley and Los Angeles: University of California Press, 1986), p. 149.
31. Swayne, *Story of Concord*, p. 93.
32. Ibid., p. 247.
33. ESS, p. 28.
34. Ibid., p. 29.
35. Ibid.
36. Ibid.
37. Ibid., p. 39.
38. Ibid., p. 47.
39. Ibid., p. 45.
40. Ibid.
41. Ibid., p. 46.
42. Ibid.
43. Ibid., p. 47.
44. Ibid.
45. In a footnote, Ives observed that he intended *Thoreau* to be performed on a smaller, more intimate scale than the preceding movements: "To be played in a lower dynamic ration than usual; i.e., the F here is about the mf of the preceding movements. Both pedals are used almost constantly." Charles Ives, *Piano Sonata No. 2*, 2d ed. (New York: Associated Music Publishers, 1947).
46. KCAT, p. 91.
47. Ibid., p. 199.
48. ESS, p. 51.
49. Ibid., p. 69.
50. Ibid., p. 53.
51. Ibid., p. 52.
52. Ibid., p. 65.
53. Ibid., p. 62.
54. Ibid., p. 68. Quoted by Ives with his elisions. See Henry David Thoreau, *A Week, Walden, Maine Woods, Cape Cod* (New York: Library of America, 1985), p. 420.
55. Ibid., p. 67.
56. Ibid.
57. Thoreau, *A Week*, p. 155.
58. *114*, no. 48.
59. ESS, p. 69.
60. Ralph Waldo Emerson, *Emerson in His Journals*, selected and edited by Joel Porte (Cambridge, Mass.: Belknap Press, Harvard University Press, 1982), p. 292.

18: JOURNEY'S END

1. John Kirkpatrick, preface to Charles Ives, *Symphony No. 4* (New York: Associated Music Publishers, 1965).
2. Henry Bellaman, program notes to Ives's *Fourth Symphony*, Pro Musica program, January 29, 1927.
3. Ives, *Symphony No. 4*.
4. Ibid.
5. IMEM, p. 129.
6. Ibid.
7. BUR, p. 103.
8. KMEM, p. 278.
9. ARCH, diaries, Commuter's Diary, box 45, note of June 11, 1915.
10. ROS, p. 131.
11. KCAT, p. 125.
12. Ibid.
13. Nathaniel Hawthorne, "The Celestial Rail-Road," in *Tales and Sketches* (New York: Library of America, 1982), p. 823.
14. Ibid.
15. Kirkpatrick, preface to Ives, *Symphony No. 4*.
16. It is no coincidence that the author of "The Celestial Rail-Road" is also the chronicler of sin, and indeed this is one of the themes in the story. The theme is avoided completely in the Hawthorne movement of the *Concord Sonata* but is latent in the underlying aesthetic program of the *Fourth Symphony*.
17. KCAT, p. 57.
18. IMEM, pp. 66, 154–55.
19. *114*, postface.
20. Kurt Stone, "Ives's Fourth Symphony: A Review," *Musical Quarterly* 52, no. 1 (January 1966), p. 14.
21. Ibid., p. 15.
22. Ibid., p. 16.
23. Ibid., p. 11.
24. Ibid.
25. KCAT, p. 200
26. KMEM, p. 271.
27. Ibid.
28. VP, p. 82.
29. KCAT, pp. 200–201, *114*, no. 50.
30. *114*, no. 50.
31. Ibid., no. 51.

19: SHADOW ON THE GRASS

1. KCAT, p. 51.
2. *114*, no. 24.
3. IMEM, p. 112.
4. CEI to "Tom," headed "7 Iola Place Asheville, N.C.," n.d.
5. COW, p. 76.
6. Ibid., p. 75.
7. BUR, p. 95.
8. COW, p. 76.
9. Wooldridge, *From the Steeples and Mountains*, p. 185.
10. ARCH, copies of correspondence and medical reports from Joslin Clinic, box 39.
11. Medical Records, Roosevelt Hospital, New York. Admissions of April 26, 1954, and May 9, 1954.
12. Wooldridge, *From the Steeples and Mountains*, pp. 185–86.
13. VP, p. 36.
14. *Our Book*, December 1918.
15. *114*, no. 112.
16. IMEM, p. 82. On January 20, Harmony noted: "Charlie finishing up copy of Sonata Prologue." The following day, "C worked at Thoreau, trying to write something to make people think Thoreau movement sounds like Thoreau." This was evidently the essay that he finished early in February and had typed by a local stenographer. By the middle of February, he was busily copying music, and a note in his hand on February 20 reads, "Emerson, Alcotts & Thoreau all finished and copied— three movements." The Hawthorne movement remained to be completed.

ARCH, diaries, *Our Book*, February 1919.

17. Ibid., March 18, 1919.
18. Ibid.

20: UNIVERSE

1. KCAT, pp. 26–28.
2. IMEM, p. 106.
3. Ibid.
4. Ibid.
5. Ibid.
6. Ibid.
7. KCAT, p. 27.
8. Phyllis Greenacre, "The Childhood of the Artist: Libidinal Phase Development and Giftedness," in vol. 2 (New York: International Universities Press, 1971), pp. 489–90.
9. KCAT, p. 28.
10. Ibid.
11. IMEM, pp. 106–07.
12. Ibid., pp. 124–25.
13. Ibid., p. 108.
14. Greenacre, "The Childhood of the Artist," p. 495.
15. KCAT, pp. 126–27.
16. Phillip Edward Newman, "The Songs of Charles Ives" (Ph.D. diss., University of Iowa, 1967), vol. 2, p. 377.
17. KCAT, p. 127.
18. ESS, p. 136.
19. Ibid., p. 137.
20. KMEM, p. 205.
21. Ibid.
22. Ibid., p. 224.
23. ARCH, box 38, folder 1.
24. ESS, p. 241.
25. Ibid., p. 142.
26. Ibid., p. 160.
27. Ibid., p. 145.
28. Ibid., p. 186.
29. Ibid., p. 197.
30. Ibid., pp. 198–99.
31. Ibid., p. 199.
32. ESS, pp. 204–209.
33. ARCH, box 25, folder 3–4.
34. ESS, p. 213.
35. *114*, no. 22.
36. KCAT, p. 128.
37. "It strikes me that . . . / some men and women get tired of a big job; / but over there our men did not quit. . . . / Too many readers go by the headlines; / party men will muddle up the facts. / So a good many citizens voted / as grandpa always did. . . . / "It's raining, let's throw out the weather man, / Kick him out! Kick him out! Kick him out! . . . / Prejudice and politics, and the standpatters / came in strong, and yelled, / "Slide back! Now you're safe, that's the easy way!" / Then the timid smiled and looked relieved, / "We've got enough to eat, to hell with ideals!" / All the old women, male and female, / had their day today; / and the hog-heart came out of his hole; / But he won't stay out long, / God always drives him back! / Oh Captain, my Captain! / A heritage we've thrown away; / But we'll find it again, / My Captain, Captain, oh my Captain!
38. Newman, "The Songs of Charles Ives," vol. 1, p. 105.
39. *114*, p. 55.
40. COW, p. 119.
41. VP, pp. 6–7.
42. Ibid., p. 56.
43. Ibid., p. 58.
44. Ibid., p. 54.
45. Ibid., p. 51.
46. Ibid., p. 41.
47. Ibid., p. 55.
48. Ibid., p. 63.
49. ESS, p. 241.
50. KMEM, pp. 229–35.

21: AUTOBIOGRAPHIES I, 1920–22

1. IMEM.
2. Elizabeth W. Bruss, *Autobiographical Acts* (Baltimore: Johns Hopkins University Press, 1976).
3. *114*.
4. IMEM, p. 11.
5. *114*, postface following p. 260, two unnumbered pages.
6. Ibid., second page.
7. Ibid.
8. Ibid.
9. Ibid.
10. Ibid.
11. *114*, p. 119.
12. Ibid., no. 2.
13. Ibid., no. 114.
14. IMEM, p. 127.
15. Ibid., p. 126.
16. *114*, no. 19.
17. Ibid., no. 51.
18. Ibid., unnumbered, following p. 269.
19. Ibid., no. 5.
20. Ibid., no. 10.
21. Ibid., postface, p. 2.
22. Ibid.
23. COW, p. 21.
24. *Musical Courier*, September 2, 1922.
25. CEI to *Musical Courier*, September 21, 1924.
26. CEI to Walter Damrosch, December 14, 1911.
27. CEI to Damrosch, June 24, 1915.
28. CEI to Josef Stransky, April 27, 1920.
29. CEI to Leopold Stokowski, June 17, 1921.
30. Elizabeth Sprague Coolidge to HTI, March 15, 1921.
31. CEI to E. S. Coolidge, March 1921.
32. Rita Meade, *Henry Cowell's New Music, 1925–1936* (Ann Arbor: UMI Research Press, 1981), p. 12.
33. IMEM, p. 12.
34. Meade, *Henry Cowell's New Music*, p. 115.
35. Henry Bellaman, "The Music of Charles Ives," *Pro Music Quarterly*, March 1927, pp. 16–22.
36. IMEM, p. 279.
37. Meade, *Henry Cowell's New Music*.
38. Sidney R. Cowell, "Ivesiana: 'More Than Just Something Unusual,'" *Musical America*, October 1974, p. 16.
39. ARCH, correspondence, HC to CEI, July 27, 1927.
40. Meade, *Henry Cowell's New Music*, p. xv.
41. Ibid., p. xvii.
42. Ibid., p. 89.
43. Ibid., p. 113.
44. CEI to Nicholas Slonimsky, July 14, 1929.
45. *Eastern Underwriter*, September 19, 1930. See VP, p. 41.
46. Ibid.
47. Charles Ives, *Eleven Songs and Two Harmonizations*, ed. John Kirkpatrick (New York: Associated Music Publishers, 1968), p. 50.
48. KCAT, p. 212.
49. Stuart Feder, "Charles Ives and the Unanswered Question," *Psychoanalytic Study of Society* 10 (1984), pp. 321–51.
50. Meade, *Henry Cowell's New Music*, p. 114.

22: AUTOBIOGRAPHIES II, 1931–34

1. ARCH, diaries of Edith Ives, 1924.
2. VP, p. 106.
3. *New Music Quarterly*, October 1927.
4. ARCH, box 56, Lucille Fletcher, "A Connecticut Yankee in Music," unpublished article written for the *New Yorker*, 1939.
5. This account is drawn largely from KMEM, preface, pp. 12–15.

6. Ibid., p. 15.
7. Ibid., p. 27.
8. Ibid., pp. 26–27.
9. Ibid., p. 29.
10. Ibid., p. 20.
11. Ibid., p. 25.
12. Ibid., pp. 25–26.
13. Ibid., p. 26.
14. Ibid.
15. VP, p. 88.
16. Ibid., p. 225.
17. IMEM, p. 140. For instance, father used to say, 'If one can use chords of 3rds and make them mean something, why not chords of 4ths? If you can have a chord of three notes and [one of] four, alternating and following, why not measures of 3/4 then 4/4, alternating and following? If the whole tones can be divided equally, why not half tones? That is, if one has twelve notes in an octave, why not more or less? If you can learn to like and use a consonance (so called), why not a dissonance (so called)? If the piano can be tuned out of tune to make it more practicable (that is, imperfect intervals), why can't the ear learn a hundred other intervals if it wants to try?— and why shouldn't it want to try? If the mind can learn to use a two against (or rather with) a three why not nine vs. eleven?—or even better (or worse)? If the mind can learn to use two rhythms together, why can't it [use] five or worse together?—and the measure referred to above? If the mind can understand one key, why can't it learn to understand another key with it?'
18. Ravel was "weak, morbid and monotonous," Hindemith "a nice German boy," and Sibelius (toward whom Ives could wax eloquently vitriolic) platitudinous at best—"a nice mixture of Grieg, Wagner, and Tchaikovsky," all of whom he also criticized. As for older masters, Mozart was "emasculated." Only Bach, Beethoven, and Brahms escape scathing, and even Brahms, on further reflection, receives an appended "No."

19. IMEM, p. 52.
20. Ibid., p. 135.
21. Ibid., p. 138.
22. Ibid.
23. Ibid., p. 47–48.
24. Maynard Solomon, "Charles Ives: Some Questions of Veracity," *Journal of the American Musicological Association* 40, no. 3 (Fall 1987), pp. 443–70.
25. IMEM, p. 47.
26. ROS, p. 32.
27. IMEM, p. 43.
28. Ibid., p. 44.
29. Ibid.
30. Ibid.
31. Ibid.
32. Ibid., p. 125.
33. VP, p. 138.
34. ESS, p. 83.
35. IMEM, p. 41.
36. Ibid., p. 28.
37. Ibid., p. 38.
38. Ibid., p. 30.
39. Ibid., p. 26.
40. Ibid., p. 30.
41. Ibid., p. 50.
42. Ibid., pp. 133–34.
43. Ibid.
44. Ibid., p. 135.
45. ROS, p. 185.
46. William Lyons Phelps to CEI, June 17, 1920.
47. CEI to WLP, December 21, 1920. ROS, p. 198.
48. Edward Wagenknecht, *Mark Twain: The Man and His Work* (New Haven: Yale University Press, 1935).
49. CEI to WLP, January 6, 1937, cited in BUR, p. 136.
50. CEI to WLP, January 4, 1937 (handwritten draft).

23: FINAL COLLABORATIONS

1. IMEM, p. 114.
2. Ibid., p. 71.
3. KCAT, p. 60.
4. Henry Cowell to CEI, April 28, 1936.
5. KMEM, p. 135, note.
6. Don C. Gillespie, "John Becker, Musical Crusader of Saint Paul," *Musical Quarterly* 52, no. 2 (April 1976), pp. 195–217, quotations at pp. 208, 195.
7. Ibid., p. 200.
8. Ibid., p. 202.
9. Ibid., p. 204, citing CEI to John J. Becker, November 9, 1933.
10. Ibid.
11. CEI to Guggenheim Foundation, December 1932.
12. CEI to JJB, August 9, 1937.
13. CEI to JJB, before January 30, 1938, and June 30, 1938.
14. Gillespie, "John Becker," p. 204.
15. KCAT, p. 122.
16. Ibid., p. 125.
17. Gillespie, "John Becker," p. 204. Throughout this period of collaboration with Becker, Cowell, and Harrison, Ives also employed copyists to prepare scores under his supervision.
18. Meade, *Henry Cowell's New Music*, p. 331.
19. Ibid., p. 330.
20. SRC, personal communication. See also Michael Hicks, "The Imprisonment of Henry Cowell," *Journal of the American Musicological Society* 44, no. 1 (Spring 1991), pp. 92–119. The first complete biography of Henry Cowell, using the full resources of the Cowell collection at the New York Public Library, is being prepared by Joel Sachs.
21. HC to Mary Bell, January 19, 1939.
22. Meade, *Henry Cowell's New Music*, p. 355.
23. New York *Herald Tribune*, May 23, 1936.
24. HTI to CSR, July 3, 1936.
25. HTI to CSR, July 12, 1936.
26. HTI to HC, August 14, 1940.
27. HC to HTI, March 31, 1941.
28. HC to HTI, September 15, 1941.
29. CEI to HC, September 1941.
30. SRC, personal communication, August 1989.
31. VP, p. 82.
32. Ibid., p. 86.
33. Ibid., p. 93.
34. Ibid.
35. Ibid., p. 87.
36. Gillespie, "John Becker," pp. 213, 196.
37. ARCH, correspondence, LH to CEI, October 23, 1944.
38. Ibid.
39. HTI to LH, November 1944.
40. HTI to LH, February 19, 1946.
41. LH to CEI, "Thurs.," [May 16,] 1946.
42. CEI to LH, June 28, 1946.
43. HTI to LH, June 16, 1946.
44. John Cage to CEI, May 13, 1947.
45. CEI to LH, [mid-May,] 1947.
46. CEI to JB, July 14, 1947.
47. COW, p. 125.
48. HC to HTI, February 15, 1947.
49. COW, p. v.
50. VP, p. 203.
51. KCAT, p. 212.
52. HTI to HC, September 29, 1944.
53. Ibid.
54. Sidney R. Cowell, "Ivesiana: 'More than Just Something Unusual.'" *Musical America*, October 1974, p. 16.
55. VP, p. 117.
56. Bigelow Ives, Personal Communication.
57. Sidney Cowell, "Ivesiana."

APPENDIX A

1. Maynard Solomon, "Charles Ives: Some Questions of Veracity," *Journal of the American Musicological Society* 40, no. 3 (Fall 1987), pp. 443–70.

2. See Stuart Feder, "Charles and George Ives: The Veneration of Boyhood," *Annual of Psychoanalysis* 9 (1981), pp. 265–316. "There is no question about the presence of conflict and certain problem areas will emerge clearly enough in the ensuing account. Especially noteworthy are those of sexual identity and the threat of homosexuality, the aggressive component in character, and limitations in mourning. However, . . . pathology is not the whole story."

3. Peter Blos, *Son and Father: Before and Beyond the Oedipus Complex* (New York: Free Press, 1985).

4. Sissela Bok, *Lying* (New York: Pantheon, 1978).

5. VP, p. 138.

6. Ibid.

7. W. H. Hitchcock and Vivian Perlis, eds., *An Ives Celebration* (Urbana: University of Illinois Press, 1977), p. 69.

8. Solomon, "Charles Ives."

9. Carol Baron, "Dating Charles Ives's Music: Facts and Fictions," *Perspectives of New Music* 28, no. 1 (Winter 1990).

10. Ibid.

11. See E. M. Forster, *Aspects of the Novel* (London: Edward Arnold, 1927), pp. 116ff.

12. VP, p. 138.

13. Ralph Waldo Emerson, "Representative Men," in *Essays and Lectures* (New York: Library of America, 1983), p. 615.

14. Solomon, "Charles Ives," p. 466.

INDEX